Quality Instruction and Intervention

Strategies for Secondary Educators

Edited by
Brittany L. Hott, PhD, BCBA-D

ROWMAN & LITTLEFIELD
Lanham • Boulder • New York • London

For Luke

Associate Acquisitions Editor: Courtney Packard
Assistant Acquisitions Editor: Sarah Rinehart
Sales and Marketing Inquiries: textbooks@rowman.com

Published by Rowman & Littlefield
An imprint of The Rowman & Littlefield Publishing Group, Inc.
4501 Forbes Boulevard, Suite 200, Lanham, Maryland 20706
www.rowman.com

86-90 Paul Street, London EC2A 4NE

Copyright © 2023 by The Rowman & Littlefield Publishing Group, Inc.

All rights reserved. No part of this book may be reproduced in any form or by any electronic or mechanical means, including information storage and retrieval systems, without written permission from the publisher, except by a reviewer who may quote passages in a review.

British Library Cataloguing in Publication Information Available

Library of Congress Cataloging-in-Publication Data
Names: Hott, Brittany L., editor.
Title: Quality instruction and intervention : strategies for secondary educators / Edited by Brittany L. Hott, PhD, BCBA-D.
Description: Lanham, Maryland : Rowman & Littlefield, [2023] | Includes bibliographical references and index.
Identifiers: LCCN 2023003330 (print) | LCCN 2023003331 (ebook) | ISBN 9781538143766 (hardback) | ISBN 9781538143773 (paperback) | ISBN 9781538143780 (epub)
Subjects: LCSH: High school teaching. | Youth with disabilities—Education, Secondary. | Effective teaching. | Educational psychology. | Education, Secondary—Aims and objectives.
Classification: LCC LB1625 .Q35 2023 (print) | LCC LB1625 (ebook) | DDC 373.1102—dc23/eng/20230215
LC record available at https://lccn.loc.gov/2023003330
LC ebook record available at https://lccn.loc.gov/2023003331

Brief Contents

Acknowledgments — xii

1. **Introduction to Quality Instruction and Intervention** — 1
   Brittany L. Hott and Angela Green

2. **High-Quality Core Classroom Reading Instruction** — 6
   Pamela Williamson, Kelly J. Williams, Dave Furjanic, and Jessica R. Toste

3. **Reading Intervention Methods for Secondary Students** — 23
   Jessica R. Toste, Brennan Chandler, Erica Fry, and Kelly J. Williams

4. **Quality 6–12 Mathematics Instruction** — 44
   Bradley S. Witzel, Tricia K. Strickland, and Jonté A. Myers

5. **Mathematics Interventions for Secondary Students with Disabilities** — 63
   Tricia K. Strickland, Bradley S. Witzel, and Jonté A. Myers

6. **Teaching the Podcast: Using a Genre Approach to Secondary Writing Instruction** — 87
   Amber Curlee and Jessica Singer Early

7. **Writing Intervention** — 108
   Amber B. Ray and John Romig

8. **Science and Social Studies Content** — 127
   Sami Kahn, Timothy Lintner, Darren Minarik, and Jonte' C. Taylor

9. **Science and Social Studies Intervention** — 147
   Jonte' C. Taylor, Darren Minarik, Sami Kahn, and Timothy Lintner

10. **Quality Behavior Instruction: Classroom Management** — 168
    Ashley MacSuga-Gage, Jasmine Justus, Nicholas A. Gage, and Brittany Batton

11. **Social, Emotional, and Behavioral Intervention** — 189
    Kathleen M. Randolph, Glenna Billingsley, and Jasmine Justus

12. **Good Study Strategies** — 212
    B. Keith Ben-Hanania Lenz

13. **Additional Resources** — 232
    Julie Atwood and Jacquelyn Purser

References 237
Index 270
About the Contributors 278

Contents

Acknowledgments	xii
1 Introduction to Quality Instruction and Intervention	1
Brittany L. Hott and Angela Green	
References	5
2 High-Quality Core Classroom Reading Instruction	6
Pamela Williamson, Kelly J. Williams, Dave Furjanic, and Jessica R. Toste	
Underlying Policies, Standards, Theories, and Research	7
Educational Policy	7
Academic Standards	7
Foundational Theories	8
Guiding Research	10
Reading Assessment and Instruction in Secondary English Language Arts Classrooms	12
Assessments to Guide Instructional Planning and Decision-Making	13
Instructional Methods for Core Reading Instruction	14
Effective and Explicit Instruction	15
Vocabulary Instruction	16
Comprehension Instruction	17
Conclusion	18
Bridge from Instruction to Intervention	18
References	19
3 Reading Intervention Methods for Secondary Students	23
Jessica R. Toste, Brennan Chandler, Erica Fry, and Kelly J. Williams	
Theories Informing Reading Interventions for Secondary Students	24
Evidence Base on Reading Interventions	25
Assessment Methods to Guide Instructional Decision-Making	26
Data-Based Instruction	27
Progress Monitoring	27
Diagnostic Assessment	28
Intervention Adjustments	29
Key Intervention Methods	29
Prerequisite Skills Instruction	30
Foundational Skills Routine	30
Letter-Sound Review	30

      Blending Practice   30
      Read and Write Words   31
      New Concept   31
      Read Connected Text   31
    Multisyllabic Word Reading Fluency   31
      Multisyllabic Word Reading Instructional Routine   32
        Affix Learning   32
        Peel Off Reading.   32
        Word-Building Activity   32
        Word Reading Fluency   33
        Connected Text Reading   33
    Fluency Building   33
      Oral Reading Fluency Routine   33
    Content-Area Knowledge Building   35
      Vocabulary Routine   35
      Topic Introduction Routine   36
    Building and Monitoring Reading Comprehension   37
      Context Clues   37
      Greek and Latin Roots   37
      Question Types   38
      Summarizing   38
        Get the Gist Routine   38
  Conclusion   39
  References   39

4   Quality 6–12 Mathematics Instruction   44
Bradley S. Witzel, Tricia K. Strickland, and Jonté A. Myers

  Chapter Objectives   46
  Setting Goals in Secondary Mathematics   46
  Planned Outcomes   47
  Progressions Across Grade and Content   50
  Systematic Instruction   52
    Task Analysis Steps   52
    Task Analysis Example of Division of Fractions   52
    Task Analysis Example of Logs   53
  Practice Standards   53
  Practice and Homework   55
    Immediate Practice   55
    Completed with Potential Assistance   56
    Mixed Problems of Multiple Math Skills   56
    Completed in a Reasonable Amount of Time   56
  Instructional Strategies   57
    Cognitive Strategies   57
    Visuals   57
  Assessment to Drive Differentiation   60
    Differentiation   61
  Conclusion   61
  References   62

Contents

5 Mathematics Interventions for Secondary Students with Disabilities — 63
Tricia K. Strickland, Bradley S. Witzel, and Jonté A. Myers

- Characteristics of Students with Mathematics Learning Disabilities — 64
- Taxonomy of Intervention Intensity — 65
- Research-Based Instructional Practices — 66
  - Explicit Instruction — 66
  - Guided Practice Worksheet — 72
  - Quadratic Functions Cue Card — 73
  - Multiple Representations — 74
  - Strategy Instruction — 77
  - Prompt Cards and Structured Worksheets — 79
- Linear, Quadratic, and Exponential Functions — 80
  - Linear Functions — 80
  - Quadratic Functions — 80
  - Exponential Functions — 80
  - Classwide Peer Tutoring (CWPT) — 81
  - Progress Monitoring — 82
- Conclusion — 83
- References — 83

6 Teaching the Podcast: Using a Genre Approach to Secondary Writing Instruction — 87
Amber Curlee and Jessica Singer Early

- Objectives — 88
- Foundational Learning Theory — 88
- Guiding Research and Policy — 89
- Connection to Standards — 90
- Professional Groups — 93
- Formative/Summative Assessment Methods — 93
- Teaching the Podcast Genre — 94
- Assignment Examples — 96
- Mentor Texts — 101
- Writing Workshop Tip: Scriptwriting — 102
  - Finding Focus for Your Podcast — 102
  - Digital Tools — 103
- Celebrating Writing and Making It Public — 104
- Conclusion — 105
- References — 105

7 Writing Intervention — 108
Amber B. Ray and John Romig

- Formative Writing Assessments — 109
  - Curriculum-Based Measurement — 109
  - Exit Slips — 111
  - Error Analysis — 111
  - Holistic Ratings — 111
  - Generic Rubrics — 112
  - Genre-Specific Elements — 112

Teaching Writing Strategies for the Writing Process	112
Theory Guiding Self-Regulated Strategy Development	113
Self-Regulated Strategy Development	113
Six Stages of Instruction	114
Stage 1: Develop and Activate Background Knowledge	114
Stage 2: Discuss It	114
Stage 3: Model It	114
Stage 4: Memorize It	115
Stage 5: Support It	115
Stage 6: Independent Performance	116
Writing Strategies	116
Self-Regulation Strategies	118
Case Study Example Using SRSD for the ACT Argumentative Essay	118
Paul's Independently Written Argumentative Essay	121
Writing to Learn	122
Technology Tools	122
Sentence Construction	123
Conclusion	123
References	124

8 Science and Social Studies Content — 127
Sami Kahn, Timothy Lintner, Darren Minarik, and Jonte' C. Taylor

Why Science and Social Studies?	127
What Is Science?	129
Nature of Science (NOS)	130
Scientific Inquiry	130
Scientific Literacy	131
The Framework for K–12 Science Education and the Next Generation Science Standards (NGSS)	132
Quality Assessment in Science Education	132
Some Key Instructional Methods in Science Education	133
Project-Based Learning (PBL)	133
Socioscientific Issues (SSI)	133
Engineering Design Challenges	133
Models and Simulations	134
What Is Social Studies?	134
Nature of Social Studies	134
Social Studies Inquiry	135
Social Studies Literacy	135
The College, Career, and Civic Life (C3) Framework for Social Studies State Standards	136
Quality Assessment in Social Studies	137
Key Instructional Strategies in Social Studies Education	137
Engagement	137
Analysis	138
Project-Based Learning	138
Applying Best Practices in Science and Social Studies through a Case Study	138

Planning Instruction for All Students	140
Science Assessments Explained	141
Planning Instruction for All Students	142
Social Studies Assessment Explained	142
Conclusion	144
References	145

9 Science and Social Studies Intervention — 147
Jonte' C. Taylor, Darren Minarik, Sami Kahn, and Timothy Lintner

Evidence-Based and High-Leverage Practices in Science and Social Studies	148
General Literacy and Content Acquisition Interventions for Science and Social Studies	149
General Literacy Interventions in Science and Social Studies	150
Supported Inquiry	150
Science-Based Inquiry Research	151
Social Studies–Based Inquiry Research	151
Higher-Order Thinking and Reasoning	152
Concept Comparison	153
Question Exploration	154
Cause and Effect	155
Decision-Making	156
Cross-Curricular Argumentation	157
Key Points	158
Content Acquisition Interventions in Science and Social Studies	158
Mnemonics	158
Science-Based Mnemonics Research	159
Social Studies–Based Mnemonics Research	159
Graphic Organizers	159
Science-Based Graphic Organizer Research	159
Social Studies–Based Graphic Organizer Research	160
Peer-Mediated Support Strategies	160
Science-Based Peer-Mediated Strategies Research	160
Social Studies–Based Peer-Mediated Strategies Research	160
Key Points	161
Conclusion	161
References	162

10 Quality Behavior Instruction: Classroom Management — 168
Ashley MacSuga-Gage, Jasmine Justus, Nicholas A. Gage, and Brittany Batton

Theoretical Foundations of Evidence-Based Classroom Management	169
Relevant Educational Policy Associated with Classroom Management	171
Classroom Management and Professional Standards of Educational Practice	172
Evidence-Based Classroom Management	172
Maximize Classroom Structure	173
Description of the Skill	173
Research Support	174
How to Implement the Skill	175

Post, Teach, Review, Monitor, and Reinforce Positively Stated Rules
and Expectations 175
  Description of the Skill 175
  Research Support 176
  How to Implement the Skill 177
Actively Engage Students in Observable Ways 178
  Description of the Skill 178
  Research Support 178
  How to Implement the Skill 179
Establish a Continuum of Acknowledging Appropriate Behaviors ... 179
  Description of the Skill 179
  Research Support 180
  How to Implement the Skill 181
Establish a Continuum of Strategies to Respond to
Inappropriate Behaviors 181
  Description of the Skill 181
  Research Support 182
  How to Implement the Skill 183
Conclusion 183
References 185

11 Social, Emotional, and Behavioral Intervention 189
Kathleen M. Randolph, Glenna Billingsley, and Jasmine Justus
Chapter Objectives 190
Operational Definitions of Behavior 191
Explicit Social Skills Instruction 191
Tier 2 Evidence-Based Interventions Classroom Management ... 194
  Check-In/Check-Out 195
    Description of the Intervention 195
    Research Support 195
    How to Implement the Intervention 195
  High-Probability (High-P) Sequence 195
    Description of the Intervention 195
    Research Support 196
    How to Implement the Intervention 196
  Self-Monitoring 196
    Description of the Intervention 196
    Research Support 196
    How to Implement the Intervention 197
  Group Contingencies 197
    Description of the Intervention 197
    Research Support 198
    How to Implement the Intervention 198
Adding Intensive Interventions 198
  Behavior Contracting 199
    Description of the Intervention 199
    Research Support 199
    How to Implement the Intervention 199

Daily Behavior Report Cards	200
Description of the Intervention	200
Research Support	201
How to Implement the Intervention	201
FBA/BIP	202
Description of the Intervention	202
Research Support	202
How to Implement the Intervention	203
Relevant Educational Policy	203
Foundational Learning Theory	204
Guiding Research	205
Professional Standards	206
Formative and Summative Assessment	207
Conclusion	207
References	207

12 Good Study Strategies — 212
B. Keith Ben-Hanania Lenz

What Should Be Studied?	213
Teaching Students with Poor Study Strategies	213
Features of Good Study Strategies	215
Approaches to Teaching Good Study Strategies	216
Good Ways to Study	218
Organizing Information to Structure Study	218
Listening and Note-Taking	219
Structuring Good Study	220
The Overall Study Plan	225
Progress Monitoring and Studying	226
Conclusion	229
References	230

13 Additional Resources — 232
Julie Atwood and Jacquelyn Purser

References	236
References	237
Index	270
About the Contributors	278

Acknowledgments

THIS BOOK IS POSSIBLE BECAUSE of the time that Dr. Cathy Newman Thomas invested in conceptualizing the integration of quality instruction and intervention. Her work is centered in enhancing the education of our children and their teachers. Cathy has been a mentor for over a decade and a dedicated and kind colleague. This work is as much hers as mine.

From submission of the book proposal to copyediting and completion, Rowman & Littlefield has provided excellent support. Mark Kerr, Courtney Packard, and Sarah Rinehart are top notch. Their feedback, advice, and encouragement were nothing short of amazing.

I wish to thank the reviewers listed below. Their thoughtful comments and expertise guided the writing and revisions for the development of this book. As always, any errors and omissions are my own.

Robin Brewer, University of Northern Colorado
Debi Gartland, Towson University
Deborah Griswold, University of Kansas
Heather Haynes Smith, Trinity University
Kandace M. Hoppin, Towson University
Katrina Hovey, Western Oregon University
Marla J. Lohmann, Colorado Christian University
Francie Murry, University of Northern Colorado
Ruby L. Owiny, Minnesota State University, Mankato
Candice Styer, Western Washington University

It is an honor and privilege to have the opportunity to engage with leading scholars who authored chapters in this text. I learned much from our conversations and from their contributions to secondary education. Sarah Heiniger, doctoral student and graduate research assistant at the University of Oklahoma, assisted with editing and creating supplementary materials. This work would not be possible without her efforts.

I am appreciative of my family who continue to support me, especially my partner, Jeff, and our children, Luke, Asher, Henry, and Sylvie. I am also appreciative of Mayra, Isabelle, and Abby who provided childcare that afforded me the time to edit this book.

Finally, I am most thankful for the educators who choose to pursue professional development or graduate study to enhance practice grounded in the science of teaching and learning. Your work makes a difference, and I am hopeful that our text serves as a useful resource.

1

Introduction to Quality Instruction and Intervention

Brittany L. Hott and Angela Green

EFFECTIVE TEACHING STARTS WITH quality instruction and the majority of students respond well. However, about 35% of students will require intervention to meet academic and behavioral standards. According to the US Department of Education, approximately 7.2 million (15%) of students ages 3–21 receive special education and related services. Students with exceptionalities who are eligible to receive special education and related services and and at-risk students all deserve quality intervention grounded in the science of learning. To effectively meet the needs of diverse classrooms, knowledge of quality instruction and intervention is critical, particularly at the secondary level. Most education programs focus on academic subject matter and do not address interventions that are needed by approximately 35% of the school-age population. Conversely, the majority of special education programs focus on interventions with little attention to quality instruction.

Quality Instruction and Intervention: Strategies for Secondary Educators offers an introduction to the essential features of general education instruction grounded in the science of learning followed by the most up-to-date, empirically supported interventions. Two dedicated chapters, authored by leading content and strategy experts, are devoted to each area. The first chapter focuses on quality instruction with content-area specialists as lead authors and interventionists supporting. The second chapter focuses on effective intervention with the interventionists taking the lead author roles and content-area specialists supporting.

It is our hope that this text bridges the gap between quality instruction and effective intervention, an often overlooked component of education. The last chapters of the text include a chapter dedicated to study skills that are essential across content areas and a comprehensive resource list to support implementation of instructional practices and interventions. After reading the book, educators will be able to describe the components of effective instruction and intervention in each of the content areas, access empirically validated materials, and locate resources for continued learning.

A unifying theme across these chapters is that quality instruction and intervention are critical to ensure that every child is afforded an education that supports lifelong learning. Further, neither quality instruction nor effective intervention can occur in isolation. From expected classroom behaviors to factoring a polynomial, explicit instruction is a critical component for student success. Explicit instruction refers to practices that support learners to reduce the cognitive load. Frequent and varied opportunities to respond and appropriate affirmative or corrective feedback are given. Long-term retention is one the many benefits of explicit instruction (Riccomini et al., 2017, p. 4).

In each of the chapters, explicit instruction is centered along with exemplars in each of the content areas. Collectively, the examples of explicit instruction within these chapters support the application of this concept across domains. In the mathematics instruction chapter, Witzel and colleagues explain that "students require examples and verbal reasoning. The most essential elements of systematic instruction include task analysis preparation and a delivery system that entails a scaffolded gradual release of information: Me–We–Two–You" (p. 52). Like Witzel and colleagues, Curlee et al. share essential features of quality writing instruction including the use of mnemonics. In describing universal classroom management, Gage and colleagues remind us that "creating and explicitly teaching classroom procedures, including pencil sharpening, requesting bathroom access, entrance, and exiting, etc., ensures that students understand how to enact daily routines" (p. 173). At the secondary level, educators may assume that students understand common procedures and expectations; however, many students continue to struggle. Teaching expectations prevents most behavioral challenges. Along with explicit instruction, each of the chapters offers research-based, practical, and effective instructional practices aimed at increasing student engagement, planning for intervention and differentiation, and structuring academic conversations.

Chapter 2 presents core features of quality, evidence-based secondary reading instruction. Williamson and colleagues introduce the critical thinking skills necessary to interpret and evaluate complex literary and informational texts from a range of genres. Empirically supported recommendations include both direct and explicit instruction, opportunities for discussion, and strategies to support motivation and engagement. Reading demands exponentially increase as students transition from elementary to the secondary grades. Toste and colleagues share evidence-based interventions and curriculum-based measurement to effectively monitor student progress in grades 6–12.

Witzel and colleagues define quality mathematics instruction for secondary students in chapter 4. Beginning with the current bleak performance of secondary students on mathematics achievement tests, the authors highlight the importance of understanding both the outcomes and the progression of those outcomes for teachers tasked with mitigating the learning deficits leading to those achievement scores. After internalizing these standards, educators are led to understand the benefit of systematic instruction as a research-based practice for increasing student acquisition and retention of the more complex math skills required of secondary students.

With readily applicable examples grounded in the science of mathematics, the authors illustrate both the need for and practice of assessment for learning, systematic instruction, and the use of cognitive supports. Specific examples of cognitive supports, such as using visuals, "designed to help students plan, monitor, and modify their approach to a mathematics problem" (p. 57) are readily applicable for those striving to meet the needs of diverse learners. These cognitive strategies use a "stepwise approach to guide student processing" (p. 57) and are appropriate for students along the continuum of mathematics readiness.

Structured academic conversations, another cognitive strategy, are described as being "important for students to reason aloud but, maybe more importantly, to learn the appropriate reasoning of others" (p. 54). These conversations increase engagement as well as comprehension, and it is inherently differentiated, as students communicate their current understanding while hearing the reasoning of more or less advanced peers.

Strickland et al. begins with data about the achievement of students with disabilities on standardized math assessments, followed by the characteristics of students with math-specific learning disabilities and strategies for mitigating deficits. Cognitive weaknesses, identified by Geary in 2004 and Witzel, 2020, such as long-term memory deficits, poor sequential memory, and visuospatial deficits, are addressed in the chapter with widely applicable strategies and supports. Identifying that students with math learning disabilities may struggle additionally with decoding unfamiliar vocabulary and comprehending the text in a word problem, Witzel, Strickland, and Myers include strategies to support breaking down a word problem into manageable steps.

The taxonomy of intervention intensity is explained within a research-rich and practical discussion of strategies that embed interventions within explicit instruction. The authors provide explanations and strategies for the implementation of Concrete-Representation-Abstract Integration, which increases "conceptual understanding and promotes transfer of the concept to a range of novel situations" (p. 75).

Specific interventions such as using prompt cards, creating structured worksheets, using mnemonics for strategy instruction, and implementing classwide tutoring, are also grounded in the science of mathematics. Next, Strickland and colleagues provide actionable steps that support implementation. Finally, providing the theoretical principles and relatable examples, the authors demonstrate how to accurately, and fairly, assess learning using frequent, targeted assessments.

Curlee and Singer Early frame the writing content chapter around an engaging, process-oriented unit on podcasting. Writing and producing a podcast is one example of a genre-based project designed to allow students to "bring their whole selves to the page while sharing and making sense of new ideas and information, defining what they care about and why, and engaging with real audiences and purposes for reasons that matter to them deeply" (p. 90).

Drawing from sociocultural theory of learning, this chapter illustrates how students' backgrounds and perspectives can be captured by incorporating the needed structures and scaffolding to assist with finding and sharing their voices. The authors demonstrate how to create an outlet for and provide a model of the writing process as coaction, both between student-writers and between the writers and their background contexts and social relationships which empowers students using a strengths-based approach. Curlee and Singer Early emphasize progress rather than genre mastery. The podcast exemplar lesson and supporting resources are readily adaptable to multiple levels of ability and readiness.

The formal and informal assessment examples presented by Ray and Romig in the chapter on secondary writing interventions provide a differentiated view of assessing students. From the flexibility of curriculum-based measurement to the adaptable exit ticket strategy and rubric-referenced assessment, progress and process are emphasized over genre mastery. The authors describe a self-regulated strategy development (SRSD) model to increase students' skills in writing and provide a case-study example in a real-world context. In illustrating the SRSD model, the reader is given examples for developing lessons in each stage: developing background knowledge, discussing the strategies and process, modeling it, memorizing it, supporting it, and performing it independently. Ray and Romig describe strategies for building skills in writing as well as self-regulation to foster independence. Support strategies provided in the chapter address intervention in structure and unit-construction at tiered levels of intensity.

Unifying science and social studies as fields of inquiry, Kahn and colleagues explain, "science and social studies are inextricably linked in that they are both ways of understanding the world. Science focuses on understanding and explaining phenomena in the *natural world*. . . . Social studies focuses on understanding the *human world*; specifically, describing and explaining humans' relationships to each other and their environments" (p. 127).

This is a student-centered view of the content areas as vehicles for students to explore their physical or social environment. Inherently engaging, differentiated, and supportive of self-regulation, the investigative approach described in this chapter urges a more active role for learners. "Inquiry is often overshadowed by more 'conventional' ways of teaching social studies. Here, students are passive recipients of information unimodally relayed to them—teacher to student. The student role is simple—to sit quietly and take notes. The teacher role is just as simple—talking *at* students, not *with* them. Lost in this paradigm is inquiry" (p. 135).

Instructional methods such as Project-Based Learning (PBL), engagement opportunities, questioning strategies, and models and simulations outlined by the authors are easily translatable into other content areas and designed to meet the needs of students at different stages of readiness. With a rich discussion of literacy within science and social studies instruction, and an application-based review of the tenets of Universal Design for Learning, the instructional practices within this chapter are geared toward truly differentiated Tier 1 instruction.

Centered around evidence-based and high-leverage practices, Taylor and colleagues present intervention strategies that can be implemented within a Universal Design for Learning (UDL) framework. Planning for intervention in the content areas must include research-based strategies to mitigate literacy and content deficits. "The principles of UDL provide a conceptual planning framework for creating more inclusive units and lessons. Using UDL with a strategic planning cycle provides a way to ensure that strategic interventions align with the content and are effectively supporting learning outcomes" (p. 149).

Including Content-Enhancement Routines (CERs) as part of regular practice increases engagement and provides support for students who require intervention. The Concept Comparison Routine, Question Exploration Routine, and Cause-and-Effect Routine invite analysis rather than memorization. Additional intervention strategies for content acquisition include mnemonics, graphic organizers, and peer-mediated support.

The authors note that some may not consider science and social studies as important as math and reading. However, the focus on Science, Technology, Engineering, and Mathematics (STEM) careers and the necessity for context to support understanding in a global community make content-area instruction essential to developing successful students. With the intervention strategies in this chapter, all students can enjoy progress.

MacSuga-Gage et al. draw from learning theory and delineate how effective, research-based classroom management increases students' access to instruction while also reducing teacher burnout and increasing job satisfaction. National Education Association's micro-credentialing for classroom management skills and Council for Exceptional Children's professional standards for special educator development that encompass active engagement and motivation during instruction and support social, emotional, and behavioral growth indicate that, like content, classroom management is more than just an inherent quality that most teachers develop automatically. Randolph and colleagues provide a sound introduction to quality intervention when additional supports are needed beyond evidence-based classroom management strategies. They provide an overview of how to define a student's behavior in operational terms, a step that is often overlooked by those looking to support students struggling to regulate their behavior. Identifying the purpose of and process for teaching replacement behaviors and emphasizing explicit instruction of social skills and self-regulation, this chapter provides a guidebook for addressing behaviors that can negatively impact a student's ability to access instruction.

Intensifying interventions such as check-in/check-out and group contingencies are explained in detail with supportive research and step-by-step instructions for effective implementation. Detailed instruction of more individualized approaches for students with the most intensive needs is provided using examples based on the prerequisite definition of the targeted behavior in operational terms. Two of the interventions explored, behavior contracts and daily behavior report cards, "assist students with setting desired behavioral goals, serve as visual prompts to the student and teacher, promote frequent feedback to stakeholders, embed behavior data collection, promote independence in managing behavior, and are minimally distracting or stigmatizing to the student" (p. 199).

In a culminating chapter, Lenz shares an overview of strategies to support development of effective study skills necessary to master reading, mathematics, writing, and content-area objectives. These skills transcend into postsecondary education and beyond. Finally, a list of resources for further reading is provided in chapter 13.

REFERENCES

National Center for Education Statistics. (2022). *Students with disabilities: Fast facts*. https://nces.ed.gov/fastfacts/display.asp?id=64

Riccomini, P. J., Morano, S., & Hughes, C. A. (2017). Big ideas in special education: Specially designed instruction, high-leverage practices, explicit instruction, and intensive instruction. *TEACHING Exceptional Children, 50*(1), 20–27.

2

High-Quality Core Classroom Reading Instruction

Pamela Williamson, Kelly J. Williams,
Dave Furjanic, and Jessica R. Toste

SECONDARY ENGLISH LANGUAGE ARTS (ELA) classroom teachers are expected to support students' comprehension of complex literary and informational texts from a range of genres and in a variety of formats (Common Core State Standards, 2010). They do so by teaching students to analyze and interrogate texts to develop new knowledge and vocabulary. This is no easy feat, as schools today are increasingly more diverse than in the past and include a range of learners with unique needs and strengths (Hue, 2022). Therefore, secondary ELA teachers who work in inclusive classroom settings are responsible for educating students with disabilities (SWDs). Providing high-quality core reading instruction may be further complicated by the fact that many secondary students with and without disabilities have significant difficulty comprehending grade-level text (Hussar et al., 2020). Results from the 2019 National Assessment of Educational Progress (NAEP) reading subtest demonstrate that among students without disabilities in grades 8 and 12, only 37% and 40% (respectively) scored at or above the proficient level (Hussar et al., 2020). Even fewer SWDs in grades 8 and 12 scored at or above proficient in reading (9% and 13%, respectively) (Hussar et al., 2020). Secondary students who lack proficiency on the NAEP may have difficulty identifying information in text, recognizing main ideas, determining an author's purpose, making inferences, and interpreting the meanings of words (National Assessment Governing Board, 2019). As such, secondary ELA teachers must be prepared to implement high-quality core reading instruction that meets the needs of a diverse range of learners.

In this chapter, we first describe the foundational policies, academic standards, theories, and research that inform high-quality core reading instruction in inclusive secondary ELA classrooms. Then, we describe how assessments can be used to guide instructional planning and decision-making, and we provide evidence-based recommendations for supporting all learners. We end with a list of practical resources for educators and describe the connection between high-quality core reading instruction in secondary ELA classrooms and supplemental interventions for students who need more intensive intervention and support. The following questions guide this chapter:

- What are the policies, standards, theories, and research that inform high-quality core reading instruction in inclusive secondary ELA classrooms?
- How can assessments guide instructional planning and decision-making?
- What does high-quality core reading instruction look like in inclusive secondary ELA classrooms?
- Which evidence-based methods and practices can teachers use to meet the needs of a diverse range of learners?

UNDERLYING POLICIES, STANDARDS, THEORIES, AND RESEARCH

Educational Policy

Legislation plays an important role in inclusive secondary classrooms. The main educational law that guides elementary and secondary schools in the United States is the Every Student Succeeds Act (ESSA, 2015). ESSA has several different requirements for public schools that are applicable for secondary ELA teachers, and it requires states to set challenging academic standards in reading, test students annually in reading (in which accommodations are allowable), and set ambitious goals for underserved groups such as SWDs (ESSA, 2015). Most notably, ESSA (2015) holds schools accountable for all learners and encourages schools to implement services and practices that are "evidence-based" to the greatest extent possible. This means that school professionals (e.g., administrators, teachers) are advised to rely upon rigorous evidence to guide their instruction.

Another important law that guides inclusive secondary ELA classrooms is the Individuals with Disabilities Education Improvement Act (IDEIA), which guides special education services and supports. Among other things, IDEIA stipulates that SWDs are entitled to a free appropriate public education (FAPE). Appropriate, in the eyes of the law, means that schools provide sufficient support for SWDs to access and benefit from public education. This is typically achieved through an Individualized Education Plan (IEP) that includes specially designed instruction (SDI) in which teachers adapt the content, methodology, or delivery of their instruction to meet students' unique needs. SDI also should be based on peer-reviewed research. Additionally, IDEIA dictates that SWDs be educated alongside their peers without disabilities to the maximum extent appropriate, a concept known as the Least Restrictive Environment (LRE). Over the past two decades, the number of SWDs educated in general education classrooms has significantly increased. In fact, data from the US Department of Education in 2020 indicates that the majority of SWDs (over 66%) spent more than 80% of the school day in general education classrooms and another 17% spent 40–70% of their day in general education classrooms (National Center for Education Statistics [NCES], 2022).

Academic Standards

Core reading instruction in secondary ELA classrooms is also guided by academic standards. Most states have adopted the Common Core State Standards (CCSS) for English language arts or have created their own standards based on the CCSS. The CCSS outline the grade-level expectations in reading, writing, speaking, listening, and language (i.e., what students should know and be able to do) and aim to ensure that all students are college- and career-ready upon graduation from high school

(National Governors Association Center for Best Practices & Council of Chief State School Officers [NGA CBP & CCSSO], 2010). In reading, students are expected to read complex text from different genres and in different mediums (e.g., print, digital) to support the development of their reading comprehension (NGA CBP & CCSSO, 2010). The CCSS emphasize the comprehension of literary and informational text in the areas of key ideas and details (e.g., making inferences, citing textual evidence, drawing conclusions, determining and analyzing central ideas or themes, summarizing main ideas and supporting details), craft and structure (e.g., interpreting words and phrases, analyzing text structure, assessing a point of view or purpose), and integration of knowledge and ideas (e.g., integrating and evaluating content in different formats; explaining and evaluating arguments, claims, and evidence; analyzing similarities and differences across texts) (NGA CBP & CCSSO, 2010). The CCSS in ELA do not address how these standards should be taught nor do they provide guidance about how teachers can incorporate supports to provide access for SWDs or students who are acquiring English as an additional language; however, the standards do allow for "the widest possible range of students to participate fully from the onset" and permit "appropriate accommodations to ensure maximum participation of students with special education needs" (NGA CBP & CCSSO, 2010, p. 6).

What do the CCSS, IDEIA, and ESSA mean for secondary ELA teachers? Essentially, teachers are not only responsible for providing evidence-based core reading instruction to all students, they are also responsible for ensuring that SWDs receive SDI to meet their unique needs. In other words, teachers are responsible for ensuring that all students have access to the texts in the general education classroom, which means they may need to incorporate appropriate supports (e.g., accommodations, modifications, assistive technology, accessible educational materials). It is clear that secondary ELA classroom teachers play a critical role in the education of all learners.

Foundational Theories

The goal of reading is to comprehend or construct meaning from text (RAND, 2002), and there are several theories and models of reading comprehension that are useful for secondary ELA teachers to know. The first important model is the Simple View of Reading (SVR), a component skills model of reading comprehension. In the SVR, comprehension is defined as the product of two component skills: decoding and linguistic comprehension (Gough & Tunmer, 1986; Hoover & Gough, 1990). Students must be able to identify printed words in text (i.e., decoding/word-recognition) and understand what those words mean (i.e., linguistic/language comprehension) to comprehend text (Hoover & Tunmer, 2018). For example, students must be able to read (i.e., pronounce orally or silently) words like "determine," "analyze," "compare," and "contrast," in addition to understanding the meanings of those words in context. Although both components are essential, their contribution to reading comprehension changes as students transition from the primary grades (K–2) to the upper-elementary and secondary grades. For students in the primary grades, decoding contributes more to reading comprehension; however, for older students, reading comprehension is more dependent upon language comprehension (Foorman et al., 2020; Lonigan et al., 2018).

Although the SVR is a useful framework to understand the basic components necessary for proficient reading comprehension, it does not demonstrate the complex nature of comprehension, nor does it provide information about other processes that support students' comprehension (Barnes et al., 2015). Therefore, a second important model that informs core reading instruction is the Reading Systems Framework (RSF), which emphasizes the importance of knowledge, processes, and general cognitive resources in skilled reading comprehension (Castles et al., 2018; Perfetti & Stafura, 2014). To comprehend text, students must have knowledge about vocabulary words (i.e., semantics) in isolation and in context, sentence structure (e.g., syntax or grammar, causal connections within and across sentences), text genres (e.g., story grammar, text structure), and background knowledge about the text's topic (Castles et al., 2018; Perfetti & Stafura, 2014). There are also several processes that are necessary for comprehending text, such as the ability to activate meanings, make inferences, and monitor comprehension (Castles et al., 2018). Lastly, text comprehension requires general cognitive resources, including executive functioning skills (i.e., working memory, cognitive flexibility, and inhibitory control) (Castles et al., 2018).

What do these theories mean for core reading instruction in inclusive secondary ELA classrooms? First, teachers must understand that both word recognition and language comprehension are necessary (but not sufficient in isolation) to support proficient reading comprehension. The majority of students will need support with language comprehension to improve their reading comprehension, but students with the most persistent reading difficulties and disabilities may also need additional support to address their word recognition difficulties. Second, reading comprehension is

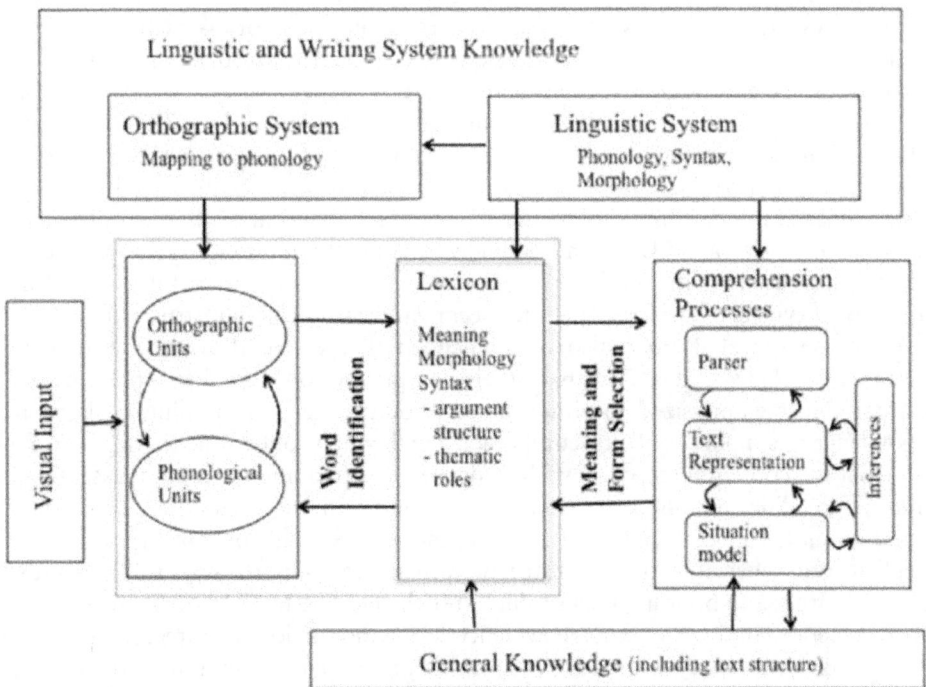

Figure 2.1 Reading Systems Framework: Integrating Word Knowledge and a Theory of Reading Comprehension

Source: Perfetti & Safura (2014). Used by permission.

complex and multifaceted, and therefore much more difficult to improve than word recognition (Castles et al., 2022; Lervåg & Melby-Lervåg, 2022). Secondary teachers must be prepared to help students develop different types of knowledge (e.g., vocabulary, syntax, background knowledge, text genres) while simultaneously incorporating practices that help students build/activate prior knowledge, make different kinds of inferences to support text base inferences (i.e., included by the author) as well as inferences that involve personal experiences (e.g., cultural), and monitor their comprehension. To support and develop executive functioning skills, core reading instruction should help students direct their attention to what's important in a text. Finally, secondary teachers must also be prepared to motivate and engage readers (Klauda et al., 2012).

Guiding Research

Despite the legislative mandate for SWDs to be educated to the greatest extent possible in general education settings, a large gap still exists in the reading achievement between SWDs and their peers without disabilities. Gilmour et al. (2019) conducted a meta-analysis of the reading achievement of K–12 students with and without disabilities, and found that on average, SWDs were reading approximately three years behind their peers. One potential explanation for this gap is the lack of evidence-based practices and SDI in secondary core ELA classrooms (Ciullo et al., 2016; McKenna et al., 2015; Wexler et al., 2018).

Wexler et al. (2018) conducted an observation study to examine the co-teaching practices of sixteen pairs of special and general education co-teachers in middle school ELA classes. During the observations, teachers spent 31.2% of instructional time on literacy activities (e.g., text reading, background knowledge instruction, comprehension strategies) and 16.9% of the time observed was spent on oral or silent reading with no literacy instruction (Wexler et al., 2018). Most notably, SWDs were more likely to interact with the general education teacher than the special educator (Wexler et al., 2018). For SWDs, time spent on oral or silent reading might have been better spent engaged in specialized instruction. While practicing oral reading with feedback is evidence-based for SWDs, silent reading without structure is not. Improving access to evidence-based practices during core reading instruction is critical for SWDs. What are known evidence-based practices for secondary, core reading instruction?

Torgesen et al. (2007) also recommended that essential content knowledge be taught to help students improve their comprehension. In other words, he and his colleagues emphasized the importance of activating and building background knowledge to support students' comprehension through content instruction. In addition, pairing content instruction with evidence-based reading practices is essential to improve reading outcomes for students with and without disabilities. These practices, grounded in the science of reading, include explicit vocabulary instruction, explicit comprehension strategy instruction, structured opportunities to discuss text, and activating and building background knowledge. The Institute of Education Sciences Practice Guide provides five evidence-based instructional strategies, including: (1) explicit vocabulary instruction, (2) direct and explicit comprehension strategy instruction, (3) opportunities for extended discussion of text meaning and interpretation, (4) increasing student motivation and engagement in literacy learning, and

(5) making intensive and individualized interventions available for struggling readers that can be provided by trained specialists (Kamil et al., 2008).

Two recent literature reviews have contributed to our understanding of evidence-based instructional practices in reading for students in the secondary grades. First, Herrera et al. (2016) examined effective programs and practices in general education English language arts and content-area classes for students in grades 6–12. They identified twelve programs and practices that demonstrated positive or potentially positive effects on reading outcomes, such as cooperative learning, explicit instruction in vocabulary and reading comprehension, feedback, fluency building, instructional routines, and writing. Swanson and colleagues' (2017) meta-analysis of reading practices delivered by general education teachers in content-area classrooms found, most notably, that core reading instruction had a significant positive effect on reading comprehension and vocabulary outcomes for all students, regardless of disability status. Students with reading difficulties also had improved reading comprehension outcomes when they received core reading instruction that emphasized explicit vocabulary and comprehension instruction; however, the authors noted that these students likely needed supplemental reading interventions in addition to high-quality core reading instruction (Swanson & Wexler, 2017).

What do all of these reviews, meta-analyses, and studies have in common? Although SWDs may not be getting evidence-based core reading instruction in practice (e.g., Wexler et al., 2018), numerous studies have demonstrated the positive effects of high-quality reading instruction and intervention for students with and without disabilities. Thus, implementing evidence-based practices is essential to improve reading outcomes for students with and without disabilities. Second, it appears that practices such as explicit vocabulary instruction, explicit comprehension strategy instruction, structured opportunities to discuss text, and activating and building background knowledge are supported by research and lead to improved reading outcomes for secondary students.

TEXTBOX 2.1. EVIDENCE-BASED PRACTICES FOR SECONDARY CORE READING INSTRUCTION

- ***Essential content knowledge instruction.*** All students need access to rich, content knowledge instruction to develop their general knowledge, including vocabulary.
- ***Attention to student motivation and engagement (e.g., interest, choice, cooperative learning).*** Not all students are motivated to learn about all topics. Engagement strategies, including cooperative learning and choice can support students' learning.
- ***Activating or building background knowledge before reading.*** Before reading, secondary teachers should activate students' background knowledge (e.g., remind me what we know about how people behave when they care deeply for someone), or build students' background knowledge around novel topics (e.g., show a video clip of bridge designs before reading a chapter about them).

- **Structured opportunities to discuss texts.** Students are given opportunities to ask and answer important questions about texts. Ensuring structure and engagement is key (e.g., reciprocal questioning strategy, Socratic questioning).
- **Explicit vocabulary instruction.** While it is impossible to explicitly teach all words, secondary teachers should explicitly teach words that are critical to text comprehension, or words that are useful across content areas (e.g., Tier 2 words, such as summarize).
- **Explicit comprehension strategy instruction (e.g., text structure, story grammar).** Despite current critiques that teachers should simply teach content to students, explicitly teaching text structures for expository text and story grammar for narratives supports students' comprehension, especially when background knowledge is lacking.
- **Intensive reading interventions for those who need them (e.g., fluency building).** Although ensuring that all students have access to critical content taught in secondary classrooms is vital, intensive reading interventions might be needed for some.

Note: This summary of EBPs included in this chapter is not an exhaustive list; however, the practices included here have well-documented support.

READING ASSESSMENT AND INSTRUCTION IN SECONDARY ENGLISH LANGUAGE ARTS CLASSROOMS

Ms. Cynthia James is beginning her first year teaching English language arts (ELA) at Sun Hill High School and she has been assigned to teach five sections of ninth grade English Literature and Composition. She wants to be prepared to start the year off right, so she takes a closer look at the data available in Sun Hill's student information system. Across all classes, she sees that her students mirror the greater neighborhood community, bringing diverse cultural and linguistic backgrounds. She also notices that a number of students are receiving special education services. One of her classes is Honors English Literature and Composition 9 and many of her students in this class are identified as gifted or talented. Additionally, two classes are labeled "inclusion" classes and she has been assigned to co-teach those classes with a special education teacher, Mr. Juan Martinez, who has ten years of teaching experience. Ms. James quickly realizes that meeting the needs of such a diverse group of learners will be challenging, but recognizes that Mr. Martinez will be a partner with her to ensure students' needs are met.

Formerly found mostly in elementary schools, Sun Hill uses a multi-tiered system of support (MTSS), which integrates the use of assessment data to identify which students might need additional support. Since the new school year has not yet started, Ms. James looked at available assessment data for her students from eighth grade. Using class rosters, she noted which students in each class did well on end-of-year exams. She hypothesizes these students will be less likely to need additional support to access the ELA content.

Next, she turns her attention to the available formative assessment scores included in her dashboard. At Sun Hill, STAR reading was selected as the benchmark assessment and the diagnostic assessment. Since Ms. James was not familiar with STAR, she visited the academic screen tools chart (https://charts.intensive intervention.org/ascreening) on the National Center on Intensive Intervention website. From that website, she noted that the benchmark assessments had convincing evidence of their classification accuracy and that the tool was valid and reliable. She learned the tool used multiple choice question answering to assess comprehension, it took 18 minutes to administer, it was computer scored, and reported scores in a variety of metrics (e.g., grade equivalent, percentiles). Next, she looked up the tool on the publisher's website. There she learned that it in addition to reading comprehension, it also measured vocabulary and that it could be given in Spanish. Collecting her thoughts, she surmised that it did not assess basic reading skills. She made notes to discuss all of this with Mr. Martinez.

Multi-Tiered Systems of Support (MTSS) is a school-based framework that integrates data and instruction (American Institutes for Research [AIR], 2022). Schools like Sun Hill High School collect MTSS data from various sources and then use that data to guide instructional planning and decision-making for all students. The goal of MTSS frameworks is prevention and early identification of potential academic difficulties through screening and early intervention through multiple increasingly intense tiers of instruction and intervention (Fuchs et al., 2010; Reed et al., 2012; Vaughn & Fletcher, 2012). Tier 1 is considered core instruction. Core instruction should support 80–85% of all learners. Tier 2 instruction typically occurs in the general education classroom and involves supplemental instruction and progress monitoring. Tier 3 is considered special education services and is typically provided by interventionists. Students are screened for risk for reading difficulties 2–3 times per year (see chapter 3 for additional information about Tier 2 and 3 instruction).

In the next two sections, we describe how secondary teachers like Ms. James and Mr. Martinez can use assessments to plan instruction and make decisions in the core ELA classroom. Additionally, we describe several evidence-based practices that support all learners from diverse cultural and linguistic backgrounds, including SWDs.

Assessments to Guide Instructional Planning and Decision-Making

At the secondary level, there are several important sources of data that schools and teachers can use to guide instructional planning and decision-making in core ELA classrooms. Ms. James and Mr. Martinez have access to summative assessments, or the assessments that reveal what was learned related to grade-level academic standards (Rissman et al., 2009). Because reading is a complex construct, comprehensive reading assessment systems also include screeners and diagnostics (Wixson, 2017). Screeners take little time to administer and can be used for multiple purposes. For example, they can be used to screen students for potential reading problems—they answer the question: Which students do I need to give a diagnostic assessment to? They can also be used as benchmarks. When used as a benchmark, they help teachers gauge the student's progress. Diagnostics take longer to give, but they provide far more information about what the student knows and can do during reading. They also suggest areas where students need additional instruction. Finally, there are reading assessment tools that are more comprehensive, such as the STAR reading assessment described earlier.

Finally, it is important to note that since reading is comprised of multiple components (e.g., vocabulary, comprehension), there are many tools available to assess reading performance. Schools typically purchase one or more for teachers to use. As illustrated in the above vignette, teachers are encouraged to learn as much as possible about the assessment tools they are given.

> # TEXTBOX 2.2.
> # AFFORDABLE ASSESSMENT TOOLS
>
> - **Bear, D. R., Invernizzi, M., Templeton, S., & Johnston, F. (2012).** *Words their way* **(5th ed.). Pearson.**
>   - This is an assessment tool that includes a spelling assessment for secondary students that can be given to an entire class of secondary students. Better understanding the kinds of word errors made by students can inform instruction.
> - **Diamond, L., & Thorsnes, B. J. (2018).** *Assessing reading: Multiple measures for all educators working to improve reading achievement* **(2nd ed.). Arena Press.**
>   - This assessment includes screeners and diagnostic assessments for many components of reading, including vocabulary, phonics, and comprehension. Some may be given to the whole class, while others are given one-on-one to students.
> - **Leslie, L., & Caldwell, J. S. (2021).** *Qualitative reading inventory* **(7th ed.). Pearson.**
>   - This comprehensive diagnostic assessment tool can be used flexibly to better understand students' reading challenges. For example, it can be used to assess students' knowledge of the macrostructures of text through retelling, reading levels in different content, or students use of strategies for reading. It can be administered to the whole class, but it is often used with individual students.
>
> *Note*: This is a collection of affordable assessment materials teachers can use to support literacy learning.

Instructional Methods for Core Reading Instruction

At their first planning meeting, the teachers recognize that the goal of Tier 1 instruction is to ensure 80–85% of students' needs are met through core instruction. Together, they decide to teach the short story "The Gift of the Magi" by O. Henry. This short story is useful for developing the concept of irony. In it, Jim and Della, the main characters, sell their most beloved possession to buy something beautiful for the other. Ms. James and Mr. Martinez plan their instruction using universal design for learning (UDL) for whole class activities to ensure all students have access to the ELA content (i.e., planning for multiple means of engagement, representation, and action/expression). To promote engagement, the teachers plan to recruit students' interest by discussing the importance of loved ones in our lives. This short story is accessible, as it is available in both text and movie formats. Finally, the teachers plan multiple ways for students to share what they learned from the story.

Next, they plan to use differentiated instruction (DI) to meet the individualized needs of students as part of classroom-based, Tier 2 instruction. They plan small group instruction using data from the STAR assessment. Group sizes will vary, with the smallest group size reserved for students who need the most support. Although differentiated, the instructional target for all groups will remain the same—irony.

With UDL and DI as instructional frameworks, evidence-based practices will be used to delivered content instruction, including (a) explicit instruction, (b) vocabulary instruction, and (c) comprehension instruction. Perhaps most importantly, supporting secondary students' motivation and engagement in ELA content is critical. Often these terms are used interchangeably, there are important distinctions between the two, especially for reading (Cambria & Guthrie, 2012). In the context of reading, motivation to read includes interest, dedication, and confidence (Cambria & Guthrie, 2012). Two of these reside within the student. Students who are interested in the topic, or who are dedicated to doing well in school are easy for teachers—they are motivated. Interested students will have an abundance of background knowledge on topics that supports their motivation. Dedicated students will persist even if they have challenges during reading. They will put forth the effort necessary to be successful with a challenging text. On the other hand, students who lack confidence in their reading abilities, those who struggle with reading, are dependent on teachers to support their motivation.

Teachers' attention to task difficulty is critical for students who lack confidence or who struggle to read (Lipson & Wixson, 2013). For these students, ELA texts must be accessible through technology or varying the readability of texts. This is critical since the focus of ELA content is related to developing comprehension and vocabulary. High-quality ELA instruction includes choice, relevance, and collaboration with peers—evidence-based practices known to support motivation and engagement among secondary students (Cambria & Guthrie, 2012).

Effective and Explicit Instruction

The foundation of explicit instruction is effective instruction (Archer & Hughes, 2011). Principles of effective instruction include (a) optimizing engaged time or time on task, (b) promoting high levels of success, (c) increasing content coverage, (d) spending more time in teacher-led instructional groups, (e) providing scaffolded instruction, and (f) addressing different forms of knowledge. Applied to ELA instruction in secondary classrooms, optimizing engagement includes high-quality discussions about texts, focusing on differentiated vocabulary instruction in small groups, and reading copious amounts of engaging texts to develop new knowledge and vocabulary. Finally, explicitly teaching students how to strategically use their academic skills and knowledge to address different forms of information is key. For example, when students learn strategy routines they should also learn when and where to use them.

Explicit instruction in the secondary ELA classroom should provide students with well-designed, focused lessons that support students' organization of new knowledge. Thinking back to RSF, well-developed general knowledge is critical to reading comprehension. Explicit instruction includes modeling, guided, and independent practice. This is particularly important when students are learning new vocabulary and comprehension strategies. Finally, explicit instruction supposes that students are expected to provide frequent responses, which draw immediate affirmative and corrective feedback from their teachers.

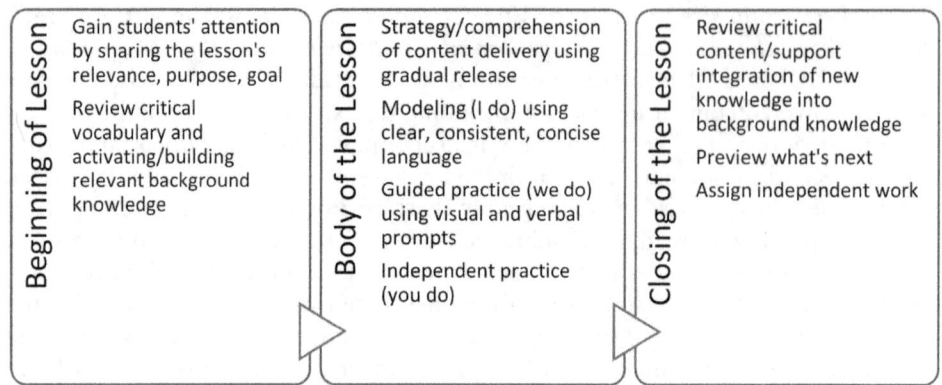

Figure 2.2 Closing the Lesson Plan for Secondary Core Literacy
Source: Adapted from Archer & Hughes (2011).

Vocabulary Instruction

Vocabulary instruction is a key component of core ELA reading instruction. It is the index of what we know (Lipson & Wixson, 2013). Vocabulary is developed indirectly through wide reading, fostering word consciousness, and through read-alouds (Beck et al., 2013). Vocabulary should also be taught through explicit instruction (Archer & Hughes, 2011). Beck and her colleagues (2013) developed a tiered system of vocabulary. Tier 1 words are those words that are used in everyday language (e.g., family). Tier 2 words are high frequency words that are used by sophisticated learners (e.g., perseverance, coincidence, absurd). Tier 2 words typically cut across content areas (e.g., summarize). Finally, Tier 3 words are low-frequency content-specific words (e.g., nucleus). In the ELA classroom, Tier 2 and 3 words are considered instructional targets for explicit instruction.

Guidelines for selecting appropriate vocabulary words for explicit instruction include selecting (a) unknown words, (b) words that are important to comprehending the text, (c) words that students will find useful in the future, and (d) words that are difficult to learn (Archer & Hughes, 2011). Recall that in our vignette, Ms. James and Mr. Martinez selected a text to begin teaching students about the concept of irony. Irony represents a difficult-to-learn concept that is highly relevant to later ELA instruction. It is also a word that challenges the bounds of making meaning from word parts. The word *iron* is not related to *irony*, which might both interest and flummox readers.

Evidence-based vocabulary instructional methods include using the Frayer model and morphemic decoding. For the Frayer model, students complete graphic organizers on paper or electronically. The vocabulary word sits in the center of four quadrants. In the upper right-hand quadrant, a student-friendly definition is recorded. Notice this does not say to record the dictionary definition here. In the lower right-hand quadrant, examples of the term are generated. This quadrant should include synonyms, concrete applications, or relevant illustrations of the word. In the upper left-hand quadrant, characteristics of the term are noted. These are features that help students identify, recognize, or distinguish the term. Finally, the lower left-hand quadrant should have non-examples required. This could include antonyms, inaccurate applications, or illustrations of the word. In figure 2.3, we illustrate a completed Frayer model for *irony*.

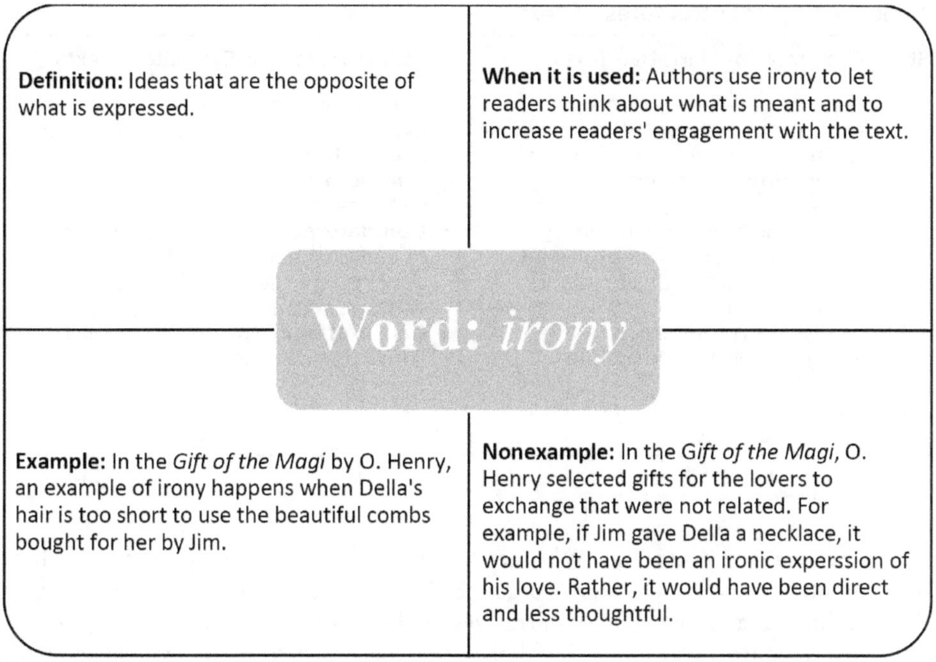

Definition: Ideas that are the opposite of what is expressed.	**When it is used:** Authors use irony to let readers think about what is meant and to increase readers' engagement with the text.
Example: In the *Gift of the Magi* by O. Henry, an example of irony happens when Della's hair is too short to use the beautiful combs bought for her by Jim.	**Nonexample:** In the *Gift of the Magi*, O. Henry selected gifts for the lovers to exchange that were not related. For example, if Jim gave Della a necklace, it would not have been an ironic experssion of his love. Rather, it would have been direct and less thoughtful.

Word: *irony*

Figure 2.3 Frayer Model Example
Source: Frayer et al. (1969).

There is convincing evidence of a relationship between morphological skills and reading comprehension (see e.g., Carlisle & Goodwin, 2013). Archer and her colleagues (2003) developed the Overt Strategy to help students pronounce multisyllabic words. Students are taught to identify and underline root and base words and to identify and circle affixes. Next, students are instructed to pronounce each morpheme in the order they are written. Once that's accomplished, they are instructed to make it a *real* word. This decoding strategy can be used in conjunction with the Word Mapping Strategy. This strategy teaches students to use morphological analysis to break a word into morphemes and define each morpheme to come up with a tentative definition of the word (Harris, Schumaker, & Deshler, 2011). Students are then taught to use these strategies during reading to support pronunciation and meaning-making of unknown multisyllabic words.

Comprehension Instruction

There is ample evidence to support the use of comprehension strategy instruction to support the reading comprehension of students with disabilities (see e.g., Jitendra & Gajria, 2011). Strategy instruction should include the use of explicit instruction (e.g., I do, we do, you do). For many students with disabilities, attending to the macrostructure of the text is particularly challenging (see e.g., McNamara, 2007). The macrostructure of the text embeds the global meaning of the text. For narratives, the macrostructure is story grammar, and for expository texts, it's text structure. Story maps are used to document story grammar elements included in a story. Story grammar elements include characters, setting, problem, and resolution. Variations of this strategy range from embedding stops during reading to address questions related to

Table 2.1. Macro Structures of Text

Story Grammar for Narrative Texts	Text Structures for Expository Texts
• **Characters:** Develop students' understandings of how authors used characters within the story (e.g., main characters drive plots and are well developed). • **Settings:** Where and when a story takes place. Contextualize explaining why authors selected this time and place for their story. • **Plot:** The linear progression of the story (e.g., problem/conflict, attempts, twists of the story). • **Resolution:** How the tale ends, either neatly or otherwise.	• **Sequence/process** (e.g., steps in an experiment, how to make something). • **Description** (e.g., definitions). • **Chronology** (e.g., sequence of historical events). • **Compare/contrast** (e.g., comparison of a known concept with an unknown concept, frequently used in conjunction with description in expository texts). • **Cause/effect** (e.g., used to explain why something happened).

Note: Macrostructures of texts are challenging for students with disabilities. Explicitly teaching them improves reading comprehension.

story grammar elements (e.g., Who are the main characters of the story, and how do you know?) (Crabtree, Alber-Morgan, & Konrad, 2010) to using character event maps to build comprehension of narratives (Williamson et al., 2015).

Text structure instruction highlights the macrostructure of expository texts (Jitendra & Gajria, 2011). Using explicit instruction, students are systematically taught to identify structures used by authors to convey the meanings of a text. Common text structures include description, compare/contrast, sequence, problem solution, and cause and effect. Teachers identify which structures are found in the text, explicitly teach students to recognize the signal words for each structure (e.g., conversely, similarly for compare/contrast) as well as the graphic organizer associated with the structure (e.g., Venn diagram for compare/contrast). This directs attention to what's important in the text and improves comprehension (Carnahan et al., 2016).

CONCLUSION

Using the MTSS approach to assessment and support, along with UDL and differentiated instruction in the secondary ELA classroom, enhances the possibility that the vast majority of learners' needs will be met. Effective delivery of both explicit vocabulary instruction and explicit comprehension strategy instruction comports with what is known about the science of reading instruction. Finally, close attention to students' motivation and engagement provides the necessary context to support all learners.

Bridge from Instruction to Intervention

High-quality core reading instruction will be sufficient for most secondary students; however, those who continue to experience significant difficulty comprehending complex, grade-level text will likely require supplemental reading interventions delivered with sufficient intensity to improve their reading achievement (Solis et al., 2014; Vaughn & Fletcher, 2012; Vaughn et al., 2022). In the next chapter, we describe how to support secondary students with more significant needs.

REFERENCES

American Institutes for Research (2022). Center on Multi-Tiered Systems of Support. https://www.air.org/centers/center-multi-tiered-system-supports-mtss-center

Archer, A. L., Gleason, M. M., & Vachon, V. L. (2003). Decoding and fluency: Foundation skills for struggling older readers. *Learning Disability Quarterly*, 26(2), 89–101. https://doi.org/10.2307/1593592

Archer, A., & Hughes, C. A. (2011). *Explicit instruction: Efficient and effective teaching*. New York: Guilford.

Barnes, M. A., Ahmed, Y., Barth, A., & Francis, D. J. (2015). The relation of knowledge-text integration processes and reading comprehension in 7th- to 12th-grade students. *Scientific Studies of Reading*, 19(4), 253–72. https://doi:10.1080/10888438.2015.1022650

Boardman, A. G., Roberts, G., Vaughn, S., Wexler, J., Murray, C. S., & Kosanovich, M. (2008). *Effective instruction for adolescent struggling readers: A practice brief*. RMC Research Corporation, Center on Instruction. https://files.eric.ed.gov/fulltext/ED521836.pdf

Carlisle, J. F., & Goodwin, A. (2013). Morphemes matter: How morphological knowledge contributes to reading and writing. In C. A. Stone, E. R. Silliman, B. J. Ehren, & G. P. Wallach (Eds.), *Handbook of language and literacy: Development and disorders* (2nd ed., pp. 265–82). Guilford.

Carnahan, C., Williamson, P., Birri, N., Swoboda, C., & Snyder, K. (2016). Increasing comprehension of expository science text for students with autism spectrum disorder. *Focus on Autism and Other Developmental Disabilities*, 31(3), 208–20. https://doi:10.1177/1088357615610539

Castles, A., & Nation, K. (2022). Learning to read words. In M. J. Snowling, C. A. Hulme, & K. Nation (Eds.), *The science of reading: A handbook* (2nd ed., pp. 165–80). Wiley-Blackwell.

Castles, A., Rastle, K., & Nation, K. (2018). Ending the reading wars: Reading acquisition from novice to expert. *Psychological Science in the Public Interest*, 19(1), 5–51. https://doi.org/10.1177/1529100618772271

Ciullo, S., Lembke, E. S., Carlisle, A., Thomas, C. N., Goodwin, M., & Judd, L. (2016). Implementation of evidence-based literacy practices in middle school response to intervention: An observation study. *Learning Disability Quarterly*, 39(1), 44–57. https://doi.org/10.1177/0731948714566120

Common Core State Standards Initiative. (2010). National Governors Association Center for Best Practices and Council of Chief State School Officers.

Crabtree, T., Alber-Morgan, S. R., & Konrad, M. (2010). The effects of self-monitoring of story elements on the reading comprehension of high school seniors with learning disabilities. *Education & Treatment of Children*, 33(2), 187–203.

Denton, C. A., Vaughn, S., Wexler, J., Bryan, D., & Reed, D. (2012). *Effective instruction for middle school students with reading difficulties: The reading teacher's sourcebook*. Brookes.

Every Student Succeeds Act, 20 U.S.C. 6301 (2015). Public Law 114–95, 114th Congress. https://www.congress.gov/114/plaws/publ95/PLAW-114publ95.pdf

Filderman, M. J., Austin, C. R., Boucher, A. N., O'Donnell, K., & Swanson, E. A. (2021). A meta-analysis of the effects of reading comprehension interventions on reading comprehension outcomes of struggling readers in third through 12th grades. *Exceptional Children, 88*(2), 163–84. https://doi.org/10.1177/00144029211050860

Foorman, B. R., Wu, Y-C., Quinn, J. M., & Petscher, Y. (2020). How do latent decoding and language predict latent reading comprehension: Across two years in grades 5, 7, and 9? *Reading and Writing, 33*(9), 2281–2309.

Fuchs, L. S., Fuchs, D., & Compton, D. L. (2010). Rethinking response to intervention at middle and high school. *School Psychology Review, 39*(1), 22–28.

Gilmour, A. F., Fuchs, D., & Wehby, J. H. (2019). Are students with disabilities accessing the curriculum? A meta-analysis of the reading achievement gap between students with and without disabilities. *Exceptional Children, 85*(3), 329–46. https://doi.org/10.1177/0014402918795830

Gough, P. B., & Tunmer, W. E. (1986). Decoding, reading, and reading disability. *Remedial and Special Education, 7*(1), 6–10. https://doi.org/10.1177/074193258600700104

Harris, M. L., Schumaker, J. B., & Deshler, D. D. (2011). The effects of strategic morphological analysis instruction on the vocabulary performance of secondary students with and without disabilities. *Learning Disability Quarterly, 34*(1), 17–33.

Herrera, S., Truckenmiller, A. J., & Foorman, B. R. (2016). *Summary of 20 years of research on the effectiveness of adolescent literacy programs and practices*. REL 2016-178. Regional Educational Laboratory Southeast.

Hoover, W. A., & Gough, P. B. (1990). The simple view of reading. *Reading and Writing, 2*, 127–60. http://dx.doi.org/10.1007/BF00401799

Hoover, W. A., & Tunmer, W. E. (2018). The simple view of reading: Three assessments of its adequacy. *Remedial and Special Education, 39*(5), 304–12. https://doi.org/10.1177/0741932518773154

Hue, M. T. (2022). Inclusive education: Equal opportunities for all. In K. J. Kennedy, M. Pavlova, & J. C-K. Lee (Eds.), *Soft skills and hard values* (pp. 93–111). Routledge.

Hussar, B., Zhang, J., Hein, S., Wang, K., Roberts, A., Cui, J., Smith, M., Bullock, F., Barmer, A., & Dilig, R. (2020). *The condition of education 2020* (NCES 2020-144). US Department of Education: National Center for Education Statistics. https://nces.ed.gov/pubsearch/pubsinfo.asp?pubid=2020144

Jitendra, A. K., & Gajria, M. (2011). Reading comprehension instruction for students with learning disabilities. *Focus on Exceptional Children, 43*(8), 1–16. https://doi.org/10.17161/foec.v43i8.6690

Kamil, M. L., Borman, G. D., Dole, J., Kral, C. C., Salinger, T., & Torgesen, J. (2008). *Improving adolescent literacy: Effective classroom and intervention practices*. IES Practice Guide. NCEE 2008-4027. National Center for Education Evaluation and Regional Assistance.

Klauda, S. L., Wigfield, A., & Cambria, J. (2012). Struggling readers' information text comprehension and motivation in early adolescence. In J. T. Guthrie, A. Wigfield, & S. L. Klauda (Eds.), *Adolescents' engagement in academic literacy* (pp. 295–351). College Park: University of Maryland.

Lervåg, A., & Melby-Lervåg, M. (2022). Early prediction of learning outcomes in reading. In M. Skeide (Ed.), *The Cambridge Handbook of Dyslexia and Dyscalculia* (Cambridge Handbooks in Psychology, pp. 305–17). Cambridge: Cambridge University Press. https://doi.org/10.1017/9781108973595.024

Lonigan, C. J., Burgess, S. R., & Schatschneider, C. (2018). Examining the simple view of reading with elementary school children: Still simple after all these years. *Remedial and Special Education, 39*(5), 260–73. https://doi:10.1177/0741932518764833

McKenna, J. W., Shin, M., & Ciullo, S. (2015). Evaluating reading and mathematics instruction for students with learning disabilities: A synthesis of observation research. *Learning Disability Quarterly, 38*(4), 195–207.

McNamara, D. S. (2007). *Reading comprehension strategies: Theories, interventions, and technologies.* Taylor & Francis Group.

National Assessment Governing Board. (2019). *Reading framework for the 2019 national assessment of educational progress.* US Department of Education. https://www.nagb.gov/content/dam/nagb/en/documents/publications/frameworks/reading/2019-reading-framework.pdf

National Governors Association Center for Best Practices & Council of Chief State School Officers. (2010). Common core state standards. Washington, DC: Authors.

Perfetti, C., & Stafura, J. (2014). Word knowledge in a theory of reading comprehension. *Scientific Studies of Reading, 18*(1), 22–37.

RAND Reading Study Group: Snow, C. (2002). *Reading for understanding: Toward an R&D program in reading comprehension.* Santa Monica, CA: RAND.

Reed, D. K. (2008). A synthesis of morphology interventions and effects on reading outcomes for students in grades K–12. *Learning Disabilities Research & Practice, 23*(1), 36–49. https://doi.org/10.1111/j.1540-5826.2007.00261.x

Reed, D. K., Wexler, J., & Vaughn, S. (2012). *RTI for reading at the secondary level: Recommended literacy practices and remaining questions.* Guilford.

Rissman, L. M., Miller, D. H., & Torgesen, J. K. (2009). *Adolescent Literacy Walk-Through for Principals: A Guide for Instructional Leaders.* RMC Research Corporation, Center on Instruction.

Santi, K. L., & Reed, D. K. (2015). *Improving reading comprehension of middle and high school students.* Springer International.

Scammacca, N. K., Roberts, G., Vaughn, S., & Stuebing, K. K. (2015). A meta-analysis of interventions for struggling readers in grades 4–12, 1980–2011. *Journal of Learning Disabilities, 48*(4), 369–90. https://doi.org/10.1177/0022219413504995

Scammacca, N. K., Roberts, G., Cho, E., Williams, K. J., Roberts, G., Vaughn, S. R., & Carroll, M. (2016). A century of progress: Reading interventions for students in grades 4–12, 1914–2014. *Review of Educational Research, 86*(3), 756–800. https://doi.org/10.3102/0034654316652942

Scammacca, N. K., Roberts, G., Vaughn, S., Edmonds, M., Wexler, J., Reutebuch, C. K., & Torgesen, J. K. (2007). *Interventions for adolescent struggling readers: A meta-analysis with implications for practice.* RMC Research Corporation, Center on Instruction.

Solis, M., Miciak, J., Vaughn, S., & Fletcher, J. (2014). Why intensive interventions matter: Longitudinal studies of adolescents with reading disabilities and poor reading comprehension. *Learning Disability Quarterly, 37*(4), 218–29. https://doi.org/10.1177/0731948714528806

Swanson, E., & Wexler, J. (2017). Selecting appropriate text for adolescents with disabilities. *TEACHING Exceptional Children, 49*(3), 160–67.

Torgesen, J. K., Houston, D. D., Rissman, L. M., Decker, S. M., Roberts, G., Vaughn, S., Wexler, J., Francis, D. J., Rivera, M. O., & Lesaux, N. (2007). *Academic literacy instruction for adolescents: A guidance document from the Center on Instruction*. RMC Research Corporation, Center on Instruction. https://media.carnegie.org/filer_public/a7/9b/a79bee13-b82e-47bd-ab63-9190baa31975/ccny_report_2007_guidance.pdf

US Department of Education. (2022, July). *Students with disabilities*. Institute of Education Sciences, National Center for Education Statistics. https://nces.ed.gov/programs/coe/indicator/cgg

Vaughn, S., & Fletcher, J. M. (2012). Response to intervention with secondary school students with reading difficulties. *Journal of Learning Disabilities, 45*(3), 244–56. https://doi.org/10.1177/0022219412442157

Vaughn, S., & Fletcher, J. M. (2021). Explicit instruction as the essential tool for executing the science of reading. *Reading League Journal, 2*(2), 13–20.

Vaughn, S., Roberts, G., Wexler, J., Vaughn, M. G., Fall, A. M., & Schnakenberg, J. B. (2015). High school students with reading comprehension difficulties: Results of a randomized control trial of a two-year reading intervention. *Journal of Learning Disabilities, 48*(5), 546–58. http://dx.doi.org/10.1177/0022219413515511

Vaughn, S., Gersten, R., Dimino, J., Taylor, M. J., Newman-Gonchar, R., Krowka, S., Kieffer, M. J., McKeown, M., Reed, D., Sanchez, M., St. Martin, K., Wexler, J., Morgan, S., Yañez, A., & Jayanthi, M. (2022). *Providing reading interventions for students in grades 4–9* (WWC 2022007). National Center for Education Evaluation and Regional Assistance (NCEE), Institute of Education Sciences, US Department of Education. https://ies.ed.gov/ncee/wwc/Docs/PracticeGuide/WWC-practice-guide-reading-intervention-full-text.pdf

Wexler, J., Kearns, D. M., Lemons, C. J., Mitchell, M., Clancy, E., Davidson, K. A., Sinclair, A. C., & Wei, Y. (2018). Reading comprehension and co-teaching practices in middle school English language arts classrooms. *Exceptional Children, 84*(4), 384–402. https://doi.org/10.1177/0014402918771543

Williamson, P., Carnahan, C., Birri, N., & Swoboda, C. (2015). Improving comprehension of narrative using character event maps for high school students with autism spectrum disorder. *Journal of Special Education, 49*(1), 28–38. https://journals.sagepub.com/doi/10.1177/0022466914521301

Wixson, K. K. (2017). An interactive view of reading comprehension: Implications for assessment. *Language, Speech, and Hearing Services in Schools, 48*(2), 77–83.

3

Reading Intervention Methods for Secondary Students

Jessica R. Toste, Brennan Chandler,
Erica Fry, and Kelly J. Williams

LITERACY IS A HIGH-STAKES EDUCATIONAL ISSUE due to its impact on students' lives, as well its impact on society, the economy, and public health more broadly. Students with reading difficulties are at heightened risk for a range adverse education and health outcomes (see DeWalt & Pignone, 2005; Reynolds & Ou, 2004). Concerningly, national data indicate that two-thirds of upper elementary students are struggling with reading (National Center for Education Statistics [NCES], 2019) and this number is even greater among those with identified disabilities. Only 12% of students with disabilities read at or above proficient levels in fourth grade, compared to 39% of their peers without disabilities (NCES, 2019). Further, the recently released long-term trend report from the National Assessment of Educational Progress indicated that reading scores declined overall between 2020 and 2022 (pre- to post-pandemic assessments)—backtracking on decades of incremental progress, and further widening the gaps for students with disabilities and students of color (NCES, 2022).

Thus, the delivery of effective intervention supports is critical. This is especially important as students move beyond the elementary grades as there is evidence that those who have not attained proficiency by fourth grade rarely catch up across their school years (Francis et al., 1996; Vaughn et al., 2003). The secondary grades represent a unique challenge for students with reading difficulties. By this time, it is generally expected that students will be able to read a variety of complex texts to gain content knowledge and to read for understanding (Chall & Jacobs, 2003; Wanzek et al., 2010). Specifically, the Common Core State Standards suggest that students must read and comprehend complex literary and informational texts "proficiently and independently" (National Governors Association, Council of Chief State School Officers [NGA CCSSO], 2010). These reading demands continue to increase dramatically as students transition from middle to high school and, at the same time, formal literacy instruction largely disappears (Kamil et al., 2008).

The purpose of this chapter is to describe scientifically based practices related to delivery of reading intervention for students in grades 6–12. These practices should work in tandem with high-quality reading instruction being provided in the core curriculum. While interventions may promote access to grade-level curriculum, it is critical that students with persistent reading difficulties receive supplemental interventions that target foundational skills development and address any existing gaps in students' reading skills. This chapter will address five questions:

1. What are the essential skills required for proficient reading in the secondary grades?
2. What are the theories that inform reading intervention delivery for secondary students?
3. What assessment methods should guide instructional decision-making for secondary students receiving reading intervention?
4. How is student data used to intensify and individualize reading intervention?
5. What are key scientifically based reading intervention methods?

THEORIES INFORMING READING INTERVENTIONS FOR SECONDARY STUDENTS

We know that reading skills follow typical developmental trajectories, with the most growth in reading acquisition taking place throughout the primary grades (Cunningham & Stanovich, 1991; Rayner et al., 2001); however, there is considerable ongoing development in the later grades. Reading comprehension, as the ultimate goal of accessing text, has been the primary outcome of interest in over three decades of research investigating reading development (e.g., Cain & Oakhill, 2009). Reading comprehension involves the proficient use and integration of a complex set of skills with the ultimate goal of gaining meaning from text (Perfetti et al., 2005; Perfetti et al., 1996; Scarborough, 2001; Stanovich & West, 1989). These component skills have been investigated to help understand the variance in students' reading comprehension—for example, the student who has difficulty decoding words is likely to have lower comprehension than their peer who decodes words quickly and accurately. These component skills are most frequently represented in the Simple View of Reading (SVR; Gough & Tunmer, 1986; Hoover & Gough, 1990). The SVR posits that disruption in either decoding skill or listening comprehension can result in difficulties with reading comprehension. The first element represents those skills related to printed word recognition, while the other group includes the factors that reading shares with oral language. The interdependent nature of these key components increases as students move from the early to the later grades. For example, word recognition accounts for a higher proportion of unique variance in students' reading comprehension in early elementary grades but considerably less variance by middle and high school (Catts et al., 2005). However, there is evidence to suggest that this is not a clear trajectory for all students (Cain & Oakhill, 2009; Silva & Cain, 2015). For secondary students with persistent reading difficulties, word recognition may continue to account for much of their reading performance, and they require targeted interventions to support these skills.

This skill instruction must also be explicit and systematic. Explicit instruction has long been considered essential to specialized instruction for students with or at risk for disability—and is well-established as a best practice for delivery of effective academic interventions (Hughes et al., 2017). Explicit instruction is defined as a direct, purposeful, and engaging way of teaching skills. We use the terms explicit and direct instruction interchangeably here, though we note the differentiation with Direct Instruction (DI) as a particular scripted instructional program used for the delivery of direct instruction ("little di"). Explicit instruction is teacher-led and has clearly defined content, instructional delivery, and learner outcomes. The introduction of skills is systematic (e.g., follows a carefully planned sequence) and cumulative (e.g., builds on previously taught skills). Teachers use clear and concise language, include step-by-step demonstrations and guided practice opportunities, and ensure frequent and active student engagement (see Archer & Hughes, 2011; Engelmann, 1980).

Accumulated evidence has indicated this instructional approach is essential to the skill development of both emerging readers and struggling readers. Evidence supporting the effectiveness of DI programs is substantial. For example, Stockard and colleagues (2018) conducted a meta-analytic review including 328 studies and reported consistently positive effects across five decades, different outcome measures, student and implementer characteristics, and other control variables. There were stronger results for students who began DI in kindergarten, but also cumulative effects for more years of intervention. Studies that use these explicit or direct instructional approaches outside of DI-branded programs find similar effects. The publication of the report of the National Reading Panel (NRP, 2000) clearly pointed to the evidence supporting the use of explicit, systematic instruction to develop foundational reading skills—and has been supported by decades of evidence since that time (see Foorman et al., 2016; Gersten et al., 2017).

EVIDENCE BASE ON READING INTERVENTIONS

The NRP report emphasized the importance of instruction across five essential reading components (i.e., phonological awareness, phonics, fluency, vocabulary, comprehension), and recommended that individual student's development across each of these components be considered in order to design and deliver effective interventions. The Education Sciences Reform Act (2002) established the Institute of Education Sciences (IES) as a separate research arm of the US Department of Education. A range of funding priorities were identified, including identification of scientifically based interventions to improve students' literacy skills. As a result, the past two decades have seen an increase in research focused on development and testing of reading interventions, and a particular interest in how to support older students.

Connor and colleagues (2014) synthesized contributions from research funded by IES related to improving outcomes for students with or at risk for reading disability. This report highlighted evidence of the effectiveness of fluency interventions, vocabulary interventions, and intensive, individualized instruction. The conclusions from this report have been supported from findings of systematic reviews of reading intervention research for students in grades 4–12. For example, Scammacca et al. (2016) synthesized evidence that older students with reading difficulties can make measurable gains when interventions are appropriately aligned with their needs. They described findings to suggest that struggling readers often require interventions over a long period of time, and some may benefit from individualized interventions. Finally, the IES Educator's Practice Guide on reading interventions for students in grades 4–9 (Vaughn et al., 2022) provides explicit recommendations to promote student achievement. This guide includes practices focused on building students' decoding skills for multisyllabic words, providing purposeful fluency-building activities, and routinely using a set of comprehension-building practices to help students make sense of text. These recommendations are supported by substantial evidence and considered best practice.

ASSESSMENT METHODS TO GUIDE INSTRUCTIONAL DECISION-MAKING

When delivering reading intervention, teachers must rely on student assessment data to select a validated intervention program that will meet the student's needs. There is strong evidence that validated and targeted reading interventions will be effective for many students who struggle with reading; however, there remain a significant number of students for whom these interventions will not be sufficient (e.g., Al Otaiba & Fuchs, 2006; McMaster et al., 2005; O'Connor & Fuchs, 2013; Torgesen, 2004). This group of students experience persistent and seemingly intractable difficulties, and these difficulties are often exacerbated as students enter secondary settings where they face mounting challenges and literacy demands. Students with persistent difficulties require support via *intensive* and *individualized* reading interventions. Research has demonstrated that data-based instruction (DBI)—also referred to as data-based individualization (NCII, 2013) or data-based program modification (Deno, 1985)—is a method of informing instructional decision with substantial evidence for effectiveness.

The DBI process generally begins with a standardized, supplemental intervention, which is then customized based on collection and interpretation of ongoing formative assessment data (Fuchs & Fuchs, 2016). Progress monitoring data is used to assess students' responsiveness to intervention methods and determine when instructional adjustments are needed, while diagnostic assessment data are important for understanding students' skills profiles. To illustrate, we turn to the case scenario of Ms. Oliver—a high school reading intervention teacher who is committed to meeting the needs of struggling readers in the secondary grades.

Ms. Oliver serves students with a diverse range of needs. She provides targeted reading interventions, supplemental to her students' core grade-level curriculum. Her students' needs vary greatly, with some who struggle with efficiently using text to gain new information and others who are unable to decode words due to lack of foundational skills. After learning about DBI, Ms. Oliver is eager to use these assessment methods to intensify intervention for some of the students on her caseload for whom her standard interventions do not seem to be enough.

To be effective, the DBI process must build on an intervention program with evidence for effectiveness. Thus, before intensifying intervention, teachers should consider:

- Has the student been taught using a scientifically based intervention that is appropriate for their needs? That is to say, the intervention program must be aligned with the student's current skills and area(s) of need. If a student is lacking foundational word reading skills, then it would not be surprising to find that they weren't making adequate progress if their intervention focused solely on connected text and reading for information.
- Has the program been implemented with fidelity? Before we can make a claim that an intervention is not effective for a student, it is essential to ensure that the intervention has been implemented as designed (e.g., content, dosage or length of sessions, group size).

- Has the program been implemented for a sufficient amount of time to determine response? Intensive intervention often requires additional time and resources; as such, before we determine that a student needs something more, we should ensure that we have allowed time for them to learn, practice, and use new skills.

Data-Based Instruction

If a student has not demonstrated the expected level of progress even though their intervention program is appropriately aligned with their needs and has been implemented with fidelity for a sufficient amount of time, they may require intensive and individualized supports. Research has demonstrated that DBI results in significant improvements in the academic performance of students with or at risk for learning disabilities (Filderman et al., 2018; Jung et al., 2018), and even greater gains associated with greater use of data (Fuchs et al., 2021).

The DBI process is often presented as a five-step process: (1) teacher delivers an intervention program targeting the student's needs; (2) student progress is monitored on an ongoing basis; (3) when data indicate the student is not making expected progress, the teacher conducts a diagnostic assessment to determine the student's specific needs and whether the intervention is meeting those needs; (4) the intervention or instructional delivery is adjusted accordingly; and (5) monitoring of student progress continues after the instructional adjustment (National Center on Intensive Intervention [NCII], 2013).

Progress Monitoring

During reading intervention, the teacher collects frequent progress monitoring data. DBI most commonly incorporates data collected through curriculum-based measurement (CBM; Deno, 1985), an ongoing progress monitoring system used to evaluate effectiveness of instruction. CBM scores are reliable and valid global indicators of performance in reading (Reschly et al., 2009; Shin & McMaster, 2019; Wayman et al., 2007; Yeo, 2010). It is generally recommended to use a CBM that assesses oral reading fluency (ORF), which involves the student reading a passage aloud for one minute and the teacher scoring the number of words read correctly. ORF scores have been found to be strongly associated with standardized measures of reading achievement (Wayman et al., 2007). For secondary students, teachers may also consider a CBM that assesses reading comprehension (e.g., Maze). Maze typically involves a 3-minute timed text reading task wherein every seventh word is missing, and the student selects the correct word for each blank to restore meaning to the sentence (Hosp et al., 2016).

First, set an individualized goal for student performance at the end of the intervention period. Multiple goal-setting methods are available, so the one best aligned with the individual student can be selected. For example, *benchmarking* involves selecting a goal that has been predetermined by a publisher or school district and may be an appropriate method when the student is achieving near grade level. If the benchmark goal is unrealistically high, the *expected rate of improvement* method, which provides a formula for calculating a goal based on peer performance, may be a better fit. A third option is the *intra-individual rate of improvement* method, which provides a formula based on the individual student's past performance. This approach is used when data suggest the other methods will not result in an appropriately ambitious, yet attainable, goal.

28   Chapter 3: Reading Intervention Methods for Secondary Students

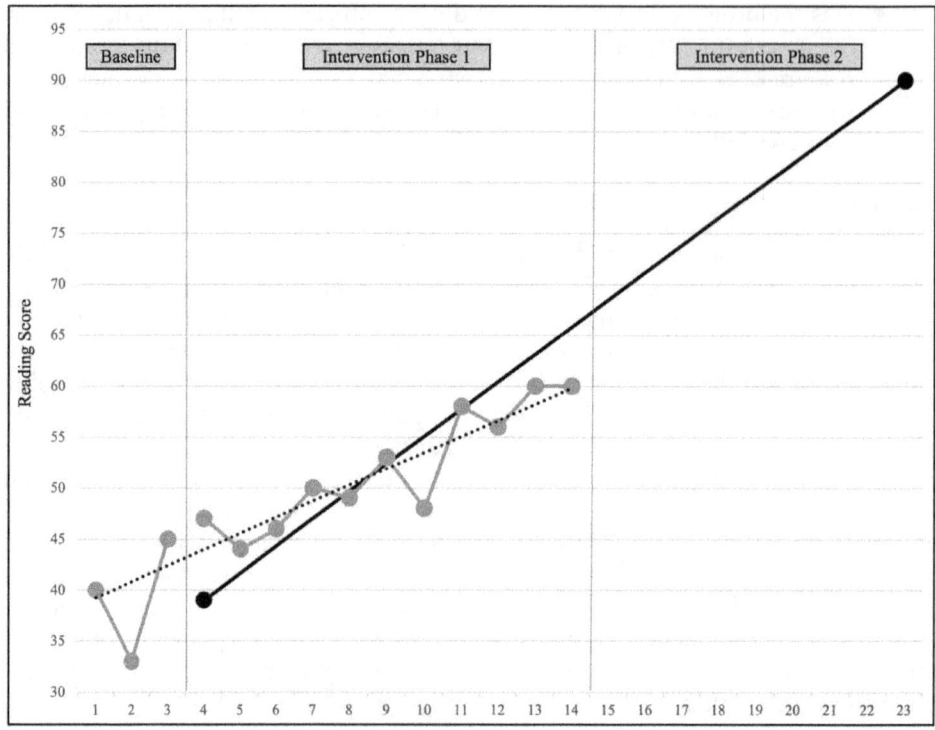

Figure 3.1   Sample CBM Progress Graph

To implement CBM, teachers measure student progress on a frequent (e.g., weekly) basis and place scores on a graph to depict progress. The CBM graph guides teachers in decision-making (Filderman & Toste, 2018). Figure 3.1 presents a sample CBM progress graph for an individual student named Sam. Key features of the graph include scores on weekly CBM probes; the long-range goal line (solid line) which is the expected or desired rate of growth; and the slope or trend line (dotted line), which is the student's rate of growth under the instructional program. To make instructional decisions, Sam's teacher first implements the intervention (Phase 1) and, after 10 to 12 weeks, inspects the graph to compare actual rate of growth (blue slope line) to expected rate of growth (orange goal line). If the actual rate of growth is lower than expected, it signals a need for an instructional adjustment. Sam's teacher adjusts the intervention, and then continues to collect data to evaluate the effects.

Diagnostic Assessment

There are two key decision points in the DBI process: (1) deciding *whether* to adjust instruction, and (2) deciding *how* to adjust instruction when necessary. Interpretation of CBM progress graphs (as described above) supports the teacher in making the first decision, but the second decision requires additional assessment data. Diagnostic assessment data will provide additional information specific to the student's areas of strength and need. For example, when graphed CBM data reflect a lack of progress over a period of several weeks, the teacher determines that there is a need to adjust instruction but may need more information to understand why intervention is not effective for this student. There are various types of diagnostic assessments that teachers may use to inform their instructional decision-making. If they have been collecting ORF CBM data, they might conduct an error analysis. Teachers might also consider conducting a spelling error analysis or administering a phonics inventory. These assessments provide more specific information about students' current skills.

Diagnostic assessment can also provide valuable information about behavioral and psychosocial factors that may be impacting student performance. These factors include motivation, attention, engagement, and emotional regulation. Teachers may seek additional information in these areas through a variety of methods including observation, student interviewing, and data from behavior charts. If the student has a recent functional behavior assessment, this may be a rich data source, illuminating not only the function of student behavior but also recommended strategies for supporting student learning.

Finally, consider the instructional environment. Environmental factors impacting student learning and achievement include classroom management, group size, homogeneity of group needs, and interpersonal dynamics within the group. Environmental data sources include observations conducted by the teacher or an outside observer, student interviewing, and group skills inventories. Enlisting the support of another adult in the building may be particularly beneficial in identifying factors related to classroom management such as routines, procedures, noise level, and sources of interruption or distraction from the intervention.

Intervention Adjustments

Finally, based on the collection and interpretation of both CBM progress data and diagnostic assessment data, the teacher will make decisions about instructional adjustments that may better align the intervention to student needs. Adaptations must be strategically aligned with all available data as students receiving intensive interventions cannot afford to lose valuable learning time. The teacher considers the range of adjustments that may result in more positive student outcomes. These include adjustments to dosage, learning environment, cognitive and behavioral supports, alignment to targeted skills, and instructional delivery.

Adjustments to dosage may involve changes to the length of intervention sessions, frequency of intervention sessions, group size, frequency and amount of feedback provided, amount of practice time provided, and number of opportunities to respond. The learning environment may be adjusted by moving from heterogeneous to homogeneous grouping, providing alternate seating, reducing distractions, or changing the location of intervention. Cognitive and behavioral supports include the use of graphic organizers, note-taking strategies, timers, self-regulation, self-monitoring, and self-recording strategies. Based on diagnostic assessment data, it may become evident that a student requires more instructional time focused on specific skills. Adjustments may also be made to instructional delivery by increasing explicit instruction; this may include providing additional modeling, increasing guided practice time before moving to independent practice, and providing more detailed and immediate feedback.

KEY INTERVENTION METHODS

Secondary students with persistent reading difficulties benefit from targeted, supplemental, and explicit reading intervention that ranges from the word- to text-level. In this section, we outline five intervention domains and summarize key methods and instructional routines that optimize student learning within each domain.

Prerequisite Skills Instruction

After assessing the students on her caseload, Ms. Oliver noticed that Nico, one of her ninth grade students with severe reading difficulties, struggled the most on the diagnostic phonics inventory. Nico had trouble recalling vowel sounds and reading one-syllable words with various vowel patterns like "break" and" poke." After reviewing the results of the phonics inventory, it was evident to Ms. Oliver that Nico required foundational decoding skills instruction, but she was not sure where to begin.

In secondary schools across the United States, there are students with severe reading difficulties like Nico who lack foundational reading skills. Although these skills are taught in the elementary grades, it is imperative that these skills are addressed when students in the secondary grades have gaps in their knowledge and application of these foundational skills. As noted in the previous chapter, students must be able to decode words in order to comprehend text. Students with reading difficulties at the monosyllabic word level benefit from explicit instruction in decoding skills with opportunities to apply taught skills through connected text reading.

Foundational Skills Routine

Teachers can use a supplemental and targeted foundational skills routine that encompasses explicit instruction in phonemic awareness and phonics instruction with multiple opportunities to respond. Before teachers begin this instructional routine with students, they should review diagnostic assessment data to determine which skills and concepts students need targeted instruction in. Following this, they can use a phonics scope and sequence to determine where to start instruction. This five-step instructional routine that can be done in as little as 15 minutes includes: (a) letter-sound review, (b) blending practice, (c) read and write words, (d) new concept, and (e) read connected text.

Letter-Sound Review. The letter-sound review is an efficient way for students to gain fluency in their grapheme-phoneme correspondences (GPCs) with flash cards. Teachers can create their own deck of flash cards by choosing 8–10 previously introduced GPCs and preparing them on cards. Students will say the sound(s) that is represented by the grapheme on each card. If students' do not say the correct sound or hesitate, the teacher provides the correct sound and moves the card to the back of the deck.

Following the flash card GPC review, teachers will have students encode (i.e., spell) some of the review sounds. Teachers will select and pronounce 5–7 sounds; students will then spell all graphemes that represent the sound. If students write the incorrect grapheme, teachers can model the correct spellings of the graphemes on the student paper. The spelling portion of this review might sound something like this: *The sound is /ā/. What sound? Write the letter that represents the sound /ā/.*

Blending Practice. To facilitate phonemic awareness skills—the ability to manipulate individual sounds—necessary for decoding, blending practice can be advantageous. The focus of this part of the routine is for students to blend GPCs together with corrective feedback from the teacher. Using the same grapheme index cards from the letter-sound review, teachers present single-syllable words with three to four sounds (e.g., /b/ /r/ /ea/ /k/). The teacher directs students to say each sound individually (e.g., /b/ /r/ /ea/ /k/) and then blend the sounds together (e.g., break). Teachers can repeat this with 5–10 words.

Read and Write Words. Fluent word recognition is essential to decoding words, therefore repetitive word reading practice is necessary. Using previously mastered and introduced GPCs, teachers create word lists of 15–20 words for students to read and write. As students read and write the decodable words, teachers provide corrective feedback as necessary.

New Concept. Up until this point, the foundational skills routine has been a review of previously mastered and introduced concepts. The new concept portion of the routine is where the teacher explicitly teaches one—or a few—GPCs that the student has not yet mastered. For secondary students with persistent reading difficulties, this usually means providing explicit instruction in vowel teams (e.g., ea, oi, ie) and patterns. During this part of the routine, the teacher employs explicit instruction by modeling the GPC(s) and providing brief opportunities to practice reading and spelling a handful of words with target GPC(s). Instruction in a portion of the lesson might sound something like this: *Today we are going to learn the vowel teams ai and ay. What vowel teams? Both vowel teams usually make the sound ā. What sound?* The teacher would then have the student read and write a handful of preselected words with the vowel team.

Read Connected Text. In the final portion of the foundational skills routine, students move from the word-level to the text-level and apply the word reading skills students targeted in the previous parts of the routine. Teachers can generate sentences or paragraphs that focus on patterns and word reading skills that the student is working toward. It is important to build students' confidence in reading sentences and short passages they can decode with support before moving on to more challenging text.

Ms. Oliver began implementing the foundational skills routine with Nico right away. She used assessment data from the phonics inventory to guide her selection of word reading skills to target. Ms. Oliver found the routine straightforward to apply due to its simplicity and ease of implementation. She was impressed to see incremental increases in Nico's skills—and confidence—over the weeks that the routine was implemented.

Multisyllabic Word Reading Fluency

In reviewing other diagnostic data, Ms. Oliver noticed that Jade—a tenth grade student on her caseload—could fluently read single-syllable words but struggled to read longer, more complex words. For example, when Jade came to the word "transportation," she read it as "tr-ans-p-or-tat-ian." Additionally, Jade read "re-lăt-able" for "relatable" and "basket" for "basketball." It was evident to Ms. Oliver that Jade would benefit from explicit instruction in multisyllabic word reading.

Multisyllabic words bring unique challenges for readers who have mastered single-syllable words and most vowel patterns. This is in part because the complex letter patterns found in multisyllabic words place a burden on students' working memory and make accurate, fluent reading even more of a challenge for students with reading difficulties. When students struggle to read these words, it is vital for teachers to provide targeted intervention as students encounter more than 200,000 multisyllabic words, and such words are often critical to the meaning of the text (Kearns et al., 2016; Vaughn et al., 2022).

Multisyllabic Word Reading Instructional Routine

One way to provide targeted intervention in multisyllabic word reading is to employ a research-based routine that focuses on explicit instruction in long word reading with multiple opportunities for purposeful practice and fluency building (Lovett et al., 2000; Toste et al., 2017; Toste et al., 2019). This entire routine is appropriate within daily intervention; however, as with the foundational skills routine, teachers may choose to use any combination of these components to support the individual needs of their students. This 30-minute routine is comprised of five parts: (a) affix learning, (b) "peel off" reading, (c) word-building activity, (d) word reading fluency, and (e) connected text reading.

Affix Learning. Because many multisyllabic words are comprised of affixes, it is vital to explicitly teach the pronunciation and meaning of affixes (i.e., prefixes and suffixes) along with words that contain them. During affix learning, the teacher introduces around three high-frequency affixes (see White et al., 1989, for a list of commonly used affixes). The teacher first introduces the affix by reading it aloud, writing it out, and having students read the affix. The teacher then provides a sample word with the affix being targeted. Following the introduction, the teacher provides a student-friendly definition of the affix and invites students to generate sample words with the affix. Finally, students write each new affix and the sample word taught. It is important to regularly review previously learned affixes as new affixes are introduced.

After reviewing the list of high-frequency affixes, Ms. Oliver decided to introduce Jade to the prefix "dis-" during her first time employing the multisyllabic word reading routine. Ms. Oliver used the following language and instructional moves to introduce the affix:

> "This is the prefix dis-." Ms. Oliver wrote the affix on the whiteboard. "One word that I know begins with the "dis-" is "disagree." Ms. Oliver wrote out "disagree" on the board. "This affix means not or the opposite of. Because dis- means opposite of, then we know the word disagree means to not agree. Can you think of other words that begin with the prefix dis-?" Jade responded with the word "disappoint." Ms. Oliver provided Jade with affirmative feedback and then asked her to add "dis-" to her affix chart.

Peel Off Reading. In the next step of this routine, students are provided with a strategy for decoding multisyllabic words that contain affixes. The peel off strategy guides students to segment a word into affixes, read the affixes in the word, and then read the whole word. The objective of this strategy is to equip students with the skills and practice necessary to decode tricky multisyllabic words fluently and accurately.

To begin, teachers present a list of 20–30 multisyllabic words varying in difficulty to students. First, the teacher guides students to underline affixes in each word. Students then read underlined affixes as teachers provide corrective feedback to ensure all students are correctly pronouncing affixes. Next, students read the whole words together with the teacher. Following this practice, teachers can provide students with timed fluency practice by reading the list of words. To do this, each student is timed while reading the entire list aloud twice. The first read is focused on accuracy while the second read is focused on both accuracy and beating the clock (i.e., improving their previous time).

Word-Building Activity. After students have explicit instruction in affixes along with a strategy to read multisyllabic words, teachers can provide students with a structured activity where they assemble and blend word parts together to practice reading words. There are a variety of ways to gamify this part of the routine (see Toste et al., 2017), but each activity follows a similar format. Before starting the activity, teachers select and introduce a handful of base words (e.g., happy, build, help, read, teach) on index cards. After the teacher presents each base word, students repeat each word. Next, the teacher quickly reviews previously taught affixes if necessary. Students then attach prefixes and/or suffixes (e.g., un-, -ful, re-, -ing) written on index cards to the base word to build a new word. After this, the students read the word by pointing to each word part (e.g., re-/teach/-ing/). Finally, the student blends the word parts together and says the whole word (e.g., reteaching). The teacher provides corrective feedback and repeats the steps so that students receive multiple opportunities to practice.

Word Reading Fluency. Fluency in reading multisyllabic words is necessary for reading comprehension. An effective way to focus on word reading fluency is the use of targeted word lists with a timed component. Speedy Read—a structured instructional practice—is simple and has high utility in reading intervention (Toste et al., 2017). To employ Speedy Read, students are given a word list (with similar phonetic patterns) and are asked to read the list chorally with the teacher. Then, the students read for 30 seconds while the teacher tracks the students' responses. After reading, teachers provide feedback and have students reread incorrectly pronounced words.

Connected Text Reading. As with the foundational skills routine, it is important for students to go beyond single-word reading and practice sentence and passage reading. For students with reading disabilities and difficulties, teachers should be careful not to select texts that are too challenging for them to read by first generating sentences that target the multisyllabic word reading skills that students have been practicing in the routine before moving on to paragraph and passage reading.

Ms. Oliver appreciated this routine because it was simple, efficient, and engaging. She found she could adapt the routine to meet the needs of her students, as some of her students only needed instruction in affixes and the peel off strategy, while others benefited from the entire routine.

Fluency Building

A handful of students that Ms. Oliver supports can read words in isolation but struggle reading them connected in a passage. Some read word by word in a choppy, laborious manner while others read in a robotic fashion. She noticed these same students struggled to comprehend the text and turned to research to find ways to help build students' reading fluency that is engaging and easy to implement.

Fluency—the ability to read text with accuracy, speed, and proper expression—undergirds reading comprehension (Schreiber, 1980). As Ms. Oliver has noticed, some students need opportunities to practice moving from the word level to the text level. Fluent reading can be supported and developed by using various engaging activities that focus on reading speed, automaticity, and expression.

Oral Reading Fluency Routine

One way to build students' reading fluency is to use a structured routine to support students in multiple opportunities to read the same text. Repeated reading—which has been shown to be effective at improving reading rate, accuracy, and comprehension for students with reading disabilities (Chard et al., 2002; Rashotte & Torgesen, 1985; Therrien, 2004)—can be easily embedded into structured fluency practice. Whenever possible, teachers should choose texts on topics students are learning about in their content-area classes. See table 3.1 for a description and example of this five-step routine.

In addition to automaticity and reading speed, prosody (i.e., expression) is important in helping students understand what they are reading. Proficient oral reading prosody sounds much like speech with appropriate phrasing and stress, pausing, rise and fall patterns, and general expressiveness (Schwanenflugel et al., 2004). To support prosodic reading, explicit modeling and opportunities to practice are vital. Teachers can model the importance of expressive reading by reading a short paragraph aloud twice. The first time, the teacher reads it quickly without expression. The second time, the teacher reads the passage at a conversational pace with prosody. The teacher can then have a conversation with the students about what was different about the two reads. Next, the students can practice prosodic reading by echoing their teachers or by working with peers. Additionally, explicitly teaching students to pause at commas, stop at periods, raise or lower their voice at question marks, and show emotion at an exclamation point is important and will support their reading comprehension.

Table 3.1. Fluency Building Routine

Steps	Description	Example
1. Introduce the passage	The teacher introduces the passage the students will be reading.	Today we are going to read a passage about the impact of the meat industry on climate change.
2. Define key words	The teacher preselects, introduces, and defines words that are essential to meaning of the text.	We will see the word emission in this text. Emission means the discharge of something, especially gas or radiation. What does emission mean? We will also see the word "pollution," which is the introduction of harmful materials into the environment.
3. Students underline words they do not know how to decode or understand	Students look over the text and underline words that they do not know or do not understand. The teacher guides the students as they read the unknown word and provides brief meanings of words they do not understand.	Scan the passage and underline any words you cannot read or do not understand. [Teacher goes over any words with students]. Micah, that word is greenhouse. What word? Greenhouse gases are gases in the earth's atmosphere that trap heat.
4. Provide repeated reading practice	The teacher leads students in repeated text reading. Students read the text aloud at least two times using various practices (e.g., choral read, whisper read, echo read).	First, we are going to read the text together. Then, you are going to whisper read. Finally, I will read a section and then you will echo my reading.
5. Check for understanding	After reading the passage, the teacher asks comprehension questions to check for understanding. Questions can range from lower- to higher-order, depending on lesson focus and student groupings.	I'm going to ask you three questions about what we just read: What is responsible for a third of all planet-heating gases? What should societies be aware of when addressing the climate crisis? What did the author recommend people do if they are concerned about climate change?

Note: Adapted from Toste et al. (2017) and Vaughn et al. (2022).

To help build students' fluency and content-area knowledge, Ms. Oliver worked with her students' subject-area teachers to gather texts on topics students are learning about in their content-area classes. Mr. Burns—one of the tenth grade science teachers—shared his lesson plans with Ms. Oliver about his upcoming climate change unit. This helped Ms. Oliver choose texts that were not only the appropriate reading level for her students but also supported their content-area knowledge. This alignment gave her students access to the grade-level curriculum.

Content-Area Knowledge Building

Imagine being presented with a passage on the structure, care, and maintenance of a *coracle*. You learn that a *coracle* should not be occupied by more than one person, that willow beds must be carefully tended to ensure *coracle* materials are healthy, and that a *coracle* may be coated in coconut oil. Although your literal comprehension of each of these details is strong, you may struggle to build meaning from the passage unless you already know that a *coracle* is a small, bowl-shaped fishing boat often made from interwoven bamboo or willow rods. In this case, you need both *word* knowledge (What is the definition of *coracle*?) and *world* knowledge (What is a fishing boat? Who uses fishing boats? Where are they used? What do they look like?) to make meaning from the passage.

World knowledge, also known as background knowledge or content-area knowledge, supports the development of mental models for understanding the meaning of a text (Neuman et al., 2014). This background knowledge allows readers to make inferences, understand the specific intent of a word that has multiple meanings, and visualize what is happening in the text as they read. Core instructional strategies activate and build upon background knowledge students already possess, but students may arrive with little to no experience in some areas and require intensive pre-reading supports if they are to comprehend academic texts. When there is no prior knowledge on a topic, the teacher establishes a knowledge base through targeted, brief, explicit instruction that supports *word knowledge* (vocabulary background) and *world knowledge* (content background) before reading (Vaughn et al., 2022).

Vocabulary Routine

Vocabulary is a critical component of reading comprehension (Perfetti & Stafura, 2014) that is often underdeveloped in students with reading difficulties; therefore, it is crucial that secondary students with reading difficulties are provided with explicit vocabulary instruction. To further support students' word knowledge, aligning and integrating vocabulary words from students' content-area classes proves advantageous. One way to support students' content-area vocabulary is to employ an explicit vocabulary instructional routine (Archer & Hughes, 2011). This efficient routine contains the following steps, with a sample provided in table 3.2:

- **Step 1: Introduce the word.** First, teachers tell students the pronunciation of the word and invite students to repeat the word. If students struggle to pronounce the word, teachers can model the pronunciation and have the student repeat it again.
- **Step 2: Introduce the meaning of the word.** Next, teachers introduce the meaning of the word using a student-friendly definition. If the word contains affixes that are currently being targeted in instruction (e.g., -sion in erosion), teachers can guide students' in analyzing the meaningful parts of the word.

Table 3.2. Vocabulary Routine Example

Step	Description
Step 1: Introduce the word	[Teacher displays the word]. This word is erosion. What word? Erosion.
Step 2: Introduce meaning of the word	This word has an affix in it. Look to see if you can spot the affix. [Students point to the affix]. The suffix "-sion" means the state or process of. Erosion is the process of wearing down of land by wind or water. What is erosion? The wearing down of land by wind or water.
Step 3: Illustrate with examples	Wind breaking down rocks and carrying the particles away is a type of erosion. Ocean waves can cause coastline erosion. Rivers can create a significant amount of erosion over time because they break up the particles along the river bottom and carry them downstream. [Teacher shows visual examples of erosion].
Step 4: Check understanding	I'm going to ask you a question. When I say, "show me," put your thumbs-up for yes or thumbs-down for no. Could rainfall cause erosion? [Students respond with thumbs-up]. How could rainfall cause erosion? [Students respond.]

- **Step 3: Illustrate with examples.** The third step in the routine is to illustrate the word with a handful of visual or verbal examples.
- **Step 4: Check students' understanding.** Finally, teachers check students' understanding of the vocabulary term through interaction with the word. To do this, teachers can have students discriminate between examples and non-examples, ask students to produce their own examples, or ask students questions that necessitate processing of the word's meaning.

To further support her students' learning in the general education classroom, Ms. Oliver sought to use the explicit vocabulary routine with words that her students would be learning in their content-area courses. She collaborated with Mr. Burns and other content-area teachers to determine essential vocabulary words that her students would come across in text. She knew the alignment between content-area classes would benefit her students in building word-level knowledge.

Topic Introduction Routine

To construct meaning from an unfamiliar text, readers must have an existing organizing framework or mental model based on prior instruction, knowledge, or experience with the subject matter. Missing or limited prior knowledge presents a barrier to reading comprehension. When teachers provide explicit instruction of relevant content, texts are more comprehensible. One approach to building this world knowledge is the Topic Introduction Routine.

- **Step 1: Provide a 3- to 5-minute introduction to the topic.** This introduction may be delivered via a variety of media and formats. Teachers select the modality that will be most engaging and accessible to students.
    a. Provide students a short passage on the same topic that is easier to read than the instructional text.

b. Use a brief video or podcast to introduce the topic in an age-appropriate way.
  c. Deliver a quick lecture on the topic with visual supports (e.g., illustrations, photos).

- **Step 2: Summarize and clarify.** Briefly restate the most relevant points from the introduction. When student comments indicate misconceptions, teachers take this opportunity to clarify understandings.
- **Step 3: Ask questions.** Topic-specific questions allow students to reflect on what they have just learned. These questions should also prepare students for what they are about to read. As students respond, teachers provide feedback and clarify understandings.

Based on Mr. Burns' lesson plans, Ms. Oliver knew the students would be reading a newspaper article in class about greenhouse gases produced by the meat industry. After informally assessing her students' existing climate science knowledge, she realized they did not know the difference between traditional farming and factory farming. To build knowledge around the scope and size of modern meat-producing farms, Ms. Oliver showed a 2-minute video about technological advances in modern farming.

Pre-reading routines that establish and reinforce word and world knowledge allow students to engage meaningfully with texts. This meaningful engagement, in turn, adds to their word and world knowledge and equips them for reading to learn.

Building and Monitoring Reading Comprehension

Comprehension is the ultimate goal of reading instruction. Whether the purpose for reading is to gather information about a current event, learn a new skill, appreciate a collection of poetry, escape into a fantasy novel, or quickly scan pages of listings for summer jobs, the reader must be able to make meaning of the words on the page and to recognize when that meaning-making process breaks down. Students with reading difficulties often struggle to build and monitor reading comprehension. Although decoding ability may be the factor with the greatest impact on reading comprehension (McNamara et al., 2004; Perfetti et al., 1985), strong evidence exists for several comprehension-building practices that support secondary students in making meaning of texts (Vaughn et al., 2022).

Context Clues

When students encounter unfamiliar words in texts, poor comprehension may result. Rather than skipping the word or waiting for help, students can use context clues to identify the meanings of unknown words. One effective process is to (1) mark the unknown word, (2) look for clues in the sentence, and (3) look for clues in the surrounding sentences. If the word meaning is still unknown after reading and thinking about the surrounding sentences, teachers instruct student to look up the definition.

Greek and Latin Roots

Many unfamiliar words contain word parts that students know. Particularly in math, science, and social studies texts, content-area vocabulary words are likely to contain Greek and Latin root words. By explicitly teaching these common roots, teachers equip students to think about meanings of individual word parts, including prefixes and suffixes, to arrive at a working definition for many words. This instruction also allows students to identify important relationships across a variety of related words.

Question Types

Secondary students need to be able to justify their answers to different question types by returning to the text for evidence. Comprehension questions can be placed in three categories based on the type of evidence needed to answer them. *Right there* questions are text-dependent, and readers will often locate the words in the question and the words needed to answer it in a single sentence. *Think and search* questions are also text-dependent, but readers will need to pull information from multiple parts of the text in order to answer them fully. *Author and me* questions require readers to make inferences based on connecting what they already know to a portion of the text. There are typically the most challenging question type and require repeated practice opportunities across a variety of texts.

Summarizing

When readers have adequate comprehension, they are able to communicate their understanding by synthesizing information from the text into short summary statements. Summarizing requires readers to distinguish between essential and inessential information and to find connections between main ideas.

Get the Gist Routine. Readers craft gist statements for each paragraph in a passage. The gist statement should be one complete sentence, make sense, and include the important information from the paragraph. This is accomplished by completing the following steps:

- Identify who or what the paragraph is about (the subject).
- List the most important information about the subject of the paragraph.
- Combine the important information to form a gist statement.
- Write the gist statement using your own words.

In addition to working with her students in small-group intervention, Ms. Oliver collaborated with her content-area team to facilitate supports for her students' generalization of these routines and strategies in their other classes. Some of her colleagues supported use of strategies when working in small groups in their classes, while others opted to introduce the practices related to building and monitoring reading comprehension to their entire class because they saw how these routines could benefit all students.

Overall, Ms. Oliver was happy to observe academic gains among students who had experienced persistent reading difficulties. She felt confident in her selection and application of research-based instructional routines and the ongoing data-based decision-making she was using to inform her instruction. Although it took time to grow accustomed to these intervention methods, they provided her—and her students—with efficient and effective structures. As her confidence in these intervention methods increased, she noticed that her students' reading performance and confidence also continued to grow.

CONCLUSION

In addition to high-quality core instruction, struggling readers require supplemental intervention. For students in the secondary grades, interventions should be informed by both theories of reading development and explicit instruction in order to ensure alignment with students' specific areas of need and to optimize effectiveness. Students with persistent and severe reading difficulties often require intensive, individualized interventions, which must be informed by ongoing and frequent collection of student assessment data. In this chapter, we summarized instructional practices and routines aligned with five key intervention methods that meet the needs of secondary students. These key methods—prerequisite skills instruction, multisyllabic word reading fluency, fluency building, content-area knowledge building, and building and monitoring reading comprehension—can be employed in a variety of settings to meet school scheduling needs. At the secondary level, time is a precious resource. Further, the decisions made about instruction and intervention can have high-stakes impacts for students with persistent reading difficulties as they progress through the secondary grades. Thus, it is essential that reading interventions apply scientifically based practices to optimize the benefits that students gain from this supplemental intervention time. Implementation of the methods described in this chapter can ultimately help struggling readers overcome difficulties and achieve reading success.

REFERENCES

Al Otaiba, S., & Fuchs, D. (2006). Who are the young children for whom best practices in reading are ineffective? An experimental and longitudinal study. *Journal of Learning Disabilities, 39*(5), 414–31.

Archer, A. L., & Hughes, C. A. (2011). *Explicit instruction: Effective and efficient teaching*. Guilford.

Cain, K., & Oakhill, J. V. (2009). Reading comprehension development from 8 to 14 years: The contribution of component skills and processes. In R. K. Wagner, C. Schatschneider, & C. Phythian-Sence (Eds.), *Beyond decoding: The behavioral and biological foundations of reading comprehension* (pp. 143–75). Guilford.

Catts, H., Hogan, T., & Adolf, S. (2005). Developmental changes in reading and reading disabilities. In H. Catts & A. Kamhi (Eds.), *Connections between language and reading disabilities*. Erlbaum.

Chall, J. S., & Jacobs, V. A. (1983). Writing and reading in the elementary grades: Developmental trends among low SES children. *Language Arts, 60*(5), 617–26.

Chard, D. J., Vaughn, S., & Tyler, B-J. (2002). A synthesis of research on effective interventions for building reading fluency with elementary students with learning disabilities. *Journal of Learning Disabilities, 35*(5), 386–406.

Connor, C. M., Alberto, P. A., Compton, D. L., & O'Connor, R. E. (2014). *Improving reading outcomes for students with or at risk for reading disabilities: A synthesis of the contributions from the Institute of Education Sciences Research Centers* (NCSER 2014-3000). National Center for Special Education Research, Institute of Education Sciences, US Department of Education.

Cunningham, A. E., & Stanovich, K. E. (1991). Tracking the unique effects of print exposure in children: Associations with vocabulary, general knowledge, and spelling. *Journal of Educational Psychology, 83*(2), 264–74.

Deno, S. L. (1985). Curriculum-based measurement: The emerging alternative. *Exceptional Children, 52*(3), 219–32.

DeWalt, D. A., & Pignone, M. P. (2005). The role of literacy in health and health care. *American Family Physician, 72*(3), 387–8.

Engelmann, S. (1980). *Direct instruction.* Educational Technology.

Filderman, M. J., & Toste, J. R. (2018). Decisions, decisions, decisions: Using data to make instructional decisions for struggling readers. *TEACHING Exceptional Children, 50*(3), 130–40.

Filderman, M. J., Toste, J. R., Didion, L. A., Peng, P., & Clemens, N. H. (2018). Data-based decision making in reading interventions: A synthesis and meta-analysis of the effects for struggling readers. *Journal of Special Education, 52*(3), 174–87. https://doi.org/10.1177/0022466918790001

Foorman, B., Beyler, N., Borradaile, K., Coyne, M., Denton, C. A., Dimino, J., Furgeson, J., Hayes, L., Henke, J., Justice, L., Keating, B., Lewis, W., Sattar, S., Streke, A., Wagner, R., & Wissel, S. (2016). *Foundational skills to support reading for understanding in kindergarten through 3rd grade* (NCEE 2016-4008). National Center for Education Evaluation and Regional Assistance (NCEE), Institute of Education Sciences, US Department of Education. Retrieved from the NCEE website: https://ies.ed.gov/ncee/wwc/practiceguide/21

Francis, D. J., Shaywitz, S. E., Stuebing, K. K., Shaywitz, B. A., & Fletcher, J. M. (1996). Developmental lag versus deficit models of reading disability: A longitudinal, individual growth curves analysis. *Journal of Educational Psychology, 88*(1), 3–17.

Fuchs, D., & Fuchs, L. S. (2016). Responsiveness-to-intervention: A "systems" approach to instructional adaptation. *Theory Into Practice, 55*(3), 225–33.

Fuchs, D., Fuchs, L. S., & Vaughn, S. (2014). What is intensive instruction and why is it important? *TEACHING Exceptional Children, 46*(4), 13–18.

Fuchs, L. S., Fuchs, D., Hamlett, C. L., & Stecker, P. M. (2021). Bringing data-based individualization to scale: A call for the next-generation technology of teacher supports. *Journal of Learning Disabilities, 54*(5), 319–33.

Gersten, R., Newman-Gonchar, R., Haymond, K. S., & Dimino, J. (2017). What is the evidence base to support reading interventions for improving student outcomes in grades 1–3? (REL 2017-271). *Regional Educational Laboratory Southeast.*

Gough, P., & Tunmer, W. (1986). Decoding, reading, and reading disability. *Remedial and Special Education, 7*, 6–10.

Honig, B., Diamond, L., Gutlohn, L., Fertig, B., Daniel, H., Zemelman, S., & Steineke, N. (2018). *Teaching reading sourcebook* (3rd ed.). Arena.

Hoover, W. A., & Gough, P. B. (1990). The simple view of reading. *Reading and Writing: An Interdisciplinary Journal, 2*(2), 127–60.

Hosp, M. K., Hosp, J. L., & Howell, K. W. (2016). *The ABCs of CBM: A practical guide to curriculum-based measurement.* Guilford.

Hughes, C. A., Morris, J. R., Therrien, W. J., & Benson, S. K. (2017). Explicit instruction: Historical contemporary contexts. *Learning Disabilities Research & Practice, 32*(3), 140–48.

Jung, P. G., McMaster, K. L., Kunkel, A. K., Shin, J., & Stecker, P. M. (2018). Effects of data-based individualization for students with intensive learning needs: A meta-analysis. *Learning Disabilities Research and Practice, 33*(3), 144–55.

Kamil, M. L., Borman, G. D., Dole, J., Kral, C. C., Salinger, T., & Torgesen, J. (2008). Improving adolescent literacy: Effective classroom and intervention practices

(NCEE 2008-4027). National Center for Education Evaluation and Regional Assistance. https://ies.ed.gov/ncee/wwc/docs/practiceguide/adlit_pg_082608.pdf

Kearns, D. M., Steacy, L. M., Compton, D. L., Gilbert, J. K., Goodwin, A. P., Cho, E., Lindstrom, E. R., & Collins, A. A. (2016). Modeling polymorphemic word recognition: Exploring differences among children with early-emerging and late-emerging word reading difficulty. *Journal of Learning Disabilities, 49*(4), 368–94.

Lovett, M. W., Lacerenza, L., Borden, S. L., Frijters, J. C., Steinbach, K. A., & De Palma, M. (2000). Components of effective remediation for developmental reading disabilities: Combining phonological and strategy-based instruction to improve outcomes. *Journal of Educational Psychology, 92*(2), 263–83.

Malatesha Joshi, R. (2005). Vocabulary: A critical component of comprehension. *Reading & Writing Quarterly, 21*(3), 209–19.

McMaster, K. L., Fuchs, D., Fuchs, L. S., & Compton, D. L. (2005). Responding to nonresponders: An experimental field trial of identification and intervention methods. *Exceptional Children, 71*(4), 445–63.

McNamara, D. S., Floyd, R. G., Best, R., & Louwerse, M. (2004). World knowledge driving young readers' comprehension difficulties. In *Proceedings of the 6th international conference on learning sciences* (pp. 326–33). International Society of the Learning Sciences.

National Center for Education Statistics. (2019). *Explore results for the 2019 NAEP reading assessment.* The Nation's Report Card. https://www.nationsreportcard.gov/reading?grade=4

National Center for Education Statistics. (2022). *Reading and mathematics scores decline during COVID-19 pandemic.* The Nation's Report Card. https://www.nationsreportcard.gov/highlights/ltt/2022/

National Center on Intensive Intervention. (2013). *Data-based individualization: A framework for intensive intervention.* American Institutes for Research (AIR). https://intensiveintervention.org/sites/default/files/DBI_Framework.pdf

National Governors Association, Council of Chief State School Officers (NGA CCSSO). (2010). *Common core state standards for English language arts.* Washington, DC: NGA Center for Best Practices and CCSSO.

National Reading Panel. (2000). *Report of the national reading panel: Teaching children to read: An evidence-based assessment of the scientific research literature on reading and its implications for reading instruction,* Vol. 1. National Institute of Child Health and Human Development.

Neuman, S. B., Kaefer, T., & Pinkham, A. (2014). Building background knowledge. *Reading Teacher, 68*(2), 145–48.

O'Connor, R., & Fuchs, L. S. (2013). Responsiveness to intervention in the elementary grades: Implications for early childhood education. In V. Buysse & E. S. Peisner-Feinberg (Eds.), *Handbook of response to intervention (RTI) in early childhood education* (pp. 41–56). Brookes.

Perfetti, C., & Stafura, J. (2014). Word knowledge in a theory of reading comprehension. *Scientific Studies of Reading, 18*(1), 22–37.

Perfetti, C. A., Landi, N., & Oakhill, J. (2005). The acquisition of reading comprehension skill. In M. J. Snowling & C. Hulme (Eds.), *The science of reading: A handbook* (pp. 227–47). Blackwell.

Perfetti, C. A., Marron, M. A., & Foltz, P. W. (1996). Sources of comprehension failure: Theoretical perspectives and case studies. In C. Cornoldi & J. Oakhill (Eds.),

Reading comprehension difficulties: Processes and interventions (pp. 137–65). Lawrence Erlbaum.

Rashotte, C. A., & Torgesen, J. K. (1985). Repeated reading and reading fluency in learning disabled children. *Reading Research Quarterly, 20,* 180–88.

Rayner, K., Foorman, B., Perfetti, C. A., Pesetsky, D., & Seidenberg, M. S. (2001). How psychological science informs the teaching of reading. *Psychological Science in the Public Interest, 2*(2), 31–74.

Reschly, A. L., Busch, T. W., Betts, J., Deno, S. L., & Long, J. D. (2009). Curriculum-based measurement oral reading as an indicator of reading achievement: A meta-analysis of the correlational evidence. *Journal of School Psychology, 47*(6), 427–69.

Reynolds, A. J., & Ou, S. (2004). Alterable predictors of child well-being in the Chicago longitudinal study. *Children and Youth Services Review, 26*(1), 1–14.

Scammacca, N. K., Roberts, G. J., Cho, E., Williams, K. J., Roberts, G., Vaughn, S. R., & Carroll, M. (2016). A century of progress: Reading interventions for students in grades 4–12, 1914–2014. *Review of Educational Research, 86*(3), 756–800.

Scarborough, H. S. (2001). Connecting early language and literacy to later reading (dis)abilities: Evidence, theory, and practice. In S. B. Neuman & D. K. Dickinson (Eds.), *Handbook of early literacy research.* Guilford.

Schreiber, P. A. (1980). On the acquisition of reading fluency. *Journal of Reading Behavior, 12*(3), 177–86.

Schwanenflugel, P. J., Hamilton, A. M., Wisenbaker, J. M., Kuhn, M. R., & Stahl, S. A. (2004). Becoming a fluent reader: Reading skill and prosodic features in the oral reading of young readers. *Journal of Educational Psychology, 96*(1), 119–29.

Shanahan, T., Callison, K., Carriere, C., Duke, N. K., Pearson, P. D., Schatschneider, C., & Torgesen, J. (2010). Improving reading comprehension in kindergarten through 3rd grade: IES practice guide (NCEE 2010-4038). What Works Clearinghouse, National Center for Education Evaluation and Regional Assistance (NCEE), Institute of Education Sciences, US Department of Education.

Shin, J., & McMaster, K. (2019). Relations between CBM (oral reading and maze) and reading comprehension on state achievement tests: A meta-analysis. *Journal of School Psychology, 73,* 131–49.

Silva, M., & Cain, K. (2015). The relations between lower and higher level comprehension skills and their role in prediction of early reading comprehension. *Journal of Educational Psychology, 107*(2), 321–31.

Stanovich, K. E., & West, R. F. (1989). Exposure to print and orthographic processing. *Reading Research Quarterly, 24*(4), 402–33.

Stevens, E. A., Vaughn, S., Swanson, E., & Scammacca, N. (2020). Examining the effects of a tier 2 reading comprehension intervention aligned to tier 1 instruction for fourth-grade struggling readers. *Exceptional Children, 86*(4), 430–48.

Stockard, J., Wood, T. W., Coughlin, C., & Khoury, C. R. (2018). The effectiveness of direct instruction curricula: A meta-analysis of a half century of research. *Review of Educational Research, 88*(4), 479–507.

Swanson, E., Stevens, E. A., Scammacca, N. K., Capin, P., Stewart, A. A., & Austin, C. R. (2017). The impact of tier 1 reading instruction on reading outcomes for students in grades 4–12: A meta-analysis. *Reading and Writing, 30*(8), 1639–65.

Therrien, W. J. (2004). Fluency and comprehension gains as a result of repeated reading: A meta-analysis. *Remedial and Special Education, 25*(4), 252–61.

Torgesen, J. K. (2004). Lessons learned from research on interventions for students who have difficulty learning to read. In P. McCardle & V. Chhabra (Eds.), *The voice of evidence in reading research* (pp. 355–82). Paul H. Brookes.

Toste, J. R., Williams, K. J., & Capin, P. (2017). Reading big words: Instructional practices to promote multisyllabic word reading fluency. *Intervention in School and Clinic*, 52(5), 270–78.

Toste, J. R., Capin, P., Williams, K. J., Cho, E., & Vaughn, S. (2019). Replication of an experimental study investigating the efficacy of a multisyllabic word reading intervention with and without motivational beliefs training for struggling readers. *Journal of Learning Disabilities*, 52(1), 45–58.

Vaughn, S., & Fletcher, J. M. (2012). Response to intervention with secondary school students with reading difficulties. *Journal of Learning Disabilities*, 45(3), 244–56.

Vaughn, S., Linan-Thompson, S., Kouzekanani, K., Bryant, D. P., Dickson, S., & Blozis, S. A. (2003). Reading instruction grouping for students with reading difficulties. *Remedial and Special Education*, 24(5), 301–15.

Vaughn, S., Kieffer, M. J., McKeown, M., Reed, D. K., Sanchez, M., St. Martin, K., Wexler, J., Jayanthi, M., Gersten, R., Dimino, J., Taylor, M. J., Newman-Gonchar, R., Krowka, S., Haymond, K., Wavell, S., Lyskawa, J., Morgan, S., Keating, B., & Yañez, A. (2022). Providing reading interventions for students in grades 4–9: Educator's practice guide (WWC 2022007). What Works Clearinghouse.

Wanzek, J., Wexler, J., Vaughn, S., & Ciullo, S. (2010). Reading interventions for struggling readers in the upper elementary grades: A synthesis of 20 years of research. *Reading and Writing*, 23(8), 889–912.

Wayman, M., Wayman, T., Wallace, H., Wiley, I., Tichá, R., & Espin, C. (2007). Literature synthesis on curriculum-based measurement in reading. *Journal of Special Education*, 41(2), 85–120.

White, T. G., Power, M. A., & White, S. (1989). Morphological analysis: Implications for teaching and understanding vocabulary growth. *Reading Research Quarterly*, 24(3), 283–304.

Yeo, S. (2010). Predicting performance on state achievement tests using curriculum-based measurement in reading: A multilevel meta-analysis. *Remedial and Special Education*, 31(6), 412–22.

4

Quality 6–12 Mathematics Instruction

Bradley S. Witzel, Tricia K. Strickland, and Jonté A. Myers

SUCCESS IN MATHEMATICS LEARNING has been linked to performance in multiple subject areas (Geary, 2011), graduation, postsecondary opportunities, and technical school completion. Students who attend postsecondary training but lack understanding of Algebra 2 typically must take several additional courses toward their certificate and are more likely than their peers to drop out of programs (Adelman, 2006; Moore & Shulock, 2009). With the importance of mathematics being so well understood, millions of dollars are pumped into grant programs and curricula development to improve student performance. However, despite many efforts to improve or even reform instructional approaches, learning mathematics remains difficult for most students in the United States. The recent National Assessment of Educational Progress (NAEP) results indicate less than half of US students are meeting grade-level expectations, called proficient or advanced. Specifically, only 41% of all fourth grade students, 34% of all eighth grade students, and 24% of all twelfth grade students met grade-level expectations in end-of-year or end-of-grade mathematics assessment (Hussar et al., 2020).

While these scores are poor, the results for students with disabilities are even more alarming. For students identified with disabilities, only 17% met grade-level expectations in fourth grade, while only 9% and 7% met grade-level expectations in eighth and twelfth grade, respectively (Hussar et al., 2020). Even though students are often identified with disabilities based on academic performance, this disparity between those with identified disabilities and those not identified is disheartening. Action must be taken to improve the mathematics education of all students, regardless of disability identification.

Three critical inferences can be drawn about students' mathematics performance nationally based on data from the NAEP 2019 mathematics assessment: (a) scores are low across all grade levels, (b) scores decrease with grade level, and (c) students with disabilities fare far worse than their general education peers. The fourth grade scores being under 50% already show a concern in mathematics, highlighting the need for better mathematics instruction as early as possible. However, waiting until fourth grade doesn't paint a clear picture as to where the issues in mathematics learning begin. That said, early understanding of mathematics may predict students' overall achievement (Geary, 2011). The percentage of students meeting expectations falls in every successive testing year. This highlights the compressibility in mathematics. Some of the most important tenets of mathematics are learned in early childhood and practiced throughout elementary school. If these skills aren't adequately acquired and retained, then learning proceeding to related skills is difficult at best. Even students who appear to have understood elementary mathematics struggle in secondary math courses. This is known as the arithmetic to algebra gap (Witzel & Little, 2016). Students' performance in secondary mathematics is highly contingent upon students' procedural and conceptual understanding of key arithmetic skills. For students with disabilities, this last point is particularly troubling. Being diagnosed with an academic disability means that a student had performance deficits that warranted additional and/or different instruction. In mathematics, any delay in providing services, particularly instructional supports, may mean that important skills, such as computational fluency or understanding of fractions were not achieved. These skills almost guarantee difficulties in secondary mathematics content. Understanding key areas of concern better informs core instruction, particularly in secondary mathematics where it is essential that teachers scaffold previous learning to better connect current grade-level standards. The National Mathematics Advisory Panel (NMAP, 2008) highlighted key foundational skills for secondary mathematics success. The identified skills include but should not be limited to the following: (a) fluency with whole numbers, (b) fluency with fractions, and (c) using formulas to measure aspects of two- and three-dimensional shapes.

Looking more closely, we see how the interconnected mathematics constructs are within each of these skills. Take the example of students learning to count. When students struggle with counting in preschool and kindergarten settings, these difficulties impact the students' computation performance. Difficulty counting, particularly on a number line, often leads to difficulty with addition and subtraction. Further, difficulties with addition of single-digit numbers impacts the students' proficiency with multiples, leading to difficulty in the conceptualization of multiplication. With a weakness in early understandings of multiplication, increased fluency or fast recall is less likely. This will impact students' computation with fractions. Mastery of fractions is viewed by many researchers as a precursor skill to algebra. This curriculum walk may seem extreme, but the potential dangers are real and highlight the compressibility of mathematics standards. Students' success with early mathematics learning is necessary but not sufficient for success in secondary mathematics. Secondary teachers must be aware of these pitfalls so that they can more appropriately scaffold instruction to further students' strengths and support learning of core standards. For example, knowing that many students struggle with computational proficiency, initial instruction with factoring should involve more commonly known math facts. For example, instead of factoring $(-36z - 48y + 12x)$, consider using terms with more commonly known coefficients $(15z + 20y + 5x)$.

Teachers agree with this analysis. According to the National Survey of Algebra Teachers (Hoffer et al., 2007), middle and high school teachers believe that students are ill-prepared for secondary mathematics, such as algebra, especially in the areas of computation proficiency, rational numbers, basic study skills, and word problem solving. Increased recent attention on early childhood and elementary mathematics is important to improving students' foundational skills. However, too little time and energy is spent addressing what is needed to help improve secondary mathematics instruction to help shore up gaps in learning while primarily leading students to standards-focused achievement. The focus of this chapter is to share key strategies for improving the performance of students with math difficulties in grades 6–12 mathematics. The following are chapter objectives:

1. Understand the structured outcomes of learning objectives (SOLO) approach to build proficiency at each math topic.
2. Understand progressions across grade and content to develop secondary mathematics skills.
3. Understand systematic instruction as a research-based instructional practice to support secondary students' mathematics development.
4. Identify types of practice and determine the most appropriate practice type for various situations.
5. Identify instructional practices to support students' mathematics learning, including cognitive strategies, visuals, and differentiation.

SETTING GOALS IN SECONDARY MATHEMATICS

As stated earlier, Algebra 2 understanding is linked to a number of postsecondary options. Yet, it isn't enough to pass an Algebra 2 course. Rather, students must develop understanding of key concepts and solve problems with efficiency. With the goal of a minimum of Algebra 2 understanding for most students, curriculum should be paced to build students' achievement steadily, scaffolding one concept to the next.

While Algebra 2 should be set as the minimum goal, there shouldn't be a maximum goal. According to NMAP (2008), major topics that must be achieved include proficiency with symbols and expressions, linear equations, quadratic equations, functions, polynomials, and combinatorics. Key concepts per major topic include the following:

- Symbols and Expressions
    - Polynomial expressions
    - Rational expressions
    - Arithmetic and finite geometric series
- Linear Equations
    - Real numbers as points on the number line
    - Linear equations and their graphs
    - Solving problems with linear equations
    - Linear inequalities and their graphs
    - Graphing and solving systems of simultaneous linear equations
- Quadratic Equations
    - Factors and factoring of quadratic polynomials with integer coefficients
    - Completing the square in quadratic expressions

- Quadratic formula and factoring of general quadratic polynomials
- Using the quadratic formula to solve equations

- Functions
  - Linear functions
  - Quadratic functions—word problems involving quadratic polynomials
  - Graph of quadratic functions and completing the square
  - Polynomial functions (including graphs of basic functions)
  - Simple nonlinear functions (e.g., square and cube root functions; absolute value; rational functions; step functions)
  - Rational expressions, radical expressions, and exponential functions
  - Logarithmic functions
  - Trigonometric functions
  - Fitting simple mathematical models to data

- Algebra of Polynomials
  - Roots and factorization of polynomials
  - Complex numbers and operations
  - Fundamental theorem of algebra
  - Binomial coefficients (and Pascal's Triangle)
  - Mathematical induction and the binomial theorem

- Combinatorics of Finite Probability
  - Combinations and permutations, as application of the binomial theorem and Pascal's Triangle

Historically, not every student learns every aspect of secondary mathematics through Algebra 2; curriculum streamlining should be considered for students who need more time learning mathematics. Increasing the focus on learning foundational skills and key secondary topics (previously listed) will help most students (1) build success through Algebra 2, and (2) increase opportunities in postsecondary settings.

PLANNED OUTCOMES

Within courses, students must gain mathematical proficiency. Consider the structured outcomes of learning objectives (SOLO) approach to build proficiency at each math topic. SOLO (Biggs & Collis, 1982) starts with the student learning at a prestructural level. A prestructural level means that the student does not have background information sufficient to make sense of a given mathematical problem. For a student presented with the challenge of solving for x, in $6 - 3x = 15$, if the student answers 15, then that may indicate the student is unfamiliar with this type of problem. The goal for a student at the prestructural level is to advance to unistructural.

At the unistructural level, the student learns the concepts and procedure of one strategy to solve a mathematical problem. A unistructural approach would be to

48   Chapter 4: Quality 6–12 Mathematics Instruction

subtract 6 from both sides of the equal sign and then divide by the coefficient, –3, to reach the answer of –3. The goal of a student at the unistructural level is to develop a relational understanding. This means that the student can relate two different approaches to solving a problem.

To gain relational understanding, the student must first develop a multistructural understanding, knowing the concepts and procedures of at least two different approaches to solving the problem. An alternate problem for the example would be to first divide all terms by –3 and then add 2 to both sides to reach the answer of –3. Once two approaches are learned, the student develops the connections between the two approaches. The connection between both approaches in this example is the multiplicative property of equality. Without knowing the connection between approaches, the student is merely memorizing procedures without understanding why. While SOLO may be used consistently throughout mathematics learning, it is particularly useful for secondary mathematics, where multiple approaches to problem solving are highly related to one another.

When a middle school teacher is applying the SOLO taxonomy to their teaching, they must keep in mind the expected learning outcome of the student as well as the time dedicated to take the student to that outcome. For instance, when a sixth grade math teacher is teaching students a unit on applying number theory concepts to find common factors and multiples (CC.2.1.6.E.3), an early lesson may be to find the greatest common factors (GCF) of two whole numbers. Goals for this lesson should be based on each student's understanding.

Likewise, an Algebra teacher who is teaching students to simplify expressions involving polynomials (CC.2.2.HS.D.3) and applying the SOLO taxonomy must consider where students are in their learning in order to set goals for their teaching. For a lesson on simplifying expressions involving polynomials, the following might be considered as indicators of each level of learning:

With SOLO in mind, the minimal goal throughout secondary mathematics coursework is unistructural understanding. However, to develop student success across math topics and courses, teachers should emphasize developing a student's understanding across structural levels, such as unistructural to relational. To improve the ability to build to relational thinking, teachers encourage students to verbally reason their mathematic approach to solving a problem. In the practice guide aimed at improving students in algebra, Star and colleagues (2019) recommend students

Table 4.1. Student Performance on the Objective (CC.2.1.6.E.3)

Prestructural	Unistructural	Multistructural	Relational
Student **does not accurately find the GCF** of two whole numbers	Student **accurately finds the GCF** of two whole numbers using memorized multiplication recall	Student accurately finds the GCF of two whole numbers **using two multiplication approaches** (e.g., factor trees and memorized multiplication recall)	Student accurately finds the GCF of two whole numbers and **explains the relationship between two or more approaches**

Table 4.2. Student Performance on the Objective (CC.2.2.HS.D.3)

Prestructural	Unistructural	Multistructural	Relational
Student **does not accurately compute two polynomial expressions**	Student **accurately computes two polynomial expressions** and provides the answer in simplest form using a single consistent method	Student accurately computes two polynomial expressions and provides the answer in simplest form **using multiple methods** (e.g., performing all computations and factoring first or factoring first and performing all computation afterward)	Student accurately computes two polynomial expressions and provides the answer in simplest form using multiple methods and **explaining the mathematical relationship between the methods**

dialogue with the teacher or each other to clarify their understanding and learn alternate, and sometimes more advanced, strategies.

We use solving quadratic equations in the general form $ax^2 + bx + c$ to demonstrate how to advance students from the unistructural to the relational level. For example, when solving the expression $6x^2 - 14x + 4 = 0$, there are multiple approaches that a student could take. One way is for the student to factor the expression and then use knowledge of computation to develop the factors.

$$2(3x2 - 7x + 2) = 0$$

Factors of A[3&1]; C[–1& –2]

$$2(3x - 1)(1x - 2) = 0$$

$$x = \frac{1}{3}, 2$$

Another approach is to use the quadratic formula

$$\left(x = \frac{-b \pm \sqrt{b^2 - 4ac}}{2a} \right)$$

In the example, $a = 6$, $b = 14$, and $c = 4$.

$$\frac{-(-14) + \sqrt{196-96}}{12} = \frac{14 + 10}{12} = \frac{24}{12} = 2$$

$$\frac{-(-14) - \sqrt{196-96}}{12} = \frac{14 - 10}{12} = \frac{4}{12} = \frac{1}{3}$$

$$x = \frac{1}{3}, 2$$

Have students discuss the mathematics similarities of these approaches. Both use greatest common factors, but the quadratic formula is derived from completing the square. Without connecting these approaches mathematically, students are stuck at the multistructural level.

For students who struggle in mathematics, unistructural success may be a reasonable goal. However, while unistructural may be minimal but reasonable, setting up an accurate and efficient way of completing mathematics places increased stress of planning on teachers who will need to plan the most appropriate approach that links topics across math topics.

PROGRESSIONS ACROSS GRADE AND CONTENT

Students who appear to perform well in early grades mathematics do not always succeed in courses from algebra and beyond—a phenomenon described as the "arithmetic to algebra gap." This is particularly troubling since most students in the United States do not perform proficiently in grade-level standards as early as fourth grade. One of the reasons for this disparity is that the attainment of benchmarks for math success in the early grades may not contribute to success later. It is increasingly important to intentionally scaffold student learning from key elements of elementary learning to those in secondary mathematics. Take, for example, how subtraction is taught in elementary mathematics and how it inefficiently transitions to secondary mathematics standards.

A child in the early grades who learns to count to 1,000 by rote may look impressive to their family or even to their teacher, but if this skill is not coupled with understandings of measurement, number patterns, and place value, then such excitement may be misguided. A student who counts from 0, identifying distance from 0 to 1, and shares number patterns based on place value (i.e., one 10 and one 1; one 10 and two 1s; one 10 and three 1s—instead of eleven, twelve, thirteen) shows a higher likelihood of building number sense which can applied to later learning. Additionally, some students who show exceptional strengths in some areas of mathematics but not necessarily foundational skills, such as proficiency with whole number computation, may not actually be growing their foundation to becoming successful at later mathematics. Take, for example, the terminal skill of borrowing in multi-digit subtraction. A third grade student may spend weeks learning to "Take from the bigger number" to make a column subtraction problem easier. However, this doesn't support place value pattern building.

$$\begin{array}{r} 74 \\ -38 \\ \hline \end{array}$$

The student works from right to left starting with, "I can't take 8 from 4." So, the student borrows from the 7, redistributing the ten.

$$\begin{array}{r} 6\,\cancel{7}^{1}4 \\ -3\,8 \\ \hline 3\,6 \end{array}$$

The student subtracts 8 from 14 to get 6. Then the student subtracts 3 from 6 to get 3. A 3 then a 6 is interpreted as thirty-six in this problem.

While this approach allows the student to arrive at the correct answer, it doesn't support future work with polynomials. Take, for example, the subtraction of the expressions $7x + 4 - (3x + 8)$.

$$\begin{array}{r} 7x + 4 \\ -\ 3x - 8 \\ \hline 4x - 4 \end{array}$$

After distributing the subtraction, the computation may appear as $7x + 4 - 3x - 8$. Without the need to regroup or "borrow" the student subtracts based on like terms. This is quite dissimilar from the approach above.

Therefore, we recommend either of the following approaches in third grade. These approaches aid scaffolding from arithmetic to algebra through the structure of the strategy and the connected language (Witzel & Little, 2016).

Student A   *Student B*

$$\begin{array}{r} 74 \\ -\ 38 \\ +\ 70 + 4 \\ -\ 30 - 8 \\ +\ 60 + 14 \\ -\ 30 - 8 \\ \hline +\ 30 + 6 = 36 \end{array} \qquad \begin{array}{r} 74 \\ -\ 38 \\ +\ 70 + 4 \\ -\ 30 - 8 \\ \hline +\ 40 - 4 = 36 \end{array}$$

While student A closely resembles the polynomial expression computation through the use of the distributive property and computation by term, the regrouping to answer only positive differences does not cleanly align with what is done in algebraic computation. Student B subtracts the integers to find a negative difference, which is a process similar in strategy and approach to the polynomial expression. However, if you increase student focus on this approach, we recommend teaching computation on a number line (rather than a number ray) prior.

The Meadows Center at the University of Texas produced a document sharing general progression of mathematics skills toward algebra readiness in grades 5–8. As shown earlier, it is important to think beyond the direct skill as it may be currently taught and consider how to teach these foundational skills so that they can scaffold to secondary math content. Each of these key areas impacts a student's ability to achieve in algebra-level content. (http://www.meadowscenter.org/files/mstar/ResourcesPMSTARchart.pdf)

Progressions through high school courses require increased attention to details. For example, understanding of functions of rational exponents, such as $f(x) = \sqrt{x}$. Even though 10 is rational, $f(10) = \sqrt{10}$ is irrational. For more information on high school progressions, review Achieve the Core (2016) (https://achievethecore.org/page/254/progressions-documents-for-the-common-core-state-standards-for-mathematics).

Many of the above examples show how to scaffold learning to secondary mathematics. For middle school and high school teachers, this is important because when instruction prior to their courses is effective, they can start their lessons by showing what strategies were learned earlier and then connect that learning to the lesson they are presenting. Consider the power of sharing the subtraction with integers approach (Student B above) before starting computation using variable symbols. Mathematics instruction shouldn't be about clever tricks but rather how to set up students for long-term success.

SYSTEMATIC INSTRUCTION

Students deserve research-supported instruction that increases their likelihood of long-term success in math. One of the most effective instructional approaches for teaching students when learning something that is new or difficult is systematic instruction. Systematic instruction involves teaching a skill or concept in a highly structured environment using clear and direct language, a high amount of interaction, and sufficient student practice. This is no different in mathematics, where students require examples and verbal reasoning. At the most essential elements of systematic instruction is a task analysis preparation and a delivery system that entails a scaffolded gradual release of information: Me–We–Two–You.

Task analysis involves breaking down a complex skill into manageable mathematical steps that may be executed in order to solve a problem or reduce the solution into an easy-to-interpret form (Wilcox et al., 2013).

Task Analysis Steps

1. Identify the target skill that students should be able to demonstrate
2. Solve the problem and note each written step and verbal reasoning associated with each step
3. Differentiate what steps are new and which have been demonstrated by the students from prior skills
4. Write out the steps and label the steps for students
5. Teach 1–3 steps at a time having students practice steps in small chunks
6. Monitor student progress and adjust

Task Analysis Example of Division of Fractions

a. Reorganize division problem $\quad \dfrac{\dfrac{5}{8}}{\dfrac{3}{4}}$

b. Use reciprocal of denominator (divisor) $\quad \dfrac{\dfrac{5}{8}}{\dfrac{3}{4}\left(\dfrac{4}{3}\right)}$

c. Multiply numerator and denominator (identity) $\quad \dfrac{\dfrac{5}{8}\left(\dfrac{4}{3}\right)}{\dfrac{3}{4}\left(\dfrac{4}{3}\right)}$

d. Multiply fractions in the numerator and denominator

$$\frac{\frac{5}{8}\left(\frac{4}{3}\right)}{\frac{3}{4}\left(\frac{4}{3}\right)} = \frac{\frac{20}{24}}{1}$$

e. Find a simplified fraction answer using GCF

$$\frac{20 \div 4}{24 \div 4} = \frac{5}{6}$$

Task Analysis Example of Logs

a. Use log operations to solve $\log_b\left(\frac{14}{3b}\right)$ if $\log_b 2 = x$, $\log_b 7 = y$, and $\log_b 3 = w$
b. Understand that the fraction in a log can be rewritten as $\log_b$ (numerator) – $\log_b$ (denominator)
c. Apply this to get $\log_b 14 - \log_b 3b$
d. Understand that multiplication within a log such as $\log_b (7 \times 2)$ can be rewritten as $\log_b 7 + \log_b 2$
e. $\log_b 14 = \log_b (7 \times 2)$, so the equation in part c equals $\log_b 7 + \log_b 2 - \log_b 3 - \log_b b$
f. Understand that $\log_b b$ equals 1
g. Applied, the equation can now be written as $\log_b 7 + \log_b 2 - \log_b 3 - 1$
h. Use the substitutions given in part a to rewrite the equation in part (g) as $y + x - w - 1$

These task analyses should follow the systematic instruction principles of Me–We–Two–You.

Me—Teacher models the task analysis while reasoning through the process aloud.
We—Teacher dialogues with students regarding the approach to solve problems.
Two—Students dialogue in pairs or triads regarding the approach to solve problems.
You—Students engage in independent practice with multiple problems.

These steps are flexible, and some students will require more modeling (Me) or guided practice (We or Two) than others. In mathematics, systematic instruction may produce specific outcomes at least to the level of understanding obtained by the instructor. Therefore, teacher knowledge is necessary but not sufficient for student learning.

PRACTICE STANDARDS

The National Council of Teachers of Mathematics (2000) published five process standards along with their curriculum standards per grade level. These process standards were consistent across grades and helped focus instruction about the curriculum standards. The process standards include: (1) Representation, (2) Reasoning and Proof, (3) Communication, (4) Problem Solving, and (5) Connections. These are considerations within lessons and units to enhance the learning experiences of students.

The Common Core State Standards expanded these to develop the eight practice standards. These practices guide student goal setting of lessons and units but do not replace the need for systematic instruction in learning procedures and concepts of mathematics. The practice standards are described below.

Make sense of problems and persevere in solving them. Instead of simply trying to compute answers, students must be taught to analyze problems according to what is known and what is unknown. Have students share aloud what they observe and how they believe the problem should be solved. Finally, help students see how some problems take significantly more time than others. It may even be helpful to grade a problem solving incrementally, celebrating early steps and approaches rather than simply answers.

Reason abstractly and quantitatively. Importantly, students must make sense of seemingly complex abstract problems in mathematics. To do this, consider contextualization of problems using context familiar to students. For example, rather than simply having students repeatedly graph $x < -3$ on a horizontal line, give context. A penguin dives more than three feet below the surface to catch a fish. Graph the options that the penguin dove in relation to the surface. Some students might graph a line open from -3 to ∞. Other students might argue that penguins can't dive deeper than 1,500 feet. If that is their justified argument, then have those students graph $-1500 \leq x < -3$. If a student were this astute to make this argument, then it shouldn't be problematic to explain the difference in the two graphs.

Construct viable arguments and critique the reasoning of others. Verbal reasoning is a repeated recommendation in the practices. It isn't only important for students to reason aloud but, maybe more importantly, to learn the appropriate reasoning of others. Have students reason aloud in pairs or triads. However, pooling multiple struggling students together may cause more confusion. Make sure that at least one of the students in a group has evidenced accurate reasoning so that the other students may learn what to do rather than what not to do.

Model with mathematics. Mathematics should be as relevant and practical as possible, particularly for students who do not see the importance of mathematics. Connect mathematics to charts, graphs, and diagrams to what is being learned in class. Connecting complex equations to reasoning of mathematics, such as the formula for an area of triangle to an actual triangle, is helpful for students to make sense of what they see mathematically.

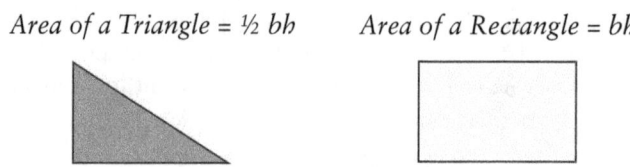

Area of a Triangle = ½ bh   Area of a Rectangle = bh

Use appropriate tools strategically. Many tools are available for mathematics, from hands-on materials to graphing calculators. Importantly, these are only tools and not the essence of mathematics so the use of mathematics tools must be explicitly taught. Use graphing calculators to show the incline of different slopes or the direction of parabolas. These visual descriptions of content should be connected to abstract mathematics learning.

Attend to precision. Mathematically proficient students accurately communicate their problem solving, verbally and visually. Students must show their work in problem solving and understand precise mathematics terms.

Look for and make use of structure. Mathematics is a study of patterns, among other things. From early number sense to later symbolic reasoning, the structure of mathematics aids in solving problems. For example,

$$\frac{6(x-1)}{x-5}$$

means that x could be all real numbers except 5 because a fraction with a denominator of 0 has an undefined value, making it not a legal fraction. This type of reasoning requires knowledge of the mathematical properties and definitions along with computational facility.

Look for and express regularity in repeated reasoning. Students should show their work when solving mathematics, especially during the acquisition stage when learning is new. A student may encounter the radical 7^{-x} and conclude that $7^{-x} = (1/7^x)$. After repeatedly practicing similar problems, the student should recognize the pattern and quickly interpret such radical expressions, $x^{-4} = (1/x^4)$. Recognizing these patterns will help the student scaffold learning to more complex mathematics. For more examples, see Illustrative Mathematics (https://illustrativemathematics.org/).

PRACTICE AND HOMEWORK

The "You" in systematic instruction refers to independent practice and deserves special consideration when teaching mathematics. Practice is important. Students must practice learned skills to develop proficiency. However, how practice is conducted impacts students learning, maintenance, and attitude. Practice should be immediately blocked, completed with potential assistance when newer, mixed of multiple math skills, and able to be completed in a reasonable amount of time.

Immediate Practice

When something has just been presented, students should work immediately on practicing that type of problem. This is called blocked practice. When learning is new, there should be blocks of problem types for students to practice. These blocks all contain similar types of problem approaches but possibly with variations in complexity only, such as more difficult numbers. Immediate practice and feedback on similar problems helps build familiarity and reasoning with the problem type. If students just learned two new things, the immediate practice might look like:

A   A   A   A   B   B   B   B

Blocked practice should be only used with recently learned materials that students haven't yet mastered.

Completed with Potential Assistance

When practicing newer problems, students may run across problems in their approach that require assistance. Immediate feedback and redirection are necessary so that the student practices problems accurately and efficiently. When assistance isn't available, the student makes a conscious decision to start guessing or stop trying. A few students may have the option of a helping family member or an online equivalent. While this is advantageous to those students, it is clearly unfair to students who do not have such support systems. Therefore, initial practice with any newly learned mathematics construct should be completed where immediate and professional assistance may be given. In most cases, this practice is done in the classroom before students are dismissed. If students leave class before fully working through problems independently, then they shouldn't be required to complete the assignment at home. In such cases, homework might best be from an earlier unit or a mixed set of problems learned prior to the lesson. If there is doubt that students will remember how to complete a homework problem, then consider including fully worked or partially worked examples to help jog the student's memory.

$$3x - 6y = 12, \text{ solve for } x.$$
$$+ 6y = \underline{}$$
$$3x = \underline{} + 12$$
$$3x/3 = \underline{}/3 + 12/3$$
$$1x = \underline{} + \underline{}$$

This partially solved problem includes targeted blanks where the student will recall the appropriate steps and solve accordingly.

Mixed Problems of Multiple Math Skills

If students only practice what was just taught, they tend to struggle with chapter and unit tests. This is because they have a difficult time recognizing the type of problem and often struggle recalling how to tackle the problem. While blocked practice is effective at recently learned mathematics, frequent cumulative reviews are important to maintaining learning. Cumulative reviews (sometimes called interleaving) mix multiple problem types together, requiring the student to identify different problems from previous learning and recall the necessary approach. Mixing problem types occurs after students demonstrate success with the recently learned information and may appear as:

X   Y   A   W   B   X   Y   A   W   B

The most recently learned information (A and B) are woven in with practicing previously learned concepts (W, X, and Y). Rohrer and colleagues (2015) found that this technique has been particularly successful in learning most advanced mathematics coursework, from algebra through calculus.

Completed in a Reasonable Amount of Time

We all know horror stories about students who spend three hours on mathematics homework. These are cases of mathematics endurance and not acquisition. If homework is restricted to only problems that require little to no assistance to solve, then homework completion times should already be lessened. Intervention Central presents different researchers' conclusions on time limits for total amount of homework per night (https://www.interventioncentral.org/blog/homework/how-choose-right-amount-daily-homework). Much debate circulates about the need for homework, at all. As a maximum, no more than two hours in total homework should be given to students. Too much homework becomes counterproductive to student learning. This is because students begin to dread a subject merely because of the endurance required to keep up rather than uncertainty regarding their own abilities. Often, the duration of time needed to complete homework increases with student confusion and doubt. When homework is assigned on mixed review material which students have already mastered, then time should be less and performance should be greater. Mathematics homework should fit within a proportional fraction of time spent on homework which should never exceed two hours.

INSTRUCTIONAL STRATEGIES

Cognitive Strategies

Mathematics requires critical thinking and problem solving (Boaler, 2019). To support student problem solving, students require a process to apply their critical thinking. Cognitive strategies apply a stepwise approach to guide student processing. Cognitive strategies are designed to help students plan, monitor, and modify their approach to a mathematics problem. Polya (1957) developed a four-step process to problem solving that has been the basis for many newer, more-researched approaches.

1. Understanding the problem,
2. Devising a plan to solve the problem,
3. Implementing the plan, and
4. Reflecting on the problem.

Pfannenstiel and colleagues (2015) developed a metacognitive approach that encourages self-regulation for students to follow sequentially:

__ Read the problem carefully
__ Identify and circle important information
__ Draw a visual that helps you find the solution
__ Identify the computation needed and write the equation to solve the problem
__ Solve and check your work

Cognitive strategies must be explicitly taught to students. Instruction of cognitive strategies typically follow these steps: (1) develop and activate background knowledge, (2) introduce the strategy, (3) model the strategy, (4) have students memorize the strategy, (5) guide the application of the strategy, and (6) have students independently practice the strategy. Use cognitive and metacognitive strategies to drive student problem solving.

Visuals

Mathematics may appear very abstract to students when it focuses on numbers and symbols alone. It is important to tie visuals to abstract notation whenever possible to build conceptual understanding and even drive procedural facility. Some visuals support mathematics concepts while also supporting procedures. One such visual is the area model (aka box method; array). This method visually represents the distributive property of multiplication and is versatile across mathematics concepts, making it a valuable visual to use over many years and courses. Using the area model, multiplication of two expressions is split between terms (i.e., numbers and variables). For whole number multiplication, such as 71 × 28, the terms are set by place value.

71 × 28	70	1
20	1400 7 tens × 2 tens = 14 hundreds	20 1 × 2 tens = 2 tens
8	560 7 tens × 8 = 56 tens	8 1 × 8 = 8

Adding the products results in 1400 + 20 + 560 + 8 = 1988

Expanding this approach to binomials shows the same language pattern.

$(3x - 1)(4x + 5)$	$3x$	-1
$4x$	$12x^2$ $(3)(4) = 12$ $(x)(x) = x^2$	$-4x$ $(-1)(4) = -4$ $(1)(x) = x$
$+5$	$15x$ $(3)(5) = 15$ $(x)(1) = x$	-5 $(-1)(5) = -5$

Adding the products results in $12x^2 - 4x + 15x - 5 = 12x^2 + 11x - 5$

For more complex polynomials, the approach remains the same.

$(2x^2 - x + 5)(7x - 9)$	$2x^2$	$-1x$	$+5$
$7x$	$14x^3$	$-7x^2$	$35x$
-9	$-18x^2$	$+9x$	-45

Adding the products reveals $14x^3 - 7x^2 + 35x - 18x^2 + 9x - 45 = 14x^3 - 25x^2 + 44x - 45$

Similarly, visuals should be flexible enough to deconstruct or decompose the mathematics. Based on the area model, factoring a quadratic would reveal a similar pattern.

Factor $3x^2 + 2x - 1$				
Steps 1 and 2	Quad			
		$3x^2$		
				-1
Step 3	Quad			
		$3x^2$		$-1x$
		$3x$		-1
Step 4	Quad		$3x$	-1
	x		$3x^2$	$-1x$
	1		$3x$	-1

To complete this process, working backward from the area model looks like this:

1. Multiply the A and C terms

    $(3x^2)(-1) = -3x^2$

2. Determine potential factors of step 1

    $(1x)(-3x); (-1x)(3x)$

3. Select the factors that add to be the B term and write the terms in the spaces provided

    $2x = -1x + 3x$

4. Find the greatest common factors for the columns and rows and write in the rows and columns

    $(3x-1)(x+1)$

While these are highly used because they reveal both concepts and procedures, some students simply struggle with procedural facility. In such cases, a procedural visual may be appropriate.

The "clues and undos" approach organizes a student's review of what is happening to an unknown and then how to reverse that process through computation. For

$$\frac{5}{6}x + 4 = 8,$$

solve for x. In this example, the student identifies that the x is being multiplied by 5/6 and then added by 4. To solve for x, the student must first subtract both sides by 4 and then divide both sides by 5/6.

This organization visual helps the student conclude that $x = 24/5$.

$$5/6x + 4 = 8$$
$$-4 = -4$$
$$5/6x = 4$$
$$5/6x \,(6/5) = 4\,(6/5)$$
$$1x = 24/5$$

ASSESSMENT TO DRIVE DIFFERENTIATION

To increase individualization of learners, assessment should detail individual understanding. Universal screeners identify approximations about who is excelling and who isn't. Progress monitoring is flexible, showing levels of growth over time toward the unit or course exam, or even within a single intervention. Importantly, use standardized assessments whenever possible to avoid inflated scores when determining growth (Myers et al., 2021). While these are important aspects of informed instruction, formative assessments align clearly with instruction and can lead directly to student needs.

Consider the systematic instruction of the lesson being taught. After students practice that skill, it is important to assess their knowledge before assigning mixed practice or moving to the next math skill. In an elementary classroom, an exit slip relies on a small number of problems to determine who understood the lesson and who didn't. Expanding on this approach is the formative checklist. Based on the steps required to solve a problem, teachers will grade each student's steps toward the problem solving of one or two problems. To do this, students will present their approach one step at a time on whiteboards or other interactive material. Teachers will check off students' accuracy to determine what students understand and what they do not.

In an earlier example, the students were applying a strategy to factor a quadratic. Those steps were:

1. Multiply the A and C terms
2. Determine potential factors of step 1
3. Select the factors that add to be the B term and write the terms in the spaces provided
4. Find the greatest common factors for the columns and rows and write in the rows and columns

The formative checklist of student answers may appear as:

Student Name	Multiply (A)(C)	Determine potential factors	Select factors that add to B	Find GCF	Answer	Score
Abby	Y	Y	N	N	N	2 out of 5
Bret	Y	Y	N	Y	N	3 out of 5
Carl	Y	Y	Y	Y	Y	5 out of 5
Devon	Y	Y	Y	Y	Y	5 out of 5
Edith	N	Y	Y	N	N	2 out of 5

In responding to the students, it is important to highlight what each student did accurately, and they all did something that could be praised. Abby accurately multiplied the correct terms and determined potential factors. Bret multiplied accurately, determined the correct potential factors, and accurately found the GCF. The last step was the accurate step, but it was based on incorrect factors. That is why the answer was wrong. With this approach, the focus is equally on what Bret did correctly as to what they could do to obtain the correct answer.

Too often, assessments are reprimands to students who struggle in mathematics. The use of a formative checklist changes the emphasis to what the student is doing accurately and what to do next time. Importantly, if a student repeats an error, then differentiation should be considered to help the student better access the needed mathematics step.

Differentiation

In the earlier case of Bret, they experienced difficulty with addition of integers. If Bret receives interventions with computation, then an accommodation should be considered until they complete that intervention. In the case of Bret, a calculator might be a possibility. This should be accounted for in the formative checklist.

Student Name	Multiply (A)(C)	Determine potential factors	Select factors that add to B	Find GCF	Answer	Score
Abby	Y	Y	N	N	N	2 out of 5
Bret	Y	Y	calculator	Y	Y	4 out of 4
Carl	Y	Y	Y	Y	Y	5 out of 5
Devon	Y	Y	Y	Y	Y	5 out of 5
Edith	N	Y	Y	N	N	2 out of 5

By including a calculator, the teacher shouldn't mark that step as correct or incorrect. So, the total number of points the problem is worth gets reduced, but it does not affect the student's grade. As the student gains in performance regarding the area that is accommodated, a teacher team should decide whether to fade that accommodation or continue to support it. With the goal of independent accuracy, the hope is that accommodations are faded over time.

CONCLUSION

All students can succeed in mathematics. With excellent instruction and focused assessment, we can find ways to help students achieve in mathematics and prepare students for success in postsecondary settings. Using the SOLO framework, teachers should emphasize developing a student's understanding across structural levels, with minimal understanding at the unistructural level but with aspiration toward the relational level. To do so, an understanding of mathematics progressions across grade and content is needed. Additionally, the use of research-based instructional practice, incorporating systematic instruction, cognitive strategies, and visuals is critical to support secondary students' mathematics development.

REFERENCES

Achieve the Core (2016). *CCSS Instructional Practice Guide.* https://achievethecore.org/page/1119/instructional-practice-guide

Adelman, C. (2006). *The toolbox revisited: Paths to degree completion from high school through college.* US Department of Education.

Biggs, J., & Collis, K. (1982). *Evaluating the quality of learning: The SOLO taxonomy.* Academic.

Boaler, J. (2019). *Limitless mind: Learn, lead, and live without barriers.* HarperOne.

Geary, D. C. (2011). Consequences, characteristics, and causes of mathematical learning disabilities and persistent low achievement in mathematics. *Journal of Developmental and Behavioral Pediatrics, 32*(3), 250–63. DOI:10.1097/DBP.0b013e318209edef

Hoffer, T. B., Venkataraman, L., Hedberg, E. C., & Shagle, S. (2007). Final report on the National Survey of Algebra Teachers for the National Math Panel: NORC at the University of Chicago.

Hussar, B., Zhang, J., Hein, S., Wang, K., Roberts, A., Cui, J., Smith, M., Bullock Mann, F., Barmer, A., & Dilig, R. (2020). *The condition of education 2020* (NCES 2020-144). US Department of Education: National Center for Education Statistics. https://nces.ed.gov/pubsearch/pubsinfo.asp?pubid=2020144

Moore, C., & Shulock, N. (2009). *Student progress toward degree completion: Lessons from the research literature.* Institute for Higher Education Leadership & Policy, California State University.

Myers, J. A., Brownell, M. T., Griffin, C. C., Hughes, E. M., Witzel, B. S., Gage, N. A., Peyton, D., Acosta, K. & Wang, J. (2021). Mathematics interventions for adolescents with mathematics difficulties: A meta-analysis. *Learning Disabilities Research & Practice, 36*(2), 145–66. https://doi.org/10.1111/ldrp.12244

National Council for Teachers of Mathematics. (2000). *Principles and standards for school mathematics.* Author.

National Mathematics Advisory Panel. (2008). *Foundations for success: The final report of the National Mathematics Advisory Panel.* US Department of Education.

Pfannenstiel, K. H., Bryant, D. P., Bryant, B. R., & Porterfield, J. A. (2015). Cognitive strategy instruction for teaching word problems to primary-level struggling students. *Intervention in school and clinic, 50*(5), 291–96. https://doi.org/10.1177/1053451214560890

Polya, G. (1957). *How to solve it. A new aspect of mathematical method* (2nd ed). Princeton University Press.

Rohrer, D., Dedrick, R. F., & Stershic, S. (2015). Interleaved practice improves mathematics learning. *Journal of Educational Psychology, 107*(3), 900–908.

Star, J. R., Caronongan, P., Foegen, A., Furgeson, J., Keating, B., Larson, M. R., Lyskawa, J., McCallum, W. G., Porath, J., & Zbiek, R. M. (2019 [2015]). Teaching strategies for improving algebra knowledge in middle and high school students (NCEE 2014-4333). National Center for Education Evaluation and Regional Assistance (NCEE), Institute of Education Sciences, US Department of Education. http://whatworks.ed.gov

Wilcox, B. R., Caballero, M. D., Rehn, D. A., & Pollock, S. J. (2013). Analytic framework for students' use of mathematics in upper-division physics. *Physical Review Special Topics–Physics Education Research, 9*(2), 020119. https://link.aps.org/doi/10.1103/PhysRevSTPER.9.020119

Witzel, B. S., & Little, M. E. (2016). *Teaching elementary mathematics to struggling learners.* Guilford.

5
Mathematics Interventions for Secondary Students with Disabilities

Tricia K. Strickland, Bradley S. Witzel, and Jonté A. Myers

IN 2008, THE NATIONAL MATHEMATICS ADVISORY PANEL (NMAP) released their final report summarizing the state of mathematics education in the United States, focusing on the preparation of students for proficiency in algebra. To obtain algebraic proficiency, students must develop: (a) conceptual understanding; (b) procedural knowledge; and (c) problem-solving skills associated with algebra. Conceptual understanding is defined as the knowledge of relations and connections (Star, 2005), while procedural knowledge refers to actions and manipulations involving rules, algorithms, and strategies (de Jong & Ferguson-Hessler, 1996). In-depth procedural knowledge coincides with in-depth conceptual knowledge and vice versa (Baroody et al., 2007). Together, conceptual understanding and procedural fluency support effective and efficient problem solving (NMAP, 2008), as students apply previously learned concepts and skills to novel problems in which the solution method is unknown (National Council of Teachers of Mathematics [NCTM], 2000). Students with disabilities must be provided with evidence-based instruction to support their progression through the high school mathematics curriculum. However, these students struggle to achieve in secondary school mathematics. According to the National Assessment of Educational Progress (NAEP, 2019), only 9% of eighth grade students with disabilities scored at or above proficient in mathematics. By twelfth grade, only 6% of students with disabilities scored at or above proficient (National Center for Education Statistics, 2015).

Historically, students with disabilities enroll in less-rigorous mathematics courses that focus on basic math rather than grade-level standards (Kortering et al., 2005; Maccini & Gagnon, 2002; Wagner et al., 2003). Additionally, they take fewer mathematics courses in high school than their non-disabled peers (Wagner et al., 2003), and Algebra 1 is often the highest-level mathematics course they complete (Wilson, 2008). Further, students with disabilities continue to be underrepresented in advanced mathematics courses, such as Geometry, Calculus, and Algebra 2. Specifically, students with disabilities make up 12% of the high school enrollment; however, their enrollment in Geometry, Algebra 2, and Calculus is 9%, 6%, and 2%, respectively.

CHARACTERISTICS OF STUDENTS WITH MATHEMATICS LEARNING DISABILITIES

Mathematics difficulties (MD) is a broad term that includes students who score in the low average range (e.g., at or below the 35th percentile) on a standardized achievement assessment (Gersten et al., 2005). Students with MD is a relatively large group that is comprised of students with identified mathematics learning disabilities (MLD) and those without an MLD diagnosis who demonstrate mathematics challenges (Strickland & Maccini, 2013). These students may share common characteristics and benefit from similar interventions (Myers et al., 2021). This chapter focuses on instructional practices which research has deemed beneficial for students with MD, including those with MLD.

Students with MLD exhibit characteristics that may impede their performance in secondary mathematics. Although this is a heterogeneous population, students with MLD may exhibit one or more of the following characteristics. Due to long-term memory deficits, they have difficulty recalling math facts (Geary, 2004) and struggle to compute arithmetic problems because of poor sequential memory with procedures (Geary, 2004). Students with MLD and Attention-Deficit Hyperactivity Disorder may also have visuospatial deficits, as evidenced by difficulty visually representing mathematical information (Witzel, 2020). Additionally, students with MLD perform significantly lower than their non-disabled peers in problem solving which requires students to decode complex vocabulary and comprehend expository or narrative text (Pongsakdi et al., 2020). To accurately complete word problems, students must separate essential information from nonessential and develop a multistep plan to solve the problem (Verschaffel et al., 2020). However, many students with MLD lack operational proficiency to eliminate routine steps in the problem-solving process and struggle to apply appropriate strategies to solve problems, and have intense language needs that impact word problem solving (Van Luit & Toll, 2018). In secondary mathematics, affective measures may also negatively impact students' algebra performance, such as low motivation, self-esteem, and/or passivity in the classroom (Gagnon & Maccini, 2001; Mazzocco, 2007). Due to these characteristics, mathematics outcomes for students with MLD, particularly in secondary mathematics, have been far below outcomes for their non-disabled peers.

Due to the importance of mathematics, specific interventions must be used in the classroom to address the learning needs of students with MLD. This chapter provides an overview of research-based intervention practices that have been found to support students with disabilities as they progress through the secondary mathematics core curriculum. Objectives include understanding of:

- The seven dimensions of the taxonomy of intervention intensity
- How to identify research-based strategies to incorporate within an intervention
- How to implement explicit instruction
- How to implement the Concrete-Representational-Abstract and Concrete-Representational-Abstract-Integration
- How to implement strategy instruction
- How to implement prompt cards/structured worksheet
- How to implement classwide peer tutoring
- How to implement progress monitoring

TAXONOMY OF INTERVENTION INTENSITY

Designing and delivering mathematics interventions is essential to helping students with learning disabilities in mathematics to attain proficiency and learn core standards. Approximately 5%–10% of the general education population requires intensive intervention via special education services (O'Connor & Fuchs, 2013). Students who qualify for special education services under the category of LD have difficulties that interfere with their ability to make academic progress at the same rate as their peers without disabilities. There is an achievement gap that requires intensive interventions for students in special education to reach comparable achievement. The Taxonomy of Intervention Intensity includes seven dimensions for evaluating and building intervention intensity to meet the needs of students with MLD: (1) strength of intervention, (2) dosage of intervention, (3) alignment to core needs, (4) attention to transfer, (5) comprehensiveness of explicit instruction, (6) behavioral support, and (7) meeting individual learning needs (Fuchs et al., 2017).

- *Strength* refers to the intervention's effect on student performance. Specifically, special educators should utilize interventions that report disaggregated effects for students with intensive intervention needs. The National Center on Intensive Intervention Tools Chart provides expert ratings on the technical rigor of interventions and can be found here https://charts.intensiveintervention.org/aintervention.
- *Dosage* refers to the size of the instruction group, the number of minutes per session, and the number of sessions provided per week. Within these parameters, special educators should focus on the number of opportunities each individual student has to respond and receive corrective feedback.
- *Alignment* reflects the extent to which the intervention focuses on the student's academic skill deficits while supporting the learning of grade-appropriate curricular standards. Using error pattern analysis helps align a student's needs with an intervention.
- *Attention* to transfer refers to a student's ability to apply skills they learned to novel contexts. Knowledge and skill transfer is challenging for many students with MLD; therefore, intensive interventions should include explicit transfer instruction to needs found in the school's core math expectations (curriculum and assessment).
- *Comprehensiveness* of explicit instruction principles promotes academic success for students with disabilities. Explicit instruction principles include activating prior knowledge, modeling, providing practice opportunities, gradual fading of supports, and cumulative reviews.
- *Behavioral* support is necessary to encourage student efforts during an intervention. Students with disabilities experience difficulties with attention, motivation, and self-regulation, especially during an intervention that targets a deficit area. Intensive interventions incorporate self-regulation and executive function to assist students with perseverance.
- *Individualization* is the hallmark of special education and is often best described in students' individualized education programs. Data-based individualization (DBI) is a process for individualizing interventions. Teachers regularly use progress monitoring data to determine appropriate adjustments to an intervention.

The goal of providing intensive intervention services is to improve educational outcomes for students with disabilities. Utilizing the seven dimensions of taxonomy (Fuchs et al., 2017) enables special educators to make appropriate decisions regarding interventions.

RESEARCH-BASED INSTRUCTIONAL PRACTICES

Students with MLD require intensive interventions using research-based instructional practices. Research-based instructional practices include strategies and activities that have empirical support for increasing their mathematics achievement. Within the field of special education, numerous instructional practices have been identified as promoting positive outcomes for students with disabilities. In the following sections, we will describe the following instructional practices: (a) explicit instruction; (b) multiple representations; (c) strategy instruction; (d) prompt cards/structured worksheets; (e) classwide peer tutoring; and (f) progress monitoring.

Explicit Instruction

In an analysis of over fifty studies on mathematics for students with MLD, an NCTM panel (2007) concluded with six recommended strategies in their practice brief. Among those, explicit instruction (EI) had the highest relative effect size for students with disabilities and the second-highest relative effect size for students with academic needs. On a related note was the demonstrated effectiveness of think-aloud, which is usually a part of EI.

EI is a systematic approach to teaching that builds students' knowledge over time using step-by-step planning (Gersten, Chard et al., 2009; Fuchs et al., 2021). It is an important strategy for the development of procedural mathematical knowledge and provides the necessary skills for engaging in problem-solving. EI is a teacher-directed instructional cycle that incorporates the following components: (a) an advanced organizer, (b) teacher demonstration, (c) guided practice, (d) student verbal reasoning, (e) independent practice, (f) corrective feedback, (g) distributed reviews for maintenance, and (h) progress monitoring and curriculum-based assessment (Hudson et al., 2006).

Students with LD should receive EI regularly during mathematics instruction as it is a highly effective method for improving mathematics outcomes (NMAP, 2008). Although EI is an effective instructional practice, it should not comprise all the mathematics instruction for students with disabilities (Gersten, Beckman et al., 2009; NMAP, 2008). Teachers should vary the number of EI components based on students' intensity needs to be successful. Additionally, teachers should also use less teacher-centered approaches, such as inquiry-based learning to help students with MLD make connections about the concepts they must learn.

Table 5.1 contains a sample lesson implementing EI to teach students with disabilities how to solve quadratic equations using the quadratic formula.

Table 5.1. Sample Explicit Instruction Lesson

Component of Explicit Instruction	Script*
Planning	General educator and special educator review state standards and students' IEPs. The example below aligns to CCSS.MATH.CONTENT.HSA.REI.B.4.B
	Solve quadratic equations by inspection (e.g., for $x^2 =$ 49), taking square roots, completing the square, the quadratic formula and factoring, as appropriate to the initial form of the equation. Recognize when the quadratic formula gives complex solutions and write them as a 3 bi *for real numbers* a *and* b.
	A curriculum-based assessment (pretest) is given to determine students' current performance.
Advance Organizer	Review prerequisite skills: Review identifying the quadratic, linear, and constant terms of a quadratic expression. Review finding the solutions to quadratic equations by factoring.
	Objective: Today we are going to solve quadratic equations using the quadratic formula.
	Rationale: Some quadratic equations cannot be factored or are very difficult to factor. We can use the quadratic formula to find the solutions to any quadratic equation.
Teacher Demonstration (The teacher uses think-alouds while solving the steps and engaging students with questions involving simple computations. Students are *not* writing anything during this demonstration. Many students with disabilities have impaired working memory therefore the act of writing may interfere with the act of listening and watching the teacher model this solution procedure.)	T: *I need to solve the equation $3x^2 + 5x - 12 = 0$ by factoring. I may be able to factor this, but I often have difficulties factoring when there is a coefficient other than 1 for the quadratic term. So, I am going to use the quadratic formula.*
	The quadratic formula is $$x = \frac{-a \pm \sqrt{b^2 - 4ac}}{2a}$$
	How do I know what a, b, *and* c *refer to? I need to make sure that the equation is in standard form. What is standard form?*
	S: $ax^2 + bx + c = 0$
	T: *Well done! So, let's look at our equation. Is it in standard form?*
	S: Yes.
	T: *Yes, it is already in standard form. The* a, b, *and* c *in the quadratic formula refers to the* a, b, *and* c *in the quadratic in standard form. I would like everyone to point to and say out loud what* a *is.* (The group pointing simultaneously encourages active engagement. Teacher walks around the room monitoring students and will provide immediate corrective feedback to individual students as needed).
	S: 3
	T: *Great! What is* b?
	S: 5
	T: *Yes! And what is* c?
	S: –12

Table 5.1. *Continued*

Component of Explicit Instruction	Script*
	T: Nice job recognizing that c is negative! Now I am going to substitute the a, b, and c values from the quadratic equation into the quadratic formula. I am going to substitute the b's with 5s, the a's with 3s, and c with negative 12. I am going to use parentheses to indicate that I will need to multiply. Here's my quadratic formula with the appropriate substitutions. $$x = \frac{-5 \pm \sqrt{5^2 - 4(3)(-12)}}{2(3)}$$ My next step is to complete the computation within the square root symbol using order of operations. What do I need to do first? S: Exponents. T: Yes, I need to compute 5 squared, which is 5 times 5. What is that class? S: 25 T: Thank you! $$x = \frac{-5 \pm \sqrt{25 - 4(3)(-12)}}{2(3)}$$ Next, I need to multiply −4 times 3 times −12. Negative 4 times 3 is what? S: Negative 12. T: And −12 times −12 is what? S: Positive 144. T: I'm going to double check that with my calculator to make sure that we remembered that math fact (modeling using the calculator). Yes! You are correct! $$x = \frac{-5 \pm \sqrt{25 + 144}}{2(3)}$$ I can add 25 plus 144 to get 169. $$x = \frac{-5 \pm \sqrt{169}}{2(3)}$$ Next, I need to find the square root of 169. Who can help me? Use your calculator if needed. S: 13 T: Great! Next, I am going to multiply 2 times 3 in the denominator. So, here's what we have so far. $$x = \frac{-5 \pm 13}{6}$$ Because we have the plus and minus symbol, I am going to set up two separate solutions like this. $$x = \frac{-5 + 13}{6}$$ $$x = \frac{-5 - 13}{6}$$

Component of Explicit Instruction	Script*
	We can now solve for x. −5 +13 is what class?
	S: 8
	T: I can simplify 8/6 to what?
	S: 4/3
	T: Yes, so 4/3 is one solution to this quadratic equation. Now let's find the second solution. −5 − 13 equals what?
	S: −18.
	T: and −18/6 can be simplified to what?
	S: −3
	T: Well done! The second solution to this quadratic equation is −3.
	Based on student performance, the teacher will model a variety of equations.
Guided Practice *Students are provided a worksheet to complete as the teacher guides them in the solution procedure. See below for the worksheet. The worksheet contains a task analysis as well as visual prompts.* *The teacher constantly walks around the classroom, monitoring student progress and providing immediate feedback.*	T: Now let's do one together. I am handing out a worksheet with our practice problem which is set up in a table. Fill in the blank spaces as we complete this problem together. Let's follow the steps listed on your worksheet to help us solve this problem. What do I first need to ask myself when I am given a quadratic equation to solve?
	S: Is it in standard form?
	T: Great! Is our problem $5x^2 - 8x - 6 = 0$ in standard form?
	S: Yes.
	T: How do you know?
	S: The quadratic term is first, then the linear term, then the constant. It's an equation because there is an equal sign.
	T: Great explanation! Our next step is to substitute the a, b, and c values in the quadratic formula. I would like everyone to do that on their worksheet. The teacher walks around the room monitoring student progress and providing immediate corrective feedback.
	T: Great job! I really like how you remembered that subtracting negative 8, or the opposite of negative 8 is positive 8. Our formula now looks like this
	$$x = \frac{8 \pm \sqrt{8^2 - 4(5)(-6)}}{2(5)}$$
	T: What is our next step?
	S: Complete the computations within the square root sign using order of operations.
	T: Yes! And what do we need to do first?
	S: Exponents.
	T: Which equals what? Remember you can check yourself with a calculator.
	S: 64

(continued)

Table 5.1. *Continued*

Component of Explicit Instruction	Script*
	T: Well done! What comes next?
	S: Multiply 4ac.
	T: And what does this equal?
	S: 184
	T: We have completed the computations so now we can find the square root. Use your calculators and round to the nearest tenths place.
	The teacher continues to walk around the room, monitoring progress and providing immediate corrective feedback as needed.
	T: Well done with your computations. Our formula now looks like this. Make sure your formula on your worksheet looks the same. If not, let me know and I will come and help.
	$$x = \frac{8 \pm 13.6}{2(5)}$$
	T: What do we do next?
	S: Multiply the numbers in the denominator.
	T: And what is our denominator now?
	S: 10
	T: Yes, so now our formula looks like this
	$$x = \frac{8 \pm 13.6}{10}$$
	What is our next step?
	S: Separate the solutions.
	T: Yes! And how many solutions will we have?
	S: Two.
	T: Great! Do that on your paper while I walk around checking.
	$$x = \frac{8 + 13.6}{10}$$
	$$x = \frac{8 - 13.6}{10}$$
	T: Nice job setting up your two solutions. Now simplify and be ready to tell me what x equals. Remember to use your calculator and round to the nearest tenths place.
	Students work while the teacher walks around the room monitoring progress and providing corrective feedback.
	T: Well done! $x = 2.2$ and $x = -0.6$
	The teacher continues to provide guided practice, gradually decreasing prompts, until the students successfully solve. Additionally, the teacher continues to monitor progress.

Component of Explicit Instruction	Script*
Paired Guided Practice	Now that the teacher has faded her guidance, it is important that students practice while thinking aloud through their problem-solving process. Having students verbalize and draw their steps helps reduce potential impulsivity to problem solving while encouraging thinking through the process of finding solutions.
	For these steps, place students in pairs or triads and each should complete a problem for their group. Each member of the group is assigned a color, such as school colors, to differentiate which problem they will present to their group.
	T: On the board, there are three problems, labeled Crimson, Gold, and Platinum. Crimson partners stand up. Now, using your whiteboard, explain to your partners how to solve your problem. Begin.
	S: Students assigned the Crimson problem stand and explain their problem to their partners. As they present, the other group members follow along and correct or guide as needed.
	T: Groups, did Crimson get theirs correct? If so, give them a thumbs-up.
	Next partner. Gold stand up. Begin.
	S: Students assigned the Gold problem stand and explain their problem to their partners. As they present, the other group members follow along and correct or guide as needed.
	T: Groups, did Gold get theirs correct? If so, give them a thumbs-up. If you are ready to begin on your own, then begin.
	For my groups of three, Platinum partners stand up. Begin.
Independent Practice	After students demonstrate that they can solve the equation using the quadratic formula, they engage in independent practice. This form of practice is independent from the teacher; however, students may work with each other. Independent practice may be in the form of a worksheet, flash cards, or computer program.
	Initially, students may use the cue card (see below) to support their learning. Use of the cue card is faded as students become familiar with the procedure.
Non-Example Corrections	While monitoring, the teacher recognizes potential error patterns emerging. So, the teacher includes two problems on the board. One problem is accurately completed while the other has one of the potential errors.
	T: In 30 seconds, I am going to stop you to do two with me.
	Waits 30 seconds.
	T: Eyes up front. One of these two problems has an error. In teams, identify the error and correct it.

(continued)

Table 5.1. *Continued*

Component of Explicit Instruction	Script*
	Students work out both problems and correct the error. By showing non-examples, the teacher highlights an error pattern before students make the error on their own. This preparation for a potential error helps students identify what to do correctly rather than waiting for them to make and even practice the mistake.
Maintenance	Factoring quadratic equations using a variety of methods (factoring, completing the square, quadratic formula) will be practiced over time (weekly, monthly). Homework problems may be a combination of review problems as well as new material.
Curriculum-Based Assessment	A curriculum-based assessment (posttest) is administered to students to determine if they have mastered this content. Results of the assessment are used to determine if students are ready to progress in the curriculum or if there is a need for remediation.

* T= Teacher, S = Student
Note: The teacher may use choral responses and/or call on individual students to respond to the questions.

Guided Practice Worksheet

The quadratic formula is:

$$x = \frac{-b \pm \sqrt{b^2 - 4ac}}{2a}$$

Complete the problem below during guided practice.

1. Write the quadratic equation in standard form.

    $5x^2 - 8x - 6 = 0$

2. Substitute a, b, and c values.

    $$x = \frac{-\_\_ \pm \sqrt{(\ )^2 - 4(\ )(\ )}}{2(\ )}$$

3. Complete computations within the square root sign using order of operations.

    $$x = \frac{-\_\_ \pm \underline{}}{2(\ )}$$

4. Multiply the numbers in the denominator.

    $$x = \frac{-\_\_ \pm \underline{}}{\underline{}}$$

5. Separate the solutions.

$$x = \frac{-\_\_ + \_\_}{\_\_} \qquad x = \frac{-\_\_ - \_\_}{\_\_}$$

6. Simplify.

$$x = \frac{-\_\_ + \_\_}{\_\_} \qquad x = \frac{-\_\_ - \_\_}{\_\_}$$

Quadratic Functions Cue Card

The quadratic formula is:

$$x = \frac{-b \pm \sqrt{b^2 - 4ac}}{2a}$$

Use the standard form of a quadratic equation to determine the values of *a*, *b*, and *c*

$$ax^2 + bx + c$$

Task analysis for solving a quadratic equation using the quadratic formula:

1. Write the quadratic equation in standard form.

   $4x^2 + 5x - 6 = 0$

2. Substitute a, b, and c values.

   $$x = \frac{-5 \pm \sqrt{5^2 - 4(4)(-6)}}{2(4)}$$

3. Complete computations within the square root sign using order of operations.

   $$x = \frac{-5 \pm \sqrt{25 + 96}}{2(4)}$$

   $$x = \frac{-5 \pm \sqrt{121}}{2(4)}$$

   $$x = \frac{-5 \pm 11}{2(4)}$$

4. Multiply the numbers in the denominator.

   $$x = \frac{-5 \pm 11}{8}$$

5. Separate the solutions.

$$x = \frac{-5 + 11}{8}$$

$$x = \frac{-5 - 11}{8}$$

6. Simplify.

$$x = \frac{\frac{6}{8}}{} \qquad x = \frac{-16}{8}$$
$$x = \frac{3}{4} \qquad x = -2$$

Multiple Representations

One especially effective instructional strategy for teaching mathematical concepts and procedures to students with MLD is the Concrete to Representational to Abstract sequence of instruction (CRA; Witzel et al., 2008). CRA has successfully helped students in multiple mathematics areas from elementary to secondary. CRA starts by using manipulatives (Concrete) to represent the mathematics concept and procedure. Once mastered, the student uses an approximate visual representation, such as a picture of the object (Representational). Finally, the student uses abstract symbols, such as tallies, to solve the problem. It is critical to connect the phases by keeping the steps similar between them, using precise and equivalent mathematics language, and connecting the C and R levels to the Abstract steps (Strickland, 2017). For example, when representing $2x$, say "two groups of x" and write $2x$, while using manipulatives to show two cups of x.

Representation	Verbal connection
Concrete = $2x$	"Two groups of x"
Pictorial = $2x$	"Two groups of x"
Abstract $2x$	"Two groups of x"

Connecting the stages using precise language also involves:

Instruction Stages	Description	Purpose	Example: $3x + 2 = 8$
Concrete	Hands-on instruction using concrete manipulative objects (e.g., base ten blocks, sticks, fraction bars) with purposeful stepwise verbal reasoning	Concept and/or procedures are modeled to students using concrete objects	(concrete representation with cylinders, x-block, +, and tally marks)
Visual Representation	Transitions from concrete to pictorial representations of targeted concepts and/or procedures (e.g., drawing pictures, tallies, dots) using the same approach and verbal reasoning	Purposeful and systematic transition from concrete objects to visual representations	$3x + 2 \neq 8$ 000 x + // ///////// - // - // $\frac{000\,x}{000\,x}$ $\frac{//////}{000}$ 0 x ≠ 2
Abstract	Transitions from visual representation to *abstract* representation using the same approach and verbal reasoning	Links the conceptual and procedural knowledge with abstract symbols	$3x + \cancel{2} = 8$ $-\cancel{2}\quad -2$ $\frac{\cancel{3}x}{\cancel{3}} = \frac{6}{3}$ $x = 2$

The Concrete-Representational-Abstract Integration (CRA-I) strategy involves the presentation of a mathematics task using concrete manipulatives, drawings of the manipulatives, and abstract notation (e.g., numbers and symbols) concurrently (Strickland, 2017). The integration of the concrete and abstract representations is recommended in the mathematics literature (Pashler et al., 2007), as integrating and connecting the concrete and the abstract representations during instruction supports students' conceptual understanding and promotes transfer of the concept to a range of novel situations. Additionally, integrating the concrete, representational, and abstract phases expedites the progress from the concrete to the abstract. Gersten, Chard, and colleagues (2009) recommend that use of manipulatives with older students should be expeditious as the goal should be facility in abstract symbolism.

Therefore, the CRA-I strategy may be an efficient strategy to promote academic gains in a timely manner, thus, reducing the achievement gap between students with disabilities and their non-disabled peers.

The following is an example of the implementation of the CRA-I strategy when introducing the concept of a quadratic expression as the product of two linear expressions: (1) *All the classrooms in our school are currently square in shape.* (2) *Our school will be renovated, and each classroom will have an increase in length by 4 feet and an increase in width by 2 feet.* Fill in the table below.

Classroom	Side of original classroom in feet	New length in feet	New width in feet	New area in square feet
Mr. Hernandez	9	**13**	**11**	**143**
Ms. Katz	10	**14**	**12**	**168**
Ms. Smith	11	**15**	**13**	**195**
Any square rec rooms	x	**x + 4**	**x + 2**	**(x + 4)(x + 2)**

Note: Bold values represent cells completed by the student.

Use **algebra blocks** to determine the area of any rec room after it is expanded. **Sketch** the blocks.

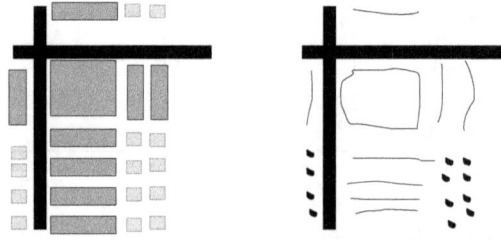

Write area equation: *length * width = area*

$$(x + 4)(x + 2) = x^2 + 6x + 8$$

The CRA-I strategy is a versatile instructional practice that can support students' understanding of algebraic concepts and procedural skills. Research has suggested that using the CRA-I strategy will enable students to develop mastery of algebraic topics such as multiplying linear expressions and factoring quadratic expressions in a timely manner (Strickland & Maccini, 2012; Strickland & Maccini, 2013), thus providing them with access that enables their progress within the high school algebra curriculum. There are benefits to both the graduated and the integrated approaches to CRA instruction and the determination of which approach to use should depend on the characteristics of the students and the algebraic topic.

Witzel, Riccomini, and Schneider (2008) developed CRAMATH, a seven-step attack strategy for planning a CRA lesson. This strategy includes sequential steps that involve:

- Choosing the math topic to be taught;
- Reviewing procedures to solve the problem;
- Adjusting the steps to eliminate notation or calculation tricks;
- Matching the abstract steps with an appropriate concrete manipulative;
- Arranging concrete and representational lessons;
- Teaching each concrete, representational, and abstract lesson to student mastery; and
- Helping students generalize what they learn through word problems.

There is a growing body of research to support the use of computer-generated virtual manipulatives instead of concrete physical objects. Virtual manipulatives may be used within a virtual-representational-abstract (VRA) framework to improve mathematics outcomes for students with disabilities (Bouck & Sprick, 2019) and may be more socially acceptable and less stigmatizing for secondary students (Bouck et al., 2019). It is important to carefully choose a virtual manipulative that promotes both conceptual and procedural understanding, and meets the unique needs of students with disabilities (Strickland, 2021). Strickland (2021) has developed an evaluation checklist to determine if a virtual manipulative is (a) an accurate representation of the mathematics content, (b) accessible for diverse learners, (c) feasible for classroom and home use, and (d) easy to use.

Strategy Instruction

Strategy instruction (SI) incorporates explicit instruction to teach students with mathematics difficulties cognitive and metacognitive processes needed to engage in problem solving or to complete complex tasks (Impecoven-Lind & Foegen, 2010). SI includes three main features. First, SI uses a memory aid (i.e., mnemonics) or attack strategy to aid in the remembering of the problem-solving steps. The second feature is the use of familiar words or phrases to cue actions (i.e., *Read the problem, Translate into an equation*). Third, SI includes a sequence of steps that the student will follow to successfully solve the problem (Maccini et al., 2008). The use of a strategy involves a general approach to solving a wide range of problems (Gersten, Chard et al., 2009) and has been found to be effective for students with LD in a wide range of educational settings, including general education classrooms and alternative settings (Maccini et al., 2008).

Below is an example of the use of the STAR strategy to solve an algebraic word problem. This strategy incorporates the mnemonic STAR, which cues students to *Search, Translate, Answer,* and *Review* when representing and solving word problems. In the *search* phase, students are prompted to read the problem carefully and write down what is known and what needs to be found out. Next, students *translate* the words into an algebraic representation, via manipulatives, pictures, or algebraic notation. To *answer* the problem, students use the manipulatives or algebraic procedures for the necessary symbolic manipulation. Lastly, students *review* the problem by rereading it, asking if the answer makes sense, and checking the answer for accuracy. It is important to remember that students need to be explicitly taught how to use the strategy. Additionally, providing students with a cue card containing the steps of the strategy is an important support especially during guided and independent practice while they are mastering fluency and internalizing the steps (Maccini et al., 2008).

SI is a promising instructional practice that supports metacognitive processes (i.e., self-regulation, strategic planning, self-monitoring, and evaluating a learning task) that are often deficient in students with disabilities (Allsopp et al., 2018; Bley & Thornton, 2001). Students can plan, monitor, and evaluate their progress in the representation and solution of algebraic word problems while using strategies such as STAR.

- Search the word problem
- Translate the words into an algebraic equation
- Answer the problem
- Review the solution

SI may also be used for solving basic computational tasks to algebraic problems. For example, Witzel, Mercer, and Miller (2003), used a mnemonic device, ISOLATE to support the connections between the stages of learning in using CRA to solve equations with a single variable, such as $2x + 3 = 7$. The mnemonic required students to:

- Identify the variables
- Set up equations
- Organize to balance
- Let equations begin
- Act on the variable side of equal sign
- Total other side
- Evaluate and check answer

In action, at the abstract level, ISOLATE may appear as the following in the sample $2x + 3 = 7$, solve for x:

Step	Student Thinking	Math Step	
Identify the variables	I am solving for x, which is on the left side of the equation. There are no other variables in this equation, but there are constants and a coefficient.	$2x + 3 = 7$	
Set up equations	To isolate x, I should subtract both sides by 3 and then divide by the coefficient 2.	Mental planning of subtracting 3	then dividing by 2.

Step	Student Thinking	Math Step	
Organize to balance	What must be done to one side must also be done to the other. That way, each calculation equals itself.	$2x + 3 = 7$ $-3 = -3$	$\dfrac{2x}{4} = \dfrac{4}{4}$
Let equations begin	a. Am I only subtracting constants from constants? b. Am I only dividing the coefficient?	$2x + 3 - 3 = 7 - 3$	$\dfrac{2x}{2} = \dfrac{4}{2}$
Act on the variable side of equal sign	a. Three minus three is 0	$2x + 0 = 7 - 3$	$\dfrac{1x}{1} = \dfrac{4}{2}$
Total other side	a. Seven minus three is 4	$2x = 4$	$\dfrac{1x}{1} = \dfrac{2}{1}$
Evaluate and check answer	One x equals 2. If I substitute that back into the original equation, does it make sense? $2(2) + 3 = 7$. Yes, $7=7$.	$1x = 2$	

With this strategy, the mnemonic is a single verb that depicts the ultimate action requested of the student. The use of single verbs for mnemonics may aid in some students' retrieval of a strategy needed to solve the problem. However, the strategy also encourages reasoning and procedural facility.

Prompt Cards and Structured Worksheets

Prompt cards and structured worksheets provide students with cues to complete a task. Additionally, these materials help students to develop a strategic plan to solve problems (Maccini et al., 2008) as they prompt students to think about important components of the problem and to ask themselves questions regarding known and unknown information. When completing an algebra problem, students with MLD often have difficulty identifying important information, understanding the nature of the problem, and organizing an efficient strategy for solving the problem (Gurganus, 2007). Prompt cards and structured worksheets guide students through these important elements to reach a reasonable problem solution. Additionally, they support students' metacognition by assisting with self-regulation. A structured worksheet was included in the EI script above. Below is an example of a prompt card to help students identify the function as linear, quadratic, or exponential.

LINEAR, QUADRATIC, AND EXPONENTIAL FUNCTIONS

Linear Functions

Ask yourself:

Is the change in x values constant? Yes
Is the change in y values constant? Yes

x	y
1	3
2	6
3	9
4	12
5	15

(+1 between each x; +3 between each y)

Quadratic Functions

Ask yourself:

Is the change in x values constant? Yes
Is the 2nd difference in y constant? Yes
Is the change in y values (1st difference) constant? No

x	y	First	Second
1	1	+3	+2
2	4	+5	+2
3	9	+7	+2
4	16	+9	
5	25		

(+1 between each x)

Exponential Functions

Ask yourself:

Is the change in x values constant? Yes
Is the change in y values (1st difference) constant? No
Are the y values getting large quickly? Yes
Are the first differences multiples? Yes

x	y	First Difference	Multiples
1	4	+3	×2
2	8	+8	×2
3	16	+16	×2
4	32	+32	
5	64		

(+1 between each x)

Classwide Peer Tutoring (CWPT)

Peer-assisted instruction, or peer tutoring, involves a student, under the supervision of the teacher, assisting a peer to learn a skill or concept. These student partnerships occur during structured math study sessions, after receiving instruction from the teacher. Peer tutoring can involve both cross-age tutoring, in which an older student tutors a younger student, and within-classroom tutoring, which involves a higher-performing student tutoring a lower-performing student (Gersten, Chard et al., 2009).

Kunsch and colleagues (2007) found that CWPT was an effective instructional math strategy for K–12, with small but positive effects at the secondary level. CWPT is an instructional strategy that has led to improved mathematics outcomes for students with disabilities (Impecoven-Lind & Foegen, 2010). Specifically, CWPT is a viable practice option to improve the algebra performance of students with disabilities addressing topics such as solving equations (Allsopp, 1997). The teacher uses CWPT after direct instruction of the skill or concept. The teacher provides explicit training in peer-tutoring social skills, transitioning from regular seating to tutoring pairs, and retrieval and return of tutoring materials. Additionally, the teacher models the tutor/tutee partnership, error correction procedures, and how to provide feedback. When implementing CWPT, students are divided into two halves based on their class grade or assessment data. A ranking procedure is then used to control for large differences in student ability levels within tutoring pairs. Students from the first half are paired with students from the second half. For example, a teacher may administer a pretest to her class of thirty students. She then ranks the students by their test scores, from highest to lowest. She separates the highest fifteen student scores (group 1) from the lowest fifteen student scores (group 2). The student with the highest score from group 1 is paired with the student with the highest score from group 2. Then the student with the second-highest score from group 1 is paired with the student with the second-highest score from group 2. This pairing system continues until all are paired. This pairing system provides an opportunity for students with differing abilities to work together, but controls for large differences between partners (Allsopp, 1997). Research has shown that both partners benefit, with the student with lower abilities benefiting differentially (Kamps et al., 2008).

In each pair, students take a turn being the tutor (or coach) and being the tutee (or player). The higher-achieving student is the tutor first. After approximately 10 minutes, they switch roles, and the lower-achieving student is now the tutor. A point system is often added to CWPT (Allsopp, 1997). Two points are awarded for every correct answer. If the tutee makes an error, the tutor models the correct solution. The tutee then practices the solution correctly, and one point is awarded. Points may also be awarded for appropriate tutoring behaviors. At the end of the week, the team with the most points earns an award.

Because CWPT is an opportunity for students to practice skills, the teacher must provide the practice problems. Including a variety of skills relating to a specific topic is beneficial for students with disabilities who may have difficulty with retention and recall of previously learned concepts and skills. These problems may be used to create flash cards with the problem on the front and the solution on the back. In this case, students should be provided with a cue card. Or the teacher may create a worksheet, providing the tutor with an answer key. It is important for the answer key to include the steps and cues for solving the problem, not only the solution.

In addition to improving algebraic skills, CWPT also provides the opportunity for students to engage in practice toward mastery of Common Core Standards in Mathematics (CCSSO, 2010), in this case, specifically CCSS.MATH.PRACTICE. MP3, which states that students construct viable arguments and critique the reasoning of others. Furthermore, tutoring partnerships may promote active engagement of students with disabilities, who often are passive learners (Gagnon & Maccini, 2001).

Progress Monitoring

Progress monitoring involves the frequent administrations of curriculum-based measurement (CBM) to assess students' learning and provide objective data to track student performance. CBM have empirically documented reliability and criterion validity to ensure that they are consistently measuring the specific content that they claim to measure. These tools are brief assessments, which should take approximately five minutes for a student to complete, but are administered frequently (Foegen, 2008). CBM should be administered at least three times a year (i.e., the beginning, middle, and end of the school year), but may be administered weekly to more sensitively measure progress for students with Individualized Education Programs (IEPs) or for students at risk for academic difficulties (Lembke et al., 2016). Data from progress monitoring help teachers determine if the instruction is leading to academic gains or if instructional changes are required to meet the needs of students who are not progressing (Foegen, 2008).

Project AAIMS (Algebra Assessment and Instruction: Meeting Standards) is one of a few reliable and valid tools for monitoring student progress in algebra content to date (Foegen, 2008). Specifically, three measures (i.e., Basic Skills, Algebra Foundations, and Algebra Content Analysis) are available at the Project AAIMS website: https://faculty.sites.iastate.edu/afoegen/project/algebra-assessment-instruction-meeting-standards-aaims.

These measures may be administered weekly to determine if a student is making progress toward achieving IEP goals relating to algebraic concepts and skills. Below is an example scenario.

> Juan is a ninth grade student with a learning disability that interferes with his mathematics progress. He has difficulty with recalling math facts and struggles with multi-step problems as he frequently confuses procedural steps. Juan's IEP contains goals and objectives addressing algebraic readiness concepts such as solving one- and two-step linear equations, graphing linear equations, graphing a linear function, and solving and graphing linear equations.
>
> As Juan was failing in his current Algebra 1 class, the IEP team determined that additional math support was needed. Specifically, Juan receives an intervention that implements explicit instruction on foundational algebra skills and concepts necessary for success in Algebra 1. The intervention includes the use of concrete-representational-abstract instruction. To determine if the intervention is meeting Juan's needs, his teacher decides to administer the AAIMS Basic Skills measure on a weekly basis. Based on the data collected below, is the intervention effective?

Every week Juan is given the Basic Skills measure. His scores are graphed in the dotted line. The data points to the left of the vertical line indicates scores prior to intervention, while the data points to the right of the vertical line indicate scores after intervention. A goal line is drawn in the solid black line from his first baseline data point to his goal, which is marked with an X. Juan's goal is 48 or 80% of the items. A viable method to analyze this data is to focus on the most recent four scores. If they fall below the goal line, then the teacher needs to make an instructional change (Lembke et al., 2016). Based on the data, Juan has reached his goal. His teacher now decides to focus on important algebra concepts and will continue monitoring Juan's progress by using the Algebra Foundations measure.

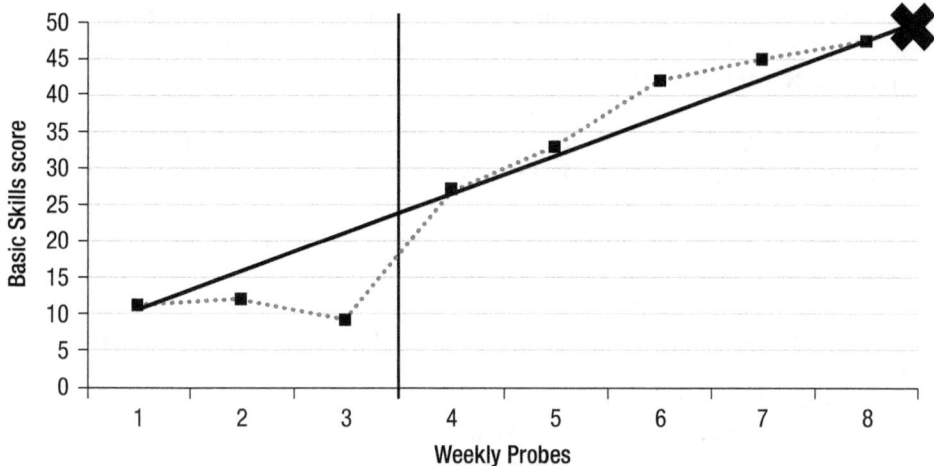

CONCLUSION

To meet the needs of secondary school students with MLD, consideration must be given to their unique learning needs. Based on these unique needs, special education teachers may consider the seven dimensions of the Taxonomy of Intervention Intensity. Interventions must include the implementation of research-based instructional practices. Finally, progress monitoring must occur on a frequent basis to determine if the student is making adequate progress. Interventions and instructional practices may need to be altered based on the progress monitoring data to ensure that students with disabilities are on track to achieve their IEP goals and make progress within the grade-level curricular standards.

REFERENCES

Allsopp, D. H. (1997). Using classwide peer tutoring to teach beginning algebra problem-solving skills in heterogeneous classrooms. *Remedial and Special Education, 18*(6), 367–79.

Allsopp, D. H., Lovin, L. H., & van Ingen, S. (2018). *Teaching mathematics meaningfully. Solutions for reaching struggling learners* (2nd ed.). Paul H. Brookes.

Baroody, A. J., Feil, Y., & Johnson, A. R. (2007). An alternative reconceptualization of procedural and conceptual knowledge. *Journal for Research in Mathematics Education, 38*(2), 115–31.

Bley, N. S., & Thorton, C. A. (2001). *Teaching mathematics to students with learning disabilities* (4th ed.). PRO-ED.

Bouck, E. C., & Sprick, J. (2019). The virtual-representational-abstract framework to support students with disabilities in mathematics. *Intervention in School and Clinic, 54*(3), 173–80.

Bouck, E. C., Park, J., Satsangi, R., Cwiakala, K., & Levy, K. (2019). Using virtual-abstract instructional sequence to support acquisition of algebra. *Journal of Special Education Technology, 34*(4), 253–68.

Council of Chief State School Officers (CCSSO). (2010). *Common core state standards for mathematics*. Common Core State Standards Initiative. https://learning.ccsso.org/wp-content/uploads/2022/11/Math_Standards1.pdf

de Jong, T., & Ferguson-Hessler, M. G. M. (1996). Types and qualities of knowledge. *Educational Psychologist, 31*(2), 105–13.

Foegen, A. (2008). Algebra progress monitoring and intervention for students with learning disabilities. *Learning Disabilities Quarterly, 31*(2), 65–78.

Fuchs, L. S., Fuchs, D., & Malone, A. S. (2017). The taxonomy of intervention intensity. *TEACHING Exceptional Children, 50*(1), 35–43.

Fuchs, L. S., Newman-Gonchar, R., Schumacher, R., Dougherty, B., Bucka, N., Karp, K. S., Woodward, J., Clarke, B., Jordan, N. C., Gersten, R., Jayanthi, M., Keating, B., & Morgan, S. (2021). *Assisting students struggling with mathematics: Intervention in the elementary grades* (WWC 2021006). National Center for Education Evaluation and Regional Assistance (NCEE), Institute of Education Sciences, US Department of Education. http://whatworks.ed.gov/

Gagnon, J. C., & Maccini, P. (2001). Preparing students with disabilities for algebra. *TEACHING Exceptional Children, 34*(1), 8–15.

Geary, D. C. (2004). Mathematics and learning disabilities. *Journal of Learning Disabilities, 37*(1), 4–15.

Gersten, R., Jordan, N. C., & Flojo, R. (2005). Early identification and interventions for students with mathematics difficulties. *Journal of Learning Disabilities, 38*(4), 293–304.

Gersten, R., Chard, D. J., Jayanthi, M., Baker, S. K., Morphy, P., Flojo, J. (2009). *A meta-analysis of mathematical instructional interventions for students with learning disabilities: Technical report*. Instructional Research Group.

Gersten, R., Beckmann, S., Clarke, B., Foegen, A., Marsh, L., Star, J. R., & Witzel, B. (2009). *Assisting students struggling with mathematics: Response to intervention (RtI) for elementary and middle schools* (NCEE 2009-4060). National Center for Education Evaluation and Regional Assistance, Institute of Education Sciences, US Department of Education. https://ies.ed.gov/ncee/wwc/Docs/PracticeGuide/rti_math_pg_042109.pdf

Gurganus, S. P. (2007). *Math instruction for students with learning problems*. Pearson Education.

Hudson, P., Miller, S. P., & Butler, F. (2006). Adapting and merging explicit instruction within reform based mathematics classrooms. *American Secondary Education, 35*(1), 19–32.

Impecoven-Lind, L. S., & Foegen, A. (2010). Teaching algebra to students with learning disabilities. *Intervention in School and Clinic, 46*(1), 31–37.

Kamps, D. M., Greenwood, C., Arreaga-Mayer, C., Veerkamp, M. B., Utley, C., Tapia, Y., Bowman-Perrott, L., & Bannister, H. (2008). The efficacy of classwide peer tutoring in middle schools. *Education and Treatment of Children, 31*(2), 119–52.

Kortering, L. J., deBettencourt, L. U., & Braziel, P. M. (2005). Improving performance in high school algebra: What students with learning disabilities are saying. *Learning Disability Quarterly, 28*, 191–203.

Kunsch, C. A., Jitendra, A. K., & Sood, S. (2007). The effects of peer-mediated instruction in mathematics for students with learning problems: A research synthesis. *Learning Disabilities Research & Practice, 22*(1), 1–12.

Lembke, E. S., Strickland, T. K., & Powell, S. R. (2016). Monitoring student progress to determine instructional effectiveness. In B. Witzel (Ed.) *Bridging the gap between arithmetic & algebra.* Council for Exceptional Children.

Maccini, P., & Gagnon, J. C. (2002). Perceptions and application of NCTM standards by special and general education teachers. *Exceptional Children, 68*(3), 325–44.

Maccini, P., Strickland, T., Gagnon, J. C., & Malmgren, K. (2008). Accessing the general education math curriculum for secondary students with high-incidence disabilities. *Focus on Exceptional Children, 40*(8), 1–32.

Mazzocco, M. M. M. (2007). Defining and differentiating mathematical learning disabilities and difficulties. In D. B. Berch & M. M. M. Mazzocco (Eds.), *Why is math so hard for some children? The nature and origins of mathematical learning difficulties and disabilities* (pp. 29–48). Paul H. Brookes.

Myers, J. A., Brownell, M. T., Griffin, C. C., Hughes, E. M., Witzel, B. S., Gage, N. A., Peyton, D., Acosta, K., & Wang, J. (2021). Mathematics interventions for adolescents with mathematics difficulties: A meta-analysis. *Learning Disabilities Research & Practice, 36*(2), 145–66. https://doi.org/10.1111/ldrp.12244

National Center for Education Statistics. (2015). *Average mathematics score lower and reading score unchanged.* The Nation's Report Card. https://www.nationsreportcard.gov/reading_math_g12_2015/#

National Center for Education Statistics. (2019). *Explore results for the 2019 NAEP mathematics assessment.* The Nation's Report Card.

National Council of Teachers of Mathematics (2000). *Principles and standards for school mathematics.* Author.

National Mathematics Advisory Panel. (2008). *Foundations for success: The final report of the national mathematics advisory panel.* US Department of Education. https://files.eric.ed.gov/fulltext/ED500486.pdf

O'Connor, R. E., & Fuchs, L. S. (2013). Responsiveness to intervention in the elementary grades: Implications for early childhood education. In V. Buysse & E. S. Peisner-Feinberg (Eds.), *Handbook of response to intervention in early childhood* (pp. 41–55). Paul H. Brookes.

Pashler, H., Bain, P., Bottge, B., Graesser, A., Koedinger, K., McDaniel, M., and Metcalfe, J. (2007). *Organizing instruction and study to improve student learning* (NCER 2007-2004). National Center for Education Research, Institute of Education Sciences, US Department of Education. https://files.eric.ed.gov/fulltext/ED498555.pdf

Picciotto, H. (1995). *The algebra lab: Lab gear activities for Algebra 1.* Creative.

Pongsakdi, N., Kajamies, A., Veermans, K., Lertola, K., Vaurus, M., & Lehtinen, E. (2020). What makes mathematical word problem solving challenging? Exploring the roles of word problem characteristics, text comprehension, and arithmetic skills. *ZDM Mathematics Education, 52*(1), 33–44. https://link.springer.com/article/10.1007/s11858-019-01118-9

Star, J. R. (2005). Reconceptualizing procedural knowledge. *Journal for Research in Mathematics Education, 36*(4), 404–11.

Strickland, T. K. (2017). Using the CRA-I strategy to develop conceptual and procedural knowledge of quadratic expressions. *TEACHING Exceptional Children, 49*(2), 115–25.

Strickland, T. K. (2021). Algebra instruction for students with disabilities in the era of common core. *Intervention in School and Clinic, 57*(5), 306–15. https://doi.org/10.1177%2F10534512211032613

Strickland, T. K., & Maccini, P. (2012). The effects of the concrete-representational-abstract-integration strategy on the ability of students with learning disabilities to multiply linear expressions within area problems. *Remedial and Special Education, 34*(3), 142–53.

Strickland, T. K., & Maccini, P. (2013). Exploration of quadratic expressions through multiple representations for students with mathematics difficulties. *Learning Disabilities: A Multidisciplinary Journal, 19*(2), 61–71.

US Department of Education, Office for Civil Rights. (2018). *2015–2016 civil rights data collection STEM course taking.* https://www2.ed.gov/about/offices/list/ocr/docs/stem-course-taking.pdf

Van Luit, J. E. H., & Toll, S. W. M. (2018). Associative cognitive factors of math problems in students diagnosed with developmental dyscalculia. *Frontiers in Psychology, 9*, 1907. https://doi.org/10.3389/fpsyg.2018.01907

Verschaffel, L., Schukajlow, S., Star, J., & Van Dooren, W. (2020). Word problems in mathematics education: A survey. *ZDM, 52*(1), 1–16. https://doi.org/10.1007/s11858-020-01130-4

Wagner, M., Marder, C., Blackorby, J., Cameto, R., Newman, L., Levine, P., Davies-Mercer, E., Chorost, M., Garza, N., Guzman, A. M., & Sumi, C. (2003). *The achievements of youth with disabilities during secondary school: A report from the National Longitudinal Transition Study-2 (NLTS2).* SRI International. https://nlts2.sri.com/reports/2003_11/nlts2_report_2003_11_complete.pdf

Wilson, M. G. (2008). *Math course taking and achievement among secondary students with disabilities: Exploring the gap in achievement between students with and without disabilities* [Unpublished doctoral dissertation]. University of Maryland, College Park.

Witzel, B. S. (2020). Executive functioning disorder and mathematics: Three strategies to implement. *Children and Adults with Attention-Deficit/Hyperactivity Disorder* (CHADD). https://chadd.org/attention-article/executive-functioning-disorder-and-mathematics

Witzel, B., Mercer, C. D., & Miller, M. D. (2003). Teaching algebra to students with learning difficulties: An investigation of an explicit instruction model. *Learning Disabilities Research & Practice, 18*(2), 121–31.

Witzel, B., Riccomini, P., & Schneider, E. (2008). Implementing CRA with secondary students with learning disabilities in mathematics. *Intervention in School and Clinic, 43*(5), 270–76.

6

Teaching the Podcast: Using a Genre Approach to Secondary Writing Instruction

Amber Curlee and Jessica Singer Early

THE PAST THIRTY YEARS HAVE BROUGHT ABOUT significant changes in the ways writing is constructed, shared, taught, and assessed. Many of these developments have taken place as part of the onset of advanced technologies, increased access to the internet and digital and multimodal forms of literacy, and the economic and social demands of globalization. These changes have led the National Council of Teachers of English (NCTE) and the International Literacy Association (ILA), as well as other leading literacy organizations, to issue position statements on the complexities and intricacies of teaching twenty-first-century writing and on teaching writing to support reading (NCTE, 2018; ILA, 2020). As writing has become increasingly digital and multimodal, writing assessment demands in schools have placed more and more focus on teaching highly structured, formulaic, and scripted writing forms in the secondary writing curriculum. English language arts teachers have focused their writing instruction on the five-paragraph essay (Smith, 2006; Wiley, 2000), formulaic and timed writing (Jane Schaffer Writing Program, n.d.), and varying forms of highly structured argument. These practices are accentuated by a pervasive belief that formulaic and impersonal writing forms are, somehow, more serious or rigorous and what "count" as college and academic writing and that they can help underprepared students succeed on tests and for their future lives. Although these approaches to teaching writing may fit teachers' ideas and intentions to support students in preparing for high-stakes exams, they do not represent the array of written genres produced in the world, nor do they allow students to draw from their diverse lived experiences, interests, languages, cultures, and learning styles (Early, 2019).

As writing researchers and teacher educators, we take the stance that students do not have to leave themselves behind when writing for school or to prepare for college, the workplace, or civic engagement. We may be rigorous, scholarly, and academic in our approach to teaching writing without depriving students of opportunities to write from their lived experiences, cultures, values, and voices (Early, 2017; Germán, 2021). This chapter focuses on the teaching of writing at the secondary level (grades 6–12) in English language arts classrooms. We use genre as a framework and approach for teaching writing so students may learn how writing is tied to social purposes, contexts, and expectations (Prior, 2006). The genre framework offers an inclusive and expansive approach to teaching writing that allows students to bring their whole selves to the page and to experience how writing works in the world around them, while also allowing for clear guidelines and structure to support students with diverse learning backgrounds and needs. Two objectives guide this chapter:

1. Students will be able to practice written genre forms to prepare them for the kind of writing used in college, the workplace, and community.
2. Students will be able to complete classroom-based writing opportunities which share their lived experiences, cultures, and languages as well as meet their needs as diverse learners.

We share an instructional example of a genre-based writing unit focused on podcast writing to model best practices for teaching writing using a genre approach.

FOUNDATIONAL LEARNING THEORY

We draw from sociocultural learning theory as a way of conceptualizing writing and language use. From this perspective, the specific cultural activities of language learning and literacy are products of social interaction and are embedded in a larger cultural and institutional context (Vygotsky, 1978; Bazerman, 2000 [1988]; Prior, 2006). This approach diverges from a cognitive or developmental view of literacy in which meaning-making results from encoding and decoding texts, or predefined stages of thinking and learning (Hayes & Nash, 1996; MacArthur & Graham, 2016). We view writing as a social practice and are interested in the ways the teaching of writing may be enhanced through social relationships and in connection to social contexts and expectations (Bazerman, 2000 [1988]; Brandt, 2001; Early, 2010). From this lens, writing is always situated within a context, is tied to specific purposes, and changes over time with practice and guidance (Bazerman et al., 2009). Thus, learning to write is a process of coaction (Prior, 2006), meaning it is a practice embedded in the social and material world. Individuals do not learn to write alone and, even while writing, which is seemingly a solitary act, they call upon prior knowledge grounded in social relationships and contexts (Early, 2010; Early & Saidy, 2018).

Genre theory is based on the understanding of written texts as socially constructed language practices that reflect the norms and expectations of a community. Communities continually set, maintain, and shift expectations for the discourse practices that take place within their social context and, hereby, a genre or set of genres emerge (Purcell-Gates et al., 2007; Prior, 2006). While there is no simple, unified definition of what constitutes "genre," in teaching writing two accepted tenets include teaching the features of particular writing forms along with the ways these specific tasks allow writers to participate in the social actions of a discourse community (Dean, 2008). Bazerman and Prior (2005) argue that genre theory has three different perspectives: genres as text, as rhetoric, and as practice. The *genre as text* perspective focuses primarily on the features of textual form as reflection of a particular social situation and views the norms that govern particular writing forms as fluid and flexible—continually shifting to fit sociocultural values and contexts. *Genre as rhetoric* emphasizes the social situations that surround the various textual forms. The third perspective, *genre as practice*, begins with the contexts and processes of genre rather than the genre form itself. The repeated patterns and rhetorical decisions a writer makes while writing help form specific genres (Paré & Smart, 1994; Johns, 2001). Genres also create familiar communicative moves and serve as benchmarks to explore new rhetorical situations. While genre is defined by expectations, form, and an "insider" understanding of its social and contextual uses, these are continually shifting to meet new social demands and literacy technologies.

GUIDING RESEARCH AND POLICY

In the past twenty years, there have been a number of studies and commissions devoted to exploring the range of writing practices taking place in schools and in tracing the way the teaching and practice of writing has shifted with onset of advanced technologies and new literacy practices (Grabill & Hicks, 2005). In April 2003, the National Commission on Writing (NCW) in America's Schools and Colleges (2003) released a report titled *The Neglected "R": The Need for a Writing Revolution*. This landmark report called for "a writing revolution," meaning a significant increase in the time, resources, and technologies devoted to writing instruction and practice in K–12 schools. Later that year, in July 2003, the National Center for Education Statistics (NCES, 2003) released results from the 2002 NAEP in Writing, which was the most comprehensive assessment of writing ever conducted in this country. Approximately 276,000 students (grades 4, 8, and 12) from 11,000 public and private schools participated in this assessment. The study found that fewer than one in three fourth-graders, one in three eighth-graders, and one in four twelfth-graders scored at or above the "proficient" level in writing and there were significant gaps in performance between ethnically diverse and second language students and white classmates.

The NAEP report also showed that although there had been an increase in writing in classrooms throughout the United States in the period between 1988 and 1998, the majority of students were not taking part in writing assignments that required complexity, length, or real-world application. This is of significant concern for secondary students hoping to pursue higher education or enter the workforce where the demands for writing are complex and multifaceted (American Diploma Project, 2004). Equally disconcerting, reports of the types of school writing eighth grade students participated in between 2002 and 2007 show a significant drop in the practice of every form of writing students were asked about, including interpretation and analysis, persuasive letters and essays, personal and imaginative stories and observations, and professional writing (Applebee & Langer, 2009; Salahu-Din et al., 2008). Moreover, a study by ACT (2005) showed that close to one-third of high school students planning to attend postsecondary institutions did not meet readiness benchmarks for college composition courses and 50% or more of adolescents in certain ethnic groups do not meet ACT benchmarks, placing them at a great disadvantage in their transition to and overall success in college.

To address the problem of the "Neglected R," in 2004, the NCW held a year-long, four-part seminar in different parts of the country. During these seminars, classroom teachers, principals, researchers, curriculum coordinators, policymakers, and university administrators met to discuss what counts as effective writing instruction and ways to better meet the needs of all students. The commission concluded that we must personalize writing instruction, create a sense of community around writing and writers, make writing a part of policy reform, and improve professional development. They also found that models of effective writing instruction require students to be active participants in the learning process, and that educators must encourage students to write for public audiences; call on students to collect, analyze, and synthesize sources; and invite students to use their home cultures, languages, and lived experiences as a resource (NCW, 2006). Across the board, these studies have shown that while secondary students are writing more in school than they did thirty years ago, they are typically only writing a page and a half per week in English language arts classrooms, which is the subject area where the most writing takes place in secondary schooling (Applebee & Langer, 2009).

With these challenges and goals in mind, educators and policymakers across the country have set out to improve writing instruction in classrooms, including instruction at the secondary level. Graham's (2019) review of research recommends best practices for writing instruction and synthesizes research to influence policy and practice to better meet the needs of students in K–12 school settings. He argues that teachers of writing need "to create, enact, sustain, and modify (as needed) a vision for teaching writing in their particular class and context that is reasonably consistent with any school, district, state, or national goals that are applicable to their situation and context" (p. 293). With the recent implementation of the Common Core State Standards (2010), there is increased attention to teaching argumentative and persuasive written forms. Other modes, such as narrative, poetic, or creative forms, have been increasingly pushed out of the curriculum. Teachers of writing continue to teach highly structured, formulaic, and timed writing forms and these practices are accentuated by a pervasive belief that argumentative and expository modes are, somehow, more serious, or what "count" as college and academic writing. Although argumentative and persuasive modes may fit our best intentions in supporting students in preparing for their future pathways and in passing high-stakes exams, they in no way represent the diverse array of written genres produced in the world. Nor do they allow students to draw from their diverse lived experiences to communicate their ideas for audiences and purposes beyond the school walls.

This chapter offers a rigorous, scholarly, and academic approach to teaching writing using genre as a framework so students may write in connection to social purposes, contexts, and expectations. The genre framework offers an inclusive and expansive approach to teaching writing that allows students to bring their whole selves to the page while sharing and making sense of new ideas and information, defining what they care about and why, and engaging with real audiences and purposes for reasons that matter to them deeply. The genre approach to teaching writing also allows teachers of writing to move beyond narrow definitions of what counts as "college-ready" or "scholarly" writing while also providing clear guidance and structure to support diverse learning styles and interests and while meeting rigorous state standards.

CONNECTION TO STANDARDS

The Common Core State Standards operate as a driving force behind equalizing public education across all publicly funded schools. In 2010, more than forty states signed on to the Common Core State Standards Initiative to set common goals for students at each grade level of public schooling, regardless of location, racial makeup, or socioeconomic status. This was seen as a way to make goals of the 2001 No Child

Left Behind Act plausible (US Congress, 2001). These standards brought heavier focus to reading of nonfiction texts and argumentative writing, effectively pushing narrative forms of writing out of classrooms. Secondary level Common Core Standards provide the skills and abilities which students should achieve at each grade level in order to be adequately prepared for college, career, and life, upon graduation from high school. The standards focus on reading, writing, speaking, and listening, and provide detailed learning goals for teachers to focus lessons on.

In the application of standards, it is helpful to find genres which can combine the use of multiple standards into one assignment, encouraging students to explore the intersections of the skills. Podcasting serves as a multifaceted writing genre through which teachers can join the reading of informational texts for research, expository, and argumentative writing with a public-facing narrative style which achieves many common core standards while leaning into student interests and ideas and demonstrating the value of student voices. A podcast assignment, such as the one described later in the chapter, addresses a wide variety of standards of 11–12 grade Language Arts classrooms (similar standards can be found in earlier secondary levels to align with a similar podcasting assignment). Table 6.1 includes the CCSS standards addressed through the teaching of the genre-based podcasting unit introduced in this chapter.

Table 6.1. CCSS Standards

Reading Standards	Writing Standards	Speaking and Listening Standards	Language Standards
11-12.RL.1: Cite research in support of arguments and ideas presented.	**11-12.W.1:** Write arguments to support claims, utilizing valid reasoning and supportive evidence.	**11-12.SL.2:** Evaluate and integrate multiple sources of information presented in diverse formats and media in order to make informed decisions and solve problems.	**11-12.L.1:** Demonstrate understanding and command of English Language.
11-12.RI.4: Determine meanings of words and phrases in a text, and, analyze author's use of these within the text.	**11-12.W.2:** Write clear, explanatory texts to explore complex concepts.	**11-12.SL.3:** Evaluate a speaker's point of view, reasoning, use of evidence, and rhetoric, as well as other elements impacting efficacy of presentation.	**11-12.L.3:** Apply knowledge of language use to make effective choices appropriate to context.
11-12.RI.6: Determine author's purpose and point of view in a text, and, analyze impact of chosen style and content on the text.	**11-12.W.3:** Write well-structured and detailed narratives.	**11-12.SL.4:** Present information and findings with a clear message and point of view which is easily followable by audience and appropriate to task, audience, and purpose.	**11-12.L.4:** Determine and clarify the meaning of unknown words and phrases based on grade-level reading and content.

(continued)

Table 6.1. *Continued*

Reading Standards	Writing Standards	Speaking and Listening Standards	Language Standards
	11-12.W.4: Write in a clear and coherent manner which is appropriate to task, purpose, and audience.	**11-12.SL.5:** Make strategic and thoughtful use of media appropriate to task, purpose, and audience.	**11-12.L.5:** Demonstrate understanding of figurative language, word relationships, and nuance in word meaning.
	11-12.W.5: Utilize elements of the writing process (planning, editing, revising, rewriting) with a focus on specific audience and purpose.	**11-12.SL.6:** Adapt speech to fit the format and environment, proficiently utilizing formal English where appropriate.	
	11-12.W.6: Utilize technology to produce, publish, update, and share writing products in response to ongoing feedback.		
	11-12.W.7: Conduct research to solve a problem or answer a question, adjusting tactics when necessary and synthesizing information to fit the needs of the project.		
	11-12.W.8: Gather information from a variety of sources, evaluating each source's strengths and limitations as applicable to the purpose and audience of the project.		
	11-12.W.9: Draw evidence from a variety of sources to support analysis, reflection, and research.		

PROFESSIONAL GROUPS

Educators and policymakers across the United States have set out to improve writing instruction, including instruction at the secondary level. The National Writing Project (NWP), National Council of Teachers of English (NCTE), Conference on College Composition and Communication (CCCC), and Council of Writing Program Administrators (CWPA) are just some organizations that have begun to extend their networks, growing their membership and outreach and using online resources to improve writing instruction across grade levels. For example, the NWP continues to expand its professional development and leadership opportunities for K–College teachers of writing. The organization now has more than 200 university-based writing project sites, which span all fifty states, Washington, DC, Puerto Rico, and the Virgin Islands. The National Writing Project is also collaborating with the Center on English Learning and Achievement to conduct a new national study on writing instruction across grades and subjects.

Many groups also have come together to address the issue of college readiness, recognizing that writing is key to students' success in college and the workplace. The best-known example is the *Framework for Success in Postsecondary Writing* (National Council of Teachers of English [NCTE], 2011), which was developed by the CWPA, NCTE, and NWP. Based on current writing pedagogy research, the framework offers a series of mental habits and rhetorical and 21st-century skills that students need to succeed in college and college writing. One of the primary goals of the framework is to help teachers develop sound habits and skills with students through writing, reading, and critical analysis. As organizations and commissions have ramped up their efforts to improve student writing and writing instruction, there has also been a greater focus on research designed to examine the writing practices of ethnically and linguistically diverse students in academic contexts from kindergarten to graduate school, as well as out-of-school contexts like the workplace and community (Ball, 2006; Beaufort, 1999; Edelsky, 1986; Faltis & Wolfe, 1999; Guerra, 2008; Hull & Schultz, 2002; Valdés, 2001). A number of studies in ethnically and linguistically diverse school communities have focused on the impact of specific instructional strategies on students' writing development.

NCTE (2005) has offered position statements calling for the inclusion of multimodal literacy practices (designing through different genres of communication, including linguistic, visual, and audio) in the curriculum. By including these elements teachers may incorporate the rhetorical and 21st-century skills deemed vital to students' progress toward college- and career-ready writing. Teaching writing through podcasting encompasses these skills while providing an audience beyond the classroom, an opportunity for research, and demonstration of the value of each student's knowledge, ideas, interests, and voice.

FORMATIVE/SUMMATIVE ASSESSMENT METHODS

The goal of assessment in secondary writing is not only to ascertain the level of growth of each student but also to demonstrate the value of the writing process itself. As was explained in NCTE's "Framework for Success in Postsecondary Writing," the habits of mind required to achieve writing success require heavy focus on the process (NCTE, 2011). Guidelines for assessment should be clearly outlined for students for each assignment, and should only assess what they have learned within the instructional unit. Rather than focusing on genre mastery, assessment should focus on progress and process. This means thinking about the process from invention to completion as well as the genre framework, which includes audience, social purpose, and expected conventions or elements. The kinds of questions teachers can ask their students to think about as they assess their own writing or when assessing their students' writing include:

1. Does the writer take part in the stages of the writing process (not necessarily in this order):
   a. Brainstorming
   b. Close reading of model texts
   c. Drafting
   d. Researching (formal or informal)
   e. Peer or teacher reviewing
   f. Revising
   g. Making public and sharing
2. Does the writer meet the genre expectations for the particular genre assigned?
   a. Does the writer have a clear purpose?
   b. Does the writer acknowledge or write for a clear and intended audience?
   c. Does the writer take up 3–5 genre elements or repeated patterns?

TEACHING THE PODCAST GENRE

With an increase in access to and interest in digital and technological literacies, the podcast genre is experiencing a revolution. The genre was already increasing in popularity, and then when COVID-19 hit, people were home with more time on their hands, and there continues to be a surge in listening, following, and creating podcasts. According to recent data, there are currently over 2 million podcasts and 48 million episodes available, and these numbers are climbing weekly (Winn, 2021). There are podcasts covering a vast range of topics from comedy, therapy and self-help, politics, sports, cooking, and current affairs. If you have a topic or interest, you can surely find a podcast to match. According to Nielson ratings, over 50% of homes in the United States listen to podcasts and most people who follow podcasts listen to seven shows in their entirety per week (Bate, 2020; Nielsen, 2017). Comedy is the most popular podcast genre along with news and education (Winn, 2021).

The podcast represents a multimodal approach to writing. Podcasts involve writing (scriptwriting) voice-over, and music. As students create podcasts, whether individually or in groups, they must pay careful attention to writing, sound, and spoken word. The podcast also requires the writer to go through steps of composing, recording, and mixing. This allows opportunities for them to consider story line and messaging, standards of unity and presentation, as well as design, clarity, and sense of audience.

Bringing podcasts to the teaching of writing is a wonderful way to engage students in a timely and innovative multimodal literacy practice. Teaching the podcast may be tied to any topic, instead of a more traditional research or argument paper, or used as an assessment tool in response to reading or a broader unit of study. The podcast involves the same skills and analytical approaches to research required for many state and district standards but can feel more relevant and enticing than a traditional research paper. The podcast blends research, scriptwriting, music, voice performance, and editing. You can learn a great deal about this genre by inviting a fruitful conversation with your students about their connection to it. You get a read on students' prior knowledge regarding the genre along with their insight into how the genre is evolving in real time by asking students what podcasts they listen to or they have heard about.

Throughout the teaching of a podcasting unit, students become active participants in the acquisition of knowledge, and are encouraged to contribute their ideas and insights. The podcast genre provides an engaging means for building connections between new skills and habits and students' existing knowledge. At each step of the podcasting unit, from the introduction of the genre to more specific lessons, such as scriptwriting and the inclusion of sound effects, students may be provided with analytical prompts and model texts appropriate to the lesson to perform their own deep dive into the concept, discerning elements which build a successful podcast and how they operate within the genre. Asking students to become active in their acquisition of knowledge and understanding of podcasts builds a deeper and more authentic connection to the genre than is possible with a teacher-centered topic.

The podcast may be assigned as an individual project where each student creates their own or it lends itself to group work (pairs or small groups). Keeping the time limit requirement relatively short (5–10 minutes) works best when students work independently. If you want students to work in groups, they can create a longer podcast (10 minutes for a group of 2 and 20–30(ish) minutes for a group of 4). If possible, keep the groups small (3–4 students). Anything more significant makes the managing of roles and contributions unwieldy. It also helps to break down the podcasts' teaching, writing, and production into tangible steps.

You want to give students a topic for their podcasts that provides enough room for students to have agency and choice in what they decide to write about. For example, students may create podcasts on current issues or events, on topics they are deeply invested in and want others to know about, or on some aspect or realm of education they want to see changed. It is also popular to participate in fandom and young adult literature, popular culture, social media, and many more. You have endless options for the assignment's focus and can make it fit the direction of your curriculum and context. Students choose a range of topics such as homelessness, clean drinking water, body image, lack of green spaces, and funding for libraries.

We typically assign podcasts that involve making an argument and conducting research. However, there are a variety of subgenres within the broader podcast genre to choose from. This includes the following: including the podcast interview, narrative (fiction or nonfiction), conversation or panel discussion, repurposed content (contains the same message as other podcasts or texts but is delivered in a new way), or a hybrid show (a show that includes a monologue and then a conversation or panel discussion or interview). It helps to choose which of these kinds of podcasts you want students to create so you can help them navigate the necessary deliverables in creating that form of a podcast.

A podcast unit focuses on teaching the following elements:

1. Exploring Podcasting as a Genre
2. Research and Podcasting: What do I need and how will I use it?
3. Structuring a Podcast: Evaluating model texts, Outlining
4. Podcast Scripting
5. Technology and Style in Podcasting

A podcast writing unit may be expanded to accommodate deeper research, a longer podcast, or to provide additional time for students who need it (see table 6.2).

Table 6.2. Sample Podcast Unit Calendar

Week 1	Week 2
Monday	**Monday**

• Intro to Podcast Genre
• Assignment Handout
• Group Activity: Presenting sample podcasts, a mix of student and professional. Discussion of what makes each effective or engaging, or what doesn't work.
	• Outline Mini-Conferences
	• Scriptwriting
	• Due:
	  ○ Script Outline
	  ○ Complete draft works cited

Tuesday	**Tuesday**
• Exploring Research in Podcasts PP • Research Plan (handout) • Reading: How to Start a Podcast Article	• Script Conferences
Wednesday	**Wednesday**
• Podcast Structure/Analysis PP and handout • Due: Bring 3 sources	• Recording • Integrating sound effects and music
Thursday	**Thursday**
• Where do we see evidence of stereotypes? Examples in media and life • How to Script a Podcast	• Peer Review • Final Edits
Friday	**Friday**
• Technology and Style PP and Take it/Leave it handout	• Sharing and celebration of podcasts

ASSIGNMENT EXAMPLES

The following assignment presents a podcast assignment used in an English 101 composition course for first-year college students focusing on elements of the college experience (see textbox 6.1). Amber (first author) invited her students to create a podcast script exploring an element of the college experience of their choice. Students selected a variety of topics, including the importance of sleep, study habits, the impact of COVID-19, how to choose a roommate, etc. (see textbox 6.2). This podcast assignment may be easily modified for the secondary level through a simple topic change to focus on the secondary experience. Or, students can choose a stereotype to explore and identify the falsities in, incorporating source information and interviews to support their claims. The podcasting genre as a whole, and this model unit in particular, can be easily adapted to fit topics which meet the needs and interests of teacher's contexts and diverse student needs and interests.

TEXTBOX 6.1. SAMPLE PODCAST ASSIGNMENT

College Experience Podcast Assignment Sheet

250 Points

Prompt:

For this assignment, you will come up with a question regarding the college experience and perform research regarding that question. You will use this research to develop an informative podcast that will answer your question and help the audience understand why that information is important. To do this assignment well, you'll want to have a fairly narrow question that you've researched in depth. The podcast should be well researched, and clearly demonstrate why the information included is important to the audience.

Requirements:

- 5-7 minute podcast created using Anchor.
- Explain research question and its relevance to your audience.
- Answer questions using appropriate and relevant research (scholarly sources, statistics, newspaper articles, etc.) and integrate that research to establish your personal ethos, the ethos of your piece, and to shape the way you answer the question and organize that answer.
- Written works cited including 8 sources following MLA requirements.
- Use appropriate music, sound effects, etc. to make your podcast.

The final draft should be polished, and you should make significant changes from the first draft to the final.

Due Dates:

Topic, 3 sources (10 Points)	11/8
Opening 1-2 paragraphs of podcast script (20 Points)	11/10
Script Outline (20 Points)	11/17
Draft of Works Cited (20 Points)	11/17
Recording draft due to Dropbox (20 Points)	11/22
Conference (10 points)	11/22 and 11/24
Final draft and Works Cited (150 Points)	12/1

*Rough draft may be submitted in MP3 or MP4 on Canvas.
*Final podcast must be submitted via Anchor. Works Cited must be submitted via Canvas.

TEXTBOX 6.2. SAMPLE PODCAST SCRIPT

College Experience Podcast Script

First-Year College Student

Hello everyone. My name is Emma, and I am a freshman at Arizona State University. With my first semester almost over, I have been able to get fully acquainted with my college dorms. However, it wasn't as easy as I thought it would be. There were many things I didn't plan for, things I forgot to buy, and obstacles that got in the way. The purpose of this podcast is to make sure you don't run into the same problems I did by giving you feedback from other students about their time in the dorms and some hacks for you to get prepared.

The summer after my high school graduation was full of planning for college. I thought about storage, utilities, and decorations for my dorm room. I was most looking forward to living in the college dorms because I believed it was the best choice in order to experience the college life. You see college students in movies and TV shows and expect it to be similar; however, living with other people throws curveballs your way. Unexpected problems such as noise levels, sharing washing and dryer machines, and spending more money than necessary will inevitably cause you extra unwanted stress. But fret not, as we dive into getting ready for college dorm life.

College dorm expectations aren't normally far from reality; however, they can be sugarcoated. These expectations likely derive from the representation in the media. Many coming-of-age films that take place in college depict it as a place where young adults drink, party, and pull all-nighters to finish assignments. An article by the University of Texas in Austin examined how the media portrays higher education in which a lot of it contains the same tropes. The frat party practice is one of the most popular activities highlighted in movies and TV shows—a packed house with red plastic cups everywhere. In comparison, a common character is a stuffy professor that presents a cold and distant demeanor to their students. The last well-known niche in college films is that the status quo from high school sticks—jocks at one table, nerds at the other. This can cause students to focus on partying, staying up late, and staying closed off in order to avoid social alienation. These common and often unrealistic approaches toward college are a big factor in what causes students to be unprepared for living there.

A friend of mine, Zoe, is from Washington state and moved out here to pursue a degree in sports management. I asked her what she thought living in the dorms would be like. (Recording 1)

> There are many things glossed over when preparing to move into college dorms. Moving away and becoming independent is one of the biggest changes in your life. College is already stressful enough, so it would be in everyone's best interest to be fully prepared for dorms so there's one less factor contributing to stress. A study conducted by two researchers at NASPA, the National Association of Student Personnel Administrators, explored the expectations versus the reality of first-year college students. The results of the study showed that students with unrealistically high academic and social expectations had lower first-year GPAs than those who had

average or below average expectations. Students are advised to maintain realistic and attainable expectations based on the findings of this essay.

I asked Zoe if there was anything about college that didn't live up to her expectations, to see if her answer aligned with what NASPA found. (Recording 2)

While preparing to live in college dorms, it is wise that you don't hold it to such a high or low standard. Not only will students be faced with the stress that comes from academic success and healthy social life, but moving out is a huge step in life. However, our podcast is here to make the transition a little easier.

One of the best pieces of advice I can give is to talk to anyone you know who lived in the dorms during their freshman year and ask them for advice. For example, the Huff Post asked dozens of their workers to provide a one- or two-sentence response to the question, "What did you wish you knew as a college freshman?" Most of the responses have to do with your surroundings, rather than the dorm itself. Explore the city, try the local restaurants, take advantage of the gym, and learn about the places that give student discounts. Another article written by Samantha Gorski at the University of New Hampshire spoke more about what it is like living with another person. She advised communicating with them, starting to talk as soon as you can before actually moving in, and setting up quiet hours where there are no TV, music, or friends over so that homework can get done.

With this advice in mind, let's hear what our guest Zoe has to say about what helped her while living in the dorms. (Recording 3)

Now that we've gone over background information on college expectations and stressors, as well as seeing what advice people give to college freshmen, let's move on to helpful hacks you can implement to make dorm living easier. An article by One Crazy House, a website that gives you tips and organization ideas for your living space, went over some dorm hacks and products to make life easier. A great tip is to make use of vertical storage. They suggest items like over-the-door shoe racks, towel racks, and hanging baskets. They also mention maximizing under-the-bed storage like bins, drawers, or boxes. And if your bed isn't lofted very high, then you can purchase bed risers to create extra space.

Now, we'll move on to my personal college dorm hacks. I've learned to implement these through my experience; however, these may not work for everyone. It is a good idea to make use of reusable plates, bowls, and cutlery to reduce waste, but this means cleaning them afterward. I found this great brush at my local grocery store that dispenses soap into the bristles. So, replace your sponges with a soap dispensing palm brush. Next, if your room has enough space for a chair or two, it's a great idea to buy an ottoman. Not just any ottoman though. On Amazon, you can find small ottomans with a tabletop tray. So one side of the lid can be used as a foot rest or a seat, but when you flip it over, it can be used as a wood table. Lastly, one of the most convenient items I've found was a clip-on nightstand. It attaches to your bed frame and there is a wide variety of ones you can utilize. Some are pouches that can hold things like your phone, water bottle, and snacks. Or you can find one that acts as a mini table to keep books or your computer on. Using all of these on a daily basis has made living in a small room a little more bearable.

My last question for Zoe was to tell us about one thing that she wasn't prepared for in college dorms.

Moving into college dorms brings a lot of unwanted stress regarding living with a stranger, moving all of your belongings, and making sure you account for everything you will have to buy. Then it gets added onto getting used to college classes, making friends, and possibly joining clubs. However, the stress of moving can easily be avoided. Using the information from this podcast coupled with the opinions from students who have spent time in the dorms, you can adequately prepare for dorm life. Make good use of the tips listed in the podcast, and do research on your college's dorms, since each college is a little different. Thank you so much for listening and good luck!

Interview Questions:

1. What were your expectations for living in the dorms before move-in day?
2. What didn't live up to your expectations? Or what were you not prepared for?
3. Do you have any advice for incoming freshmen who will be moving into the dorms?
4. Is there anything you wish you knew before moving into the dorms?

TEXTBOX 6.3. SAMPLE PODCAST ASSESSMENT RUBRIC

An "A" Podcast:

1. Demonstrates clear understanding of the podcast genre developed through exploration of a variety of example podcasts (model texts).
2. Shows thoughtful consideration of the intended audience. Theme, tone, vocabulary, and syntax are appropriate for engaging the intended audience in the topic.
3. Establishes the purpose of the podcast in a manner which is clear to the audience, and includes all necessary information to establish purpose.
4. Presents necessary background information needed for the audience to understand the topic and purpose of the podcast. Gives clear definitions of vocabulary or jargon related to the topic.
5. Explains relevance and importance of topic in the student's life, demonstrating connections to student's funds of knowledge and real-world experiences.
6. Uses technology in meaningful ways to increase engagement with information—such as but not limited to quality recordings, appropriate sound effects, and background music—made accessible for presentation through publication on chosen podcast application.
7. Demonstrates thorough research of topic through interaction with a variety of resources and artifacts.
8. Cites research from a variety of sources including but not limited to one recorded interview. Sources are identified by name, author, or title during the podcast, and a complete works cited list is submitted.

A "B" Podcast:

1. Demonstrates clear understanding of the podcast genre developed through exploration of some example podcasts (model texts).
2. Shows some consideration of the intended audience. Theme, tone, vocabulary, and syntax are mostly appropriate for engaging the intended audience in the topic.
3. Establishes purpose of podcast in a mostly clear fashion, and includes most necessary information to establish purpose.
4. Presents some necessary background information needed for the audience to understand the topic and purpose of the podcast, but some elements may need clarification. Defines some but not all vocabulary or jargon related to the topic.
5. Explains relevance and importance of topic in the student's life.
6. Uses some technology to increase interest, but does not make best use of sound effects, background music, and other such tools. Made accessible for presentation through publication on chosen podcast application.
7. Demonstrates thorough research of the topic, but resources are somewhat limited.
8. Cites research including one recorded interview. Sources are identified, but not clearly, in podcasts, as well as in works cited.

A "C" Podcast:

1. Demonstrates little understanding of the podcast genre.
2. Does not show thought into the needs and preferences of the audience.
3. Leaves audience questioning purpose of podcast.
4. Gives some background information, but leaves the audience with questions.
5. Does not build connections between a student's life and the topic of a podcast.
6. Is recorded but does not use technology to enhance engagement with elements such as sound effects or background music, or uses elements in a way which distracts from the message of the podcast.
7. Includes some elements of research but lacks in depth and variety of resources.
8. Does not name all sources in the podcast. Works cited are incomplete.

MENTOR TEXTS

As you introduce each element of the podcasting genre, or any new genre for that matter, model texts are a vital resource in giving students an understanding of the expectations of a genre. In a podcasting unit, this means finding podcasts to explore with students to understand how each element comes into play, what works, what doesn't, and why. Through this analysis, students become more familiar with the "rules" and possibilities of the genre (see model lesson below for more details). Students should be exposed to examples of successful student podcasts as well as professional podcasts, to present models at a level they feel is within their reach. Both National Public Radio (NPR) and the *New York Times* hold student podcast competitions, and share winning and high-achieving submissions online. Model texts are chosen to exemplify strengths and/or weaknesses in use of the element which is the focus of the lesson. For example, when teaching the lesson on Research and Podcasting, a model is presented which uses no identifiable research to support the author's claims, alongside a model which uses evidence but fails to identify the source of the information, and finally a model which uses strong and clearly identifiable evidence to support claims. By engaging with models achieving varying levels of success in their inclusion of evidence, students are able to discern how to include evidence, common pitfalls to avoid, and the impact of supporting their ideas in a clear and strong manner.

> ## TEXTBOX 6.4. WHERE TO FIND PODCAST MODELS
>
> StoryCorps: https://storycorps.org/
> New York Times Contest Winners: https://www.nytimes.com/2021/07/01/learning/winners-of-our-fourth-annual-podcast-contest.html
> NPR Student Examples: https://www.npr.org/2019/06/08/729605772/eight-student-made-podcasts-that-made-us-smile
> Youth Radio Media: https://yr.media/
> This I Believe: https://thisibelieve.org/

WRITING WORKSHOP TIP: SCRIPTWRITING

As students gather and read external sources, they can hone their focus or argument before scriptwriting. Here are a series of reflection questions to help them think about their investment in the topic and the main idea, argument, or message they hope to convey to their audience.

Finding Focus for Your Podcast

1. What is your topic, and why do you care about it?
2. What are the root causes of this issue?
3. What is making the issue worse? What could make it better?
4. Now that you've started to think about your position on this topic, articulate your opinions as an argument. Draw from some of the facts you read or heard in your group work.
5. Keep it simple.

As students focus their arguments, they can begin scriptwriting. You can provide a podcast scriptwriting template to help students plan and draft the different elements of their podcasts (see table 6.3). The template is just a suggestion for including elements but should not be used as a formula. The details may appear in the podcast in a different order, or an element may not apply and could be left out.

Students may read their scripts as a part of their editing and revision process to listen for places they stumble or places that seem unclear. The more they practice reading the scripts aloud, the more successful their recordings will be. Creating

Table 6.3. Podcast Scriptwriting Template

Time (seconds or minutes)	Script
	Opening Music and Sound Effects
	Introduction: Set the stage for your episode. • This should be 3–5 minutes. • Identify yourself and all members of the podcast (names and grades and your investment in or connection to the topic). • Tell why your show has come into being and what you hope it offers, and what the listener can expect in this show.
	Segue: Use music, sound, or a brief phrase to transition or move the piece forward.
	Main Idea/Argument & Topic Background: You might also discuss the background or relevance of the topic and define the problem or issue if there is one. Include your main point and 1–2 supporting details (e.g., data or quotes to back you up).
	Segue: Use music, sound, or a brief phrase to transition or move the piece forward.
	Support for Argument with Story Example(s), Interview, Panel, or Data: *Note*: If you have a guest, plan out the interview questions so the guest knows what to expect and say.
	Segue: Use music, sound, or a brief phrase to transition or move the piece forward.
	Opinion(s): Share your perspective, thoughts, and opinions about the topic along with the perspectives of others. Do not hold back. Be honest and be you. Be sure to provide a diversity of views along with your own.
	Closing: Summarize the episode, share major takeaways and why they matter, offer a call to action, and include a simple sign-off/goodbye.
	Closing Music and Sound Effects/Fade-Out
Total Time: _____	

podcasts is as much about listening as it is about the act of writing. You also want to have them time themselves to make sure the writing is clear, easy to read, and falls within the allotted time frame. You can review their podcast scripts before they record to get a sense that everyone has what they need to succeed and that the script follows the key genre elements you are assessing.

Digital Tools

Students just need a microphone, a free online account, and the internet. Audio tools are easily accessible and free, which is important in thinking and planning for equity and inclusion in the writing classroom. The easiest way for students to record the audio is with Audacity, GarageBand (available only for Mac and Apple devices), or Anchor, which are free applications for recording, editing, and publishing podcasts.

Students may download and use these apps on smartphones, tablets, or other digital devices. These are all user-friendly and easy to work with in the classroom. There are also YouTube tutorials on how to use each of these, which are helpful to show or make accessible for students and in case you feel less tech-savvy. Most devices have integrated microphones, which work well. If students have access to an internet-connected Chromebook, laptop, or mobile device, they are set to record their audio.

Almost all learning management services, like Blackboard and Canvas, have a recording component students can use. Because of the quiet required to record a high-quality podcast, students should record outside of the classroom in a quiet and controlled setting. You can ask the librarian if there are spaces available in the library for students to record or have students record in quiet nooks and crannies of the school.

After recording, it's time for students to edit their audio. You want to encourage students to record their audio chronologically in conjunction with their scripts. Sometimes they mess up a particular part and need to re-record and splice and clip to fix it. Their first step is to arrange the audio in order and then trip and cut any mistakes, pauses, or interruptions. Next, they can add music and sound effects. If they have access to MacBooks and GarageBand, they can easily mix music loops into their audio recordings. Audacity users cannot compose music within the software, so they need to find music elsewhere to include. Students may want to use their favorite music clips for their podcasts, and it is a perfect opportunity to talk about fair usage and royalties. Students' music choices need to be Podsafe, meaning it is legal to distribute online for others to listen to and download freely. There is a ton of Podsafe music to choose from, and students appreciate having time in class to listen and choose music that fits. This is part of curating a multimodal text, and the music and editing choices are just as important as the scriptwriting in forming a polished podcast. Here are sites that offer Podsafe music:

- Podsafe Audio: https://www.podsafeaudio.com
- Soundsnap: https://www.soundsnap.com
- Soundstripe: https://www.soundstripe.com/music-library

Accommodations can be made for different learning styles and needs by providing additional structure, such as an outline, peer writing support and feedback, and teacher-led writing conferences for those who would benefit from more guidance. While some students may have technology and a quiet setting outside of school in which to record their podcast, some may not. Providing students time, space, and technology within the school setting keeps the assignment accessible to all.

CELEBRATING WRITING AND MAKING IT PUBLIC

There are many fun ways to extend the podcast unit by finding audiences and purposes for students to share their work beyond the classroom community. One of the ways to do this is to have a podcast listening party or set up listening stations around the room (laptops or tablets with headphones) and have students rotate from one podcast to another, and leave feedback on sticky notes for the authors. You can extend the podcast listening party to include family and friends and hold a public exhibition of podcasts where students' podcasts are linked to QR codes, and the event guests can invite guests, or you can invite other classes to attend. You can also have students create podcasts connected to student podcast contests or challenges and then, at the end of the unit, submit them to these publication venues.

There are so many ways to remix writing instruction to bring diverse written genre forms to our students. Instead of listening to the swarming buzz of standardized writing that too often expects students to reach higher standards by writing uniform, impersonal, timed, or formulaic essays, without enough direct engagement with or relevance to their lives, we can offer students opportunities to write across a range of genres that allow them to bring their voices and ideas and experiences to their pages.

CONCLUSION

Ultimately, we hope you take up the teaching of secondary writing using diverse genres in whatever way fits your students, context, curriculum requirements, and tried and true approaches. The goal is to meet adolescents where they are and tap into what they care about and what they are interested in through writing. The podcast is just one of many genres that allow students to practice the kinds of literacies used in this digital age of communication that will prepare all students for their future pathways in college, the workplace, and the community.

REFERENCES

ACT. (2005). *Crisis at the core: Preparing all students for college and work*. Iowa City, IA: ACT, Inc. https://www.act.org/content/dam/act/unsecured/documents/crisis_report.pdf

American Diploma Project. (2004) *Ready or not: Creating a high school diploma that counts*. Washington, DC: Achieve, Inc. https://files.eric.ed.gov/fulltext/ED494733.pdf

Applebee, A. N., & Langer, J. A. (2009). EJ Extra: What is happening in the teaching of writing? *English Journal, 98*(5), 18–28.

Ball, A. (2006). Teaching writing in culturally diverse classrooms. In C. MacArthur, S. Graham, & J. Fitzgerald (Eds.), *Handbook of writing research* (pp. 293–310). New York: Guilford.

Bate, J. (2020, March 4). *The growing popularity of podcasts*. PPL PRS United for Music. https://pplprs.co.uk/popularity-of-podcasts

Bazerman, C. (2000 [1988]). *Shaping written knowledge: The genre and activity of the experimental article in science*. WAC Clearinghouse. (Originally published in 1988 by University of Wisconsin Press).

Bazerman, C., & Prior, P. (2005). Participating in emergent socio-literate worlds: Genre, disciplinarity, interdisciplinarity. In R. Beach, J. Green, M. Kamil, & T. Shanahan (Eds.), *Multidisciplinary perspectives on literacy research* (2nd ed., pp. 133–78). Hampton.

Bazerman, C., Bonini, A., & Figueiredo, D. (Eds.). (2009). *Genre in a changing world*. Parlor.

Beaufort, A. (1999). *Writing in the real world: Making the transition from school to work*. Teachers College Press.

Brandt, D. (2001). *Literacy in American lives*. Cambridge University Press.

Common Core State Standards. (2010). *ELA: National Governors Association Center for Best Practices & Council of Chief State School Officers*. Washington, DC: Authors.

Dean., D. (2008). *Genre theory: Teaching, writing, and being*. National Council of Teachers of English.

Early, J. S. (2019). A case for teaching biography-driven writing in ELA classrooms. *English Journal, 108*(3), 89–94.

Early, J. S. (2017). Escribiendo juntos: Toward a collaborative model of multiliterate family literacy in English only and anti-immigrant contexts. *Research in the Teaching of English, 52*(2), 156–80.

Early, J. S. (2010). "Mi hija, you should be a writer": The role of parental support and learning to write. *Bilingual Research Journal, 33*(3), 277–91.

Early, J. S. (2022). *Next generation genres: Teaching writing for civic and academic engagement*. Norton.

Early, J. S., & Saidy, C. (2018). *Creating literacy communities as pathways to success: Equity and access for Latina students*. Routledge.

Edelsky, C. (1986). *Writing in a bilingual program: Había una vez*. Ablex. https://eric.ed.gov/?id=ED305192

Faltis, C., & Wolfe, P. M. (1999). *So much to say: Adolescents, bilingualism, and ESL in the secondary school*. Teachers College Press.

Germán, L. E. (2021). *Textured teaching: A framework for culturally sustaining practices*. Heinemann.

Grabill, J. T., & Hicks, T. (2005). Multiliteracies meet methods: The case for digital writing in English education. *English Education, 37*(4), 301–11. http://www.jstor.org/stable/40173204

Graham, S. (2019). Changing how writing is taught. *Review of Research in Education, 43*(1), 277–303. https://doi.org/10.3102/0091732X18821125

Guerra, J. (2008). Cultivating transcultural citizenship: A writing across communities model. *Language Arts, 85*(4), 296–304.

Hayes, J. R., & Nash, J. G. (1996). On the nature of planning in writing. In C. M. Levy & S. Ransdell (Eds.), *The science of writing: Theories, methods, individual differences, and applications* (pp. 29–55). Lawrence Erlbaum.

Hull, G. A., & Schultz, K. (2002). *School's out! Bridging out-of-school literacies with classroom practice*. Teachers College Press.

International Literacy Association. (2020). *Research advisory: Teaching writing to improve reading skills*. https://www.literacyworldwide.org/docs/default-source/where-we-stand/ila-teaching-writing-to-improve-reading-skills.pdf

Jane Schaffer Academic Writing Program. (n.d.). *Writing is about thinking*. Louis Educational Concepts. https://janeschaffer.com/

Johns, A. M. (2001). *Genre in the classroom: Multiple perspectives*. Routledge.

KQED Teach. (2023). *Bring media literacy and media making to your teaching*. KQED Teach. https://teach.kqed.org

Lombardo, C. (2019). *8 student-made podcasts that made us smile*. NPR. https://www.npr.org/2019/06/08/729605772/eight-student-made-podcasts-that-made-us-smile

MacArthur, C. A., & Graham, S. (2016). Writing research from a cognitive perspective. In C. A. MacArthur, S. Graham, & J. Fitzgerald (Eds.), *Handbook of writing research* (pp. 24–40). Guilford.

National Assessment of Education Progress. (2009, July 21). *The nation's report card*. https://www.nationsreportcard.gov/reading_math_grade12_2005/s0206.asp

National Center for Education Statistics. (2003). *The nation's report card: Writing 2002, NCES 2003–529*, by H. R. Persky, M. C. Daane, & Y. Jin. Washington, DC: US Department of Education. Institute of Education Sciences.

National Commission on Writing in America's Schools and Colleges. (2003). *The neglected "R": The need for a writing revolution*. College Entrance Examination Board.

National Commission on Writing in America's Schools and Colleges. (2006). *Writing and school reform*. College Board.

National Council of Teachers of English. (2005). *Multimodal literacies*. NCTE. https://ncte.org/statement/multimodalliteracies

National Council of Teachers of English. (2011). *Framework for success in postsecondary writing*. NCTE. Distributed by ERIC Clearinghouse. https://files.eric.ed.gov/fulltext/ED516360.pdf

New York Times. (2021, July 1). Winners of our Fourth annual podcast contest. Learning Network. https://www.nytimes.com/2021/07/01/learning/winners-of-our-fourth-annual-podcast-contest.html

Nielsen Company. (2017). Nielsen podcast insights. https://www.nielsen.com/us/en/insights/report/2017/nielsen-podcast-insights-q3-2017

NPR. *This I Believe*. (n.d.). https://www.npr.org/series/4538138/this-i-believe

Paré, A., & Smart, G. (1994). Observing genres in action: Towards a research methodology. In A. Freedman & P. Medway (Eds.), *Genre and the new rhetoric* (pp. 146–54). Routledge. https://doi.org/10.4324/9780203393277

Prior, P. (2006). A sociocultural theory of writing. In C. A. MacArthur, S. Graham, & J. Fitzgerald (Eds.), *The handbook of writing research* (pp. 54–66). Guilford.

Purcell-Gates, V., Duke, N. K., & Martineau, J. A. (2007). Learning to read and write genre-specific text: Roles of authentic experience and explicit teaching. *Reading Research Quarterly*, 42(1), 8–45. https://doi.org/10.1598/RRQ.42.1.1

Salahu-Din, D., Persky, H., & Miller, J. (2008). The nation's report card[TM]: Writing 2007. National assessment of educational progress at grades 8 and 12: National, state, and trial urban district results. NCES 2008-468. Distributed by ERIC Clearinghouse.

Smith, K. (2006). In defense of the five-paragraph essay. *English Journal*, 95(4), 16–17.

StoryCorps. (2003–2023). https://storycorps.org

United States Congress, 107th, 1st session. (2001). No Child Left Behind Act of 2001: Conference Report to Accompany H.R.1, Report 107–334. US Government Printing Office.

Valdés, G. (2001). *Learning and not learning English: Latino students in American schools*. Teachers College Press.

Vygotsky, L. S. (1978). *Mind in society: The development of higher psychological processes*. Harvard University Press.

Wiley, M. (2000). The popularity of formulaic writing (and why we need to resist). *English Journal*, 90(1), 61–67.

Winn, R. (2021, April). *2021 Podcast stats and facts: New research from April 2021*. Podcast Insights. https://www.podcastinsights.com/podcast-statistics

Youth Radio Media. (2021, November 23). YR Media. https://yr.media

7

Writing Intervention

Amber B. Ray and John Romig

THIS CHAPTER PRESENTS METHODS OF assessment and instruction for secondary writing intervention. Writing is a process whereby writers communicate a message through an intelligible code of symbols. Writing can be brief (e.g., taking notes, short-answer responses, worksheets, and summaries of read material) or longer compositions (paragraphs, essays, stories, etc.). The Common Core State Standards (CCSS) place increased emphasis on writing instruction at all grade levels (Sundeen, 2015). Within writing instruction, the CCSS place decreased emphasis on writing mechanics (spelling, punctuation, capitalization) and increased emphasis on writing process: prewriting, drafting, revising, editing, publishing (Troia & Olinghouse, 2013). Another emphasis within the CCSS is producing compositions. When selecting writing activities, teachers often rely on brief writing activities (short-answer responses, worksheets, and summaries of read material). However, these activities alone will be insufficient for meeting the demands of the CCSS. This chapter focuses primarily on paragraph-level and essay-level writing interventions—interventions that will help students meet the demands of the CCSS. First, we present methods of formative writing assessments. Then, we present a model for teaching writing strategies in the context of the writing process. We demonstrate this model—self-regulated strategy development (SRSD)—through a case study of a high school writer receiving intervention to improve writing on the ACT exam. Next, we present strategies for using writing as a learning tool and incorporating technology tools into writing. We close with a summary of sentence construction strategies and resources.

After reading this chapter, readers should be able to:

- Identify approaches to formatively assessing students' writing
- Describe the self-regulated strategy development model for teaching writing
- Identify effective interventions for sentence, paragraph, and essay writing
- Summarize relevant research related to writing intervention

FORMATIVE WRITING ASSESSMENTS

Writing assessments can be categorized in multiple ways. One categorization is between summative and formative assessments. Summative assessments are assessments that can be used to screen students at risk for writing difficulty, determine eligibility for special education, identify strengths and weaknesses in students' writing, and other evaluative purposes. Formative assessment is a process whereby teachers repeatedly collect data on students' writing and use the data to make instructional adaptations. In this chapter, we focus on formative assessment strategies.

On average, formative assessment has been an effective strategy for improving writing achievement of kindergarten through eighth grade students (Graham et al., 2015). Although some studies in Graham et al.'s analysis did include students in grades 6–8, there is generally a lack of studies examining formative assessment for students in secondary grades. Graham et al. (2017) evaluated the evidence base of formative assessment for secondary writers and categorized the use of formative assessment as having minimal evidence according to *What Works Clearinghouse* guidelines. "Minimal evidence" may not sound like a ringing endorsement, but being included in the Graham et al. (2017) practice report at all indicates some level of research supporting its use. When formatively assessing writing, teachers have several strategies to consider. In the following section, we will present curriculum-based measurement, exit slips, error analysis, holistic ratings, genre rubrics, and genre-specific elements assessment strategies that can be used in a formative assessment process.

Curriculum-Based Measurement

When using curriculum-based measurement (CBM) to formatively assess writing, teachers have several decisions to make. First, teachers select a writing task. Writing tasks generally include a type of writing prompt and writing duration. Prompt types include descriptive, narrative, and persuasive prompts. Writing durations can range from 3 to 10 minutes. Before the writing duration, students usually have some time (e.g., 1 minute) to read the prompt and brainstorm or engage in other prewriting activities. Research examining writing prompts has generally found different prompt types do not impact the validity of CBM-Writing (CBM-W) tasks (Romig et al., 2020). Some commercial progress monitoring programs offer writing prompts for teachers to use. Alternatively, Intervention Central (www.interventioncentral.org) has a bank of story-starter writing prompts teachers can access for free.

Researchers have examined durations ranging from 3 to 10 minutes; generally, longer durations led to increased validity for CBM tasks (Romig et al., 2020). When creating the writing task, students generally have one minute to read the prompt and generate ideas. After one minute of thinking time, teachers signal students to begin writing, and the writing duration begins. When the predetermined amount of time has passed, the teacher signals for students to stop writing and collects the writing samples. It is important to use a consistent writing prompt type and duration when using a CBM for progress monitoring.

Once teachers have selected a writing task, they select a scoring procedure. Dozens of scoring procedures have been tested for CBM (Romig et al., 2017). Again, it is important for teachers to be consistent with scoring procedures when using CBM for progress monitoring. CBM scoring procedures are countable indices of observable writing features. The four most commonly researched CBM scoring procedures are the number of words written (WW), the number of words spelled correctly (WSC), the number of correct word sequences (CWS), and the number of correct minus incorrect word sequences (CIWS).

When scoring the number of WW, teachers simply count the total number of words students wrote in the given time. A word is defined as any two adjacent letters (plus single letter words "I" and "a") offset on either side by a space. That is, words do not have to make sense, be spelled correctly, or even be remotely close to real words. When scoring the number of WSC, teachers count the number of correctly spelled words students wrote in the given time. Correctly spelled words are defined as any word that is spelled correctly according to standard rules of English spelling. Much like early computer spell checkers, the spelling of words is considered without respect to their usage. For example, if students use the wrong form of their/there/they're but spell their chosen form correctly, it is counted as a correctly spelled word.

Unlike WW and WSC, the number of CWS and CIWS scoring procedures do take word usage and context into consideration. Another difference is that these two scoring procedures (CWS and CIWS) do not count individual words. They count sequences between words. Both words in the sequence must be spelled, punctuated, and used correctly. When scoring for CWS, teachers count the number of sequences that are correct according to this definition. When scoring for CIWS, teachers count the number of correct word sequences and the number of incorrect word sequences. The total score is the difference between correct and incorrect word sequences. See Hosp et al. (2016) for further details on scoring procedures.

CIWS has slightly higher validity than CWS; both are generally considered to have acceptable validity (Romig et al., 2017). However, because the number of incorrect word sequences is subtracted from correct word sequences, the CIWS scoring procedure can sometimes result in a negative score for students. For this reason, teachers may consider using CWS rather than CIWS for students who make a high number of incorrect sequences in their writing to avoid assigning them a negative score for their writing sample. Although CWS and CIWS have the highest validity of these four scoring procedures, teachers may choose to use the WW or WSC scoring procedures based on individual student needs. For example, if a student has extreme writing anxiety and refuses to produce any text, it may be more appropriate to monitor the number of WW. Likewise, for students who struggle primarily with spelling, assessing the number of WSC might be the most appropriate strategy.

After collecting data using the chosen writing task and scoring procedure, teachers use CBM data to guide instruction in a process called data-based decision-making, or intensive intervention. After scoring CBM writing samples frequently (e.g., weekly), teachers graph students' performance on a line graph and make instructional decisions based on whether student performance appears on track to meet an end-of-year goal. If a student appears on track to reach the end-of-year goal, the teacher will continue collecting data and implementing current instructional routine. However, if the student does not appear on track to reach the end-of-year goal, the teacher will make an instructional change. Instructional changes could include changing the strength or dosage of an intervention, increasing the explicitness of instruction, addressing student behavior and motivation, or individualizing instruction (Fuchs et al., 2017).

CBM has several advantages as a formative assessment strategy. It produces multiple forms of the same assessment (i.e., different writing prompts) and is simple and efficient to administer and score, easily understood, and inexpensive to administer. However, there are significant challenges to using a CBM approach to formative assessment. First, criterion validity is a quantitative method of measuring an assessment's validity. CBM for writing generally has moderate criterion validity for secondary writers, lower than CBM for reading (Romig et al., 2017, 2020). Second, a significant assumption when using CBM to guide writing instruction is that CBM is sensitive to changes in student performance (e.g., growth in writing achievement) over short periods of time. This sensitivity to change is essential if teachers are to use CBM to guide instruction on a week-to-week basis. However, researchers investigating the sensitivity to growth of CBM-W have generally examined growth over long periods of time (e.g., months or an academic year). Research examining CBM-W over shorter periods has raised significant questions about its usefulness as a progress monitoring measure (Romig et al., 2021). Finally, aside from these concerns, there is generally very little research examining CBM-W in secondary grade levels.

Exit Slips

Aside from CBM, teachers have less formal options for formative assessment strategies. Exit slips are brief assessments teachers give at the end of a class period to determine whether students mastered the period's lesson. For example, in a lesson on imagery in narrative writing, the exit slip might ask students to write a description of a scene that uses imagery. If students demonstrate mastery of imagery on the exit slip, the teacher knows students mastered the lesson and can move to a new skill in the next lesson. If students did not demonstrate mastery of imagery, the teacher can reteach the material at the beginning of the next lesson.

Error Analysis

Error analysis is another informal formative assessment strategy. When conducting error analysis, the teacher examines students' writing for specific errors. Teachers can focus specifically on spelling, noting which words were misspelled and how the student misspelled them. When teachers identify trends in students' spelling errors, they can use this data to inform instruction (i.e., remediate specific student weaknesses). Error analysis does not have to be limited to spelling. Other stylistic errors can be recorded and examined for common trends in errors such as noun, verb, or pronoun usage; omitted or substituted words; punctuation errors; capitalization errors; or paragraph errors (e.g., starting new paragraphs on a new indented line). Again, teachers analyze these errors for common trends and remediate specific weaknesses (e.g., the student frequently does not use end-of-sentence punctuation, or perhaps the student does not use question marks at the end of interrogative sentences).

Holistic Ratings

When using holistic ratings, teachers assign a single rating to a writing sample that encompasses all aspects of writing (organization, syntax, word choice, vocabulary, etc.). Like the process for using CBM data to guide instruction, teachers can graph holistic ratings and use the graphs to monitor students' progress and guide instructional decisions. A limitation of holistic ratings is that students may need to make a substantial amount of improvement to increase their rating. Students may remain at the same rating level for a long time and appear to be making no progress. However, in reality, students might be making important growth in writing skills that is undetected by the holistic rating system.

Generic Rubrics

Generic rubrics are a very common method of writing assessment. These rubrics are intended to be used with all genres of writing (e.g., informative, narrative, argumentative, etc.). The rubric items and ratings are broad and—as the name would suggest—generic to genre elements. Teachers can create their own writing rubric, use one developed by districts, or use other rubrics developed by writing experts. The 6 + 1 Trait Writing rubric is a common rubric used in secondary classrooms. However, research on this tool as a formative assessment strategy has found quite small positive effects (Graham et al., 2015).

Genre-Specific Elements

As the name would suggest, genre-specific elements are elements of writing that are specific to different genres (e.g., descriptive, narrative, and persuasive). For example, characterization (description and development of characters) may be an important component of narrative writing but is generally not considered an important element of persuasive essays. Alternatively, persuasive essays should include a clear thesis statement that is generally not included in narrative writing. When assessing students' writing using genre-specific elements, teachers can develop a list of genre-specific elements and then track the number of elements students include in their writing over time. Figure 7.2 below provides an example where a student self-evaluated his writing for persuasive genre elements and tracked progress on a bar graph.

Research on writing assessments does not clearly indicate which of these assessment strategies is best for improving student outcomes. Teachers have wide freedom when selecting assessment strategies. However, no matter which assessment strategy teachers choose, researchers have identified essential components. First, students need to receive feedback on their writing (Graham et al., 2015). Feedback can come from teachers (e.g., Wolter, 1975), peers (e.g., Boscolo & Ascorti, 2004), or computers (e.g., Caccamise et al., 2007) and can be given verbally or in writing. Second, teachers should use pre-assessments to students' strengths and weaknesses before teaching skills and strategies (Graham et al., 2016). Third, writing instruction should be informed by writing assessment (Graham et al., 2016). It is not enough for teachers to simply collect writing assessment data. These data must be used to shape instruction for assessment to lead to meaningful improvements in students' writing. Finally, teachers should regularly monitor students' writing progress (Graham et al., 2016). Regular monitoring may vary depending on the nature of the skill or strategy being monitored. Simple writing skills may be monitored frequently (i.e., weekly) while more complex writing skills or strategies may only be monitored 3–5 times throughout the year.

TEACHING WRITING STRATEGIES FOR THE WRITING PROCESS

Explicitly teaching writing strategies is the most effective approach when instructing students to write effectively (Graham et al., 2016). A writing strategy provides step-by-step procedures for a writing task. Writing strategy instruction teaches students strategies for completing one or more aspects of the writing process (Graham et al., 2020). Self-regulated strategy development (SRSD) is the most effective writing intervention for students in grades 1–12 in improving writing quality with an effect size of 1.59 (Graham & Harris, 2018), indicating a very large positive effect.

Theory Guiding Self-Regulated Strategy Development

SRSD is an instructional model that has many theoretical influences (Harris & Graham, 2018). SRSD has several core components: criterion-based learning; active and engaged learning; scaffolding; a focus on attitudes toward writing, self-efficacy, and attributions; and explicit development of self-regulation (Harris & Graham, 2018). These components are supported by multiple, eclectic theories including behavioral theory, cognitive-behavioral theory, motivation theory, social-cognitive theory, constructivism, sociocultural theory, attribution theory, self-efficacy theory, and expertise theory (Harris & Graham, 2018). The foundation of SRSD was influenced by a fusion of behavior modification and cognitivist approaches to learning. Additionally, SRSD instruction includes metacognitive strategies to help students develop their abilities to select learning strategies and reflect upon their success which was developed by drawing on metacognitive theory. Over time SRSD has been influenced by many theories, guided by research on SRSD with students with disabilities and other struggling writers.

Self-Regulated Strategy Development

The SRSD instructional model incorporates three essential components: (1) six stages of instruction, (2) task-specific writing strategies, and (3) self-regulation strategies (see figure 7.1).

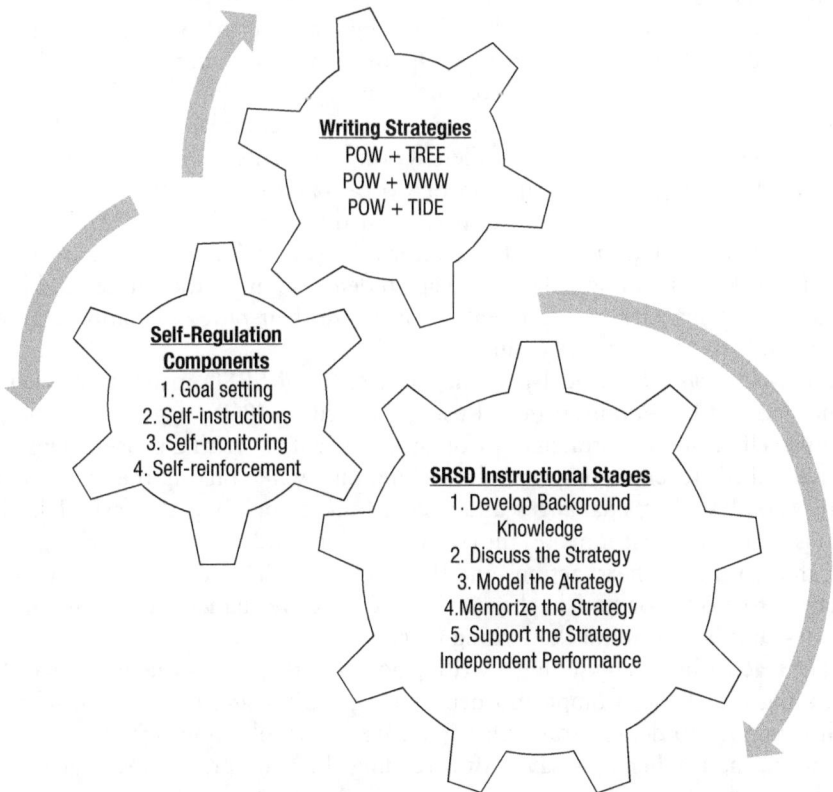

Figure 7.1 Essential Components of the Self-Regulated Strategy Development Instructional Model

Six Stages of Instruction

When using the SRSD instructional model, there are six stages of instruction: (1) develop and activate background knowledge, (2) discuss it (the strategies and writing process), (3) model it, (4) memorize it, (5) support it (gradual release of control), and (6) independent performance. Multiple lessons occur within each of the stages.

Stage 1: Develop and Activate Background Knowledge. Developing and activating background knowledge is the first stage of instruction. During this stage, teachers facilitate a discussion to activate students' prior knowledge related to the current writing task and develop additional knowledge students will need (e.g., key vocabulary terms). Teachers and students collaboratively examine well-written and poorly written sample essays within the current genre and identify what the writer did well and what needs to be improved. It is important that exemplar writing pieces be written at the students' writing level for students to view the writing task as achievable. For example, if students are going to be writing informative essays, it can be beneficial for the class to brainstorm examples of informative writing such as a science textbook, a newspaper article, or manuals. Students then need to read and analyze exemplar informative essays similar to what they are being expected to write. These exemplars can be essays written by students in previous years or other classes or created by the teacher.

Stage 2: Discuss It. Stage two of SRSD is discuss it. During this stage, the teacher and students discuss the writing and self-regulation strategies within the context of the writing process. Many teachers begin by teaching the writing strategy POW, which stands for **P**ull apart the prompt, **O**rganize my notes, and **W**rite and say more. This is a useful strategy when approaching any type of writing as it is essential that students determine the task they are being expected to complete based on the writing prompt. To enhance the quality of their writing, students should then make a plan for what they are going to write through organizing notes, often using a graphic organizer. There are several genre-specific writing strategies (e.g., TREE or HIT SONGS[3] for argumentative, TIDE for informative, and CSPACE for narrative; see section below) that can be utilized to help students organize their notes and include all necessary genre elements. Students then utilize their notes to compose an essay that expands upon what they included in their notes.

Stage 3: Model It. Model it is the third stage of SRSD instruction where the teacher uses a think-aloud to model using the writing (POW + genre-specific strategy) and self-regulation strategies throughout the entire writing process. During the think-aloud the teacher completes the writing task while talking their way through the process, handling challenges and successfully completing the task. The think-aloud is critical because it makes the covert decisions and steps of the writing process overt though the teachers' actions and thinking aloud. The teacher also uses self-instructions to model for students how to handle affective challenges such as emotions, attitudes, and beliefs about the writing task.

The teacher begins by setting a writing goal and then starts the first step of POW by reading aloud the prompt and determining the writing task. The teacher uses self-instructions to demonstrate what good writers think about when pulling apart a prompt. The teacher may say, "After reading the prompt, I know that my topic is endangered species. Hmmm . . . I need to find some key words in the prompt to determine the writing task and genre. I see the word persuade, which means I need to write an argumentative essay. What do I need to persuade my reader about and who is my reader? I need to look at this prompt carefully. [Rereads prompt aloud]. I'm supposed to persuade my classmates about the importance of protecting endangered species." Students with disabilities and ELs may need additional support when pulling apart the prompt; it can be helpful for the teacher to model circling, highlighting, and/or underlining key words within a prompt. Additionally, when analyzing a longer prompt, students can be taught to create a DO/WHAT chart (Olson et al., 2013). This is a two-column chart where the right column is labeled Do and the left column is labeled What. In the do column students write verbs from the prompt that describe what they need to do (e.g., write, discuss, explain, persuade) and in the what column they write words from the prompt that indicate the task (e.g., an essay, why the theme is significant).

The teacher continues modeling the writing process by organizing notes. The teacher may say, "I need to organize my notes for a persuasive essay using the TREE strategy." The teacher then models utilizing a graphic organizer to make notes. The teacher should model using short phrases, not complete sentences, when making notes. The teacher can also demonstrate how notes can change by drawing lines through what was written and adding different notes and how to add additional components of good writing, such as transition words, in the margins of notes. Finally, the teacher models how to write and say more by utilizing the notes from the graphic organizer to write a complete essay. This is done by having the notes next to where the essay is being composed. Then the teacher starts by reading aloud the first part of their notes and then models how to transform that idea into one or more complete sentences. It is important that the teacher models writing the complete essay to support the learning of all students within the class.

After the complete essay is written, the teacher should model self-monitoring by rereading the essay and making revisions and edits as needed. The focus of the revision process should be based on the writing goal. For example, a writing goal may be to write an argumentative essay using the TREE strategy. The teacher should model rereading the essay and labeling the parts of TREE or using a TREE checklist to identify the part of TREE within the essay. The teacher can then demonstrate how to record progress toward the writing goal on a graph and model self-reinforcement by saying, "I wrote an essay that incorporated all the argumentative genre elements. My writing is really improving!"

Stage 4: Memorize It. The fourth stage of SRSD instruction is memorize it. It is important for students to memorize the strategies being used in order to promote automaticity of strategy use. When using a mnemonic, the students need to memorize what each letter stands for and what it means. Additionally, students see the benefit of memorizing the strategies because the strategies help the students tackle the challenging task of essay writing. Additionally, students will not always have the graphic organizer or classroom poster with the strategy for reference. Memorizing the strategy begins early during SRSD instruction as students are introduced to and begin practicing the strategy. Teachers can support the memorization of strategies through choral response, partner practice, flash cards, memory games, and written ungraded quizzes.

Stage 5: Support It. Support it is the fifth instructional stage. This stage begins with collaborative writing practice where the teacher leads students through the entire writing process using POW and the genre-specific writing strategy, but this time students contribute ideas for the essay. The teacher can also ask students what step should be completed next. This guided instruction allows the teacher and students to practice together and the teacher can provide immediate feedback and correction as needed. The whole class collaborative writing process can be repeated as many times as needed. Through collaborative writing sessions, the teacher gradually shifts more of the responsibility to the students. There are numerous ways teachers can start this gradual release of responsibility; for example, the whole class could collaboratively pull apart the prompt and organize notes and then students work with partners to write the essay. More responsibility can be shifted to students by having them collaboratively complete the entire writing process in small groups or in pairs with coaching and feedback from the teacher as needed. If there are still some students who are struggling, the teacher can lead that group of students through the writing process while the rest of the class works with partners to collaboratively write essays. If the teacher realizes that students are struggling with any portion of the writing process, the teacher can do another think-aloud modeling the steps or collaboratively work with students to help them work toward independent use of the strategies. This recursive nature of SRSD instruction helps all students achieve their writing goals.

Stage 6: Independent Performance. The final instructional stage of SRSD is independent performance. This stage is when students can independently apply the writing and self-regulation strategies on their own with support and encouragement from the teacher, as necessary. Even once students achieve independent performance, it is important that the teacher review the strategies and give students the opportunity to practice applying the strategies when writing an essay throughout the school year to help students maintain their skills. Furthermore, the teacher and students should discuss transferring their learning to different situations and students should have the opportunity to use the strategies in other contexts. For example, if the students learned how to write an argumentative essay using POW + TREE in a social studies course, to generalize their knowledge, skills, and use of the strategies they could write an argumentative essay in their science or English language arts class.

Writing Strategies

When preparing to teach writing, teachers need to identify the skill(s) they want to focus on and select appropriate writing strategies to help students with the writing process. Many writing strategies help students during the planning and drafting stages of writing by providing them with an organizational structure that incorporates the key elements within that genre (i.e., argumentative, informative, and narrative). Additionally, there are writing strategies that target other writing skills such as summary writing, paragraph writing, and revising and editing. There are a variety of strategies that can support each writing skill and it is up to the teacher to select that strategy that will best support their students. Table 7.1 highlights a variety of writing strategies; this is by no means an exhaustive list but an overview of some of the strategies that have been developed and taught using SRSD (see Ray, in press, for more information).

Table 7.1. Writing Strategies

Genre or Writing Skill	Writing Strategy	Source
Argumentative	**TREE:** **T**opic, **R**eason, **E**xplanation, **E**nding	Geres-Smith et al., 2019; Hoover et al., 2012; Mason et al., 2013; Straub & Vasquez, 2015
	HIT SONGS[3]: **H**ook, **I**ntroduce the topic, **T**hesis, **S**tate the perspective, **O**utlook on the perspective, **N**eed examples, **G**ive your opinion, **S**upport your thesis, **S**tate the relationships between your thesis and the perspectives given in the prompt, **S**ummary	Ray & Graham, 2020; Ray et al., 2019
	DARE: **D**evelop topic sentence, **A**dd supporting detail, **R**eject arguments from the other side, **E**nd with a conclusion	Chalk et al., 2005; Eissa, 2009
Informative / Expository	**TIDE[2]:** **T**opic sentence, **I**mportant **D**etails, **E**laborations, **E**nding sentence	Benedek-Wood et al., 2014
	PLAN and WRITE: **P**ay attention to the prompt, **L**ist main ideas, **A**dd supporting details, **N**umber your ideas, **W**ork from your plan to develop thesis statement, **R**emember your goals, **I**nclude transition words in your paragraph, **T**ry to use different kinds of sentences, **E**xciting/ interesting/ $100,000 words	Burke et al., 2017; De La Paz, 1999
	IBC: **I**ntroduction, **B**ody, **C**onclusion	MacArthur & Philippakos, 2010
Narrative	**STACS:** **S**etting, **T**ension, rising **A**ction, **C**limax, **S**olution	Foxworth et al., 2017
	MIND: **M**ain, **I**dea, **N**umbered subtopics, **D**etails	Sundeen 2012
Summary Writing	**WINDOW:** **W**rite a topic sentence, **I**dentify important information, **N**umber the pieces of identified information, **D**evelop sentences, **O**rganize sentences using transition words, **W**rite an ending sentence	Asaro-Saddler et al., 2018; Saddler et al., 2019
Paragraph Writing	**GO 4 IT . . . NOW!:** **G**oal statement (topic sentence), **O**bjectives (**4** of them, supporting details), **I**dentify a **T**imeline . . . **N**ame topic, **O**rder details, **W**rap it up and restate topic	Konrad & Test, 2007
Revising and Editing	**COPS:** **C**apitalization, **O**verall appearance, **P**unctuation, **S**pelling	Reid et al., 2013

Self-Regulation Strategies

The final essential component of SRSD instruction is the explicit teaching and use of self-regulation strategies to support students in managing the writing process. The four main self-regulation strategies embedded into SRSD instruction are goal setting, self-monitoring, self-instruction, and self-reinforcement. The teacher and students should work together to set writing goals related to the target skill of instruction. It can be beneficial to set a goal that the entire class is working on and an individual goal for each student. For example, the class goal may be to write a narrative that incorporates all the parts of STACS. An individualized goal should be an aspect of their writing that needs to be improved but may not directly apply to all the students in the class. There are endless possibilities for individualized goals, some examples are goals about using transition words at the beginning and within paragraphs, using a variety of word choices, and using commas after prepositional phrases. Throughout the writing process, the teacher and students should refer to the writing goals and monitor their progress toward achieving their goals.

Teaching students to self-monitor throughout the writing process will help them consciously think about and reflect on their writing. Students can self-monitor their use of a strategy by writing down the strategy they are using and checking steps off as they complete them. Students also need to reread their writing and self-assess their own writing. They can then self-record their progress on a graph. Graphing progress provides students with a visual representation of their progress which can increase their motivation and commitment to continue to utilize the writing strategies. The graphs can also allow students to see where additional improvement is needed.

Self-instruction is a metacognitive strategy that helps students use a strategy and work through the writing process. Self-instruction is a tool that can help students with problem definition (e.g., "What is my purpose for writing?"), focusing attention and planning (e.g., "Take a deep breath, good ideas will come to me."), strategy use (e.g., "I can use WINDOW to help me write my summary."), self-evaluation and error correcting (e.g., "Did I follow all the steps? Oops, I missed one. That's okay, I can revise."), coping and self-control (e.g., "I can slow down and take my time."), and self-reinforcement (e.g., "I completed my essay. I'm getting better at this!"). Using self-reinforcement helps to promote intrinsic motivation. Students can reinforce themselves when they make progress toward or meet their goal.

Case Study Example Using SRSD for the ACT Argumentative Essay

Paul is a junior in high school with a learning disability (LD) in reading and writing. He scored well below the writing benchmark on the state test and earned a C in English language arts the previous semester. Paul aspires to attend college and excels in many subjects, especially math and science. However, his writing skills continually impede his ability to showcase his knowledge. Paul is preparing to take the ACT and many of the colleges he is applying to require the essay component of the ACT exam, which is an argumentative essay. His teacher decides to use SRSD instruction to teach Paul the writing strategy HIT SONGS[3] and self-regulation strategies to prepare him for this writing exam. Table 7.2 is the outline of the teacher's instructional plan aligned with the stages of SRSD.

Table 7.2. SRSD Instructional Stages with Objectives and Activities for ACT Argumentative Writing

SRSD Stage	Objective(s)	Activities
Develop and Activate Background Knowledge	Students will be able to identify strong and weak argumentative elements and identify parts of an argumentative essay.	Instructor (a) explains elements of an argumentative essay, (b) explains how to analyze different perspectives of an argument, (c) helps students identify well-written and poorly written argumentative essays, and (d) explains the college entrance exam writing test procedures.
Discuss the Strategy	Students will be able to identify the purpose of the strategy and when to use it.	Instructor introduces the strategy and explains that students will be learning to apply the strategy for writing argumentative essays based on an ACT prompt.
Model the Strategy	Students will be able to describe how the strategy is applied.	Instructor models strategy use through analyzing the prompt and using the strategy to plan and compose an essay with an introduction paragraph, three body paragraphs, and a conclusion paragraph.
Memorize the Strategy	Students will be able to memorize the strategy.	Instructor uses flash cards and other memory activities to help students memorize the mnemonic devices.
Support the Strategy	Students will be able to write an argumentative essay based on an ACT prompt with assistance from the instructor.	Instructor assists as students use the strategy graphic organizer to plan and compose argumentative essays based on ACT writing prompts.
Independent Performance	Students will be able to independently plan, compose, and edit an argumentative essay based on an ACT prompt.	Instructor has students write an argumentative essay based on an ACT writing prompt. Students write argumentative essays independently, with verbal reminders to use the strategy. When finished, students and the instructor use the ACT essay scoring guide to edit the essay. Process is repeated until students achieve mastery.

The teacher begins by having Paul take a practice ACT essay exam to gain an understanding of what he is currently able to write. The teacher and Paul then work together to analyze the practice essay and set a writing goal. The teacher has Paul record his writing goal. As the instruction continues as outlined in table 7.2, Paul self-evaluates and graphs (see figure 7.2) the number of persuasive elements he includes in each practice essay he writes. This allows him to visually see his progress and reinforces learning and utilizing the writing and self-regulation strategies.

The teacher also has Paul develop his own list of self-instructions (see textbox 7.1). These personalized self-instructions provide Paul with positive things he can say to himself to help him through the writing process. These statements can help him think of good ideas, support him while working, and help him when he is checking his work.

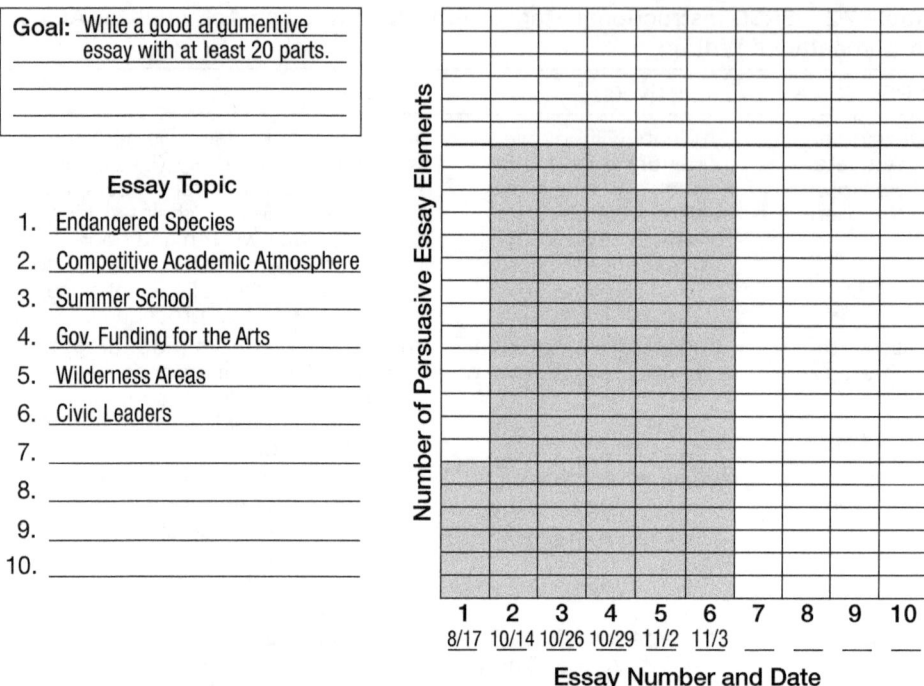

Figure 7.2 Sample Student Goal and Self-Evaluation Graph

TEXTBOX 7.1. PAUL'S SELF-INSTRUCTIONS

Self-Statements

To think of good ideas:

- Know about topic
- Keep on topic

While I work:

- Pace yourself
- Do your best
- Use better words
- Use HIT SONGS[3]
- Transitions

To check my work:

- Planning sheet check-off
- Reread
- Make sure it's logical
- Compliment yourself

Once Paul is able to independently plan, compose, and edit an argumentative essay based on an ACT prompt, his teacher has him practice writing an essay under similar conditions to the actual ACT exam by providing him with the directions, prompts, and lined paper in the same format as the ACT and completing the essay under the specified time conditions. After the SRSD instruction, textbox 7.2 is Paul's independent planning in response to a prompt whether a soft drink company should be allowed to advertise in schools and below is the full text of Paul's independent response to the prompt.

> ## TEXTBOX 7.2. PAUL'S PLANNING PAGE—ORGANIZING NOTES
>
> H—Battle on school ad
> I—Soft drink ad on bus and school generates money but parent organization opposes
> T—Should keep it until a better opportunity for funds comes
>
> S—School may as well get money benefits
> O—Strong—shows both sides
> N—Kids see commercials
> G—Agree
>
> S—School is not right place
> O—Weak, doesn't talk about funds
> N—Kids informed with eating habits less likely to be obese
> G—Disagree
>
> S—Should keep it
> S—Will not generate as much funds
> S—Perspective 3
> S—School will probably try to find new funds; determine the meeting point

Paul's Independently Written Argumentative Essay (original student essay, spelling has been corrected):

Right now there is an ongoing battle on whether a school should have an advertisement for a soft drink company. The debate was brought up from a parent organization after the school used the ad. The ad generates $200,000 annually for the school which is a lot more than fundraisers have made. I believe the school should only keep the ad until a better opportunity for funds comes.

To start off, perspective one states that soft drink are bad for you, but also other foods are the same. It says that people will eat what they want, and that the school might as well benefit from it. This perspective is strong because it shows that it agrees that soft drinks are bad, but also that schools need funding. For example, if the ad gets taken down, the school loses money but they still see the ad around town or on commercials. I agree with this perspective because it allows the school to earn funds.

Next, the second perspective states that school is not the place for the ad and that it should be removed. It takes on how the ad installs bad habits and choices for the kids. This argument is weak because it does not have a plan for how the school can get funds. For instance, if the ad were to be removed, the school would lose funding and it is not certain that the kids would then have good habits. I disagree with this perspective because it removes funding from the school.

Lastly, in perspective three, it states that it is unfortunate that the school has to be funded by a soft drink ad. But, gaining funds for the school is the better choice, until other opportunities come up. This perspective is strong because it knows soft drinks are bad, but funding the school balances it out, and it even states that it should be removed when better ways to fund come up. An example would be that the school uses this ad, but finds new ways to get funds and then uses that. I agree with this perspective because it provides another way for the school to get funds when an opportunity comes up.

As stated earlier, the school should keep the ad until a better solution for funds comes up. If the school removes the ad, it also will remove a good source of its funding. My thesis agrees mostly with perspective 3 because it says that the school should keep the ad until better options come up. Ultimately, the school needs funds, so it will most likely keep the ad or find a new way to generate funds. Health is important for the youth, but educating them is also of great importance.

When evaluating Paul's essay, the teacher and Paul determine that he did well organizing his notes through using the HIT SONGS[3] strategy. He used words or short phrases to plan and then expanded upon his notes in the essay. His essay was well organized and incorporated the necessary argumentative genre elements. Furthermore, he analyzed a variety of perspectives and provided development and support for his thesis. He also utilized transition words at the beginning and within paragraphs. Paul then graphs his essay on his goal sheet to continue to self-monitor his writing progress.

Writing to Learn

Writing is a tool that can support and enhance student learning of material. It can be especially helpful to have students write after reading. Some examples of writing after reading are taking notes, using a learning journal, summarizing, synthesizing, or writing an essay in one of the genre areas. Note-taking helps students process the information they are learning and encourages students to identify main ideas and key information from a reading. Learning journals are when students reflect on what they have learned and write down what they learned and how it relates to their personal knowledge and experiences. After reading, additional thought is required when students are asked to transform a mental summary into writing. Writing a summary enhances learning of the material identifying the main concepts and putting information into their own words. Writing a synthesis pushes students' learning beyond summary writing because students must integrate information and connect ideas across multiple texts. Overall, providing students with brief, frequent writing activities throughout the school year leads to greater learning of material (Klein et al., 2019).

Technology Tools

With the advance and accessibility of technology, students are expected to produce written work using computers (CCSSO, 2020). Technology tools can support students during all the stages of the writing process. For example, the prewriting / planning stage can be done by creating an outline on a digital document or a mind-mapping program. Drafting using technology tools can include input via keyboard or speech to text. Making revisions can be easier when using technology because students can reorganize their thoughts and make edits without having to rewrite their paper. Digital tools also provide various applications that support editing, with features such as spelling and grammar checks and a thesaurus to enhance word choice. Finally, technology also offers a wide variety of formats for students to publish their written work whether it is simply printing a document or posting on a virtual platform (e.g., Google Classroom, blog, website).

Sentence Construction

There are some students in middle and high school who need more intensive writing interventions. Often these students need to develop the writing skill of sentence construction. Students need explicit instruction in sentence construction to convey their thoughts in writing. One approach for learning sentence construction is through teaching sentence combining where students receive direct and specific practice in rewriting basic sentences into complex and compound sentences (Saddler, 2019). For example, a student may write "Newton's first law has two parts. It says an object at rest will stay at rest until a force acts upon it. It also says a moving object will continue to move until a force acts upon it." These sentences could be combined to, "Newton's first law states that an object at rest will stay at rest and object in motion will stay in motion unless a force acts upon the object." Another way to develop students' writing at the sentence level is to use sentence starters or sentence frames to provide students with a structure for writing sentences. For example, "The most likely reason for the Revolutionary War was _____ because _____." This strategy can be especially helpful for students with disabilities and ELs.

Furthermore, students' simple sentence writing fluency can be enhanced through explicit instruction and timed practice. One sentence intervention that has been developed for secondary students uses the gradual release of responsibility instructional method and picture word prompts to explicitly teach students how to write sentences (Datchuk, 2017; Datchuk & Kubina, 2017; Datchuk & Rogers, 2019). This intervention combines explicit sentence instruction and frequency building to a performance criterion. It also incorporates self-regulation components such as goal setting and graphing performance. Intervention materials are available at shawndatchuk.com.

CONCLUSION

To borrow a sports analogy, students with writing difficulties face many challenges and are much like an athlete sitting on the sidelines—they lack the essential skills and strategies to be a star player on the team or even in the starting lineup. Writing interventions equip students with the essential skills and strategies they need to get off the sidelines and onto the playing field. They may not become the star player but, by using evidence-based interventions, struggling writers can get off the bench. The use of this sports analogy is meant to highlight the importance of implementing effective interventions for students with writing difficulties. Writing skills are essential to succeeding in middle and high school and will make a substantial contribution in preparing students to be successful in college and beyond. This chapter provided multiple research-based interventions for sentence, paragraph, and essay writing with a detailed example of using the evidence-based practice of SRSD to teach writing. Additionally, multiple approaches for formatively assessing students' writing and tracking their writing progress were described. By no means does this chapter include all known secondary writing interventions; however, it does provide many research-based approaches which serve as a good starting point for teachers to address the challenges and writing needs of secondary students struggling with writing.

REFERENCES

Asaro-Saddler, K., Muir-Knox, H., & Meredith, H. (2018). The effects of a summary writing strategy on the literacy skills of adolescents with disabilities. *Exceptionality, 26*(2), 106–18. https://doi.org/10.1080/09362835.2017.1283626

Benedek-Wood, E., Mason, L. H., Wood, P. H., Hoffman, K. E., & McGuire, A. (2014). An experimental examination of quick writing in the middle school science classroom. *Learning Disabilities: A Contemporary Journal, 12*(1), 69–92.

Boscolo, P., & Ascorti, K. (2004). Effects of collaborative revision on children's ability to write understandable narrative texts. In L. Allal, L. Chanquoy, & P. Largy (Eds.), *Revision: Cognitive and instructional processes* (pp. 157–70). Kluwer.

Burke, L., Poll, G., & Fiene, J. (2017). Response to an expository writing strategy across middle school RtI tiers. *Learning Disabilities: A Contemporary Journal, 15*(1), 85–101.

Caccamise, D., Franzke, M., Eckhoff, A., Kintsch, E., & Kintsch, W. (2007). Guided practice in technology-based summary writing. In D. S. McNamara (Ed.), *Reading comprehension strategies: Theories, interventions, and technologies* (pp. 375–96). Erlbaum.

Chalk, J. C., Hagan-Burke, S., & Burke, M. D. (2005). The effects of self-regulated strategy development on the writing process for high school students with learning disabilities. *Learning Disability Quarterly, 28*(1), 75–87. https://doi.org/10.2307/4126974

Council of Chief State School Officers (CCSSO). (2020). *Common core state standards for English language arts*. Common Core State Standards Initiative. https://learning.ccsso.org/wp-content/uploads/2022/11/ELA_Standards1.pdf

Datchuk, S. M. (2017). A direct instruction and precision teaching intervention to improve the sentence construction of middle school students with writing difficulties. *Journal of Special Education, 51*(2), 62–71. https://doi.org/10.1177/0022466916665588

Datchuk, S. M., & Kubina, R. M. (2017). A writing intervention to teach simple sentences and descriptive paragraphs to adolescents with writing difficulties. *Education and Treatment of Children, 40*(3), 303–26.

Datchuk, S. M., & Rogers, D. B. (2019). Text writing within simple sentences: A writing fluency intervention for students with high-incidence disabilities. *Learning Disabilities Research & Practice, 34*(1), 23–34. https://doi.org/10.1111/ldrp.12185

De La Paz, S. (1999). Self-regulated strategy instruction in regular education settings: Improving outcomes for students with and without learning disabilities. *Learning Disabilities Research and Practice, 14*(2), 92–106.

Eissa, M. A. (2009). The effectiveness of a program based on self-regulated strategy development on the writing skills of writing-disabled secondary school students. *Electronic Journal of Research in Educational Psychology, 7*(1), 5–24.

Foxworth, L. L., Mason, L. H., & Hughes, C. A. (2017). Improving narrative writing skills of secondary students with disabilities using strategy instruction. *Exceptionality, 25*(4), 217–34. http://doi.org/10.1080/09362835.2016.1196452

Fuchs, L. S., Fuchs, D., & Malone, A. S. (2017). The taxonomy of intervention intensity. *TEACHING Exceptional Children, 50*(4), 35–43. https://doi.org/10.1177/0040059918758166

Geres-Smith, R., Mercer, S. H., Archambault, C., & Bartfai, J. M. (2019). A preliminary component analysis of self-regulated strategy development for persuasive writing in grades 5 to 7 in British Columbia. *Canadian Journal of School Psychology, 34*(1), 38–55. https://doi.org/10.1177/0829573517739085

Graham, S., & Harris, K. R. (2018). Evidence-based writing practices: A meta-analysis of existing meta-analyses. In M. Braaksma, K. R. Harris, & R. Fidalgo (Eds.). *Design principles for teaching effective writing: Theoretical and empirical grounded principles* (pp. 13–37). Brill Academic.

Graham, S., Hebert, M., & Harris, K. R. (2015). Formative assessment and writing: A meta-analysis. *Elementary School Journal, 115*(4), 523–47. https://doi.org/10.1086/681947

Graham, S., Bañales, G., Ahumada, S., Muñoz, P., Alvarez, P., & Harris, K. R. (2020). Writing strategies interventions. In D. L. Dinsmore, L. K. Fryer, & M. M. Parkinson (Eds.), *Handbook of strategies and strategic processing* (pp. 141–58). Routledge.

Graham, S., Bruch, J., Fitzgerald, J., Friedrich, L., Furgeson, J., Greene, K., Kim, J., Lyskawa, J., Olson, C. B., & Smither Wulsin, C. (2016). Teaching secondary students to write effectively (NCEE 2017-4002). National Center for Education Evaluation and Regional Assistance (NCEE), Institute of Education Sciences, US Department of Education. Retrieved from the NCEE website: http://whatworks.ed.gov

Harris, K. R., & Graham, S. (2018). Self-regulated strategy development: Theoretical bases, critical instructional elements, and future research. In M. Braaksma, K. R. Harris, & R. Fidalgo (Eds.). *Design principles for teaching effective writing: Theoretical and empirical principles* (Studies in Writing, vol. 34, pp. 119–51). Brill Academic. https://doi.org/10.1163/9789004270480_007

Hoover, T. M., Kubina, R. M., & Mason, L. H. (2012). Effects of self-regulated strategy development for POW+TREE on high school students with learning disabilities. *Exceptionality: A Special Education Journal, 20*(1), 20–38. https://doi.org/10.1080/09362835.2012.640903

Hosp, M. K., Hosp, J. L., & Howell, K. W. (2016). *The ABCs of CBM* (2nd ed.). Guilford.

Klein, P. D., Haug, K. N., & Bildfell, A. (2019). Writing to learn. In S. Graham, C. A. MacArthur, & M. Hebert (Eds.), *Best practices in writing instruction* (3rd ed., pp. 162–184). Guilford.

Konrad, M., & Test, D. W. (2007). Effects of GO 4 IT ... NOW! strategy instruction on the written IEP goal articulation and paragraph-writing skills of middle school students with disabilities. *Remedial and Special Education, 28*(5), 277–91. https://doi.org/10.1177/07419325070280050301

MacArthur, C. A., & Philippakos, Z. (2010). Instruction in a strategy for compare-contrast writing. *Exceptional Children, 76*(4), 438–56. https://doi.org/10.1177/001440291007600404

Mason, L. H., Kubina Jr., R. M., Kostewicz, D. E., Cramer, A. M., & Datchuk, S. (2013). Improving quick writing performance of middle-school struggling learners. *Contemporary Educational Psychology, 38*(3), 236–46. https://doi.org/10.1016/j.cedpsych.2013.04.002

Olson, C. B., Scarcella, R., & Matuchniak, T. (2013). Best practices in teaching writing to English learners: Reducing constraints to facilitate writing development. In S. Graham, C. A. MacArthur, & J. Fitzgerald (Eds.), *Best practices in writing instruction* (2nd ed., pp. 381–402). Guilford.

Ray, A. B. (in press). Writing interventions using SRSD for secondary students with and at-risk for learning disabilities: A review of empirical research. In Xinghua Liu, Michael Hebert, & Rui A. Alves (Eds.), *The Hitchhiker's Guide to Writing Research*. Springer.

Ray, A. B., & Graham, S. (2020). A college entrance essay exam intervention for students with high-incidence disabilities and struggling writers. *Learning Disability Quarterly, 44*(4), 275–87. Advanced online publication. https://doi.org/10.1177/0731948720917761

Ray, A. B., Graham, S., & Liu, X. (2019). Effects SRSD of college entrance essay exam instruction for high school students with disabilities or at-risk for writing difficulties. *Reading and Writing: An Interdisciplinary Journal, 32*(6), 1507–29. https://doi.org/ 10.1007/s11145-018-9900-3

Reid, R., Ortiz Lienemann, T., & Hagaman, J. L. (2013). *Strategy instruction for students with learning disabilities* (2nd ed.). Guilford.

Romig, J. E., & Olsen, A. A. (2021). Technical features of slopes for curriculum-based measures of secondary writing. *Reading and Writing Quarterly, 37*(6), 535–51. https://www.tandfonline.com/doi/abs/10.1080/10573569.2020.1860841

Romig, J. E., Therrien, W. J., & Lloyd, J. W. (2017). Meta-analysis of criterion validity for curriculum-based measurement in written language. *Journal of Special Education, 51*(2), 72–82. https://doi.org/10.1177/0022466916670637

Romig, J. E., Miller, A. A., Therrien, W. J., & Lloyd, J. W. (2020). Meta-analysis of prompt and duration for curriculum-based measurement of written language. *Exceptionality*. Advance online publication. https://doi.org/10.1080/09362835.2020.1743706

Saddler, B. (2019). Sentence Construction. In S. Graham, C. A. MacArthur, & M. Hebert (Eds.), *Best practices in writing instruction* (3rd ed., pp. 240–60). Guilford.

Saddler, B., Asaro-Saddler, K., Moeyaert, M., & Cuccio-Slichko, J. (2019). Teaching summary writing to students with learning disabilities via strategy instruction. *Reading & Writing Quarterly, 35*(6), 572–86. https://doi.org/10.1080/10573569.2019.1600085

Straub, C. L., & Vasquez, E. (2015). Effects of synchronous online writing instruction for students with learning disabilities. *Journal of Special Education Technology, 30*(4), 213–22. https://doi.org/10.1177/0162643415618929

Sundeen, T. H. (2012). Explicit prewriting instruction: Effect on writing quality of adolescents with learning disabilities. *Learning Disabilities: A Multidisciplinary Journal, 18*(1), 23–33.

Sundeen, T. H. (2015). Writing instruction for adolescents in the shadow of the common core state standards. *Journal of Adolescent and Adult Literacy, 59*(2), 197–206. https://doi.org/10.1002/jaal.444

Troia, G. A., & Olinghouse, N. G. (2013). The common core state standards and evidence-based educational practices: The case of writing. *School Psychology Review, 42*(3), 343–57.

Wolter, D. R. (1975). *Effect of feedback on performance on a creative writing task* [Unpublished doctoral dissertation]. University of Michigan, Ann Arbor.

8

Science and Social Studies Content

Sami Kahn, Timothy Lintner, Darren Minarik, and Jonte' C. Taylor

WHY SCIENCE AND SOCIAL STUDIES?

YOU MIGHT BE SURPRISED TO FIND science and social studies discussed together in a single chapter; after all, K–12 schools and universities commonly teach these two content areas as distinct and siloed. However, science and social studies are inextricably linked in that they are both ways of understanding the world. Science focuses on understanding and explaining phenomena in the *natural world*, such as how weather patterns form, how forces impact the way objects move through space, or how living things breathe and grow. Social studies focuses on understanding the *human world*; specifically, describing and explaining humans' relationships to each other and their environments. Some topics in social studies include how economic and legal systems form, how geography impacts societies (and vice versa), and what societal conditions might lead to war or peace.

Both science and social studies are considered sciences because they both rely on gathering and interpreting data to form knowledge. Traditionally, science, including subfields such as biology, chemistry, physics, and earth science, is referred to as a *natural science*, because it deals with understanding the natural world, whereas social studies, including subfields such as history, geography, economics, law, philosophy, and political science, is referred to as a *social science*, because it deals with human societies. Much of the data used in both disciplines is *empirical evidence*, which is based on observations, including documentation of patterns and behaviors, and is often gathered through experimentation. Scientists and social scientists may use historical and/or current data for their research, and they may use the data to predict future events. For example, a scientist may study historical weather patterns over time to make predictions about future weather patterns, while a social scientist may look at historical human migration patterns to make predictions about future migration patterns.

While the specific questions that scientists and social scientists ask may differ, the issues that arise in science and social studies are often intertwined because human activities often impact the natural world, and vice versa. For example, both scientists and social scientists might be interested in examining the impacts of human development in a wetland area; a scientist might focus on the impacts of development on a specific frog population or to the entire wetland ecosystem, while a social scientist might examine the economic or political impacts of the development on local human communities. Similarly, while scientists may investigate the biological basis of disease spread and the development of vaccines during a pandemic, social scientists might investigate the manner in which political, economic, and/or religious beliefs influence the decisions people make regarding mask wearing, travel, or vaccinations. Although scientists and social scientists focus on different aspects of the issues, both approaches are needed by society in order to gain a holistic understanding of the issues' impacts on the human and natural world and to make informed decisions. Understanding these different perspectives is also important to scientists and social scientists themselves, as societal influences necessarily impact scientists' choice of research topic, funding for their research, and the like, while scientific developments necessarily create societal questions and dilemmas that interest and influence social scientists.

From a teaching perspective, science and social studies share many similarities, but not always for the better. Sadly, both subjects are often associated with memorization of facts, figures, and dates and are often taught in this manner. In reality, science and social studies are both vibrant disciplines that are based on inquiry, which is the process of asking and investigating questions. Effective science and social studies teaching should emphasize constructivist approaches such as having students interact with objects in their environment, engage in discourse with others, develop their own investigations, and experience and overcome struggles in their pursuit of answers to their questions. We discuss these approaches in more detail later in this chapter.

In addition, science and social studies are often taught as subjects that are detached from students' lives when, in fact, science and social studies are arguably the most relevant subjects to students' lives. Take, for example, the study of astronomy in science or the history of space exploration in social studies. While teachers could teach these subjects through textbook readings, videos, and other relatively passive means, teachers could opt for approaches that make the subject more personally meaningful to students and engage students actively in their learning. For example, in science, students could be challenged to make their own observations and predictions about planetary motion, thereby allowing students to engage in practice *as* scientists while addressing their own understandings and misconceptions. Similarly, teachers can embed science and social studies content within societal controversies about space, ranging from Galileo's heliocentric ("sun-centered") view of the solar system, a historical controversy that put Galileo at odds with the Catholic church in the 1600s, to the "Space Race" during the 1960s Cold War era between the United States and the Soviet Union, to debating today's issues of whether space exploration is valuable or whether colonization in space is feasible. This approach would prompt students to examine their own values and positions on issues in relation to space and engage them in real-world issues as empowered decision-makers and developers of knowledge. This approach also integrates science and social studies in an authentic, interdisciplinary manner that emulates the way students are likely to experience the world, as opposed to experiencing these subjects in distinct, siloed parts of their day.

Quality science and social studies teaching also pushes students to feel uncomfortable. While this might, at first, sound antithetical to good teaching, having students' ideas, conceptions, and beliefs challenged is an essential part of learning. Cognitive dissonance occurs when learners are introduced to information that is unfamiliar to them, or is contradictory to their existing knowledge or beliefs. Learners often try to make sense of this dissonance by looking for information or "proof" that supports their prior knowledge. This propensity can reinforce misconceptions and even biases. Both science and social studies emphasize teaching students how to assess and integrate evidence so that they can analyze (and reanalyze) the bases of their knowledge, opening them up to new and often more sophisticated levels of understanding.

Helping students to grapple with challenging material also helps them to become more understanding of others' perspectives. Applying science and social studies in the real world necessarily involves complexity because real-world issues involve different interests and constituencies. Giving students the opportunity to hear or read about others' perspectives, or even to position themselves in another's shoes, such as through role play, can allow students to appreciate the consequences of their actions or inactions on others, and to experience empathy, both of which are foundational elements of character and moral development. In addition, by focusing on the importance of civic engagement and advocacy, teachers can ensure that students are actively engaged in their learning, have purpose in their learning, and are not bored.

While there is ample reason to consider science and social studies together due to their strong overlap in content and approach, there are also aspects of these disciplines that are distinctive and warrant further explanation. In the following sections, we identify some central ideas and background theories for each of the disciplines, discuss the national standards and their impact on assessment, and provide a case study that puts some best practices in both science and social studies into action! After reaching this chapter, you should be able to:

- Identify central ideas and key definitions for science and social studies;
- Compare and contrast science and social studies as related yet distinctive disciplines;
- Relate key background theories to best practices for science and social studies teaching;
- Discuss the critical role of national standards in developing rigorous and equitable curriculum and assessments;
- Provide examples of practices that ensure equitable participation in science and social studies for all students by drawing from the chapter case study.

WHAT IS SCIENCE?

Science is the systematic study of the natural world through observation and experimentation. Scientists work to gain understanding of phenomena by developing testable questions, formulating hypotheses, engaging in data collection and analysis, and developing conclusions based on their findings. While science in school is often taught as a singular "scientific method," in reality, scientists may take different routes to gain knowledge. Rather than thinking of science as a step-by-step recipe, many scholars attempt to capture the complexity of science by describing the Nature of

Science (NOS; Lederman, 2007), which identifies the practices, characteristics, and values of scientific endeavors. The National Science Teaching Association's (NSTA) Position Statement on Nature of Science (2020) is summarized and discussed below.

Nature of Science (NOS)

1. Scientific knowledge is both reliable and subject to change. Scientific knowledge often changes due to the discovery of new evidence or reconceptualizing existing knowledge. While this tentativeness can lead people to lose confidence in scientific findings, change is actually evidence of the rigor of science, which demands continued questioning, testing, challenging existing understandings, and reconceptualizing.
2. There is no one "scientific method" but rather shared standards for what constitutes science. These include making observations and inferences, developing explanations that are testable and based on empirical evidence, rational argument, skepticism, peer review, and reproducibility of the work.
3. Scientific knowledge is based on both observations and inferences. Because human senses are limited, scientists often need to make inferences about phenomena that can't be directly observed.
4. Creativity is necessary for scientific endeavors. Although science is often viewed as sterile and rigid, science is actually a very creative endeavor that relies on innovative thinking and problem solving.
5. Scientific inquiry is subjective, even though objectivity is often sought. Science is done by humans and therefore, is necessarily subjective. People, including scientists, bring their own biases and beliefs to their work. Scientists work to overcome these subjectivities by being transparent in their thinking and designing experiments and studies that attempt to eliminate bias.
6. Science is based in naturalistic observation and inquiry which excludes supernatural explanations for phenomena. Science is empirical, meaning that it is based on evidence gleaned from observation, experimentation, and data collection.
7. Scientific inquiry leads to laws and theories that each have specific definitions in science. Laws are generalizations about the way certain phenomena occur under certain conditions. Theories are generally accepted, rigorously tested explanations of laws. Theories explain laws but never become laws. Contrary to the public's common use of the phrase, "it's just a theory," scientific theories are well-tested and scrutinized.
8. Science is undertaken and influenced by people around the world and reflects cultural and societal influences. As discussed in the chapter introduction, science is impacted by society and vice versa.

Scientific Inquiry

Science is a way of understanding the natural world by asking questions and seeking explanations through observation and experimentation. Ideally, students should learn about science practice by emulating the work of scientists, by asking questions and designing experiments to answer the questions. This process is referred to as inquiry. Inquiry-based science teaching engages students in authentic science practice; however, this is a very challenging process, and so teachers must scaffold stu-

Table 8.1. How much information is given to the student?

Level of Inquiry	Question?	Methods?	Solution/Results?
1—Confirmation	X	X	X
2—Structured	X	X	
3—Guided	X		
4—Open			

dents' efforts. A helpful way to understand how this is done was presented by Bell et al. (2005), who think about the levels of inquiry as a series of questions about how much information is given to the students versus how much the students decide upon on their own. For example, when the question being investigated, the procedure to be followed, and the expected solution/results are all given to the students, so that the students are simply confirming something that they already know, it is considered the lowest level of inquiry, or "confirmation inquiry." This may be appropriate as a review at the end of a chapter study, for example. When students are given the question and the procedure, and are tasked only with finding the results, it is referred to as "structured inquiry." This type of investigation might be appropriate for emphasizing lab procedures, data analysis, and the like. Both of these levels are often referred to as "cookbook labs" because students are simply following directions, like a cookbook. This isn't necessarily a bad thing, as students may need to focus on skills such as following procedures, making measurements and observations, and collecting and analyzing data before they are able to identify a question and methodology. However, the idea is that teachers should work to move students toward greater independence in inquiry, so ensuring that lab investigations build toward higher levels of inquiry throughout the year. When teachers provide students with a question to investigate but students develop the procedures, it is referred to as "guided inquiry." The highest level of inquiry tasks students to identify questions, develop procedures, and collect and analyze data. This is known as "open inquiry." The levels of inquiry are depicted in table 8.1.

Scientific Literacy

The goal of science education is often stated as "scientific literacy," but the definition of scientific literacy is ambiguous and has evolved over time. Early views of scientific literacy are what Roberts (2009) referred to as Vision I, which involved canonical lists of what students should know in science, often through memorization and confirmation labs. More contemporary views, referred to as Vision II, emphasize the application of science knowledge to students' everyday lives. The *Next Generation Science Standards*, which are described in more detail in the next section, attempt to address both of these views by emphasizing competence in science content knowledge and the application of that knowledge, in order to support an educated and competitive workforce and to develop informed and engaged citizens. As K–12 science educators, we have the daunting task of developing scientifically literate students who are prepared for standardized tests, for college or vocational programs, for potential careers in science, and to apply science to everyday decision-making, from deciphering which products are safe and effective to recognizing how their choices can impact climate change. And perhaps, most importantly, we aspire to prepare students who appreciate and enjoy science.

The Framework for K–12 Science Education and the Next Generation Science Standards (NGSS)

The *Next Generation Science Standards*, which were published in 2013, provide teachers and schools with a schema, or roadmap, for promoting and assessing scientific literacy for students in K–12 classrooms. Each of the standards in the NGSS is written as a "performance expectation" that indicates precisely what a proficient student should be able to do to demonstrate their knowledge. Each standard is also built upon three major dimensions: scientific and engineering practices; crosscutting concepts that unify the study of science and engineering; and core ideas in the major disciplines of natural science. For example, fourth grade physical science standard "4-PS3-2" states that a proficient student should be able to: "Make observations to provide evidence that energy can be transferred from place to place by sound, light, heat, and electric currents." In this standard, "make observations to provide evidence" represents a science and engineering practice of making observations to serve as evidence for an explanation of a phenomenon, "that energy can be transferred" represents disciplinary core ideas about energy's definition and transfer, and "from place to place by sound, light, heat, and electric currents" represents a crosscutting concept about the various ways that energy can be transferred between objects. These standards marked a significant departure from the earlier standards for science education, which were very vague and provided little guidance for teachers about assessment. That said, the NGSS don't provide any specific curriculum or testing materials for teachers; rather, the standards serve as guides for what curriculum and assessment should address. Specific "Evidence Statements" are included for teachers to recognize the observable features of student performance that should be present by the end of the grade. The standards are also aligned with the Common Core State Standards for ELA/Literacy and Math.

Quality Assessment in Science Education

Quality assessment in science education requires teachers to give tremendous thought to the learning objectives they establish for their students. Teachers need to ask themselves, "What do I expect my students to understand?" and "How will I know whether they have achieved that understanding?" Learning objectives should be observable and measurable. For example, saying, "Students will understand photosynthesis" isn't an effective learning objective because "understanding" itself isn't observable and, even if it were, it's not clear how much "understanding" would be satisfactory. Alternatively, we can construct a measurable and observable objective about photosynthesis such as, "Students will develop a model in which they identify and describe the three inputs and two outputs of photosynthesis."

Science assessment should also give students the opportunity to show what they know. That might sound obvious, but, too often, science assessments are simplistic multiple-choice or true-and-false questions that test students' abilities to memorize definitions or processes without demonstrating deep understanding of scientific phenomena. In addition, science assessments sometimes rely on reading achievement in a way that allows students with strong reading skills to do well, regardless of whether they understand the concepts, while students who have deep understanding of the concepts but do not read or write well do poorly. Both of these scenarios are failures of the assessment process, not the students. Science teachers can provide options for the ways that students can share their understanding. For example, in the photosynthesis learning objective discussed above, students could be given options for the type of "model" they create. Models can be physical models (two- or three-dimensional), computer models, mathematical models, and so on. For this learning objective, the students could be given flexibility in the materials that they use or the type of model that they develop. They could also be given options for the manner in which they "describe" the inputs and outputs of photosynthesis. Descriptions could conceivably be written, oral, pictorial, or even kinesthetic! Providing options for the way students present their knowledge is in concert with a universal design for learning (UDL; CAST, 2018) and, as long as the learning objective criteria are met, maintains rigor and consistency among expectations.

In addition, science assessment should be both formative and summative. Teachers can use data from pre-assessments to determine students' background knowledge and plan accordingly, and continue to assess student learning throughout teaching units to determine what areas need further clarification and which students need additional assistance.

There are times in science when performance assessments make sense. For example, students might be asked to demonstrate that they understand how to use a microscope, prepare a slide, and interpret their findings from their observations.

Some Key Instructional Methods in Science Education

Project-Based Learning (PBL)

Project-based learning (PBL) is a method of teaching in which students address complex, authentic, engaging problems over an extended period of time. By challenging students to address meaningful problems, they become more invested in their work, have greater content understanding, and are more likely to remember and generalize what they have learned. PBL's theoretical foundation can be found in the work of John Dewey (1959), whose research and scholarship supported the importance of engaging students in meaningful, real-world learning. He advocated for allowing students to construct their own learning through interaction with real-world materials and problems, a philosophical approach known as constructivism, as opposed to the traditional form of teaching at the time, which was teacher-directed and positioned students as passive learners. Specifically in science, PBL is supported by a number of studies (Kokotsaki et al., 2016; Krajcik et al., 1999).

Socioscientific Issues (SSI)

Socioscientific issues (SSI) is a framework in which students investigate complex, controversial societal issues related to science as a way of promoting scientific literacy and engaged citizenship (Zeidler & Newton, 2017). Sample issues might include genetic engineering, water fluoridation, animal testing, and rebuilding in disaster-prone regions, among many others. Teachers implementing SSI encourage classroom discourse and debate as a means of encouraging evidence-based argumentation and decision-making. As students negotiate these issues, they improve in their ability to take others' perspectives, evaluate sources of evidence, and recognize the consequences of their actions (or inactions) on others.

Engineering Design Challenges. Engineering is a discipline that applies science to address real-world problems. Engineers need to solve problems in order to meet certain criteria (e.g., a building of a certain height or capacity) within given constraints (e.g., cost, time, materials). Since engineering practices are now a foundational part of the NGSS, science teachers must work to incorporate them into their curriculum. An easy and enjoyable way to do this is to give students design challenges in which they must meet criteria within constraints. Students can then work to address the challenge. As students become comfortable with this process, they can be tasked with identifying problems to solve or questions to answer themselves. The engineering design cycle is often considered to have multiple steps which include: ask questions/identify problems, imagine/plan solutions, build, test, and revise/improve.

Models and Simulations. Scientists and engineers often use models and simulations to test and communicate about phenomena that are too difficult to observe or variables that can't be manipulated directly in the real world. For example, climatologists use physical and computer models to understand the impact of different variables on sea level rise while virologists might run simulations to understand the progression of disease spread under different conditions. Science educators can encourage students to develop and use models to understand these complex interactions within and between systems.

WHAT IS SOCIAL STUDIES?

In many respects, social studies has an image problem. Trying to define social studies has been an ageless struggle as social studies means different things to different people, often at different times and usually within different contexts. Generally, it describes the loose federation of specific social science courses: history (world and United States), geography, government, economics, sociology, psychology, and anthropology (Parker, 2010), with the "big four" being history, geography, government, and economics.

There are two "schools of thought" regarding the definition and resultant purpose of social studies. The first camp ascribes to a content-centric approach which defines social studies as the teaching and learning of specific, often prescribed information (standards) correlated to each of the discipline strands (i.e., history, geography, etc.) The purpose of social studies is for students to "understand geography" or to "understand world history." Simply, social studies facilitates student understanding of the social sciences.

The second faction ascribes to a more application-based approach that views social studies as a vehicle for facilitating inquiry, discovery, advocacy, and action. It admittedly provides students with a working content-knowledge threshold or baseline of understanding. Yet it is what students *do* with this baseline of understanding that is most important. Such action is rooted in a more contemporary perspective that proports that, at its core, social studies—or more accurately, social education—encourages social engagement and civic participation designed to both model and support the tenets of a democratic society. Here, social studies encourages students to "participate in civic thought and action" and to "participate as active members in and of a democracy."

Nature of Social Studies

Similar to science, social studies is both reliable and predictable yet alternately fluid and dynamic. There are "absolutes" in social studies: names, dates, key concepts, permanent locations, etc. These absolutes ground social studies by providing baseline information—and often baseline understandings—for students.

Running counter to this absolutism is a fluid, ever-present reexamination or repositioning of social studies. Past events are open to interpretations. Motives are examined. Outcomes are reconfigured in light of new, often revolutionary information. The nature of social studies is rooted in absolutes yet open to—and supportive of—new interpretations, new insights, and new ways of presenting information.

Yet the fluidity inherent in social studies leads to new interpretations that, often, rub against these absolutes. New interpretations may be contentious at best if not heretical at worst. The resultant theoretical, conceptual, and practical division often leads to contention, confusion, and the encampment of particular dogmas or "schools of thought." Though some may see such divisions as counterproductive (and at times, they are) or of little educational heft, many in the field of social studies education find such "disagreements" reflective of the nature of our discipline. The human condition—which is central to social studies—is not a linear composite of objectivity but an amalgam of disparate thoughts, actions, and outcomes. It is through the presentation of and support for divergent views and voices that social studies reflects, values, and advances the shared and diverse experiences of all humans.

Social Studies Inquiry

The centrality of inquiry to sound social studies teaching and learning cannot be overestimated. It guides and shapes not only how social studies is taught but the multiple ways in which students can demonstrate their understanding(s) of the content. At its most basic form, inquiry facilitates hands in the air and encourages critical thought and participatory action. Inquiry asks student to *think* about and *act* upon social studies.

Yet inquiry is often overshadowed by more "conventional" ways of teaching social studies. Here, students are passive recipients of information unimodally relayed to them—teacher to student. The student role is simple—to sit quietly and take notes. The teacher role is equally simple—talking *at* students, not *with* them. Lost in this paradigm is inquiry.

A dynamic, inquiry-centered social studies classroom facilitates a sustained conversation between teacher and student and student to student as well. Questions are posed. Heads are scratched. Wheels turn. Hands are raised. Positions are taken and refuted. The inquiry-centered classroom encourages students to generate their own questions, pose their own hypotheses, gather and evaluate source information, and both reach and share their own conclusions. At its most primitive yet powerful, inquiry asks students to wrestle with the most important question in social studies—"why?"

Social Studies Literacy

Similar to science, social studies "literacy" was originally evidenced through rote memorization of isolated, disconnected bits of information deemed essential for student "understanding" of social studies content. Such understanding was often (and, unfortunately, still is) displayed through multiple-choice exams that cover marginally relevant facts. This rather esoteric practice was replaced by a more progressive view which grounds social studies literacy in and through inquiry, criticality, application, and advocacy. The ultimate goal is for social studies educators to prepare students to be critical consumers of and in their world (Wolk, 2003). Here, social studies literacy is dependent upon the creation of multiple opportunities to explore and process the content. It is only through the analysis of varied perspectives that students can make reasoned, informed decisions that facilitate recognition and preservation of the common good.

The College, Career, and Civic Life (C3) Framework for Social Studies State Standards

At its core, the C3 Framework, published in 2010, provides social studies educators with both a theoretical and practical blueprint for creating engaging, rigorous, inquiry-based learning opportunities. The C3 Framework offers guidance to states as they reimagine their social studies standards and encourages states to design and adopt civics, geography, history, and economics standards that ultimately produce students who are well-informed, participatory citizens of and in a democratic society.

The guiding conceptual underpinning of the C3 Framework is the Inquiry Arc—a set of mutually affirming ideas that serve to frame how students learn social studies content. With inquiry as the foundation of social studies teaching and learning, the framework serves to scaffold and extend students' capacity to know, analyze, explain, and argue about the interconnected complexities of their social world. Simply, the Inquiry Arc seeks to uncover understandings through the ubiquity of questions (Grant, 2013; Grant et al., 2015; National Council for the Social Studies, 2013).

There are four strands or dimensions to the Inquiry Arc: developing questions and planning inquiries; applying disciplinary concepts and tools; evaluating sources and using evidence; and communicating conclusions and taking informed action.

The first dimension, developing questions and planning inquiries, encourages both teachers and students to use compelling and supporting questions to uncover the layered nuances of social studies. A compelling question frames inquiry through an initial, admittedly broad lens (e.g., "Can actions be justified in a time of war?"). Supporting questions are more direct, refined, and guide instruction as they collectively seek to answer the compelling question (e.g., "What propaganda did the Japanese use leading up to the Nanking Massacre?").

The second dimension of the Inquiry Arc addresses the application of disciplinary concepts and tools in answering the compelling question. With teacher guidance, students incorporate various learning tools (i.e., historical documents, charts, maps, photographs, videos, music) into forming their understanding(s) of social studies content. Sound social studies teaching and learning is premised on the diversity of information available to examine the topic at hand.

Evaluating sources and using evidence is the third dimension of the Inquiry Arc. Here students gather, evaluate, and use information to make claims and counterclaims. It is imperative that students have exposure to an array of source-types that allow a more holistic, complete mosaic of potential understandings and interpretations.

The final dimension asks students to communicate conclusions and take informed action. As participatory citizenship lies at the heart of social studies, this may arguably be the most imperative step in the Inquiry Arc. With teacher guidance, students use multiple means to share their findings and put them into action. Information is idle if not acted upon. From a simple presentation, to running for an elected position, to volunteering at a local agency, the imperative is to facilitate student action and advocacy through direct participation.

Quality Assessment in Social Studies

Quality assessment in social studies is dependent upon teachers asking themselves a few seminal questions. "What is *truly* important that my students understand?" "What is this information going to do for them, now and in the future?" And lastly, "How can I provide multiple ways in which my students can demonstrate their understanding(s)?" Only by asking these questions can we move toward an assessment paradigm that is powerful, personal, and purposeful.

So often, social studies assessment is relegated to knowing who the sixteenth President of the United States was. Though important for a hearty game of trivia, this isolated, baseless, and superficial fact provides students with no context in which to understand, analyze, and evaluate Lincoln and his resultant actions. A more suitably provoking question may be, "Why is Lincoln revered? Is it his personality or his actions?" Though we often ask our students who, what, when, and where, we regularly forget to ask the most important question in social studies—"why?"

Quality social studies assessment is rooted in inquiry. It is constructed from a theoretical framework that asks students to analyze, evaluate, synthesize, and take informed action. Similar to social studies instruction, social studies assessment is not passive (e.g., multiple-choice exams, matching, etc.) but actively encourages innovation in how students demonstrate understanding. Instead of the ubiquitous paper-and-pencil exams, teachers can provide opportunities for students to draw, create, act, sing, display, and videotape their content understanding.

Lastly, social studies assessment must be authentic. How students demonstrate their understanding must "make sense" to them; it must tap into their strengths, motivations, and levels of expertise. Authentic social studies assessment serves not only to reflect content understanding but to reinforce the rather personal nature of social studies—that student voice, student action matters.

Key Instructional Strategies in Social Studies Education

The question is simple: How do you engage students in the social studies classroom? This rather simple question becomes somewhat daunting, particularly when students perceive social studies as disconnected from their lives, grounded in the ubiquitous lecture-read-write model of instruction and therefore patently boring.

Such disconnection and boredom are directly correlated to the way(s) in which social studies is taught. In an effort to reduce student passivity by increasing student engagement, we offer three ways in which social studies teaching and learning can validate student experiences, pique student curiosity, and facilitate student innovation and action.

Engagement

There are several ways to get students engaged both inside and outside of the social studies classroom. The most direct in-class strategy is to embed probing, pointed questions throughout the lesson. Such questions can be leading or "loaded," rhetorical, evaluative, application-based, or merely to gauge student comprehension. Irrespective of question type, asking questions—any type of questions—facilitates student engagement and action. Students become active learners.

Get students engaged outside of the classroom as well. This entails designing research or inquiry opportunities for students to engage in and with the community. This can be through service-learning opportunities, direct participation, or volunteerism. Through such direct involvement, students now put social studies into action!

Analysis

There are numerous strategies teachers can use to support analysis in the social studies classroom. Providing students with multiple perspectives of a singular issue or idea creates opportunities for students to evaluate and articulate their interpretations. Teachers can ask students to evaluate texts, pictures, artwork, music, or symbols. Stemming directly from the C3 Framework, analysis allows students to make sense of their social world by thinking deeply about it.

Project-Based Learning

A strategy perfectly suited to both the science and the social studies classroom is project-based learning (PBL). PBL is student- and activity-centered, takes students' personal experiences and differences into consideration, and encourages student interactions with their surrounding environment. PBL can be both simple and conversely multifaceted. Yet the key is to create opportunities for students to examine and (hopefully) solve real and relevant issues using inquiry, analysis, advocacy, and action.

APPLYING BEST PRACTICES IN SCIENCE AND SOCIAL STUDIES THROUGH A CASE STUDY

Ms. Herrera, a ninth grade science teacher and Mr. Ogden, a ninth grade social studies teacher, both at Kennedy Secondary School, were waiting for a meeting to start when they began discussing some of the news of the day. Mr. Ogden mentioned that their state legislature was considering introducing a requirement that schools mandate vaccinations for HPV, or human papillomavirus, a set of sexually transmitted viruses that can cause genital warts and cancers of the mouth, throat, genitals, and cervix. Ms. Herrera nodded and added that, although a highly effective vaccine called Gardasil has been available to combat HPV since 2006, and that the Centers for Disease Control and Prevention (CDC) recommends vaccinations for girls and boys between ages 11 and 12, only a handful of states require the vaccine for school attendance. The teachers discussed some of the reasons for this, which include concerns around state mandates in general, moral objections to vaccines associated with sexual behavior, vaccine costs and safety, the rights of parents to refuse vaccines for their children, whether states and insurance companies should have to pay for the vaccine, and so on.

As Ms. Herrera and Mr. Ogden spoke, they began to realize that this topic touched directly on their courses. Ms. Herrera's science curriculum included the study of human body systems, including the immune and reproductive systems, how vaccines work, and cellular reproduction. Mr. Ogden's social studies curriculum included the proper scope and limits of power and authority; how governments make economic decisions; the roles, rights, and responsibilities of individuals, groups, and institutions in society. Both science and social studies curricula consider issues of science, technology, and society, specifically, how advances in science and technology, past and present, impact and are impacted by society.

The teachers agreed to codevelop an engaging unit that addressed the question of whether the Gardasil vaccine should be mandatory. The unit would address the personal, societal, and economic impacts of scientific innovations and demonstrate the importance of informed participation in scientific policy debates.

The next day, the teachers met to begin identifying resources. They also both reviewed their standards, which included the following:

NGSS:

- HS-LS1-2. Develop and use a model to illustrate the hierarchical organization of interacting systems that provide specific functions within multicellular organisms.
- HS-LS1-4. Use a model to illustrate the role of cellular division (mitosis) and differentiation in producing and maintaining complex organisms.
- HS-ETS1-3. Evaluate a solution to a complex real-world problem based on prioritized criteria and trade-offs that account for a range of constraints, including cost, safety, reliability, and aesthetics, as well as possible social, cultural, and environmental impacts.

NCSS and C3:

- D2.Civ.10.9-12. Analyze the impact and the appropriate roles of personal interests and perspectives on the application of civic virtues, democratic principles, constitutional rights, and human rights.
- D2.Civ.6.9-12. Critique relationships among governments, civil societies, and economic markets.
- D2.Civ.12.9-12. Analyze how people use and challenge local, state, national, and international laws to address a variety of public issues.

Given that both teachers were quite busy (as teachers always are), they began by looking at some resources that already exist in their subject areas. Ms. Herrera identified a lesson in Zeidler & Kahn's (2014) book on socioscientific issues that addressed this very issue. She thought it made sense to take some of the aspects of the lesson, while also combining it with some of her preexisting lessons for the unit. Table 8.2 outlines the science lessons and objectives that Ms. Herrera identified.

Table 8.2. Science Lessons

Lesson	Topic	Objectives
Week 1	Compelling Question: Should the Gardasil vaccination be required for all 11- to 17-year-olds? Inquiry: How do vaccinations and the immune system work?	Students will begin to identify the moral, scientific, and societal implications of this controversy as the foundation for making a sound decision on the issue. **(SSI)** Using text and internet resources, students will work collaboratively to develop a creative project "Journey through the Immune System" that explains key content and addresses misconceptions about the immune system and vaccinations. **(Formative Assessment, Developing and Using Models)** NGSS: HS-LS1-2
Week 2	The Biology of Cancer Inquiry: How does cellular reproduction/division maintain human health? How can certain viruses cause cancer?	Students will apply their prior knowledge of cell reproduction through mitosis to the development of cancer. Students will observe, compare, and contrast microscope slides of normal and cancerous cells. Students will create physical models of normal and cancerous cells that meet certain criteria within time and material constraints. **(Engineering Design Challenge, Formative Assessment, Developing and Using Models)** NGSS: HS-LS1-4
Week 3	Sexually Transmitted Infection/Disease Inquiry: Why are STDs difficult to control and detect? What societal factors influence the spread of STDs?	Students will engage in a hands-on activity that demonstrates how STDs can travel undetected through a population. **(Developing and Using Models—Simulation)** Students will investigate credible sources of evidence to identify common misconceptions about STDs and develop public service announcements (PSAs) for their school and community to prevent the spread of STDs. **(PBL, Formative Assessment)**
Week 4	Research and Debate on Gardasil and HPV	Students will collaboratively prepare for and engage in a mock congressional debate on whether Gardasil vaccines should be mandatory for all students aged 11–17. **(SSI, Summative Assessment)** NGSS: HS-ETS1-3

Planning Instruction for All Students

To maximize accessibility and minimize barriers to learning, Ms. Herrera and Mr. Ogden think about some of the tenets of Universal Design for Learning (UDL; CAST, 2018) as they plan for all students. UDL is an approach to teaching that ensures that students' interest is engaged and sustained in many ways ("Multiple means of engagement"), information is conveyed to students using a range of approaches and supports ("Multiple means of representation"), and students have many ways of interacting with information and materials and, ultimately, showing what they know ("Multiple means of action and expression"). UDL can be used to intentionally plan for learner variability in STEM by building flexibility into instruction and ensuring that all students have meaningful, accessible entry points into the curriculum (Basham & Marino, 2013). In this lesson, the topic itself is relevant to all students since it deals with personal health, and students get to engage with the topic through hands-on activities, book and computer research, simulations, debates, and so on. Ms. Herrera will also use graphic organizers to help students to organize information. For example, she will provide them with a Yes/No T-Chart to record their reasons for and against the mandatory vaccine. She will also provide them with checklists for each of the lab activities so that they know exactly what is expected of them for success and to help students monitor their own progress. Ms. Herrera will use a concept map to review the steps of cell reproduction and how cellular reproduction fits into the "big picture" of the functions of living things. This will serve as a review and will also provide relevant context for students' learning (i.e., why it is important), which will increase students' motivation and retention of material. To help students understand how to evaluate which websites and articles are trustworthy, she will introduce the CARS rubric (Harris, 2000). CARS stands for: Credibility, Accuracy, Reasonableness, and Support. After explaining these terms and working through examples with students, she will provide them with CARS charts to help them track the criteria. For the debate, she will promote an intellectually safe classroom by discussing the difference between challenging someone's ideas and putting them down personally, and she will ensure that she and all students avoid mockery of any kind. She will also put sentence frames on the board, such as "I agree/disagree with _____ because . . ." to support students' ability to express their thoughts clearly and respectfully. Finally, she will also encourage students to share their ideas in small groups before sharing with the whole class in order to increase their confidence.

Science Assessments Explained

During this unit, Ms. Herrera is using three formative assessments to ensure that her students are applying their understanding of the key science concepts to engaging, real-world problems. In the first assessment, student teams are challenged to create a poster/PowerPoint/pamphlet/performance/poem describing a "Journey Through the Immune System" which will be presented to the class. The groups will be given a handout detailing the assignment and the required objectives in a checklist form. This list will allow the students to understand Ms. Herrera's expectations. Specific objectives might include:

- Describe the function and components of the immune system.
- Describe the relationship between vaccination and immunity.
- Describe at least one immune disorder.
- Describe the antigen-antibody reaction.

When Ms. Herrera introduces this assignment, she explains to her students that the "description" can be written, oral, pictorial, or kinesthetic. In other words, Ms. Herrera is giving her students many options for communicating their knowledge. She does this because, for this particular assessment, she isn't focused on whether students can write or speak well; she is interested in whether they understand the complexities of the immune system. Since the mode of communication that students use to share their knowledge isn't the focus of the assessment, she can be flexible and allow students to make choices. Giving students choices at any point in instruction is valuable because it helps students to feel more invested in their learning. It also allows different talents to shine! For these and other reasons, choice is a key strategy of UDL.

For the second formative assessment, Ms. Herrera challenges her students to create physical models of normal and cancerous cells after comparing and contrasting cells under the microscope. The purpose of this assessment is to ensure that students understand the distinctions between the cells that they have observed. However, to make the assessment more engaging and also to reinforce engineering design processes, she gives the students certain criteria for their models (e.g., they must be freestanding, at least 20 cm tall, and include certain features such as cell membrane, nuclei, etc.). She also gives students certain constraints, such as materials (e.g., clay, balloons, markers, string, etc.) and time (e.g., 40 minutes). By structuring the assessment this way, Ms. Herrera is able to ascertain students' understanding of the content (e.g., mitosis and cancer), while also reinforcing important scientific and engineering processes, such as modeling and design.

The third formative assessment Ms. Herrera uses probes students' understanding of both the scientific and societal factors that influence the transmission of STDs. Moreover, this assessment positions students as informed and empowered members of the school and community. After simulating the spread of an STD through a hands-on activity that uses clear cups, water, sodium hydroxide, and phenolphthalein (for a full description of the activity, see Zeidler & Kahn, 2014) students use their textbooks and the internet to research STDs and develop public service announcements (e.g., videos, podcasts, etc.) that can be shared with their school and community. To prepare students for this task, Ms. Herrera has students discuss, in small groups, why they think STDs are difficult to detect and control. She then has students come together to discuss this question as a class. Allowing students to share their ideas in a small, safe environment first before sharing in a large group is particularly important when challenging or potentially uncomfortable topics are being discussed. It is also a research-based cooperative learning strategy that encourages students who may be shy or have language difficulties to contribute. As she did for the other assessments, Ms. Herrera provides her students with a rubric that describes what she expects them to include in their PSA (public service announcement). This helps them to organize their work and to understand Ms. Herrera's expectations.

Planning Instruction for All Students

Multiple means of action, engagement and expression, cooperative learning, choice in representation of understanding and action.

Social Studies Assessment Explained

As shown in table 8.3, Mr. Ogden has designed a series of lessons/activities premised on the C3 Inquiry Arc. He wants his students to initially generate questions

Table 8.3. Social Studies Lessons

Lesson	Topic	Objectives
Week 1	Compelling Question: What factors may influence or dictate the Gardasil vaccination being required for all 11-to 17-year-olds? Inquiry: Who has (or should) have the last say? Are some interests deemed "more important" than others? What is the relationship between individual rights and the collective good?	Students will explore and identify personal, moral, economic, state and national interests, rights and responsibilities. **(SSI)** Students will work collaboratively to generate a list of seminal questions addressing personal, moral, economic, state and national rights and/or interests. **(Formative Assessment)**
Week 2	Applying Disciplinary Concepts	Students will work collaboratively to develop an disciplinary matrix that explores the historical, economic, political, and geographic factors that address the compelling question. **(Formative Assessment)**
Week 3	Evaluating Sources and Using Evidence	Students will identify and evaluate multiple sources and source types (documents, videos, advertisements, statistics, social media, public service announcements). Students will gather credible, diverse information and create a video, poster board, or written overview that situates the personal, moral, economic, state and national interests and responsibilities within disciplinary contexts. **(PBL, Formative Assessment)**
Week 4	Communicating Conclusion and Taking Informed Action	Students will facilitate a classwide debate addressing the compelling question. Students will craft a summary position statement relevant to the compelling question and send them to key stakeholders at the local, state, or national level. **(SSI, Summative Assessment)**

surrounding the Gardasil vaccination and then contextualize such questions within the broad fields of history, geography, economics, and political science. From here, Mr. Ogden asks his students to access and evaluate information regarding the potential historical, geographic, economic, and political connection(s) to and with the Gardasil vaccination. Lastly, students will communicate their conclusion(s) through action-based outreach.

Initially, Mr. Ogden wants his students to create an inquiry baseline concerning impressionistic thoughts regarding the Gardasil vaccination. Simply, students are to generate questions: "What are some moral issues involved here?" "Why is this vaccine being mandated?" "Who decides if a vaccine should be mandated?" "Whose interests are *really* at stake?" Though seemingly cursory, Mr. Ogden knows that the first step in the Inquiry Arc is to get students thinking. This initial assessment asks for nothing more than a collaborative list of student-generated questions addressing the compelling question.

From this list of questions, the second assessment asks students to examine the Gardasil vaccination through a "social studies" lens. Mr. Ogden has students explore the historical underpinnings of vaccines and mandated vaccination and any geographic variants—in terms of acceptance or refusal rates—that can be teased out. Students will also surmise as to the economic benefits such a mandate might incur as well as who, actually, has the right to make such decisions. Students can represent their understanding(s) through a simple graphic organizer (four-column matrix), poster boards spread throughout the classroom, a PowerPoint, or a simple video.

Assessment three asks students to accumulate rich, reliable, and varied sources that examine the intersection between mandated vaccinations and history, geography, economics, and political science. Mr. Ogden wants his students to become critical detectives—evaluating sources, linking (or decoupling) narratives, identifying bias, and gaining a more encompassing mosaic of understanding based upon the source types gathered and examined. To Mr. Ogden, this is the most important step in the Inquiry Arc.

To demonstrate their understanding premised on the critical evaluation of multiple source types (e.g., articles, social media posts, advertisements, relevant statistics, videos, etc.), students will work together (in groups of three) to create a composite representation of the way(s) in which history, geography, economics, and political science has or presently does influence the mandating of Gardasil. Students can create a trifold poster board, a PowerPoint or other visual representation, a skit, a video, or a written paper illustrating their newfound understanding(s).

Lastly, students need to draw conclusions and take action. To Mr. Ogden, this is the exciting part of the lesson as it allows students to creatively communicate their conclusions. Assessment four is simple: demonstrate your "position" and take action. Initially, Mr. Ogden facilitates an Inside-Out debate. A group of four randomly selected students are seated in the middle of the room. Their classmates are seated, in a circle, around them. Mr. Ogden asks the group of four, "So, based upon your research, should the Gardasil vaccination be required for all 11- to 17-year-olds?" The four students have a running conversation (often evolving into a debate) premised on their respective conclusions. After five minutes, the rest of the class joins the discussion. Such whole-class engagement allows Mr. Ogden to assess the level and scope of research performed and the depth of understanding related to the compelling question.

To supplement this debate, Mr. Ogden has each student craft a summary position statement relevant to the compelling question. Students can write a letter, tape a three-minute public service announcement, create a visual display or advertisement, or perform a skit or write a song. Mr. Ogden believes in affording students as much creativity as possible in how they communicate their conclusions to a larger audience.

CONCLUSION

In this chapter, we outlined some central tenets, background theories, and key instructional strategies for science and social studies teaching. A case study was used to highlight the incorporation of national standards and quality assessments in both disciplines, as well as the inextricable link between these two vibrant, relevant, and inspiring fields. Some of the key takeaways from the chapter include:

- Science and social studies are complementary ways of knowing about the world; while science focuses on the natural world, social studies focuses on the human world.
- Science and social studies are intertwined because human activities often impact the natural world and vice versa.
- Science and social studies involve data collection, which provides evidence to support or refute claims about the world.
- Scientific and social studies literacy are both envisioned as ways of empowering students to apply knowledge to their everyday lives, their careers, and to society.
- Science and social studies education should propel students to become developers of knowledge, critical consumers of information, and informed decision-makers.
- Good teaching practice in both disciplines emphasizes hands-on inquiry and exploratory methods, as opposed to memorization of facts and dates.
- Contemporary approaches to both science and social studies recognize a moral connection to the discipline; knowledge in both fields can and should be applied toward action, civic engagement, empathy, advocacy, and empowerment.
- Science and social studies teachers should push their students to feel challenged, uncomfortable, and engaged . . . and *never bored.*
- Quality assessment in both disciplines should not be simplistic! It should emphasize deep understanding and be equitable.

As science and social studies are both rooted in inquiry-based instruction that encourages active, participatory student engagement, it is imperative that educators design instruction with all students in mind. This entails providing strategic, sustained supports and scaffolds—interventions—that recognize and respond to the unique learning needs of *all* students and reduce barriers to learning and engagement for all students in all science and social studies classrooms. The following chapter provides educators with a number of research-based interventions that support sound, engaging, and inclusively responsive science and social studies instruction.

REFERENCES

Basham, J. D., & Marino, M. T. (2013). Understanding STEM education and supporting students through Universal Design for Learning. *TEACHING Exceptional Children, 45*(4), 8–15. https://doi.org/10.1177/004005991304500401

Bell, R. L., Smetana, L., & Binns, I. C. (2005). Simplifying inquiry instruction. *Science Teacher, 72*(7), 30–33.

CAST. (2018). *Universal Design for Learning Guidelines* version 2.2. http://udlguidelines.cast.org

Dewey, J. (1959). *The school and society.* University of Chicago Press.

Clough, M. P. (2011). Teaching and assessing the nature of science: How to effectively incorporate the nature of science in your classroom. *Science Teacher* 78(6), 56–60.

Grant, S. G. (2013). From Inquiry Arc to instructional practice: The potential of the C3 Framework. *Social Education,* 77(6), 322–26.

Grant, S. G., Lee, J., & Swan, K. (2015). *The inquiry design model.* http://www.c3teachers.org/wp-content/uploads/2014/10/IDM_Assumptions_C3-Brief.pdf

Harris, R. (2000). *WebQuester: A guidebook to the Web.* McGraw-Hill.

Kokotsaki, D., Menzies, V., & Wiggins, A. (2016). Project-based learning: A review of the literature. *Improving schools,* 19(3), 267–77.

Krajcik, J. S., Czerniak, C., & Berger, C. (1999). Teaching children science: A project-based approach. McGraw-Hill.

Lederman, N. G. (2007). Nature of science: Past, present, and future. In S. K. Abell & N. G. Lederman (Eds.), *Handbook of research on science education* (pp. 831–80). Lawrence Erlbaum.

National Council for the Social Studies (NCSS). (2013). *College, career, and civic life (C3) framework for social studies state standards.* https://www.socialstudies.org/standards/c3

National Science Teaching Association. (2020). Position statement on nature of science. https://www.nsta.org/nstas-official-positions/nature-science

Parker, W. C. (Ed.). (2010). *Social studies today: Research and practice.* Routledge.

Roberts, B. (2009). Performative social science: A consideration of skills, purpose and context. *Historical Social Research,* 34(1), 307–53.

Wolk, S. (2003). Teaching for critical literacy in social studies. *Social Studies,* 94(3), 101–6.

Zeidler, D. L., & Kahn, S. (2014). *It's debatable! Using socioscientific issues to develop scientific literacy, K–12.* NSTA Press.

Zeidler, D. L., & Newton, M. H. (2017). Using a socioscientific issues framework for climate change education: An ecojustice approach. In D. Shepardson & R. Roychoudhury (Eds.), *Teaching and learning about climate change* (pp. 56–65). Routledge.

9

Science and Social Studies Intervention

Jonte' C. Taylor, Darren Minarik,
Sami Kahn, and Timothy Lintner

THE PURPOSE OF SPECIAL EDUCATION INTERVENTIONS is to remove or mitigate academic, social, and behavioral obstacles that prevent students with disabilities from academic success. Through the use of specially designed explicit instruction and tiered supports, students receive proactive strategies designed to provide access to the general education curriculum. As noted in the previous chapter, effective science and social studies instruction is based on inquiry, where students construct knowledge through active engagement with content, asking questions, making observations, and forming ideas and positions. For students to participate in inquiry-based learning, they make connections with prior knowledge, interact with their environment, and engage in meaningful activities that involve complex content-area literacy skills. From a teaching perspective, science and social studies share many similarities, but not always for the better. Sadly, both subjects are often associated with memorization of facts, figures, vocabulary, and dates and are often taught in this manner. In reality, science and social studies are both vibrant disciplines that are based on inquiry, which is the process of asking and investigating questions. Effective science and social studies teaching should emphasize constructivist approaches to ensure that students are interacting with objects in their environment, engaging in discourse with others, developing their own investigations, and experiencing and overcoming struggles in their pursuit of answers to their questions. In this chapter, educators will:

- Examine the value of evidence-based and high-leverage practices in science and social studies.
- Identify the importance of strategic planning to support interventions within content instruction.
- Examine inquiry-based literacy interventions that support higher-order thinking and reasoning skills.
- Explore content acquisition interventions.

EVIDENCE-BASED AND HIGH-LEVERAGE PRACTICES IN SCIENCE AND SOCIAL STUDIES

In 2014, the Council for Exceptional Children (CEC), the premier organization for special educators focused on students with disabilities, established a workgroup to develop standards for determining evidence-based practices (EBPs; CEC, 2014). Cook et al. (2015) identified EBPs as effective practices that are supported by "multiple high-quality studies . . . and demonstrate robust effects on student outcomes" (p. 1). The importance of providing special education services for students with disabilities is well-documented; specifically, Cook et al. (2009) maintained the imperative that EBPs provide evidence backed by research to support students positively. The areas of focus to determine EBPs include research design, quantity of research, methodological quality, and magnitude of effect (Cook et al., 2009). As educational research must consider a number of variables as well as research designs, multiple authors have discussed what makes for quality research studies which are the basis for determining which interventions become EBPs. Research works have examined indicators for determining the quality of intervention studies using group research designs (Gersten et al., 2005), single-case research designs (Horner et al., 2005), and qualitative research (McDuffie & Scruggs, 2008). In addition to identifying quality research studies and evaluating research to determine interventions that comprise EBPs, Cook & Odom (2013) asserted "EBPs cannot have an impact unless they are implemented" (p. 142). Organizations, such as the CEC, uphold the use of EBPs to support students across disability types and content instruction.

EBPs are further encouraged by the CEC and the Collaboration for Effective Educator Development, Accountability, and Reform (CEEDAR) Center through the development and description of high-leverage practices (HLPs; McLeskey et al., 2017). HLPs are practices that support students regardless of content area, grade level, or ability. There are four broad HLP domains identified including (a) collaboration (HLPs 1–3), (b) assessment (HLPs 4–6), (c) social/emotional/behavioral practices (HLPs 7–10), and (d) instruction (HLPs 11–22). Across the four HLP domains, EBPs are directly associated with the social/emotional/behavioral practices and instruction domains (McLeskey et al., 2017). Researchers have identified using direct instruction, providing students opportunities to respond with prompting, and supplying high-quality feedback to students (Simonsen et al., 2008; Simonsen et al., 2010) as EBPs within the social/emotional/behavioral HLP domain. Additionally, functional behavioral assessments are suggested as an EBP that teachers should consider a HLP in social/emotional/behavioral instruction, even as meeting the minimal standard of being and EBP (McLeskey et al., 2017). For the HLP instruction domain, a number of cognitive strategies and instructional practices have been identified as EBPs including collaborative strategic reading, graphic organizers, text interaction strategies, self-regulated strategy development, prompting, enhanced anchored instruction, schema-based instruction, mnemonic strategies, and self-monitoring strategies (McLeskey et al., 2017). While essentially connected, HLPs are broader than EBPs and serve to offer skills and actions for implementation (Kennedy et al., 2020).

In considering HLPs and EBPs for students in inclusive science and social studies classrooms, we have identified four specific approaches and interventions that can be implemented by special and general science or social studies educators alike. Using the categories (general literacy and content acquisition) described by Ciullo et al., (2020), we provide research and descriptions of higher-order thinking and supported inquiry as general literacy interventions and mnemonics and graphic organizers as content acquisition interventions. The interventions and approaches that will be described can be considered as HLPs or EBPs or both.

GENERAL LITERACY AND CONTENT ACQUISITION INTERVENTIONS FOR SCIENCE AND SOCIAL STUDIES

Incorporating effective interventions within inclusive science and social studies classrooms begins with strategic planning for an anticipated diverse academic population (Bulgren et al., 2007; Lenz et al., 2004). Content-area teachers and special educators collaborate to support diverse learning needs by looking for ways to enhance instructional practice and content acquisition through targeted approaches that support learning as a whole while also meeting the individual needs of students with IEPs. The primary role of special educators is the implementation of specially designed instruction (SDI) for students with IEPs as mandated by the Individuals with Disabilities Education Act (IDEA, 2004). IDEA defines SDI as "adapting, as appropriate to the needs of an eligible child under this part, the content, methodology or delivery of instruction (i) to address the unique needs of the child that result from the child's disability; and (ii) ensure access of the child to the general curriculum, so that the child can meet the educational standards within the jurisdiction of the public agency that apply to all children" (34 CFR Sec. 300.39(b)(3)). To the maximum extent possible, this instruction should be delivered in the general education classroom. If it is delivered in an alternative setting, the SDI taught in the separate setting should then be generalized and supported in the general education classroom.

The principles of Universal Design for Learning (UDL) provide a conceptual planning framework for creating more inclusive units and lessons. Using UDL with a strategic planning cycle provides a way to ensure that strategic interventions align with the content and are effectively supporting learning outcomes. One such planning framework that aligns well with UDL principles is SMARTER planning, a mnemonic used to guide development of an inclusive classroom. The framework follows seven steps to ensure that the classroom teachers meet the learning needs of all students. These steps guide teachers to: (a) shape essential questions; (b) map critical content; (c) analyze the learning difficulties; (d) reach enhancement decisions; (e) teach strategically; (f) evaluate mastery; and (g) revisit outcomes (Bulgren et al., 2007; Lenz et al., 2004). This planning approach requires teachers to consider potential student learning difficulties first and then select strategic ways for students to engage with the content, participate in lesson activities, and share learning outcomes (Lowrey et al., 2017).

Table 9.1. Alignment of SMARTER Planning with Principles of UDL

SMARTER Planning	UDL Principles
Shape essential questions **M**ap critical content	**Representation**—Options for presenting information and content in different ways
Analyze the learning difficulties **R**each enhancement decisions	**Engagement**—Options for engaging student interest and motivation for learning
Teach strategically **E**valuate mastery	**Action & Expression**—Options for students to express what they learned
Revisit outcomes	**Checkpoint** to reflect and improve practice

GENERAL LITERACY INTERVENTIONS IN SCIENCE AND SOCIAL STUDIES

When providing literacy interventions in the science and social studies classroom, the general and special educator need to consider how the interventions support disciplinary literacy. Disciplinary literacy refers to students engaged in the same processes of reading, comprehending, investigating, analyzing, and writing as disciplinary experts perform in respective fields (Shanahan et al., 2011; Spires et al., 2016). Students are engaged in learning the content of the course while also modeling the processes used by disciplinary experts. Both historians and scientists collect and analyze sources, while determining the validity, reliability, and potential bias. Both have vocabulary unique to the disciplines that students need to understand. Literacy interventions that address comprehension of text through strategic reading and text interaction, identifying main ideas and details, summarizing, and writing need to consider the unique disciplinary characteristics of science and social studies in order to be included in the general education classroom.

Supported Inquiry

For deep learning to occur, students must move beyond the memorization of the content material. Students with disabilities in inclusive settings are provided with the opportunity to learn science and social studies content in an environment that, when presented well, allows for students to move to higher-order skills along Bloom's taxonomy. In effort to move students from basic general knowledge or simple comprehension of content to the ability to analyze, synthesize, and evaluate content information, instructional approaches such as inquiry-based instruction are critical. For example, Scruggs et al. (2010) reported that the use of hands-on instruction (i.e., inquiry-based instruction) was a moderately effective approach for teaching secondary content in science and social studies. When specifically focused on science and social studies content, a number of authors have advocated for inquiry-based instruction for students with disabilities (social studies—Okolo & Ferretti, 2014; science—Therrien et al., 2011, 2014; Taylor et al., 2012; 2018). The focus on inquiry instruction in science and social studies content classes at the K–12 level has been steadily encouraged by the experts in the fields and the organizations that support science and special education teachers. The National Research Council (NRC), the Next Generation Science Standards (NGSS), and the National Council for the Social Studies (NCSS) have all endorsed and highlighted the use of inquiry-based approaches as the preferred methods for instruction in science and social studies.

In addition to supporting inquiry instruction, each organization as well as a number of authors have attempted to frame and define what constitutes inquiry. Various terminology has been used to discuss inquiry as an instructional approach for students with disabilities in science and social studies including *investigative learning* (Scruggs et al., 2008), *scientific inquiry* (NRC, 2012), *guided inquiry* (Palincsar et al., 2000), *structured inquiry* (Scruggs et al., 1994), *inquiry-based learning* (Scruggs et al., 2008), *hands-on instruction* (Scruggs et al., 2011), and *inquiry arc* (NCSS, 2013), among other terms. Beyond the terminology of inquiry, experts and organizations (e.g., NRC and NCSS) in science and social studies education have theorized and described the teaching and learning practices that comprise inquiry as an instructional approach. The notion of inquiry-based instruction in science and social studies with supports (i.e., supported inquiry) is bolstered by research examining the effectiveness of inquiry-based instruction for students with disabilities. Supports used with inquiry are any practices or strategies that help scaffold students' learning during instruction or enhance learning opportunities. These supports can be established EBPs or those approaches and strategies that are backed by research.

Science-Based Inquiry Research

The NRC (2012) described a framework of scientific activity, which can be interpreted as teaching and learning practices associated with inquiry, as investigating, evaluating, and developing explanations. Aleixandre and Crujeiras (2017) expanded on the NRC scientific activity framework by describing practices associated with inquiry including: (a) asking questions, planning, observing, experimenting, and measuring (*investigating*); (b) arguing and critiquing (*evaluating*); and (c) imagining, posing hypotheses, predicting, and reasoning (*developing explanations*). The NRC (2012) and the NGSS (NGSS Lead State, 2013) both support the use of inquiry practice as a means to learn science content and to develop critical thinking skills (i.e., higher-order thinking skills).

For students with disabilities, various combinations of the inquiry practices described by NRC (2012) and Aleixandre and Crujeiras (2017) have been demonstrated to be possible through the teaching and learning dynamic. Multiple researchers have shown that students with disabilities can display science achievement through the use of inquiry. For example, inquiry-based instruction results in higher achievement in science when compared to textbook-based instruction for students with disabilities (McCarthy, 2005; Scruggs et al., 1993). Other researchers have found that inquiry can improve overall science achievement on standardized measures (Taylor et al., 2018) as well as longitudinally (Taylor et al., 2012), and can even support other skill development (e.g., self-determination, problem-solving skills) (Miller et al., 2015). Reviews of inquiry-based instruction in science have also noted that not all inquiry is the same, with its most successful implementation for students with disabilities including a number of scaffolds and supports (Mastropieri & Scruggs, 1992; Rizzo & Taylor, 2016; Scruggs et al., 1998).

Social Studies–Based Inquiry Research

In social studies, the use of inquiry was firmly established as a preferential method of instruction with the development of the College, Career, and Civic Framework for State Social Studies Standards (C3 Framework; NCSS, 2013). The C3 Framework encouraged the social studies education field to center inquiry-based instruction as the foundational approach for teaching and learning. Within the C3 Framework, the concept of an inquiry arc was described (NCSS, 2013). The inquiry arc is divided into four dimensions that include: (a) developing questions and planning inquiries, (b) applying interdisciplinary concepts and tools, (c) evaluating sources and using evidence, and (d) communicating conclusions and taking informed action. The development of the C3 Framework shifts the focus from traditional social studies teaching narratives or remembering names and dates in history to focus on students' ability "to know, analyze, explain, and argue about interdisciplinary challenges in our social world" (NCSS, 2013, p. 6). As noted by Cuenca (2020), the C3 Framework uses inquiry to support student development for sustainable civic life.

For students with disabilities in inclusive social studies classrooms, inquiry has been investigated as discipline-specific instruction from a historical perspective (Ciullo et al., 2020; Okolo & Ferretti, 2014). Prior to the establishment of the inquiry arc (NCSS, 2013), research supported the use of investigative learning or historical inquiry with additional support. For example, social studies instruction that incorporated inquiry has also included the use of (a) prepared curriculums (Scruggs et al., 2008), (b) anchor videos (Gersten et al., 2006), or (c) project-based learning (Ferretti & Okolo, 1996). All of the various uses of inquiry employed some combination of big ideas, conceptual framework learning, and/or small group and whole class discussion. Research on social studies inquiry since the establishment of the inquiry arc in the C3 Framework has focused on historical reasoning (De La Paz et al., 2017; De La Paz & Wissinger, 2016). Students were involved in the inquiry process in these studies by evaluating primary sources, forming claims for argumentation, locating supporting evidence, and writing to persuade audiences.

Higher-Order Thinking and Reasoning

Effective instruction in an inclusive classroom goes beyond foundational memorization and comprehension of content-area facts and concepts. Special education and general education teachers in middle and secondary science and social studies classrooms regularly examine complex topics and concepts that can be challenging for students with and without disabilities. Students are asked to explain main ideas, determine causes and effects, explain similarities and differences, develop informed arguments that address claims, and make decisions. As a result, students need instruction designed to facilitate critical thinking, deeper understanding, and application of content through scaffolded supports and explicit instructional steps (McLeskey et al., 2017). An effective method for addressing critical thinking and deeper understanding in an inclusive classroom is through the use of Strategic Instruction Model (SIM™) Content Enhancement Routines (CERs) that specifically address improving academic outcomes (Lenz et al., 2004).

Higher-Order Thinking and Reasoning (HOTR) CERs are evidence- and research-based ways to engage and support students in inclusive content-area classes as they respond to challenges in rigorous standards (e.g., Common Core State Standards [2010]; The College, Career, and Civic Life (C3) Framework [2013]; Next Generation Science Standards [Achieve, 2013]). HOTR CERs give teachers actionable ways to facilitate authentic inquiry and engage students with diverse learning needs in interactive dialogue about complex topics in science and social studies. HOTR CERs teach students how to make inferences from the content and connect content to other related facts and concepts through categorization and comparison. Students learn how to manipulate the content and put it together in new or novel ways, and then apply the content to find solutions to problems that appear within the topics learned. This development of thinking and reasoning skills leads to critical analysis and effective problem solving. All of the CERs provide students and teachers with a specific set of instructional steps that spell out an easy to recall acronym that students can apply to future learning opportunities. The instructional steps are organized within a visual device to organize the information.

Teachers using the CERs as an intervention tool follow an instructional sequence where they introduce the content to be learned, the purpose of the instructional device, and the expectations for the lesson. Then, teachers guide students through the co-construction of the visual device by following a set of linking steps that spell out an acronym. Finally, the teachers review the content represented in the device to determine the level of understanding that resulted from the instruction. As students use these HOTR routines within the classroom over time, they begin to self-regulate, utilizing the linking steps and higher-order thinking and reasoning skills in school-specific and real-life conditions.

Concept Comparison

The Concept Comparison Routine (Bulgren et al., 1995) is an instructional tool used to compare and contrast two or more critical concepts, events, or ideas. Teachers co-construct the comparison table using an explicit set of steps (see textbox 9.1). These linking steps prompt students to explore like and unlike characteristics and then create broader categories to help remember the similarities and differences of the content students are asked to compare (Bulgren, 2006). The routine also builds in a space for students to apply the information they learn to a new situation. Unlike other comparison tools like a Venn diagram or comparison matrix, the Concept Comparison table asks students to both categorize the like and unlike characteristics, provide a summary statement of the comparison, and apply the content to show understanding. These steps create lasting connections and provide for a deeper understanding of the content (Bulgren et al., 2009).

TEXTBOX 9.1. CONCEPT COMPARISON COMPARING LINKING STEPS

1. **C**ommunicate targeted concepts
2. **O**btain the overall concept
3. **M**ake a list of known characteristics
4. **P**in down like characteristics
5. **A**ssemble like categories
6. **R**ecord unlike characteristics
7. **I**dentify unlike categories
8. **N**ail down a summary
9. **G**o beyond the basics

Source: Bulgren et al. (1995).

In a science classroom, the teacher may choose to have students look at a larger concept like cells and then compare and categorize the characteristics of plant and animal cells. This comparison would involve working with students to determine like and unlike characteristics of each cell type and then creating larger categories to help students summarize their understanding of the characteristics. After summarizing their understanding of the cell types, students then demonstrate their understanding through a lab that explores the cell types under a microscope. They also might make physical models of cell types.

In social studies, students might be asked to understand the impact of two early leaders in US history through a comparison of their accomplishments and challenges. Students could take two leaders like Alexander Hamilton and Thomas Jefferson, identify characteristics that they share and those that make each person unique, categorize those characteristics, and then summarize their findings. Students would then demonstrate their understanding by evaluating which leader had the greatest impact on our history and why.

Question Exploration

Engaging science and social studies classrooms seek to find answers to critical questions posed within the content. The Question Exploration Routine (Bulgren et al., 2001) provides a scaffolded way to help students identify important vocabulary and break down a broad question into smaller, supporting questions. It allows students to first respond in smaller parts before formulating a more complex response. The steps of Question Exploration (see textbox 9.2) support foundational problem-solving skills that lead to higher-order thinking and reasoning. Not only do students learn how to take a complex question and break it into smaller parts before responding, they also learn how to apply what they learned to other questions or problems and relate what they learned to real-life situations (Bulgren et al., 2011).

TEXTBOX 9.2. QUESTION EXPLORATION ANSWER LINKING STEPS

1. **A**sk a critical question
2. **N**ote and explain key terms
3. **S**earch for supporting questions and answers
4. **W**ork out the main idea answer
5. **E**xplore the main idea within related area
6. **R**elate the idea to today's world

Source: Bulgren et al. (2001).

The core concepts and ideas within the Next Generation Science Standards (NGSS) align with essential and guiding questions that fit well within a device like the Question Exploration Routine. NGSS core idea LS4 examines biological evolution and students are asked, "How can there be so many similarities among organisms yet so many different kinds of plants, animals, and microorganisms?" When following the linking steps of the routine, the teacher and students using the device work together to identify essential vocabulary needed to respond to this question. They break down the question into smaller supporting questions. These supporting questions are then used to help formulate an answer to the essential question. Students following the steps of the routine also make connections between the content currently learned and previous instruction. In addition, they apply their new knowledge to a real-life situation.

Social studies curricula now incorporate the C3 Framework, which uses compelling and supporting questions to help students participate in a deeper inquiry of content. The Question Exploration Routine provides a strategic approach to help students work through an inquiry using compelling and supporting questions. When studying the Civil War, students examine the events leading up to the war and then major events and battles during the war. The compelling question for the unit might be, "Does Abraham Lincoln deserve to be called the 'Great Emancipator?'" Following the linking steps of the Question Exploration Routine, students needing more explicit instruction would be able to define key vocabulary and respond to a series of supporting questions that affirm and refute the compelling question. Students would then formulate a response to the compelling question using the supporting questions. Students might then be asked to look at abolitionist leaders during this period to determine if they better deserve the title of great emancipator. Finally, students would connect Lincoln's legacy to more recent leaders in the United States or elsewhere known for liberating a marginalized population.

Cause and Effect

Both science and social studies curricula ask students to examine events, concepts, and ideas through the process of analyzing cause-and-effect relationships. The Cause-and-Effect Routine (Bulgren, 2014) begins by asking students to explore the event provided by the teacher. The students follow explicit steps (see textbox 9.3) that guide the thinking and learning process. What makes this device powerful for higher-order thinking and reasoning is how it forces students to analyze the event and background information, whereas typical cause-and-effect graphic organizers simply ask students to identify causes and effects without a deeper analysis.

TEXTBOX 9.3. CAUSE-AND-EFFECT REASON LINKING STEPS

1. **R**estate the question
2. **E**xamine key terms
3. **A**nalyze critical event and background information
4. **S**pecify causes and connections
5. **O**rganize effects and connections
6. **N**ail down the answer

Source: Bulgren (2014).

Science classrooms frequently examine cause-and-effect relationships. For example, students might study weather phenomena and be asked to determine the major causes and effects of tornadoes. Using the Cause-and-Effect Routine, students would restate the event as a question such as, "What are the major causes and effects of tornadoes?" They would then identify key terms necessary to help complete the cause-and-effect guide. Terms like thunderstorm, wind shear, and updraft might need clarification for students to better understand the causes and effects of tornadoes. Next, students identify background information about the event itself and then describe it. From this background information, students identify the causes that lead to a tornado forming and then they identify the effects of a tornado once it touches down on the ground. Finally, the students use the information they gathered to answer the question.

Social studies is full of historical events and concepts containing cause-and-effect relationships. Students studying the Civil Rights Movement are asked to understand a number of cause-and-effect relationships related to the events of that time. One example would be the Bloody Sunday march from Selma to Montgomery, Alabama, to fight for voting rights. Students completing a cause-and-effect guide on this topic might ask, "What were the causes and effects of Bloody Sunday?" Key terms to define might include civil rights, nonviolent protest, and civil disobedience. Students would then gather background information about the event itself before considering the causes that led to the organization of the march from Selma to Montgomery. Then they would examine the effects of that day and how it influenced future marches and expanded voting rights.

Decision-Making

Another critical thinking skill vital to both science and social studies is decision-making. Bulgren (2018) noted that numerous national and state education standards in science and social studies emphasize decision-making skills like finding solutions to problems, "making choices, and constructing explanations" (p. 1). The Decision-Making Routine (Bulgren, 2018) provides students an opportunity to model these decision-making skills through a set of strategic steps (see textbox 9.4) that guide student thinking.

> ## TEXTBOX 9.4. DECISION-MAKING DECISION LINKING STEPS
>
> 1. **D**ecide the issue
> 2. **E**nter options
> 3. **C**reate a list of important information
> 4. **I**dentify reasons to support each option
> 5. **S**et rank for each reason
> 6. **I**dentify compromises or alternatives
> 7. **O**ffer a decision
> 8. **N**ame reasons for the decision
>
> *Source*: Bulgren (2018).

Experts in science use scientific evidence to examine options for addressing critical issues in areas like health or the environment. Examining science through issues is a way to connect the content and make it relatable to students. If students are studying renewable and nonrenewable resources, they might examine that topic with an issue like cars and fossil fuel consumption. Students use the decision-making guide linking steps to determine options, compromises, and alternatives that eventually lead to a decision about the topic. Options to address fossil fuel consumption with cars might include production of electric or hybrid vehicles, switching to mass transit, or increasing gas and oil prices to reduce consumption. Then, students list important information related to the topic of cars that burn fossil fuels. Students use this list to develop reasons to consider for each option and they rank the reasons by their importance in supporting the option. They also identify potential alternatives or compromises between the options. After following these steps, students come up with a decision and explain why they chose a particular option based on the information gathered.

In social studies classrooms, helping students break down options for an issue and developing an informed decision is a critical citizenship competency. Students could examine historical decisions made by leaders and use the decision-making guide as a way to better understand how people arrived at particular decisions. They could explore current political or social issues relevant to their own interests. For example, states have different ways for their citizens to vote in elections. Students could examine a few of these options and determine which option they support the most and why.

Cross-Curricular Argumentation

Science and social studies curricula are full of claims where students are asked to provide arguments and evidence to support or reject the claim. The Cross-Curricular Argumentation (Bulgren, 2020) guide provides steps (see textbox 9.5) that students follow to examine a claim. Similar to the other higher-order thinking and reasoning routines, cross-curricular argumentation requires students to deeply examine the content and develop reasoning based on evidence collected.

TABLE 9.5. CROSS-CURRICULAR CLAIMS LINKING STEPS

1. **C**larify the claim with any clarifier and define key terms
2. **L**ist the evidence
3. **A**nalyze the reasoning
4. **I**dentify other arguments for or against the claim
5. **M**ake a judgment about the quality of evidence, the reasoning, and other arguments
6. **S**tate why you accept or reject the claim

Source: Bulgren (2020).

Science and social studies teachers use claims to spark curiosity in our students. Claims create opportunities for students to explain how something works or why something happens, or to determine between truth and opinion within a claim. Students learn how to think like a scientist by identifying the claim, examining evidence and the reasoning used to support or refute a claim, determining the presence of additional arguments for or against the claim, and making a final judgment based on all of the information. For example, a science class might look at the claim that masks prevent the spread of an airborne virus. Similarly, a social studies class might examine the claim that mask mandates violate a person's personal freedom. Examining an issue like masks through the lens of different content-area disciplines provides students with information to make informed arguments and decisions.

Debate is an important part of inquiry-based social studies classrooms. All debates start with a claim and the Cross-Curricular Argumentation guide provides a tool for students to clearly break down their understanding of the topic and the reasoning behind their arguments. If students want to have a debate on the merits of masks and mask mandates to prevent spread of an airborne virus, the Cross-Curricular Argumentation guide provides the explicit steps needed to make an informed argument on the topic.

Key Points

The use of higher-order thinking skills and inquiry are essential in learning science and social studies. While it would be difficult to call the research on inquiry-based instruction in science and social studies for students with disabilities abundant, there is enough support to suggest that using an inquiry-based instructional process can be successful. It should be noted that inquiry alone may not be enough to propel students with disabilities in inclusive science and social studies classrooms to success. Encouraging students to use higher-order thinking works in tandem with inquiry. Inquiry-based instruction has been shown to be more effective when paired with additional strategies in both science and social studies (De La Paz & Wissinger, 2016; Rizzo & Taylor, 2016; Scruggs et al., 2008; Scruggs et al., 2011). Content Enhancement Routines provide both higher-order inquiry-based processes layered with explicit strategy steps for implementation (Bulgren et al., 2007). Content acquisition interventions have been used to support inquiry and science and social studies achievement for students with disabilities. These strategies have included organizational visual support (e.g., graphic organizers), mnemonic strategies (i.e., letter, keyword, pegword, acrostic), and/or peer-related strategies (e.g., classwide peer tutoring).

CONTENT ACQUISITION INTERVENTIONS IN SCIENCE AND SOCIAL STUDIES

Mnemonics

Mnemonic devices are learning strategies used to assist students with recall, connection making, and association. As expressed by Bellezza (1981), mnemonic strategies support the learning processes of organization, categorization, recall, visual support, language learning, and rehearsal. These strategies help students with "developing better ways to take in (encode) information so that it will be much easier to remember (retrieve)" for later use (Mastropieri & Scruggs, 1998, p. 202). The authors also noted that mnemonics are not meant to be a curricular method or approach or a means for comprehension but are specifically designed to support memory (Mastropieri & Scruggs, 1998). Putnam (2015) details a number of types of mnemonics including peg system (i.e., pegword), keyword, and acronym. Research on using mnemonics in science has focused on three types of mnemonic methods: keyword, pegword, and letter strategies. Keyword strategies focus on linguistics, usually tied to subject-area vocabulary, where new concepts are associated with familiar words and/or phrases. Pegword strategies are similar to keyword strategies with the added dimension of learning information that has a numerical order or sequence that is chronological. Letter strategies (i.e., acronym or acrostic) focus on the use of acronyms that spell a meaningful word or phrase. Wilson and Moffat (2014) posited that letter mnemonic strategies are effective because the information is chunked and that reduces the cognitive memory load for competing responses. As highlighted by Scruggs and Mastropieri (2000) and Mastropieri and Scruggs (2011), mnemonic strategies have been highly effective in science and social studies instruction for students with disabilities, especially related to recall of content-related facts and vocabulary.

Science-Based Mnemonics Research

The use of mnemonic strategies in science instruction has a long, well-established history. Numerous studies and meta-analytic reviews have firmly supported the use of mnemonics to teach science facts and vocabulary (Scruggs et al., 2008; Scruggs et al., 2011; Therrien et al., 2011). Specifically, Mastropieri et al. (1988) taught science vocabulary to students with EBD using keyword mnemonics with significantly higher results than students who only had flash cards with science vocabulary definitions. King-Sears et al. (1992) also focused on students with EBD and successfully used pegword mnemonics to teach science vocabulary by pairing each word with a picture. For students with LD, King-Sears et al. (1992) used a keyword mnemonic strategy, while Mastropieri et al. (1985; 1986) and Scruggs et al. (1985) used a combination of keyword and pegword strategies.

Social Studies–Based Mnemonics Research

The nature and complexity of social studies content has consistently been a challenge for students with disabilities (Lubin & Polloway, 2016). The high need to recall facts can prove to be overwhelming to students; thus, students with disabilities often experience problems with deciphering expository text from social studies readings (Hall et al., 2013; Letendre, 1993). The research on using mnemonics in social studies for students with disabilities has mostly focused on keyword and pegword strategies with success in teaching students state history (Mastropieri & Scruggs, 1989), state names and capitals (Mastropieri et al., 1992; 1994), and US presidents (Mastropieri et al., 1997).

Graphic Organizers

Graphic organizers are designed to be aids to understand concepts, and relationships between concepts and ideas. Graphic organizers allow students to compare and contrast concepts, differentiate between main ideas and supplementary information, and determine cause-and-effect relationships (Darch & Eaves, 1986). The visual aspect of graphic organizers supports students by providing a visual representation of relationships between concepts and ideas (Taylor & Hwang, 2020). As described by the IRIS Center (2020), graphic organizers can (a) show cause and effect, (b) compare and contrast, (c) describe, (d) sequence, (e) and classify items into groups.

Science-Based Graphic Organizer Research

A number of researchers have examined the efficacy of using graphic organizers for science-related content. For example, Carnahan and Williamson (2013) and Carnahan et al. (2016) used graphic organizers to support students with disabilities learning science content and in answering science-related questions. In a more specific example, Dexter et al. (2011) focused their analysis on graphic organizers specifically for students with LD in secondary grades. They found that when compared to other instructional aids, graphic organizers were significantly more successful in providing students with support in science content learning and science vocabulary.

Social Studies–Based Graphic Organizer Research

Various studies and analyses have confirmed the effectiveness of graphic organizers for students with disabilities learning social studies content. In their analysis of social studies interventions for students with EBD, Garwood (2018) found that computer-based graphic organizers effectively promote social studies learning. Research has also shown that main-idea-and-details type organizers are best when paired with social studies text for student retention of information (Boon et al., 2005). Furthermore, Ciullo et al. (2020) conducted a meta-analysis on social studies interventions for students with LD and found that graphic organizers had a large positive effect on achievement across grades.

Peer-Mediated Support Strategies

Peer-mediated support strategies entail the use of peers to assist in academic or behavioral support for students with disabilities. Support strategies that involve peers require teaching peers the academic, social, and/or communication outcomes that encourage skill development or school-based engagement that are desired for students with disabilities. Peer-mediated strategies can involve one or multiple peers and be implemented in multiple settings (Carter et al., 2014; DiSalvo & Oswald, 2002). Using peers as models and support for students with disabilities can happen in a number of ways including Classwide Peer Tutoring (CWPT; Maheady et al., 2001; Harper & Maheady, 2007), cross-age or same-age peer tutoring, Peer-Assisted Learning Strategies (PALS; Spencer et al., 2009), and Reciprocal Peer Tutoring (RPT).

Science-Based Peer-Mediated Strategies Research

The use of peer-mediated strategies in science has demonstrated varied examples of success across student categories. Mastropieri et al. (2006) used PALS for students with LD in a tiered support manner to meet the needs of individual students. For students with EBD, Bowman-Perrott et al. (2013) and Mastropieri et al. (2006) used peer tutoring and PALS strategies to improve science achievement. Additionally, Hudson et al. (2014), Jameson et al. (2008), and Jimenez et al. (2012) each used various peer-mediated strategies to support students with disabilities in science to correctly answer content and concept questions. Across those three studies, Taylor et al. (2020) found that peer-mediated strategies were moderately effective in improving science achievement for students with disabilities.

Social Studies–Based Peer-Mediated Strategies Research

In a review of social studies interventions for students the LD, Ciullo et al. (2020) found that peer-mediated strategies were moderately effective. Garwood (2018) did a review of social studies research for students with EBD. They found seventeen studies, five of which used peer-mediated strategies (i.e., CWPT and peer tutoring). They also reported strong effects in using peer-mediated strategies to support social studies learning—specifically, peer tutoring that required students with disabilities to summarize social studies facts to a peer (Garwood, 2018).

Key Points

In examining the most consistent and effective interventions and strategies that support students with disabilities in science and social studies classrooms, there is tremendous overlap. The three most consistent support strategies across the content areas are graphic organizers, mnemonic strategies, and peer-mediated strategies (see table 9.2 for summary of interventions). Each of the three interventions have been successful across grade ranges, settings, student support needs, and content material (i.e., vocabulary or content learning). Even with variations within strategy types, their effectiveness has been consistent. For example, there are multiple types of mnemonics (e.g., pegword, acrostic), yet each has been shown to be effective. Various types of graphic organizers (e.g., Venn diagrams; KWL charts) have significant research supporting their use for students with disabilities in both science and social studies settings. Lastly, peer-mediated strategies, including CWPT and PALS, have been used to great effect in supporting students with a wide variety of needs.

Table 9.2. Summary of Content Acquisition Interventions

Mnemonics	Graphic Organizers	Peer-Mediated Strategies
• Letter • Keyword • Pegword • Acrostic	• Cause and effect • Compare and contrast • Describe • Sequence • Classify	• Classwide Peer Tutoring (CWPT) • Peer-Assisted Learning Strategies (PALS) • Reciprocal Peer Tutoring (RPT)

CONCLUSION

The use of research and evidence-based strategies has been mandated by law and the zeitgeist of the educational moment to provide students with the most significant educational needs (i.e., students with disabilities) an opportunity to succeed in inclusive classrooms. These opportunities should not be limited to math and language arts. The need for the best practices in science and social studies is equally salient. These subjects are often neglected, however, it can be easily argued that science and social studies are just as vital for students, given the increasing prevalence of STEM careers as well as the fact that social and political events require an understanding of contexts that social studies knowledge can provide. In examining the general literacy and content acquisition interventions for science and social studies provided to students with disabilities, it is widely recognized that HLPs support positive outcomes. Promoting higher-order thinking skills and using supported inquiry can give teachers an opportunity to provide students with disabilities a foundation to build on in the content areas. Furthermore, using content acquisition interventions (mnemonics, graphic organizers, and peer-mediated strategies) can expand from the foundation to scaffold learning and include students with disabilities in general education science and social study classrooms.

REFERENCES

Aleixandre, M. P. J., & Crujeiras, B. (2017). Epistemic practices and scientific practices in science education. In K. S. Taber & B. B. Akpan (Eds.), *Science education: An international course companion* (pp. 69–80). Brill Sense.

Bellezza, F. S. (1981). Mnemonic devices: Classification, characteristics, and criteria. *Review of Educational Research, 51*(2), 247–75. https://www.jstor.org/stable/1170198

Boon, R. T., Fore III, C., Ayres, K., & Spencer, V. G. (2005). The effects of cognitive organizers to facilitate content-area learning for students with mild disabilities: A pilot study. *Journal of Instructional Psychology, 32*(2), 101–17. https://eric.ed.gov/?id=EJ774145

Bowman-Perrott, L., Davis, H., Vannest, K., Williams, L., Greenwood, C., & Parker, R. (2013). Academic benefits of peer tutoring: A meta-analytic review of single-case research. *School Psychology Review, 42*(1), 39–55. https://doi.org/10.1080/02796015.2013.12087490

Bulgren, J. A. (2006). Integrated content enhancement routines: Responding to the needs of adolescents with disabilities in rigorous inclusive secondary content classes. *TEACHING Exceptional Children, 38*(6), 54–58.

Bulgren, J. A. (2014). *Teaching cause and effect*. University of Kansas Center for Research on Learning.

Bulgren, J. A. (2018). *Teaching decision-making*. University of Kansas Center for Research on Learning.

Bulgren, J. A. (2020). *Cross-curricular argumentation*. University of Kansas Center for Research on Learning.

Bulgren, J., Deshler, D. D., & Lenz, B. K. (2007). Engaging adolescents with LD in higher order thinking about history concepts using integrated content enhancement routines. *Journal of Learning Disabilities, 40*(2), 121–33. https://doi.org/10.1177%2F00222194070400020301

Bulgren, J. A., Lenz, B. K., Deshler, D. D., & Schumaker, J. B. (2001). *The question exploration routine*. Edge Enterprises.

Bulgren, J. A., Lenz, K., Schumaker, J. B., & Deshler, D. D. (1995). *Concept comparison routine*. Edge Enterprises.

Bulgren, J. A., Marquis, J. G., Lenz, B. K., Deshler, D. D., & Schumaker, J. B. (2011). The effectiveness of the question-exploration routine for enhancing the content learning of secondary students. *Journal of Educational Psychology, 103*(3), 578–93.

Bulgren, J. A., Marquis, J. G., Lenz, B. K., Schumaker, J. B., & Deshler, D. D. (2009). Effectiveness of question exploration to enhance students' written expression of content knowledge and comprehension. *Reading & Writing Quarterly, 25*(4), 271–89.

Carnahan, C. R., & Williamson, P. S. (2013). Does compare-contrast text structure help students with autism spectrum disorder comprehend science text? *Exceptional Children, 79*(3), 347–63. https://doi.org/10.1177/001440291307900302

Carnahan, C. R., Williamson, P., Birri, N., Swoboda, C., & Snyder, K. K. (2016). Increasing comprehension of expository science text for students with autism spectrum disorder. *Focus on Autism and Other Developmental Disabilities, 31*(3), 208–20.

Carter, E. W., Asmus, J. M., & Moss, C. K. (2014). Peer support interventions to support inclusive schools. In J. McLeskey, F. Spooner, B. Algozzine, & N. L. Waldron (Eds.), *Handbook of effective inclusive schools: Research and practice* (pp. 387–404). Routledge.

Ciullo, S., Collins, A., Wissinger, D. R., McKenna, J. W., Lo, Y-L., & Osman, D. (2020). Students with learning disabilities in the social studies: A meta-analysis of intervention research. *Exceptional Children, 86*(4), 393–412. https://doi.org/10.1177%2F0014402919893932

Cook, B. G., & Odom, S. L. (2013). Evidence-based practices and implementation science in special education. *Exceptional Children, 79*(3), 135–44. https://doi.org/10.1177/001440291307900201

Cook, B. G., Tankersley, M., & Landrum, T. J. (2009). Determining evidence-based practices in special education. *Exceptional Children, 75*(3), 365–83. https://doi.org/10.1177%2F001440290907500306

Cook, B. G., Buysse, V., Klingner, J., Landrum, T. J., McWilliam, R. A., Tankersley, M., & Test, D. W. (2015). CEC's standards for classifying the evidence base of practices in special education. *Remedial and Special Education, 36*(4), 220–34. http://doi.org/10.1177/0741932514557271

Council for Exceptional Children. (2014). Council for exceptional children: Standards for evidence-based practices in special education. *TEACHING Exceptional Children, 46*(6), 206. http://doi.org/10.1177/0040059914531389

Cuenca, A. (2020). Proposing core practices for social studies teacher education: A qualitative content analysis of inquiry-based lessons. *Journal of Teacher Education, 72*(3), 298–313. https://doi.org/10.1177/0022487120948046

Darch, C., & Eaves, R. C. (1986). Visual displays to increase comprehension of high school learning-disabled students. *Journal of Special Education, 20*(3), 309–18. https://doi.org/10.1177/002246698602000305

De La Paz, S., & Wissinger, D. R. (2016). Improving the historical knowledge and writing of students with or at risk for LD. *Journal of Learning Disabilities, 5*(6), 658–671. https://doi.org/10.1177/0022219416659444

De La Paz, S., Monte-Sano, C., Felton, M., Croninger, R., Jackson, C., & Piantedosi, K. W. (2017). A historical writing apprenticeship for adolescents: Integrating disciplinary learning with cognitive strategies. *Reading Research Quarterly, 52*(1), 31–52. https://doi.org/10.1002/rrq.147

Dexter, D. D., Park, Y. J., & Hughes, C. A. (2011). A meta-analytic review of graphic organizers and science instruction for adolescents with learning disabilities: Implications for the intermediate and secondary science classroom. *Learning Disabilities Research & Practice, 26*(4), 204–13. https://doi.org/10.1111/j.1540-5826.2011.00341.x

DiSalvo, C. A., & Oswald, D. P. (2002). Peer-mediated interventions to increase the social interaction of children with autism: Consideration of peer expectancies. *Focus on Autism and Other Developmental Disabilities, 17*(4), 198–207. https://doi.org/10.1177/10883576020170040201

Ferretti, R. P., & Okolo, C. M. (1996). Authenticity in learning: Multimedia design projects in the social studies for students with disabilities. *Journal of Learning Disabilities, 29*(5), 450–60. https://doi.org/10.1177%2F002221949602900501

Garwood, J. D. (2018). Literacy interventions for secondary students formally identified with emotional and behavioral disorders: Trends and gaps in the research. *Journal of Behavioral Education, 27*, 23–52. http://doi.org/10.1007/s10864-017-9278-3

Gersten, R., Baker, S. K., Smith-Johnson, J., Dimino, J., & Peterson, A. (2006). Eyes on the prize: Teaching complex historical content to middle school students with learning disabilities. *Exceptional Children, 72*(3), 264–80. https://doi.org/10.1177%2F001440290607200301

Gersten, R., Fuchs, L. S., Compton, D., Coyne, M., Greenwood, C., & Innocenti, M. S. (2005). Quality indicators for group experimental and quasi-experimental research in special education. *Exceptional Children, 71*(2), 149–164. https://doi.org/10.1177%2F001440290507100202

Hall, C., Kent, S. C., McCulley, L., Davis, A., & Wanzek, J. (2013). A new look at mnemonics and graphic organizers in the secondary social studies classroom. *TEACHING Exceptional Children, 46*(1), 47–55. https://doi.org/10.1177/004005991304600106

Harper, G. F., & Maheady, L. (2007). Peer-mediated teaching and students with learning disabilities. *Intervention in School and Clinic, 43*(2), 101–7. https://doi.org/10.1177/10534512070430020101

Horner, R. H., Carr, E. G., Halle, J., McGee, G., Odom, S., & Wolery, M. (2005). The use of single-subject research to identify evidence-based practice in special education. *Exceptional Children, 71*(2), 165–79. https://doi.org/10.1177/001440290507100203

Hudson, M. E., Browder, D. M., & Jimenez, B. A. (2014). Effects of a peer-delivered system of least prompts intervention and adapted science read-alouds on listening comprehension for participants with moderate intellectual disability. *Education and Training in Autism and Developmental Disabilities, 49*(1), 60–77. https://www.jstor.org/stable/23880655

Individuals with Disabilities Education Act, 20 U.S.C. § 1400 (2004).

IRIS Center. (2020). Graphic organizers. https://iris.peabody.vanderbilt.edu/module/ss2/cresource/q1/p02/

Jameson, J. M., McDonnell, J., Polychronis, S., Riesen, T., & Taylor, S. J. (2008). Embedded, constant time delay instruction by peers without disabilities in general education classrooms. *Intellectual and Developmental Disabilities, 46*(5), 346–63. https://doi.org/10.1352/2008.46:346-363

Jimenez, B. A., Browder, D. M., Spooner, F., & Dibiase, W. (2012). Inclusive inquiry science using peer-mediated embedded instruction for students with moderate intellectual disability. *Exceptional Children, 78*(3), 301–17. https://doi.org/10.1177%2F001440291207800303

Kennedy, M. J., Cook, L., Cook, B., Brownell, M. T., & Holdheide, L. (2020). Special video: Clarifying the relationship between HLPs and EBPs. Council for Exceptional Children. https://highleveragepractices.org/clarifying-relationship-between-hlps-and-ebps

King-Sears, M. E., Mercer, C. D., & Sindelar, P. T. (1992). Toward independence with keyword mnemonics: A strategy for science vocabulary instruction. *Remedial and Special Education, 13*(5), 22–33. https://doi.org/10.1177/074193259201300505

Lenz, B. K., Bulgren, J. A., Kissam, B. R. , & Taymans, J. (2004). SMARTER planning for academic diversity. In B. K. Lenz, D. D. Deshler, with B. R. Kissam (Eds.), *Teaching content to all: Evidence-based inclusive practices in middle and secondary schools* (pp. 47–77). Pearson.

Letendre, W. (1993). Mnemonic instruction with regular and special education students in social studies. *Southern Social Studies Journal, 18*(2), 25–37.

Lowrey, K. A., Hollingshead, A., Howery, K., & Bishop, J. B. (2017). More than one way: Stories of UDL and inclusive classrooms. *Research and Practice for Persons with Severe Disabilities, 42*(4), 225–242. https://doi.org/10.1177/1540796917711668

Lubin, J., & Polloway, E. A. (2016). Mnemonic instruction in science and social studies for students with learning problems: A review. *Learning Disabilities: A Contemporary Journal, 14*(2), 207–24. http://files.eric.ed.gov/fulltext/EJ1118431.pdf

Maheady, L., Harper, G. F., & Mallette, B. (2001). Peer-mediated instruction and interventions and students with mild disabilities. *Remedial and Special Education, 22*(1), 4–14. https://doi.org/10.1177/074193250102200102

Mastropieri, M. A., & Scruggs, T. E. (1989). Mnemonic social studies instruction: Classroom applications. *Remedial and Special Education, 10*(3), 40–46. https://doi.org/10.1177/074193258901000308

Mastropieri, M. A., & Scruggs, T. E. (1992). Science for students with disabilities. *Review of Educational Research, 62*(4), 377–411. https://doi.org/10.3102/00346543062004377

Mastropieri, M. A., & Scruggs, T. E. (1998). Enhancing school success with mnemonic strategies. *Intervention in School and Clinic, 33*(4), 201–8. https://doi.org/10.1177%2F105345129803300402

Mastropieri, M. A., Scruggs, T. E., & Levin, J. R. (1986). Direct vs. mnemonic instruction: Relative benefits for exceptional learners. *Journal of Special Education, 20*(3), 299–308. https://doi.org/10.1177/002246698602000304

Mastropieri, M. A., Scruggs, T. E., & Whedon, C. (1997). Using mnemonic strategies to teach information about US presidents: A classroom-based investigation. *Learning Disability Quarterly, 20*(1), 13–21. https://doi.org/10.2307/1511089

Mastropieri, M. A., Scruggs, T. E., Bakken, J. P., & Brigham, F. J. (1992). A complex mnemonic strategy for teaching states and their capitals: Comparing forward and backward associations. *Learning Disabilities Research & Practice, 7*(2), 96–103.

Mastropieri, M. A., Scruggs, T. E, Whittaker, M. E. S., & Bakken, J. P. (1994). Applications of mnemonic strategies with students with mild mental disabilities. *Remedial and Special Education, 15*(1), 34–43. https://doi.org/10.1177/074193259401500106

Mastropieri, M. A., Scruggs, T. E., Levin, J. R., Gaffney, J., & McLoone, B. (1985). Mnemonic vocabulary instruction for learning disabled students. *Learning Disability Quarterly, 8*(1), 57–63. https://doi.org/10.2307/1510908

Mastropieri, M. A., Scruggs, T. E., Norland, J. J., Berkeley, S., McDuffie, K., Tornquist, E. H., & Connors, N. (2006). Differentiated curriculum enhancement in inclusive middle school science: Effects on classroom and high-stakes tests. *Journal of Special Education, 40*(3), 130–7. https://doi.org/10.1177/00224669060400030101

McCarthy, C. B. (2005). Effects of thematic-based, hands-on science teaching versus a textbook approach for students with disabilities. *Journal of Research in Science Teaching, 42*(3), 245–63. https://doi.org/10.1002/tea.20057

McDuffie, K. A., & Scruggs, T. E. (2008). The contributions of qualitative research to discussions of evidence-based practice in special education. *Intervention in School and Clinic, 44*(2), 91–97. https://doi.org/10.1177/1053451208321564

McLeskey, J., Barringer, M-D., Billingsley, B., Brownell, M., Jackson, D., Kennedy, M., Lewis, T., Maheady, L., Rodriguez, J., Scheeler, M. C., Winn, J., & Ziegler,

D. (2017). *High-leverage practices in special education.* Council for Exceptional Children & CEEDAR Center.

Miller, B., Doughty, T., & Krockover, G. (2015). Using science inquiry methods to promote self-determination and problem-solving skills for students with moderate intellectual disability. *Education and Training in Autism and Developmental Disabilities, 50*(3), 356–68.

National Council for the Social Studies [NCSS] (2013). *The college, career, and civic life (C3) framework for social studies state standards: Guidance for enhancing the rigor of K–12 civics, economics, geography, and history.* NCSS.

National Research Council. (2012). *A framework for K–12 science education: Practices, crosscutting concepts, and core ideas.* National Academies.

NGSS Lead State (2013). The next generation science standards: Executive summary. https://www.nextgenscience.org/sites/default/files/Final%20Release%20NGSS%20Front%20Matter%20-%206.17.13%20Update_0.pdf

Okolo, C. M., & Ferretti, R. (2014). History instruction for students with learning disabilities. In H. L. Swanson, K. Harris, & S. Graham (Eds.), *Handbook of learning disabilities* (2nd ed., pp. 462–86). Guilford.

Palincsar, A. S., Collins, K. M., Marano, N. L., & Magnusson, S. J. (2000). Investigating the engagement and learning of students with learning disabilities in guided inquiry science teaching. *Language, Speech, and Hearing Services in Schools, 31*(3), 240–51. https://doi.org/10.1044/0161-1461.3103.240

Putnam, A. L. (2015). Mnemonics in education: Current research and applications. *Translational Issues in Psychological Science, 1*(2), 130–39. https://doi.org/10.1037/tps0000023

Rizzo, K. L., & Taylor, J. C. (2016). Effects of inquiry-based instruction on science achievement for students with disabilities: An analysis of the literature. *Journal of Science Education for Students with Disabilities, 19*(1), 2. http://doi.org/10.14448/jsesd.09.0001

Scruggs, T. E., & Mastropieri, M. A. (2000). The effectiveness of mnemonic instruction for students with learning and behavior problems: An update and research synthesis. *Journal of Behavioral Education, 10*(2), 163–73. https://psycnet.apa.org/record/2001-11204-006

Scruggs, T. E., Mastropieri, M. A., & Boon, R. (1998). Science education for students with disabilities: A review of recent research. *Studies in Science Education, 32*(1), 21. https://doi.org/10.1080/03057269808560126

Scruggs, T. E., Mastropieri, M. A., & Marshak, L. I. S. A. (2011). Science and social studies. In J. M. Kauffman & D. P. Hallahan, D. P. (Eds.), *Handbook of special education* (pp. 445–55). Routledge.

Scruggs, T. E., Mastropieri, M. A., & Okolo, C. M. (2008). Science and social studies for students with disabilities. *Focus on Exceptional Children, 41*(2), 1–24. https://doi.org/10.17161/foec.v41i2.6835

Scruggs, T. E., Mastropieri, M. A., & Sullivan, G. S. (1994). Promoting relational thinking: Elaborative interrogation for students with mild disabilities. *Exceptional Children, 60*, 45–57. https://www.researchgate.net/scientific-contributions/Thomas-E-Scruggs-35534331/publications/2

Scruggs, T., Mastropieri, M., Bakken, J., & Brigham, F. J. (1993). Reading versus doing: The relative effects of textbook-based and inquiry-oriented approaches to science learning in special education classrooms. *Journal of Special Education, 27*(1), 1–15. https://doi.org/10.1177/002246699302700101

Scruggs, T. E., Mastropieri, M. A., Berkeley, S., & Graetz, J. E. (2010). Do special education interventions improve learning of secondary content? A meta-analysis. *Remedial and Special Education, 31*(6), 437–49.

Scruggs, T. E., Mastropieri, M. A., Levin, J. R., & Gaffney, J. S. (1985). Facilitating the acquisition of science facts in learning disabled students. *American Educational Research Journal, 22*(4), 575–586. https://doi.org/10.3102/00028312022004575

Shanahan, C., Shanahan, T., & Misischia, C. (2011). Analysis of expert readers in three disciplines: History, mathematics, and chemistry. *Journal of Literacy Research, 43*(4), 393–429. http://doi.org/10.1177/1086296X11424071

Simonsen, B., Myers, D., & DeLuca, C. (2010). Teaching teachers to use prompts, opportunities to respond, and specific praise. *Teacher Education and Special Education, 33*(4), 300–318. http://doi.org/10.1177/0888406409359905

Simonsen, B., Fairbanks, S., Briesch, A., Myers, D., & Sugai, G. (2008). Evidence-based practices in classroom management: Considerations for research to practice. *Education and Treatment of Children, 31*(3), 351–80. http://doi.org/10.1353/etc.0.0007

Spencer, V. G., Simpson, C. G., & Oatis, T. L. (2009). An update on the use of peer tutoring and students with emotional and behavioural disorders. *Exceptionality Education International, 19*(1). https://doi.org/10.5206/eei.v19i1.7634

Spires, H. A., Kerkhoff, S. N., & Graham A. (2016). Disciplinary literacy and inquiry: Teaching for deeper content learning. *Journal of Adolescent and Adult Literacy, 60*(2), 151–61. https://doi.org/10.1002/jaal.577

Taylor, J. C., & Hwang, J. (2021). Science, technology, engineering, arts, and mathematics remote instruction for students with disabilities. *Intervention in School and Clinic, 57*(2), 111–18. http://doi.org/10.1177/10534512211001858

Taylor, J. C., Hwang, J., Rizzo, K. L., & Hill, D. A. (2020). Supporting science-related instruction for students with intellectual and developmental disabilities: A review and analysis of research studies. *Science Educator, 27*(2), 102–13. https://eric.ed.gov/?id=EJ1259835

Taylor, J. C., Tseng, C-M., Murillo, A., Therrien, W., & Hand, B. (2018). Using argument-based science inquiry to improve science achievement for students with disabilities in inclusive classrooms. *Journal of Science Education for Students with Disabilities, 21*(1), 1–14. http://doi.org/10.14448/jsesd.10.0001

Taylor, J. C., Therrien, W. J., Kaldenberg, E., Watt, S., Chanlen, N., & Hand, B. (2012). Using an inquiry-based teaching approach to improve science outcomes for students with disabilities: Snapshot and longitudinal data. *Journal of Science Education for Students with Disabilities, 15*(1), 27–39. http://doi.org/10.14448/jsesd.04.0003

Therrien, W. J., Taylor, J. C., Hosp, J. L., Kaldenberg, E. R., & Gorsh, J. (2011). Science instruction for students with learning disabilities: A meta-analysis. *Learning Disabilities Research & Practice, 26*(4), 188–203. https://doi.org/10.1111/j.1540-5826.2011.00340.x

Therrien, W. J., Taylor, J. C., Watt, S., & Kaldenberg, E. R. (2014). Science instruction for students with emotional and behavioral disorders. *Remedial and Special Education, 35*(1), 15–27. https://doi.org/10.1177/0741932513503557

Wilson, B., & Moffat, N. (Eds.). (2014). *Clinical management of memory problems* (2nd ed.). Psychology Press. https://doi.org/10.4324/9781315774800

10

Quality Behavior Instruction: Classroom Management

Ashley MacSuga-Gage, Jasmine Justus,
Nicholas A. Gage, and Brittany Batton

CLASSROOM MANAGEMENT IS CRITICAL for student success at all grade levels. Research suggests that all students, particularly students with disabilities (SWD), have better social, behavioral, and academic outcomes in well-managed classrooms (Gage et al., 2017; Korpershoek et al., 2016; Oliver et al., 2011). These skills increase student engagement, decrease student problem behaviors, explicitly teach students what they should be doing during classroom activities, and reinforce students when they've demonstrated appropriate behaviors. Further, when teachers use effective, evidence-based classroom management skills (CMS; Simonsen et al., 2008; US Department of Education, Office of Special Education Programs [US DOE OSEP], 2016), they report higher job satisfaction and lower burnout (Aloe et al., 2014; Klassen & Chiu, 2010). Thus, it is imperative that all teachers learn and use evidence-based classroom management skills in their classrooms.

This chapter describes a series of evidence-based classroom management skills all teachers should use during instruction. These skills are considered universal prevention practices, meaning that the skills are designed to prevent problem behaviors from occurring and can and should be used frequently for all students across all instructional contexts. First, we provide a brief description of the theoretical foundations of evidence-based classroom management. Next, we will describe how classroom management aligns with relevant educational policy and professional standards of educational practice. We then describe, with actionable detail, a series of evidence-based classroom management practices organized into five domains, explaining how to: (a) maximize classroom structure; (b) post, teach, review, monitor, and reinforce positively stated rules and expectations; (c) actively engage students in observable ways; (d) establish a continuum of acknowledging appropriate behaviors; and (e) establish a continuum of strategies to respond to inappropriate behaviors (Myers et al., 2020; Simonsen et al., 2008; Simonsen & Myers, 2014). The practices within each of the five domains have extensive evidence demonstrating their effectiveness and align with recommendations by the US Department of Education's Office of Special Education Programs (2016). We will then highlight some of the limitations of the research and practice in classroom management and suggest opportunities for advancing classroom management practice in the future. The primary goal of this chapter is to provide an overview of the critical features of evidence-based classroom management skills. As such, we organize each classroom management skill as follows: (a) description of the skill; (b) brief research support; (c) how to implement the skill; and (d) resources for additional support.

THEORETICAL FOUNDATIONS OF EVIDENCE-BASED CLASSROOM MANAGEMENT

There is no one single overarching theory of learning; this is true for learning mathematics equations, improving reading comprehension, studying American history, and acquiring new prosocial behaviors and social skills. Instead, there are a number of different learning theories that are used to explain or understand how learning occurs. It is important to note that a theory, by definition, is neither a philosophy nor a law. A philosophy of learning or education is an overall value system that must be logically consistent. A law is a description of natural phenomena that are always observed to be consistent. A law describes the phenomenon but does not describe *why* it occurs. For example, Newton's law of gravitation describes the phenomenon of gravity but does not state *why* gravity works as it does. Theory is an explanation of an observed phenomenon that should always be supported by empirical evidence. In other words, a theory describes why something occurs based on the best available evidence. Thus, a philosophy is a value system that does not require evidence; a law is a phenomenon that always occurs; and a theory is a description of why a phenomenon occurs.

With regard to learning, there are philosophies and theories but no laws. By that, we mean that nothing is always true of human behavior, unlike, say gravity or thermodynamics. Therefore, to understand how and why learning occurs, we rely on logic and empirical evidence. Philosophies of learning have a history going back to the works of Plato and Aristotle. Plato (428–327 BCE) argued that knowledge was innate at birth, and the role of teachers is to "draw out" that knowledge. On the other hand, Aristotle (470–399 BCE) argued that knowledge was outside of us and that we use our senses to gather that knowledge. Skipping ahead hundreds of years, John Locke (1632–1704) argued in favor of Aristotle and suggested that humans are born with a "tabula rasa" or "blank slate," and through experiences, humans develop knowledge. In fact, learning has been an important topic in philosophy. These are only a few of the many philosophies of learning, with additional arguments forwarded in the twentieth century by the likes of John Dewey (1916) and Van Cleve Morris (1966). In essence, the fundamental component of these philosophies is that they are logically consistent with particular definitions of reality, nature, and knowledge (i.e., epistemology and ontology) but not necessarily empirically tested. By empirically tested, we mean derived from experience, experiment, and observation rather than by logic. Many philosophies of learning cannot be observed (i.e., we cannot see or measure the existence of the "tabula rasa") but instead stand as cogent intellectual arguments about knowledge and learning.

Theories of learning identify real-world events that result in learning. Unlike philosophies, theories must be tested through research, resulting in specific principles of learning and identification of events that support or result in learning. Currently, there are a number of theories of learning that have direct application to classroom instruction and classroom management. We will briefly focus on three of these here (see Schunk, 2019 for a complete review of learning theory in education): (a) behaviorism, (b) social cognitive theory, and (c) constructivism. Below, we very briefly describe each.

Behaviorism originates with the works of Thorndike's (1874–1949) connectionism and Pavlov's (1849–1936) classical conditioning but was expanded by Skinner's (1904–1990) operant conditioning. In essence, classical conditioning occurs when an unconditioned stimulus and response are manipulated with a conditioned stimulus to create a conditioned response. In contrast, operant conditioning is a controlled response with reinforcement/punishment systems according to the behavior. Behaviorism in the classroom is aligned with operant conditioning, which posits that behaviors are preceded by an antecedent and followed by a consequence (reinforcement or punishment). These three terms (antecedent, behavior, consequence) provide the basis for learning and identifying the function of a behavior. By function, we mean the "why" a behavior occurs. From a classroom management perspective, identifying the function of a problem behavior, or why the behavior is occurring, can lead to an intervention to change either the antecedent or the consequence and decrease the likelihood the problem behavior occurs. From a behavioral perspective, all behavior is functionally related to the teaching environment. To change behavior, the teacher needs to change the environment. Most evidence-based classroom management described here is based on a behavioral theory of learning.

One limitation of behaviorism is the explicit focus on only those things that can be observed and measured. There is no focus on what may or may not be happening in a child's brain as they learn. Most theories of learning that have been developed after behaviorism focus on the cognitive processes, or what mental processes may be cognitive during the learning process. The first of these is social cognitive theory. Based on the work of Albert Bandura (1986), the founding premise was that behavior could be learned through observation alone and that reinforcement is not always necessary. Instead, Bandura postulated that learning occurs through a framework of triadic reciprocity, with interactions among behaviors, the environment, and personal factors, including cognitive processes and self-efficacy, or beliefs about one's capabilities to implement actions. Learning occurs either *inactively* through actual doing or *vicariously* by observing models perform behaviors. Self-regulation then, is the process by which individuals activate and sustain behaviors learned inactively or vicariously. Key concepts regarding classroom management from a social cognitive perspective are modeling skills and opportunities for practice and building student self-efficacy and self-regulation skills.

Unlike both behaviorism and social cognitivism, constructivist theories of learning do not place emphasis on the environment but, instead, contend that learning is a process of constructing knowledge (Schunk, 2019). Constructivism has its roots in the work of Piaget and Vygotsky, two important child development psychologists. Piaget's work focused on the developmental stages of children and how learning is interrelated to a child's particular stage of development. Learning occurs when children experience cognitive conflicts, defined as an event that produces a disruption in the child's cognitive structures so that the child's beliefs do not match the observed reality and engage in assimilation, partially understood, or accommodation promotes structural change, to construct or alter internal structures. Vygotsky's work focused on the important role of social interactions and the cocreation of knowledge between individuals. For students, the critical component of learning is the zone of proximal development, or "the distance between the actual developmental level as determined by independent problem- solving and the level of potential development as determined through problem-solving under adult guidance or in collaboration with more capable peers" (Vygotsky, 1978, p. 86). At its core, the key assumption of constructivism is that people are active learners and develop knowledge for themselves. Thus, classroom management in a constructivist classroom is focused on student involvement in the management process where students control their learning. We will focus here on discrete, actionable teacher-led classroom management and less on constructivist management approaches. That being said, these two approaches need not be in opposition. For example, the Responsive Classroom®, a universal social-emotional learning program that includes classroom management, is based on a constructivist approach but incorporates most of the evidence-based classroom management skills described below (see Center for Responsive Schools, n.d.).

RELEVANT EDUCATIONAL POLICY ASSOCIATED WITH CLASSROOM MANAGEMENT

There is no explicit federal or state policy related to how teachers conduct classroom management. However, there is policy related to creating safe and supportive classroom environments that reduce the likelihood of disciplinary exclusions, such as office discipline referrals and in- and out-of-school suspension. The most recent reauthorization of the Elementary and Secondary Education Act of 1965, now called the Every Student Succeeds Act (ESSA, 2015), does include explicit language about school discipline, particularly exclusions. First, under Title I, schools are required to describe how they will improve "school conditions for student learning" (Section 1111. "State Plans") that includes plans to reduce the disciplinary practices that remove students from their classroom. Removing students as discipline for rule violation limits those students' access to the curriculum, thus reducing their learning opportunities. Second, under Title IV, districts that seek funding must assess their school conditions and their need for funds to create healthy learning environments. To receive Title IV funds, districts must create plans to foster safe, healthy, supportive, and drug-free environments that support academic achievement. A cornerstone of creating such environments is the use of universal, evidence-based classroom management.

The Individuals with Disabilities Education Act (IDEA, 2004), which provides legal and procedural protections for students with disabilities, does not describe how classroom management should be enacted but does make clear that universal, preventative approaches, which include evidence-based classroom management, are necessary for students to receive a free appropriate public education (FAPE). A recent Dear Colleague letter from the US Department of Education (DOE), Office of Special Education and Rehabilitative Services (2016), highlighted concerns about disciplinary exclusions of students with disabilities, including office discipline referrals and in- and out-of-school suspensions. Noting concerns with regard to meeting IDEA's requirement that all students with disabilities receive a FAPE, the letter recommends positive behavior supports across a continuum, from universal classroom management to more intensive interventions. The letter then recommends school personnel consider evidence-based classroom management practices outlined by the DOE's Office of Special Education Programs (OSEP, 2015). These practices are aligned with those described below and include behavior-specific praise and prompting of expected behaviors.

State-level educational policy also targets educators' need to address behavior through classroom management. Freeman and colleagues (2014) examined state policies associated with classroom management in teacher preparation programs. They found that 84% of US states had explicit policy describing classroom management in teacher preparation programs for secondary teachers and 88% for elementary teachers. However, only 55% of US states explicitly required teachers to learn research-based classroom management. A few states outlined specific evidence-based classroom management strategies, such as teaching explicit behavior expectations.

CLASSROOM MANAGEMENT AND PROFESSIONAL STANDARDS OF EDUCATIONAL PRACTICE

Effective academic instruction is contingent on student engagement with that instruction. Students cannot learn if they are not paying attention. Classroom management is a critical component of increasing the likelihood students are engaged, paying attention, and learning. Thus, classroom and instructional management practices are a critical component of teaching and aligned with professional standards of practice. The largest professional organization for educators, the National Education Association, has established a series of micro-credentials for teachers focused on classroom management practices (https://www.nea.org/professional-excellence/student-engagement/classroom-management). These include addressing challenging behaviors, classroom expectations and routines, and organizing the physical layout of the classroom, all aligned with the practices described below.

The Council for Exceptional Children (CEC), the leading special education professional organization, has established professional standards for special educator development (2021). These standards promote active engagement and motivation during instruction and support social, emotional, and behavioral growth. Within these standards are specific components aligned with evidence-based classroom management, including increased opportunities to respond and effective routines and procedures. The CEC, in partnership with the OSEP-funded Collaboration for Effective Educator Development, Accountability, and Reform Center (CEEDAR Center), developed a set of high-leverage practices all special educators should be able to demonstrate (McLeskey et al., 2017). Among them are a series of social/emotional/behavioral high-leverage practices that establish a consistent, organized, and respectful learning environment and provide positive and constructive feedback to guide students' learning and behavior.

EVIDENCE-BASED CLASSROOM MANAGEMENT

We organize classroom management into five essential practices. While it is impossible to eliminate all problem behaviors in the classroom, these practices are designed to create a positive classroom environment in which students know the expectations, are aware of the possibility of reinforcement of appropriate behaviors, and are prepared to respond to problem behaviors when they do occur. These five essential practices include:

1. Maximize classroom structure.
2. Post, teach, review, monitor, and reinforce positively stated rules and expectations.
3. Actively engage students in observable ways.
4. Establish a continuum of acknowledging appropriate behaviors.
5. Establish a continuum of strategies to respond to inappropriate behaviors. (Knoster, 2015; OSEP, 2015; Simonson et al., 2008)

Each of these five practices is aligned with a behavioral theory of learning and the belief that behavior is functionally related to the environment (Skinner, 1953). Teachers serve as the models for appropriate behavior, create systems for reinforcing appropriate behavior, and address inappropriate behaviors as they occur. Through direct instruction to teach students behavioral expectations, routines and procedures, and social skills, students learn what is expected of them during instruction and how to self-manage their behaviors. Below, we provide (a) a description of the skill; (b) brief research support; (c) how to implement the skill; and (d) resources for additional support. We provide a real-world case example of what each of the practices might look like in a secondary classroom to describe how to implement the skill. The resources for additional support are provided in textbox 10.1 for all five practices.

Maximize Classroom Structure

Description of the Skill

Maximizing structure includes both the physical environment and the rituals and routines established for the classroom. Creating a predictable classroom environment that allows for easy active supervision and movement between instructional activities prevents problem behaviors. Creating and explicitly teaching classroom procedures, including pencil sharpening, requesting bathroom access, entrance, and exiting, etc., ensures that students understand how to enact daily routines. Research suggests that a highly predictable classroom environment reduces the likelihood of problem behavior and increases a positive classroom climate (Billingsley et al., 2020).

First, teachers need to consider the physical arrangement of the classroom. Expertly designed physical arrangements minimize opportunities for disruptions and problem behaviors. Consider, for example, a theme park or department store. They are arranged to ease traffic flow and create visual prompts for expected behaviors, such as signs telling patrons "Line Starts Here" or clearly marked paths to restrooms. These arrangements and visual cues are intentional to ensure customer safety and create environments that allow for efficient service. Intentional planning in the classroom can have similar returns on investment. First, educators should consider furniture arrangement in the room to facilitate movement during transitions and create seating arrangements consistent with the type of instruction planned for (e.g., whole or small group instruction). Further, educators need to make sure that they can adequately supervise all students from anywhere in the classroom. Active supervision is a technique where educators make conscious decisions about the number of verbal and physical interactions occurring during a lesson, as it has been shown that an increase in educator interaction can increase student engagement (Gage et al., 2017). Active supervision, particularly during student-led activities such as small group or lab activities, is critical for both prevention and intervening when necessary. Ensure that furniture, bookshelves, and the like do not block lines of sight. Second, if necessary, teachers should create defined student and educator spaces, clearly articulating where students are allowed and not allowed. For example, in a high school art classroom, there may be a supply closet or pottery space where only the teacher is allowed. Third, the teacher should consider the organization of materials and supplies. Educators should keep materials in an easily accessible location for access as needed by both students and teachers. A clean and well-organized classroom reduces clutter and increases access to instructional materials.

Next, teachers must establish predictable routines for both teachers and students. Teacher routines may include planning and grading, preparing for lessons, organizing materials, and communications with parents and caregivers as well as staff who may be working in the classroom, including paraprofessionals and substitutes. Routinizing teacher duties can reduce stress and create predictable environments. Student routines should include specific procedures for transitions, group work, accessing materials, expectations for assignments, asking for help or gaining the teacher's attention, doing lab work, etc. The more students are able to know what will happen and what will happen next, the less likely they are to be distracted and off task. Another important predictable routine is the procedure a teacher uses to quickly and effectively gain student attention. Unlike elementary settings where these attention signals may include "1-2-3 eyes on me" or other rhyming phrases, in the secondary classroom, attention signals may include regional or sports team calls. For example, in schools near the University of Missouri, a teacher may say, "M-I-Z" and students respond "Z-O-U" or in New York City, a teacher may say, "Hello, Brooklyn," and students respond, "How you do?" (from a Jay-Z song). Developing attention signals appropriate for the context can help teachers and students quickly transition and increase engagement.

Research Support

Students are more engaged and on task in highly structured classrooms (Bergsmann et al., 2013). When compared to chaotic or laissez-faire classrooms, students in classrooms with high structure experience positive educational outcomes (Bergsmann et al., 2013; Brooks, 1985; Brophy, 1986, 2006; Brophy & Good, 1986; Evertson & Weinstein, 2006; Huston-Stein et al., 1977; Wallace et al., 2014), including higher rates of on-task behavior engagement (Skinner & Belmont, 1993; Tucker et al., 2002). For example, Sierens and colleagues (2009) found higher levels of classroom structure were associated with higher levels of high school students' on-task behavior and classroom engagement. Similarly, Jang, Reeve, and Deci (2010) observed 133 high school classrooms and found that teacher-provided structure was significantly correlated with students' engagement with instruction.

Like classroom structure, attention signals included as part of a broader instructional approach do not isolate the impact (e.g., Direct Instruction curricula) (Engelmann & Carnine, 1982). Attention signals can be described as a vocal statement or predetermined sound that notifies the students to return their attention to the teacher (Kwok, 2019). An example would be a teacher stating "1, 2, 3 eyes on me," with the students then directing their attention to the teacher and stating "1, 2 eyes on you." Research suggests that teachers should consider using attention signals more. For example, Stichter and colleagues (2009) observed thirty-five classrooms and found, on average, that teachers rarely used attention signals (0.03 times per minute). Active supervision, on the other hand, has been examined. A recent meta-analysis, a study that analyzes the data from a multitude of studies, of the effects of active supervision on student behavior identified twelve studies and consistent positive relationships between increased active supervision and student on-task behavior (Gage et al., 2020).

How to Implement the Skill

In her eighth grade civics classroom of twenty students, Mrs. Taylor encourages lots of group work to discuss government and social situations and has designed her classroom accordingly. Student desks are placed in groups of four facing one another. There is ample space for movement between the five groups of four in the classroom. A station of four computers has also been set up in the back of the room for groups to conduct research. Mrs. Taylor has given the students many opportunities to practice transitions from whole group to small groups and given explicit routines for the activities completed during group work. Mrs. Taylor makes sure all materials are accessible in staked file holders, and students know where to obtain them before they break out into their groups. When Mrs. Taylor is about to dismiss students for their small groups, she repeats the directions for their assignment and then says, "All set?" The students respond with, "You bet!" Students stand up from their whole group area and walk to their small groups. Brittany forgets which group she is with today and walks to look at the chart on the whiteboard serving as a reminder. When she arrives at her group, her classmate hands her a copy of their worksheet, which was in the bin in the middle of the table. Brittany reaches into the table bin and pulls out a highlighter and a pencil that she needs for the assignment. Mrs. Taylor circulates through the classroom in an unpredictable pattern to supervise.

Post, Teach, Review, Monitor, and Reinforce Positively Stated Rules and Expectations

Description of the Skill

Explicit, brief, positively stated rules and expectations set the stage for classroom success. Telling students what is expected of them reduces ambiguity and, more importantly, limits students' ability to find loopholes or gray areas in rules targeting specific behaviors that should not occur. Rather than telling students what not to do, teachers define and teach the behaviors and expectations they want to see. Teachers should develop three to five positively stated, easy-to-remember expectations or use schoolwide expectations if available in the school. These expectations should be aligned with the kind of positive classroom climate the teacher wants to construct and lets all students know what they are to do. Focusing on three to five broad expectations increases the likelihood students will remember them and they can be used to define explicit, teachable behaviors associated with each expectation by classroom routine. Examples include "Be Safe, Be Respectable, Be Responsible" or "Respect Others, Manage Self, Solve Problems Responsibly." The expectations should then be posted for all to see and for reference in the classroom.

Once established and posted, the expectations must be taught. Simply posting the expectation on the wall for all to see is not enough. Teachers need to define what each expectation looks like, particularly what it looks like by classroom routine. One way to do this is to define rules operationally and organize them using a rules-and-routines matrix. An operational definition is a description of a behavior or set of behaviors that is clear and describes what the behavior looks like. For example, a classroom expectation may be "Respect Others," and an associated behavior maybe "keep hands and feet to yourself while seated for group work." An operationally defined rule explicitly describes the behaviors a student should exhibit. Then a rules-and-routines matrix provides a framework for organizing the expectations and operationally defined rules by routine. Typically, the routines, such as whole group instruction, small group instruction, classroom exiting, etc., are listed along the top, and the expectations are listed along the left side. Operationally defined rules are listed in boxes aligned with the routine and expectation (see table 10.1). There is no minimum or maximum number of rules recommended within each box, but most matrices include two to three rules per expectation and routine, with some rules repeating across routines.

Next, teachers must explicitly teach the rules. This should be done at the beginning of the school year and then repeated as needed throughout the year. A teacher's first assumption is that each rule must be taught; do not assume that students know how to enact each rule. Since the rules are operationally defined, brief, and connected to routines, lessons should be quick (less than 5 minutes), direct, and include modeling and practice. Once taught, it is imperative that teachers monitor and reinforce students when they demonstrate each rule. Monitoring expectations and tracking the frequency of student errors identifies rules in need of reteaching. Alongside monitoring errors is reinforcing successes of rule demonstrations. Reinforcement such as verbal praise ("great job keeping your hands to yourself") or a schoolwide token economy system will increase the likelihood students do the behavior again. Reinforcement should be frequent after the lesson and faded across time. The reinforcement should immediately follow the rule demonstration, and the students should know what rule they demonstrated resulting in the reinforcement.

Research Support

Research has examined the effectiveness of establishing, posting, teaching, and reinforcing behavioral expectations at the school and classroom level. At the school level, universal prevention in schoolwide positive behavior interventions and supports (SWPBIS) is largely based on establishing, posting, teaching, and reinforcing behavioral expectations. A meta-analysis by Lee and Gage (2020) reviewed experimental group design studies and found that schools implementing universal practices, particularly behavioral expectations, have statistically significantly fewer disciplinary exclusions, including office discipline referrals and out-of-school suspensions. A review by Alter and Haydon (2017) examined classroom rules and found that two of the most effective components are directly teaching rules and tying rules to positive consequences (i.e., reinforcement).

Table 10.1. Example Rules-and-Routines Matrix

		Routines				
		Entrance	Whole Group/ Direct Instruction	Independent Work	Small Group Work/Centers	Exiting
Expectations	Be Respectful	• Greet the teacher. • Say "Hello" to table neighbors.	• Have eyes on the teacher. • Raise your hand.	• Work quietly at your desk. • Complete your own work. • Answer all the questions.	• Have your "listening ears" on when other group members are speaking. • Stay with your group. • Use inside voices.	• Keep your hands and feet to yourselves. • Use inside voices.
	Be Responsible	• Place backpack next to or under desk. • Turn in last night's homework. • Write down tonight's homework in the agenda. • Talk quietly to neighbor.	• Follow directions. • Have all materials ready. • Listen during instruction.	• Follow directions. • Place completed assignment in the bin. • Give the teacher a thumbs-up so she can come to check your work.	• Complete your task. • Help the group.	• Line up quietly. • Have all materials ready.
	Be Safe	• Walk. • Sit at your desk.	• Keep your hands and feet to yourselves. • Stay in your seat.	• Stay in your seat. • Keep your hands and feet to yourselves. • Only have needed materials.	• Use materials carefully. • Keep your hands and feet to yourselves.	• Walk. • Shoes are tied before leaving.

How to Implement the Skill

On the first day of school, Ms. Jones sits with her ninth graders and reviews their schoolwide positive behavior expectations. These include "Be Responsible," "Be Safe," and "Be Respectful." She then sits down with her students and creates a list of classroom rules that align with the schoolwide expectations. The students, guided by Ms. Jones, come up with a list of three to five positively stated, operationally defined rules for each setting in the classroom (small group, independent work, whole group, transitions). If more than five rules are created, Ms. Jones makes suggestions for consolidation or allows the students to vote between two rules of her choosing. Following the establishment of the rules, Ms. Jones plans for extra transitions between work activities and demonstrates examples and non-examples of each rule. Ms. Jones takes data on the amount of time transitions take in her classroom and realizes the average length of a transition in her class is four minutes. She would like transitions to be no longer than one minute. She reviews the expectations and corresponding rules for transitions: Be Responsible (bring your materials to your next workstation with you); Be Respectful (clean up your work area at the one-minute warning before rotating); Be Safe (move quickly and quietly to your next workstation). After reteaching the rules, she takes data again and provides lots of praise statements when the rule behaviors occur. After a week, her data indicate that the transitions take no more than two minutes.

Actively Engage Students in Observable Ways

Description of the Skill

Keeping students actively engaged with instruction is a prerequisite for learning to occur and requires that teachers intentionally involve students. The best way to involve students during teacher-led instruction is to use frequent opportunities to respond (OTR). OTR is an evidence-based classroom management practice that provides students different ways to respond, including verbal, gestural, and technology-supported responses. There are three components to all OTR. First, the teacher presents a question or academic-related prompt. We call this the antecedent. Then, the student raises their hand, gestures, or responds in some way to answer the question or prompt. The teacher provides praise or reinforcement for a correct response or an error correction with positive encouragement for an incorrect response. We call this the consequence. This sequence, the antecedent-behavior-consequence, is called the three-term contingency and is indicative of all OTR during teacher-led instruction.

Four types of teacher-directed OTR commonly used in secondary classrooms are individual, unison, or student-to-student OTR, and guided notes. Individual OTR are opportunities for the teacher to check a specific student's understanding. A unison OTR involves a choral response by the students to a question or prompt from the teacher. Both individual and unison OTR can include verbal responses, gestures (e.g., a thumbs-up), written responses on whiteboard or response mats, or technology-based response systems (see Rila et al., 2019 for a complete review of technology OTR solutions). A student-to-student opportunity to respond involves students turning and talking or discussing their answers with one another. By varying these OTR throughout the lesson and daily schedule, students are more likely to remain active participants in their learning. Guided notes involve recording key information from lectures onto a page of fill-in-the-blank spaces. The teacher cues the class to look at a particular sentence and write critical facts in the corresponding prepared spaces during the lesson.

Research Support

A handful of systematic reviews have examined the impacts of increasing OTR during instruction. MacSuga-Gage and Simonsen (2015) identified fifteen studies that demonstrated positive effects of increased OTR on student on-task behavior. The authors also highlight professional recommendations about OTR frequency during direct instruction, noting that teachers should strive to deliver three OTR per minute, with fewer OTR for more complex concepts, such as explaining the meaning of literature. A more recent systematic review by Common et al. (2020) identified twenty-one studies and, after a review, found eleven demonstrating strong internal and external validity, pointing to OTR as an evidence-based practice. Haydon and colleagues (2011) conducted a systematic review of guided notes. They identified thirteen studies, all of which demonstrated positive effects on student outcomes, including academic outcomes.

How to Implement the Skill

Mr. Smith is leading a whole group lesson with his ninth grade geometry class. He presents the information via PowerPoint on the SMART Board at the front of his classroom. He has provided students with guided notes to follow along through the lesson. He has many opportunities to respond embedded throughout his lesson. Mr. Smith circulates in the classroom throughout the lesson in an unpredictable manner. His students are permitted to scan a QR code on his first slide, which brings them to a polling app on their smartphone. Every three to four slides, he has included a polling question in which he can see the percentage of correct responses. He has provided students with whiteboards and Expo markers to solve problems on. For particularly complex problems, Mr. Smith instructs students to turn and talk to their assigned partner to work out the problem until they hear the timer ring.

Establish a Continuum of Acknowledging Appropriate Behaviors

Description of the Skill

Catching students being good is a powerful tool for increasing the likelihood students will do well again. Thus teachers should use positive reinforcement as a consequence of doing the right thing. At the universal level, positive reinforcement can be delivered in myriad ways. These different approaches fall along a continuum from least to most intensive. Intensive here refers to the amount of effort the teacher must expend to deliver positive reinforcement. The continuum consists of following specific practices from least to most intensive: (a) behavior-specific praise, (b) group contingencies, (c) token economies, and (d) behavioral contracting. Behavior-specific praise (BSP), also referred to as specific and contingent praise, involves a praise statement, followed by telling the student(s) exactly what they did right. The praise must be contingent upon a correct response and, ideally, delivered immediately after the student's positive behavior occurred. Example BSP statements include "I love the way that you walked quietly to your desk and sat down. Great job!" or "I'm so proud of how you stayed focused."

There are three types of group contingencies: interdependent, independent, and dependent (Cooper et al., 2020). An interdependent or "all for one" group contingency requires all students in the class to work together to earn one reward for everyone. A dependent or "one for all" group contingency necessitates that one student follows the prescribed expectations to earn the whole group's reward. An independent or "to each his/her own" group contingency allows each student to work on their own to achieve a reward available to all students. The most commonly used group contingency is the interdependent type. In fact, two widely researched classroom management programs, the Good Behavior Game (GBG; Barrish et al., 1969) and the classwide function-related intervention team (CW-FIT; Kamps et al., 2011), are both interdependent group contingencies.

Token economies are slightly more teacher-intensive than group contingencies as they require organization, consistency, and tracking. Token economies use a conditioned reinforcer to be later exchanged for a backup reinforcer, often including a menu of options. Put differently, token economies involve giving students a token (a gold star, a school buck, a marble in a jar, etc.) as positive reinforcement for demonstrating a rule. The tokens themselves are not meaningful or reinforcing but instead are used to gain access to a more powerful reinforcer, which may be tangible (e.g., pizza party, small toy, candy) or not tangible (extra recess time, lunch with the teacher, extra computer time, etc.). Non-tangible reinforcers are often more reinforcing than tangible items. Token economies allow for decreased satiation of reinforcers and a quick opportunity to reinforce behavior without interrupting the flow of the lesson. Token economies allow each student to individually earn tokens or for a whole class to earn tokens and access a collective reinforcer at a specified time.

The last practice, which requires the most teacher time and effort, is behavioral contracting. Behavioral contracting allows the teacher to make an explicit plan with a student or the whole class. That student or whole class must commit to following the teacher's expectations to gain access to a reinforcer. The contract must outline the expectations, how the student(s) can meet them, other staff members or stakeholders who can support the plan, the criteria needed to gain access to the reward, and, if necessary, possible consequences for not meeting the expectations. As with any contract, there is an expiration date upon which the student or class and teacher will revisit their terms and decide if the current plan is working or not and what changes can be made. The contract should then be signed by the teacher, the student or class, and in some cases the student's parent/guardian (see Majeika et al. 2020 for guidelines).

Research Support

Evidence of effectiveness has been established for practices along the continuum. Royer and colleagues (2019) reviewed six studies of BSP meeting quality standards and all found positive effects on student outcomes, including on-task behavior. Ennis and colleagues (2020) also reviewed BSP research, identifying forty-five studies and a mean effect size of 1.72 standard deviation units. As noted, the GBG is a group contingency with a great deal of research supporting effectiveness. Smith et al. (2021) conducted a meta-analysis of eight group experimental design studies of the GBG, finding a moderate effect size for student on-task behavior ($d = 0.49$). CW-FIT has been evaluated using a multisite randomized control trial, finding that students in classrooms using CW-FIT were significantly more on task and less disruptive (Wills et al., 2018). Maggin and colleagues (2011) reviewed research on token economies implemented as classroom management strategies. They identified twenty-four studies with significant and large effects on both individual students and class outcomes. Bowman-Perrott et al. (2015) conducted a systematic review and meta-analysis of behavior contracting, identifying eighteen studies and a majority of studies showed behavior contracting to have a positive effect on student behavior.

How to Implement the Skill

Ms. Perry teaches general education seventh grade math. She uses a dependent group contingency to acknowledge appropriate behaviors in her class. Each day she has an envelope hung on the whiteboard with a secret student's name at the beginning of life skills centers. She has told the students she is looking for the secret student to enter class quietly, have all the materials needed for the lesson, and complete their assigned task. If the secret student meets these expectations, the whole class will earn two tickets that could be used at the school store. Marcus is the secret student today. Ms. Perry observes that Marcus enters class quietly, has all his materials needed for class, and turns in his assignment prior to leaving class. Ms. Perry discreetly lets Marcus know that he is her secret student, and she catches him following all the rules. She asks him if he would like the class to know he was the secret student, and he says yes. Ms. Perry announces at the end of class that Marcus was the secret student and that by entering quietly, having the necessary materials for class, and completing his assignment on time, he has earned the class two tickets each that they can use at the school store.

Establish a Continuum of Strategies to Respond to Inappropriate Behaviors

Description of the Skill

Even when all preventative classroom management practices are in place, including high structure and expectations, there will still be occasions of inappropriate and problematic behavior in the classroom. Therefore, teachers need tools to respond to these behaviors. Similar to acknowledging appropriate behaviors, responding to inappropriate behaviors falls along a continuum from least to most intensive regarding teacher effort and time. The continuum includes the following practices: (a) error corrections, (b) differential reinforcement, (c) planned ignoring, (d) response cost, and (e) time out from reinforcement.

Error corrections are statements that immediately follow an inappropriate behavior. An error correction must be contingent, meaning that the correction occurs immediately after the inappropriate behavior. An error correction must be specific, telling the student exactly what they are doing incorrectly and what they should do differently in the future. An error correction must be brief and not involve lecturing, berating, or arguing. Example error correction for a student lifting the front legs of their chair up and then dropping them down, making a loud, distracting noise may be as follows: "Nick, please stop that and keep the legs of the chair on the floor." An error correction is, in essence, the same as BSP but in response to inappropriate behaviors.

Differential reinforcement (DR) is the implementation of reinforcing only the appropriate response (or behavior you wish to increase) and applying extinction too, or not reinforcing, all other responses. There are, generally speaking, four types of DR: (a) differential reinforcement of lower rates of behavior (DRL), (b) reinforcement of other behaviors (DRO), (c) reinforcement of alternative behavior (DRA), and (d) reinforcement of incompatible behavior (DRI). DRL involves the delivery of reinforcement contingent on low rates of problem behavior for a prespecified interval of time. This approach is appropriate for training a student to eventually get to nonoccurrence or if the undesirable behavior is not too intense or distracting. For example, a student may get an extra point on his homework if at least 60% of the items are answered. The threshold can then increase to 70%, then 80% across a specified period of time. DRO involves the delivery of reinforcement contingent on the nonoccurrence of the target response for a prespecified interval of time. For example, providing positive reinforcement, such as access to extra free time, contingent on not calling out answers during large group instruction. DRA is a procedure that involves systematically reinforcing behavior that is topographically dissimilar to, but not necessarily physically incompatible with, the behavior targeted for reduction. For example, providing repeated BSP for raising a hand when an OTR is presented and ignoring calling out behaviors. DRI is a procedure that involves systematically reinforcing behavior that is topographically dissimilar to and physically incompatible with the behavior targeted for reduction. For example, to reduce out-of-seat behavior, the teacher systematically reinforces the student for completion of work.

Planned ignoring is a systematic procedure for withholding attention (ignoring) when a student engages in an inappropriate behavior. The key component of planned ignoring is that it's planned. For example, for a high school student who repeatedly calls answers out instead of raising her hand, the teacher may have a one-on-one meeting with the student, reteach hand-raising when OTR is presented, and inform them that the teacher will ignore them until they demonstrate hand raising in response to an OTR. However, planned ignoring is only effective if teacher attention is a positive reinforcer maintaining the inappropriate behavior. Response cost is the same as in a token economy, but with the added procedure that tokens can be removed or taken away. For example, a classwide token economy is in place, and the class earns marbles in a jar for demonstrating compliance with rules, with the goal of ten marbles for extra Friday recess. However, when the class is not responsive to teacher instructions, such as not lining up when asked, a marble is taken out of the jar.

The last practice for addressing inappropriate behaviors is time out from reinforcement. A time-out is defined as the removal from a previously reinforcing environment or setting to one that is not reinforcing. For example, a student throws a book at another student, and, as a result, the student is sent to the administrator's office. Another example may be that a class is acting unruly and noncompliant and, as a result, does not get to go to the schoolwide pep rally. However, a critical feature of time out is that the environment the student is removed from cannot be reinforcing. For example, if the removal to the office is reinforcing, perhaps because they have access to a preferred individual there or they escape an aversive task, such as a hard worksheet, the student has not been put on time out and, instead, has been reinforced for the inappropriate behavior (see Ryan et al., 2007).

Research Support

Less research has been conducted in schools on the effectiveness of most practices addressing inappropriate behaviors. Cariveau and colleagues (2019) examined error correction research with students with developmental disabilities. They reviewed four experimental studies and found error correction paired with the adult demonstrating the appropriate skill to be the most effective for increasing the likelihood that students correctly responded. DeJager and colleagues (2020) conducted a study evaluating differences between a token economy, a response cost, and a combination of the two approaches. Results demonstrated that response cost was less effective than the token economy and combination approach but reduced classroom behavior disruptions from baseline, where no system was in place. Regarding time out, a lot of descriptive research has been conducted, but very little experimental research. Everett et al. (2010) reviewed sixty-five time-out studies conducted by parents, but only two were experimental; therefore, effectiveness could not be evaluated. Even fewer studies have focused on time-outs in school; therefore, more research is needed. However, unlike the other responding practices, DR has a robust research base, but not many are conducted in schools. Petscher et al. (2009) reviewed 116 studies of DRA, but only eight were conducted by teachers. That said, all demonstrated positive effects reducing the target problem behaviors. Another review focused on the use of DRO with students with autism (Weston et al., 2018). The authors identified forty-five studies and positive effects on target problem behaviors. However, it was unclear how many studies were conducted in schools.

How to Implement the Skill

Mr. Mack is an eleventh grade pre-calculus teacher. His class is generally engaged with instruction, but a few students are frequently off task and talking with each other. Mr. Mack decides that he would like to try using a DR procedure to respond to the students' inappropriate behaviors. He chooses DRA because it is the easiest to implement while conducting large group instruction. During his lesson, he ignores the few students' off-task behavior and chatting. However, as soon as the students are engaged with his lesson, he immediately makes eye contact and praises the students for paying attention. After three BSP statements, he drops a pen with the school logo as a tangible reinforcer for demonstrating the appropriate behaviors. He did not inform the students that he was going to give them the pens but simply presented them after three BSP on the first day of the intervention. He then returned to using frequent BSP for appropriate behavior and ignoring the off-task behaviors. After three days, Mr. Mack noticed that the students were on task and engaged with instruction much more.

CONCLUSION

Managing student behavior during instruction is critical for student success. That said, classroom management is not easy and requires training, planning, and determination for successful implementation. In this chapter, we have outlined the theoretical and legal context for classroom management and described evidence-based classroom management practices, providing a brief description of each skill, research support, and description of what the practice may look like in a secondary classroom. To further support implementation, we provide links to additional resources for each practice and skill in textbox 10.1. These resources are not exhaustive but offer a starting point for locating information and professional support to increase the likelihood that teachers will implement evidence-based classroom management.

TEXTBOX 10.1. RESOURCES FOR THE FIVE ESSENTIAL PRACTICES

Maximize Classroom Structure

- https://www.pbis.org/resource/creating-effective-classroom-environments-plan-template
- https://www.youtube.com/watch?v=6AZsS5b311c
- https://www.youtube.com/watch?v=W6stU9clh2Q

Positively State Rules and Expectations

- https://iris.peabody.vanderbilt.edu/module/ecbm/-content

Active Engagement

- https://www.education.uw.edu/ibestt/wp-content/uploads/2018/02/Opportunities-to-Respond.pdf
- https://www.gadoe.org/Curriculum-Instruction-and-Assessment/Special-Education-Services/Documents/PBIS/2016-17/PBIS in the Classroom 4/Resource Opportunities to Respond.pdf

Continuum for Acknowledging Appropriate Behaviors

- https://www.pbis.org/resource/the-student-teacher-game
- https://iris.peabody.vanderbilt.edu/wp-content/uploads/misc_media/fss/pdfs/2018/fss_behaviro_specific_praise.pdf
- https://www.interventioncentral.org/behavioral-interventions/challenging-students/behavior-contracts

Continuum for Responding to Inappropriate Behaviors

- https://www.pbis.org/resource/restorative-questions
- https://ies.ed.gov/ncee/wwc/PracticeGuide/4
- https://iris.peabody.vanderbilt.edu/module/bi1/
- https://iris.peabody.vanderbilt.edu/module/bi2/

We should note that there are universal classroom management programs and associated trainings that schools purchase, including CHAMPS, the classroom management component of Safe & Civil Schools, and Responsive Classroom®. These programs incorporate many of the practices and skills we outlined above but organize them in their own proprietary scope and sequence. Thus, instead of describing and advocating for any particular program, we focused on the explicit skills, organized in five evidence-based classroom managed practices, that are freely available and can be implemented by any and all teachers willing to try. Learning to implement these practices takes time, however, so we recommend that teachers track their use of many of these skills to evaluate their own implementation and the effects on their students' behavior. Tracking these skills can be as easy as simply putting tally marks on a Post-it or as complex as having a peer use digital data collection devices to track skill implementation (see Gage & McDaniel, 2012 for data collection approaches).

Universal classroom management is critical but is also not a magic bullet. Student problem behaviors occur in even the most well-managed classrooms. Evidence-based classroom management reduces the likelihood that rule violations will repeatedly occur, and it also helps to create predictable environments conducive to learning. Yet some students will require an additional, group, or individualized intervention, designed by either a teacher, school psychologist, or district-supported behavior analyst. For these few students, universal prevention is not enough, and they require more targeted supports not covered in this chapter. Our hope is that these students' behaviors do not discourage teachers from implementing universal practices but instead that they will see them as the first steps of prevention in a continuum of support to meet the needs of all students. We know, and research supports, that by implementing these practices, teachers can manage student behavior, deliver instruction, and actualize positive and meaningful impacts on student outcomes.

REFERENCES

Aloe, A. M., Amo, L. C., & Shanahan, M. E. (2014). Classroom management self-efficacy and burnout: A multivariate meta-analysis. *Educational Psychology Review, 26*(1), 101–26.

Alter, P., & Haydon, T. (2017). Characteristics of effective classroom rules: A review of the literature. *Teacher Education and Special Education, 40*(2), 114–27. https://doi.org/10.1177/0888406417700962

Bandura, A. (1986). *Social foundations of thought and action: A social cognitive theory*. Prentice Hall.

Barrish, H. H., Saunders, M., & Wolf, M. M. (1969). Good behavior game: Effects of individual contingencies for group consequences on disruptive behavior in a classroom. *Journal of Applied Behavior Analysis, 2*(2), 119–24.

Bergsmann, E. M., Van De Schoot, R., Schober, B., Finsterwald, M., & Spiel, C. (2013). The effect of classroom structure on verbal and physical aggression among peers: A short-term longitudinal study. *Journal of School Psychology, 51*(2), 159–74. https://doi.org/10.1016/j.jsp.2012.10.003

Billingsley, G. M., McKenzie, J. M., & Scheuermann, B. K. (2020). The effects of a structured classroom management system in Secondary Resource Classrooms. *Exceptionality, 28*(5), 317–32. https://doi.org/10.1080/09362835.2018.1522257

Bowman-Perrott, L., Burke, M. D., de Marin, S., Zhang, N., & Davis, H. (2015). A Meta-analysis of single-case research on behavior contracts: Effects on behavioral and academic outcomes among children and youth. *Behavior Modification, 39*(2), 247–69. https://doi.org/10.1177/0145445514551383

Brooks, D. (1985). The teacher's communicative competence: The first day of school. *Theory into Practice, 24*, 63–70.

Brophy, J. (1986). Teacher influences on student achievement. *American Psychologist, 41*(10), 1069–77.

Brophy, J. (2006). Observational research on generic aspects of classroom teaching. In P. A. Alexander & P. H. Winne (Eds.), *Handbook of educational psychology* (2nd ed., pp. 755–80). Erlbaum.

Brophy, J., & Good, T. (1986). Teacher behavior and student achievement. In M. C. Wittrock (Ed.), *Handbook of research on teaching* (3rd ed., pp. 328–75). Macmillan.

Cariveau, T., La Cruz Montilla, A., Gonzalez, E., & Ball, S. (2019). A review of error correction procedures during instruction for children with developmental disabilities. *Journal of Applied Behavior Analysis, 52*(2), 574–79. https://doi.org/10.1002/jaba.524

Center for Responsive Schools. (n.d.). Responsive Classroom® and PBIS: Can schools use them together? https://www.responsiveclassroom.org/sites/default/files/pdf_files/RC_PBIS_white_paper.pdf

Common, E. A., Lane, K. L., Cantwell, E. D., Brunsting, N. C., Oakes, W. P., Germer, K. A., & Bross, L. A. (2020). Teacher-delivered strategies to increase students' opportunities to respond: A systematic methodological review. *Behavioral Disorders, 45*(2), 67–84. https://doi.org/10.1177/0198742919828310

Cooper, J. O., Heron, T. E., & Heward, W. L. (2020). *Applied Behavior Analysis.* Pearson.

Council for Exceptional Children. (2021). *Initial practice-based professional preparation standards for special educators.* https://exceptionalchildren.org/standards/initial-practice-based-professional-preparation-standards-special-educators

DeJager, B., Houlihan, D., Filter, K. J., Mackie, P. F., & Klein, L. (2020). Comparing the effectiveness and ease of implementation of token economy, response cost, and a combination condition in rural elementary school classrooms. *Journal of Rural Mental Health, 44*(1), 39–46.

Dewey, J. (1916). *Democracy and education.* Macmillan.

Engelmann, S., & Carnine, D. (1982). *Theory of instruction: Principles and applications.* Irvington.

Ennis, R. P., Royer, D. J., Lane, K. L., & Dunlap, K. D. (2020). The impact of coaching on teacher-delivered behavior-specific praise in pre-K–12 settings: A systematic review. *Behavioral Disorders, 45*(3), 148–66. https://doi.org/10.1177/0198742919839221

Everett, G. E., Hupp, S. D. A., & Olmi, D. J. (2010). Time-out with parents: A descriptive analysis of 30 years of research. *Education and Treatment of Children, 33*(2), 235–59.

Evertson, C. M., & Weinstein C. S. (Eds.). (2006). *Handbook of classroom management: Research, practice, and contemporary issues.* Erlbaum.

Every Student Succeeds Act, 20 U.S.C. § 6301 (2015). https://www.congress.gov/114/plaws/publ95/PLAW-114publ95.pdf

Freeman, J., Simonsen, B., Briere, D. E., & MacSuga-Gage, A. S. (2014). Pre-service teacher training in classroom management: A review of state accreditation policy and teacher preparation programs. *Teacher Education and Special Education, 37*(2), 106–20. https://doi.org/10.1177/0888406413507002

Gage, N. A., & McDaniel, S. (2012). Creating smarter classrooms: Data-based decision making for effective classroom management. *Beyond Behavior, 22*(1), 48–55. https://doi.org/10.1177/107429561202200108

Gage, N. A., Scott, T., Hirn, R., & MacSuga-Gage, A. S. (2017). The relationship between teachers' implementation of classroom management practices and student behavior in elementary school. *Behavioral Disorders, 43*(2), 302–15. https://doi.org/10.1177/0198742917714809

Gage, N. A., Haydon, T., MacSuga-Gage, A. S., Flowers, E., & Erdy, L. (2020). An evidence-based review and meta-analysis of active supervision. *Behavioral Disorders, 45*(2), 117–28. https://doi.org/10.1177/0198742919851021

Haydon, T., Mancil, G. R., Kroeger, S. D., McLeskey, J., & Lin, W. Y. J. (2011). A review of the effectiveness of guided notes for students who struggle learning academic content. *Preventing School Failure: Alternative Education for Children and Youth, 55*(4), 226–31.

Huston-Stein, A., Friedrich-Cofer, L., & Susman, E. J. (1977). The relation of classroom structure to social behavior, imaginative play, and self-regulation of economically disadvantaged children. *Child Development, 48*(3), 908–16.

Jang, H., Reeve, J., & Deci, E. L. (2010). Engaging students in learning activities: It is not autonomy support or structure but autonomy support and structure. *Journal of Educational Psychology, 102*(3), 588–600. https://doi.org/10.1037/a0019682

Kamps, D., Wills, H., Heitzman-Powell, L., Laylin, J., Szoke, C., Petrillo, T., & Culey, A. (2011). Classwide function-related intervention teams: Effects of group contingency programs in urban classrooms. *Journal of Positive Behavior Interventions, 13*(3), 154–76. https://doi:10.1177/1098300711398935

Klassen, R. M., & Chiu, M. M. (2010). Effects on teachers' self-efficacy and job satisfaction: Teacher gender, years of experience, and job stress. *Journal of Educational Psychology, 102*(3), 741–69.

Korpershoek, H., Harms, T., de Boer, H., van Kuijk, M., & Doolaard, S. (2016). A meta-analysis of the effects of classroom management strategies and classroom management programs on students' academic, behavioral, emotional, and motivational outcomes. *Review of Educational Research, 86*(3), 643–80.

Kwok, A. (2019). Classroom management actions of beginning urban teachers. *Urban Education, 54*(3), 339–67.

Lee, A., & Gage, N. A. (2020). Updating and expanding systematic reviews and meta-analyses on the effects of school-wide positive behavior interventions and supports. *Psychology in the Schools, 57*(5), 783–804. https://doi.org/10.1002/pits.22336

MacSuga-Gage, A. S., & Simonsen, B. (2015). Examining the effects of teacher-directed opportunities to respond on student outcomes: A systematic review of the literature. *Education and Treatment of Children, 38*(2), 211–39.

Maggin, D. M., Chafouleas, S. M., Goddard, K. M., & Johnson, A. H. (2011). A systematic evaluation of token economies as a classroom management tool for students with challenging behavior. *Journal of School Psychology, 49*(5), 529–54. https://doi.org/10.1016/j.jsp.2011.05.001

Majeika, C. E., Wilkinson, S., & Kumm, S. (2020). Supporting student behavior through behavioral contracting. *TEACHING Exceptional Children, 53*(2), 132–39. https://doi.org/10.1177/0040059920952475

McLeskey, J., Barringer, M-D., Billingsley, B., Brownell, M., Jackson, D., Kennedy, M., Lewis, T., Maheady, L., Rodriguez, J., Scheeler, M. C., Winn, J., & Ziegler, D. (2017, January). *High-leverage practices in special education*. Council for Exceptional Children & CEEDAR Center.

Morris, V. O. (1966). *Existentialism in education*. Harper and Row.

Myers, D., Simonsen, B., & Freeman, J. (2020). *Implementing classwide PBIS: A guide to supporting teachers*. Guilford.

Oliver, R. M., Wehby, J. H., & Reschly, D. J. (2011). Teacher classroom management practices: Effects on disruptive or aggressive student behavior. *Campbell Systematic Reviews, 7*(1), 1–55.

Petscher, E. S., Rey, C., & Bailey, J. S. (2009). A review of empirical support for differential reinforcement of alternative behavior. *Research in Developmental Disabilities, 30*(3), 409–25. https://doi.org/10.1016/j.ridd.2008.08.008

Rila, A., Estrapala, S., & Bruhn, A. L. (2019). Using technology to increase opportunities to respond. *Beyond Behavior, 28*(1), 36–45. https://doi.org/10.1177/1074295619835207

Royer, D. J., Lane, K. L., Dunlap, K. D., & Ennis, R. P. (2019). A systematic review of teacher-delivered behavior-specific praise on K–12 student performance. *Remedial and Special Education, 40*(2), 112–128. https://doi.org/10.1177/0741932517751054

Ryan, J. B., Sanders, S., Katsiyannis, A., & Yell, M. L. (2007). Using time-out effectively in the classroom. *TEACHING Exceptional Children, 39*(4), 60–67. https://doi.org/10.1177/004005990703900407

Schunk, D. (2019). *Learning theories: An educational perspective* (8th ed.). Pearson.

Sierens, E., Vansteenkiste, M., Goossens, L., Soenens, B., & Dochy, F. (2009). The synergistic relationship of perceived autonomy support and structure in the prediction of self-regulated learning. *British Journal of Educational Psychology, 79*(1), 57–68.

Simonsen, B., & Myers, D. (2014). *Classwide positive behavior interventions and supports: A guide to proactive classroom management*. Guilford.

Simonsen, B., Fairbanks, S., Briesch, A., Myers, D., & Sugai, G. (2008). Evidence-based practices in classroom management: Considerations for research to practice. *Education and Treatment of Children, 31*(3), 351–80.

Skinner, B. F. (1953). Some contributions of an experimental analysis of behavior to psychology as a whole. *American Psychologist, 8*(2), 69–78.

Skinner, E. A., & Belmont, M. J. (1993). Motivation in the classroom: Reciprocal effects of teacher behavior and student engagement across the school year. *Journal of Educational Psychology, 85*(4), 571–81.

Smith, S., Barajas, K., Ellis, B., Moore, C., McCauley, S., & Reichow, B. (2021). A meta-analytic review of randomized controlled trials of the Good Behavior Game. *Behavior Modification, 45*(4), 641–666. https://doi.org/10.1177/0145445519878670

Stichter, J. P., Stormont, M., Lewis, T. J., & Schultz, T. (2009). Rates of specific antecedent instructional practices and differences between Title I and non-Title I schools. *Journal of Behavioral Education, 18*(4), 331–44.

Tucker, C. M., Zayco, R. A., Herman, K. C., Reinke, W. M., Trujillo, M., Carraway, K., Wallack, C., & Ivery, P. D. (2002). Teacher and child variables as predictors of academic engagement among low-income African American children. *Psychology in the Schools, 39*(4), 477–88.

US Department of Education, Office of Special Education and Rehabilitative Services (2016). *Dear colleague letter on positive behavior interventions in IEPs*. https://sites.ed.gov/idea/files/dcl-on-pbis-in-ieps-08-01-2016.pdf

US Department of Education, Office of Special Education Programs (2016). *Supporting and responding to behavior: Evidence-based classroom strategies for teachers*. https://osepideasthatwork.org/sites/default/files/ClassroomPBIS_508.pdf

Vygotsky, L. (1978). Interaction between learning and development. *Readings on the Development of Children, 23*(3), 34–41.

Wallace, T. L. B., Sung, H. C., & Williams, J. D. (2014). The defining features of teacher talk within autonomy-supportive classroom management. *Teaching and Teacher Education, 42*, 34–46. https://doi.org/10.1016/j.tate.2014.04.005

Weston, R., Hodges, A., & Davis, T. N. (2018). Differential reinforcement of other behaviors to treat challenging behaviors among children with autism: A systematic and quality review. *Behavior Modification, 42*(4), 584–609. https://doi.org/10.1177/0145445517743487

Wills, H., Wehby, J., Caldarella, P., Kamps, D., & Swinburne Romine, R. (2018). Classroom management that works: A replication trial of the CW-FIT program. *Exceptional Children, 84*(4), 437–56. https://doi.org/10.1177/0014402918771321

11

Social, Emotional, and Behavioral Intervention

Katheen M. Randolph, Glenna M. Billingsley, and Jasmine Justus

UNIVERSAL CLASSROOM MANAGEMENT PRACTICES are vital to an educator's ability to manage classroom behaviors and engage students in active learning. Without the necessary classroom management practices, otherwise well-regarded academic lessons become less effective (Ficarra & Quinn, 2014). As presented in the previous chapter, low-intensity behavior management practices that can aid in managing behaviors classwide include interventions such as precorrection, classwide group contingencies, active supervision, and opportunities to respond. These interventions are employed to prevent disruptive behaviors from occurring and increase appropriate classroom behaviors. Research (e.g., Gage et al., 2018; Greenwood et al., 2002) shows that the appropriate use of universal strategies has a larger impact on a student's educational experience than focusing on behavior only. Correlations have been found between universal practices and student engagement with instruction (Gage et al., 2018). Universal practices allow educators to increase wanted behaviors and academic retention using these practices. For example, active supervision requires the educator to move about, scan the classroom, and engage with students (Allen et al., 2020). With this practice, an educator can prevent unwanted behavior, actively correct misconceptions in student learning, and aid in the retention of information taught.

The level and intensity of behavior management practices can increase or decrease as students' behavioral needs change. Although universal practices are ideal, some students may need more intensive intervention than universal practices provide. Lane et al. (2016) conducted a study that used systematic behavior screening to determine the number of students who were at risk for needing more intensive behavioral supports. Overall, 10,000 middle and high school students were screened, showing that 15% of students were at a moderate risk and 5.49% of students were at high risk of needing intensive behavioral supports. Approximately 2,185 students out of 10,000 likely need access to more intensive behavioral supports.

Interventions such as explicit social skills instruction, independent group contingencies, and behavior contracting are invaluable to the students who need them.

Chapter 11: Social, Emotional, and Behavioral Intervention

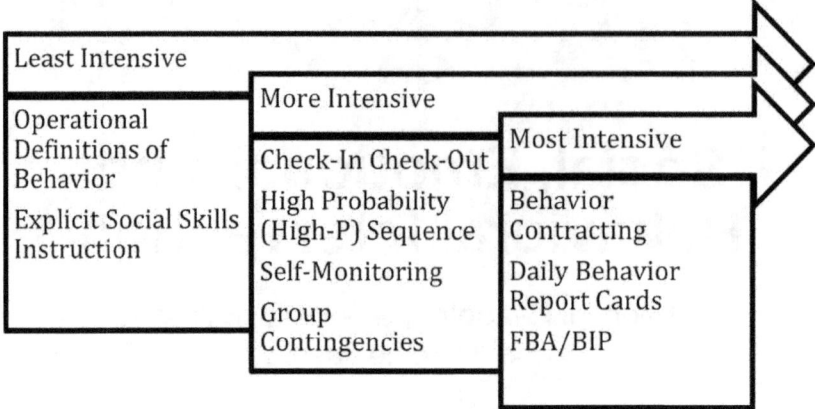

Figure 11.1 Evidence-Based Practices by Increasing Levels of Intensity

For example, precorrection is a commonly used universal classroom management strategy where the educator teaches the wanted behavior and provides modeling, examples, and non-examples. If a student needs more intensive instruction, the educator explicitly teaches a lesson utilizing a model featuring the discrete social, emotional, or self-regulation skill the student needs to learn. The intensity of the practice increases as the students need more concentrated instruction on specific social skills. Another common universal practice is a group contingency; in the Good Behavior Game (GBG), for instance, students earn points for pre-identified *good behavior*, and the class works toward reinforcement, typically a reward (Barrish et al., 1969). This evidence-based practice encourages class members to cooperate to achieve a common goal, while reinforcing desired behaviors. There are students or groups of students who may need an independent group contingency, which is an increase in intensity from a whole class contingency such as the GBG.

This chapter details several evidence-based behavior management strategies that can be used when universal strategies have been exhausted and the target behavior has not improved. All interventions within the chapter have extensive research to support their use. Figure 11.1 provides an organizational overview of the strategies outlined in the chapter. Each practice within the chapter will be presented as such: (a) description of the intervention, (b) supporting evidence, and (c) how to implement the intervention. The primary goal of this chapter is to provide a detailed overview of the need for, and the use of, intensive behavior supports.

CHAPTER OBJECTIVES

- Identify evidence-based classroom interventions to support students with challenging behaviors
- Recognize the need for progressively intensive behavioral interventions
- Determine the level of explicit instruction necessary for student success
- Identify methods for behavioral data collection in the general education classroom
- Use data to drive behavioral intervention decisions

OPERATIONAL DEFINITIONS OF BEHAVIOR

When teachers want to change student behaviors, the first step is defining the target behavior, the behavior that is being targeted for change (Cooper et al., 2020). In schools, teachers tend to focus on socially expected and acceptable behaviors, which are school-related behaviors (e.g., sitting in a chair, raising hand) that most students can perform with little to no support or instruction. To successfully identify the expected behavior, school teams should focus on defining the behavior operationally, using examples and non-examples so that multiple observers can identify the behavior across multiple settings.

The focus on defining the behavior in operational terms in schools is often overlooked or something school teams may not be aware of; the importance of high-quality operational definitions may not be sufficiently emphasized, thus school teams (i.e., teachers and paraprofessionals) may need to receive training. Behavioral definitions in schools are often subjective, vague, umbrella terms (e.g., dysregulation, off task), and leave observers to make individual interpretations when assessing the behavior. This means that one person may interpret the behavior as one thing while a different observer identifies the behavior as something else. Subjectively defining target behaviors leads to poorly measured behavioral objectives, which makes providing appropriate interventions difficult and may result in targeting the wrong behaviors or characteristics of behavior.

Target behaviors are defined one of two ways, functional or topographical. A functional definition is one that addresses the outcome of the behavior, and looks at the function (i.e., escape, attention, tangible, sensory) the behavior meets for the student (Cooper et al., 2020). A topographical definition is one that is based on the topography, or shape, of the behavior. This can be used in schools when defining behavior simply by what it *looks like*, especially when observers are not trained in behavioral practices and are participating in data collection.

Target behaviors should also include examples and non-examples. That is, what does the behavior look like when it is occurring, and what does it look like when the behavior is not occurring. Simply put, a non-example is an expected behavior that a student displays at the appropriate time. Examples and non-examples of behaviors are provided in table 11.1.

Along with target behavior identification, school teams should also identify a replacement behavior, which should serve the same function as the target behavior and be one that the student can already do (i.e., it exists in their behavioral repertoire). For example, if a student gets out of their seat when they are done with their work without teacher permission, and the function of the behavior is to escape the environment, the school team can teach the student to ask for a break when they need one, which meets that same function. The replacement behavior serves the same function (i.e., it is functionally equivalent) and provides an appropriate alternative (i.e., replacement) to the behavior that is not appropriate for the school environment (Cooper et al., 2020).

EXPLICIT SOCIAL SKILLS INSTRUCTION

Students who require additional support in learning socially expected behaviors need explicit instruction in social skills areas where they display behavioral needs (i.e.,

Table 11.1. Operational Definitions of Behavior with Examples and Non-examples

Target Behavior	Definition	Example	Non-Example
Verbal Outbursts	Bobby will say random things, unrelated to the topic at hand; ask questions that are off topic; state off-topic, sometimes sensational things; these are often when it is quiet in the classroom or during instructional time.	During whole group instruction, Bobby turns to a classmate, and says "I hate you and you're stupid!" During independent work, Bobby asks the teacher why he has an ugly shirt on.	Bobby is on task, answering questions related to the content, engaged in on-topic conversation during group work in class.
Refusal	When Sandra is given a verbal directive (do work, come inside, transition, eat lunch), she remains in the same location, says "I refuse" or "I won't go," and sits on the floor (10 minutes to entire school day).	Teacher provides direction to complete worksheet and Sandra responds, "no, I won't do it" and stays seated. Verbally redirected, looks at adult, does not respond or engage with adult. Given directive or request, does not move or comply.	When given a directive, Sandra will comply within 15 seconds.
Eloping or Attempting to Elope	When given a directive, transitioning from one setting to another (e.g., classroom to specials, returning from recess), or with an unknown antecedent, Jeremy will walk out of the classroom with the intent to go home and leave school.	When transitioning between the classroom and resource room, returning from recess, from the classroom to lunch or specials, from the bus to the classroom, Jeremy will state, "I'm going home," "My job is not to be at school," or another related statement.	Jeremy stays in area at scheduled time; transitions with peers/adults as requested.

deficits), similar to what is required academically. For example, a student who struggles with reading would not be expected to just learn the fundamentals of reading without intensive instruction, rather they would receive prescribed instruction; likewise, the use of explicit instruction in behavioral expectations is necessary. Explicit instruction is "a structured, systematic, and effective methodology for teaching academic skills" (Archer & Hughes, 2010, p. 1), and explicit instruction can be used to teach students expected social skills in all settings. It is a direct (i.e., explicit) way of teaching students the things that they need to learn, without opportunity for guessing or ambiguity, and students can apply what they learn immediately in their rehearsal and practice (Durlak et al., 2011). Explicit instruction is evidence-based instructional practice to ensure that students receive scaffolded (i.e., tiered), clear instruction.

Teachers provide explicit instruction by using the teaching functions: review, presentation, guided practice, corrections and feedback, independent practice, and review. The teaching functions ensure that students learn the skills needed, apply them, and then maintain and generalize those skills over time with the review acting as a check-in (Archer & Hughes, 2010). Durlak et al. (2011) used the acronym SAFE when describing recommended practices for teaching social skills: sequenced, active, focused, and explicit. Two nonacademic examples of skills students can learn through explicit instruction are social skills and self-regulation. Explicit behavioral instruction is sometimes referred to as skillstreaming (Goldstein, 1973), where the task is broken down into smaller incremental units like a task analysis. Skillstreaming follows similar steps: teacher introduces social skill, someone models it (adult or peer mediated), student practices skill, teacher provides feedback to the student, and student is provided with some follow-up on the skill to practice as homework (Goldstein & McGinnis, 1997). Figure 11.2 provides a side-by-side comparison of explicit instruction and skillstreaming.

Socially expected skills (i.e., prosocial skills) are necessary for students to be successful in the school setting, and using explicit instruction or skillstreaming helps

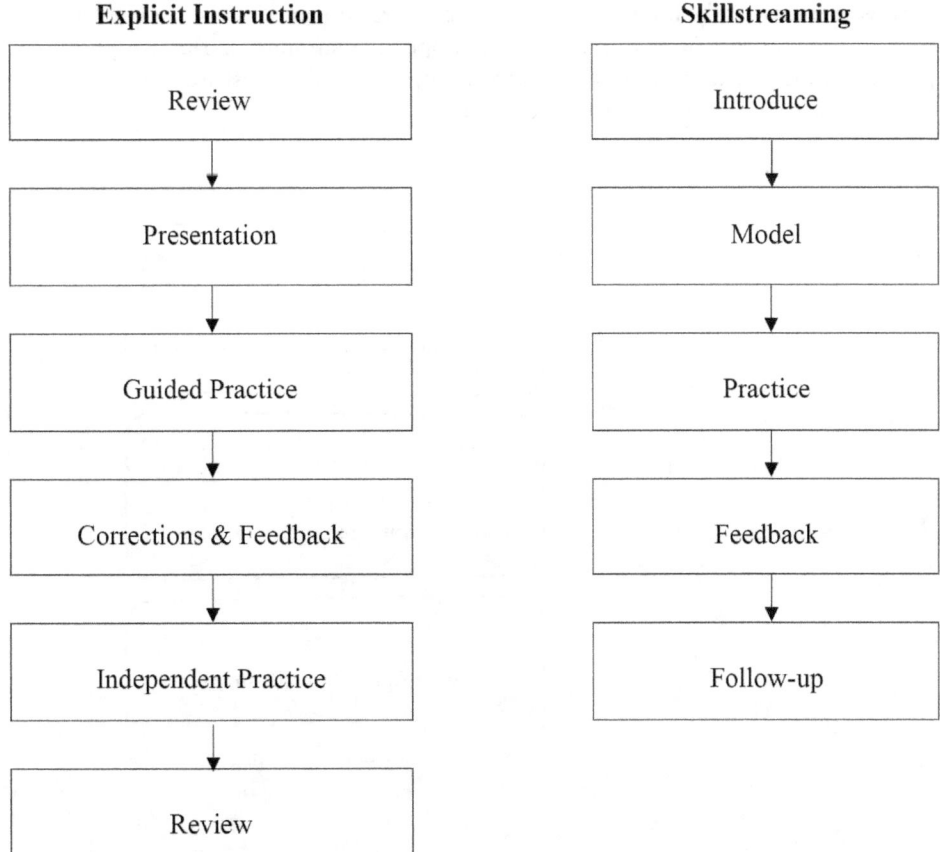

Figure 11.2 Comparison of Explicit Instruction and Skillstreaming

teach students those skills that they may be lacking with a follow-up to make sure those skills are maintained and generalized to multiple settings for student success.

TIER 2 EVIDENCE-BASED INTERVENTIONS CLASSROOM MANAGEMENT

Response to Intervention (RtI), a three-tiered system of support used for academics and behavior, incorporates evidence-based interventions for teaching, supporting, and reinforcing expected school behaviors utilizing the Positive Behavior Interventions and Supports framework (Sugai & Horner, 2002). A graphic of the three-tiered system of RtI support is provided in figure 11.3. Universal supports (i.e., Tier 1) were discussed in the previous chapter and are designed to support all students in schools. Universal supports are schoolwide measures and include behavioral expectations and reinforcement systems for all students. Tier 1 supports are typically successful with up to 80% of a school's student population (Metcalf, 2012).

Tier 2 supports are more intense, targeted, evidence-based interventions and are generally provided to students who are not meeting goals or making progress academically or behaviorally with Tier 1 (i.e., universal) supports. Students receiving Tier 2 intervention make up about 10%–15% of the school population. Tier 2 supports are provided based on student need and progress and may be applied in small groups or individually. Intervention frequency, duration, and intensity varies, and are provided to students *in addition to* Tier 1 supports. Examples of Tier 2 supports are provided in the next section, with a description of the skill, research to support the skill, and ways to implement the intervention.

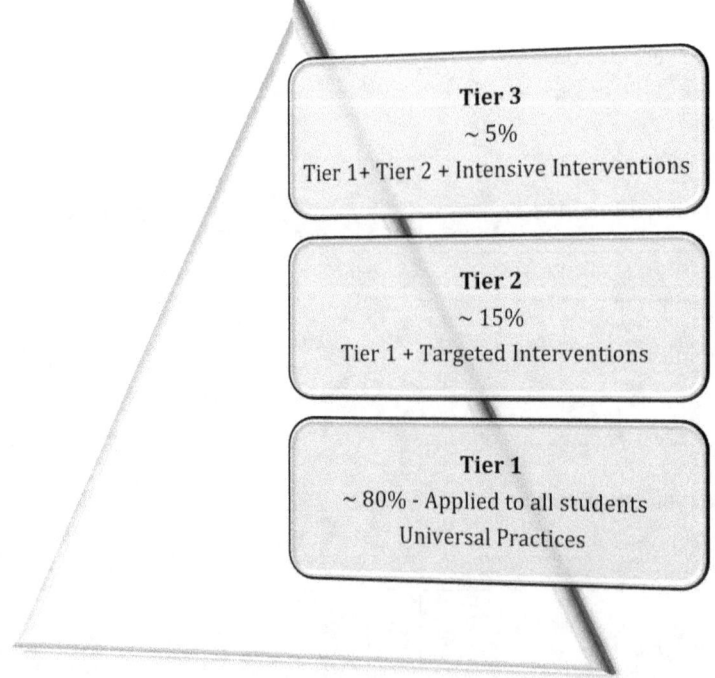

Figure 11.3 Response to Intervention Framework

Check-In/Check-Out

Description of the Intervention

Check-in check-out (CICO), also called the Behavior Education Program, involves a check-in with an adult at the beginning of the day to review behavioral expectations for the day, providing the student with a daily tracking (monitoring) report card to carry with them and either self-monitor or have teachers complete during the school day, and a check-out at the end of the day with an adult, where the student and the same teacher who conducted the check-in review the daily report card together and reflect on student progress (Drevon et al., 2019). The expected behaviors are reviewed, emphasized, and revisited during the CICO process, and the form serves as a physical reminder of those expectations. At the end of the day, the student receives incremental reinforcement (e.g., tokens) that is then exchanged for larger reinforcement (e.g., schoolwide bucks) after earning a specified amount over a period of time.

Research Support

The body of research (including Drevon et al., 2019; Maggin et al., 2015; Wolfe et al., 2016) for CICO is one that spans both general and special education and meets the Council for Exceptional Children's (CEC) quality standards (Mitchell et al., 2017) with demonstrated effectiveness both traditionally (i.e., paper and pencil) and electronically (eCICO; e.g., Hott et al., 2021). CICO and can be used in more settings than the traditional brick-and-mortar school environment. Hott and colleagues (2021) conducted a study where eCICO was used to successfully reduce inappropriate behavior on the school bus in a rural area, where two students were at risk of removal from the bus if their disruptive behavior failed to improve. CICO, like all Tier 2 interventions, is used in conjunction with Tier 1 (i.e., universal) interventions and within the schoolwide Multi-Tiered Systems of Support (MTSS) and Positive Behavior Interventions and Supports (PBIS) context.

How to Implement the Intervention

CICO is considered low intensity because it requires minimal training to immediately implement and support students. First, choose the type of monitoring that will be used: electronic or paper. Next, ensure that the school team, including the student's teachers and administrators, are aware of the intervention and able to complete the daily report card with fidelity (i.e., as it is meant to be implemented) and objectively. Determine if the student can successfully facilitate the CICO process (i.e., self-monitoring) or if a teacher will be completing the form. A short, informational meeting may be necessary for the teacher involved to guarantee that the same expectations exist across environments. More than one adult should participate in daily CICO sessions to ensure students receive the expectation reminders and positive reinforcement necessary.

High-Probability (High-P) Sequence

Description of the Intervention

The high-probability (high-p) sequence is one that reduces student escape or avoidance of tasks (i.e., non-preferred; *low-p*) including those tasks they typically try to get out of. During the high-p sequence, the teacher presents 2–5 tasks the students can complete easily followed immediately by a task they have not mastered or a non-preferred task. This process helps to build behavioral momentum, and essentially *build the student up* to completing the non-preferred task quickly and efficiently (Bross et al., 2018), and pairs that with high rates of positive reinforcement for mastered or preferred tasks.

Research Support

The high-p sequence is used to increase compliance for and completion of less-preferred academic (Lee et al., 2004) and behavioral tasks, with the initial goal of 3–5 preferred tasks to 1 non-preferred task, ultimately fading to 1:1 preferred to non-preferred tasks (Axelrod & Zank, 2012). High-p can be used to facilitate transitions from one task to another or during transitions within a singular task (Lee et al., 2008). The goal is to increase compliance with non-preferred tasks, fade the high-p requests, and decrease reliance on behavioral momentum.

How to Implement the Intervention

When implementing the high-p sequence, it's important to identify high-p versus low-p tasks and be sure to test the hypothesized task sequences. Next, implement the intervention quickly with consistency. This means the teacher should wait 5 seconds before moving on to the next task to ensure sufficient wait time while using frequent praise (i.e., for every task, 1:1) to complement the intervention without creating lag time that breaks the momentum. Teachers should collect data to measure the intervention's effectiveness, and eventually fade to 1 preferred to 1 non-preferred task to mirror a more naturalistic environment while setting up students for future academic and behavioral success (Lee et al., 2004).

Self-Monitoring

Description of the Intervention

Self-monitoring is a process of observing and recording behavior data and is done by the individual whose behavior is being recorded (i.e., the student). The student must be able to identify the behavior of their own that they are recording, which requires a clear, student-friendly, operational definition. In addition to identifying the behavior, the student needs to monitor the presence or absence of the behavior for the observation time period (i.e., class period or interval) using the predetermined type of data collection (i.e., frequency, duration) (Menzies et al., 2009). Self-monitoring can be combined with CICO to ensure the student monitors their behavior and checks in with an adult to ensure they are recording the same things. In this sense, the student serves as a side-by-side observer with an adult.

Research Support

Self-monitoring can be used with students and teachers alike. In one study, Moore Partin and colleagues (2010) implemented self-monitoring with teachers to promote their use of EBPs with students in their classroom. Results showed that teachers can implement self-monitoring to track their use of classroom practices, and this can be extended to additional techniques, as well. Self-monitoring requires a level of maturity and capability at the student level for them to identify and record the target behavior with fidelity and honesty (Menzies et al., 2009).

How to Implement the Intervention

Self-monitoring is often paired with other interventions detailed in this chapter, such as CICO and daily behavior report cards. Students who use self-monitoring must be able to understand and identify the personal behaviors they are monitoring, and be able to earnestly monitor the presence or absence of their own behavior. The following are discrete skills in which students must be trained to proficiency for effective self-monitoring:

- Students assist the teacher in determining behavior targeted for change. They must be able to recognize examples and non-examples of the operationally defined behavior, albeit in student-friendly terms.
- Students require training in monitoring their own behavior. They must practice recording their behavior by pairing up with a teacher to simultaneously record behavior, discuss inconsistencies, and reward agreement.
- After students can accurately record their behavior most of the time, the student records their behavior independently, with the teacher only spot-checking for accuracy, again reinforcing accuracy with preferred rewards.
- If interrater reliability between students and teacher is low, redefining the behavior is likely necessary.

Group Contingencies

Description of the Intervention

A group contingency places the behavioral responsibility on the group to earn the consequence (i.e., reinforcer). The benefit of group contingencies is that rather than applying single reinforcers to different students, one common consequence is applied to the entire group, which saves the teacher energy, time, and resources. Group contingencies also help with peer and classwide social interactions (Pokorski, 2019).

There are three different types of group contingencies: independent, dependent, and interdependent. Independent group contingencies present the opportunity for reinforcement to all students and apply reinforcement only to students who meet the criteria for reinforcement. Independent group contingencies can be used within a classroom token economy, where students who are meeting the expectations earn a token and those who aren't simply do not earn the reinforcement (Litow & Pumroy, 1975). Dependent group contingencies provide reinforcement to the entire group contingent on an individual student or small group performance, and this is often referred to as the *hero procedure*. If the individual (or small group) meets the criteria at the predetermined level of performance, then the entire group earns reinforcement. Teachers should use caution in implementing this procedure because it could have negative ramifications for the individual (or small group) if they do not meet the criteria for reinforcement. An interdependent group contingency is one where the entire group must meet the criteria for reinforcement, both individually and as a group, and is referred to as an *all or none* contingency. Interdependent group contingency can be used as part of the good behavior game.

Research Support

One application of group contingencies is classwide function-related intervention teams (CW-FIT), which is used to reduce target behaviors and can be implemented in a classroom as part of the daily routine (Wills et al., 2014). The study focused on three male students who displayed excessive disruptive and off-task behavior. The students were taught functionally equivalent replacement behaviors during the study and the individual students along with the class were able to earn reinforcement within the group contingency. When CW-FIT was implemented, the class was split into teams, received social skills instruction over time, demonstrated the skills that met schoolwide expectations, and the teams earned points (i.e., reinforcement) based on their participation. The three male students made improvements in their target behaviors (Wills et al., 2014).

How to Implement the Intervention

Chow and Gilmour (2016) provide a seven-step process for designing a classroom group contingency plan. Steps include: (1) identify target behaviors, (2) identify groups, (3) identify how groups get points, (4) determine how points will be awarded, (5) choose who provides points, (6) create a schedule, (7) identify rewards. Following the steps to create the group contingency and framing those within the classroom and schoolwide PBIS framework will create a positive and reinforcing classroom for all students to meet the expectations and earn the reinforcement.

ADDING INTENSIVE INTERVENTIONS

A few students, typically less than 5%, need more intensive, more individualized support (i.e., Tier 3) to be successful. When considering Tier 3 interventions, it is important to identify and consider the specific function, or purpose, the behavior is serving (Moreno & Bullock, 2011). Next, teachers need to determine consequences that maintain the behavior. Finally, the team should identify what the student receives from the misbehavior for an intervention to be effective. For students who exhibit challenging behaviors that do not improve with universal and targeted interventions (Tiers 1 and 2), a more formal process, called the functional behavioral assessment, should begin to identify the function of behavior (i.e., escape, attention, tangible, sensory). This assessment can be helpful to determine events or conditions that trigger misbehavior (antecedents) as well as what motivates or maintains the behavior (consequence).

Oftentimes classroom misbehavior is done for the purpose of getting the teacher's or other students' attention. Students sometimes exhibit behaviors to gain power, control, or status from others, which are also forms of attention-seeking behavior. Other classroom misbehaviors functionally aid students in avoiding (i.e., escaping) situations or tasks they find unpleasant. For example, a student may purposefully, although not always consciously, break classroom rules if they know that doing so will result in their removal from the learning environment. A student may actively or passively refuse to participate in lessons they deem too hard, too easy, or dislike.

The following evidence-based interventions are simple to create and complete. These multifaceted, flexible strategies assist students with setting desired behavioral goals, serve as visual prompts to the student and teacher, promote frequent feedback to stakeholders, embed behavior data collection, promote independence in managing behavior, and are minimally distracting or stigmatizing to the student, yet they are individualized to the particular function served by the behavior and offer a more intensive intervention than those previously discussed.

Behavior Contracting

Description of the Intervention

Behavior contracts, also called contingency contracts, are agreements made between the student and the teacher (administrator, counselor) which explicitly state expected behavior from each participant, and the contingency needed to earn reinforcement. Behavior contracts are formally written and signed for acknowledgment and accountability. Behavior contracting is a consequence-based intervention, meaning the contingency occurs following the behavior and either decreases or increases the target behavior. When used to support positive behavior, the contract consists of the expected behavior of the student, a criterion for completion, and a description of the reinforcer that will be received if/once the behavior occurs. A monitoring or recording form allows all parties to visually see progress toward completion of the contract.

As part of a reinforcement system, behavior contracts are used to successfully create positive behavior change because the student has input into the development of the agreement, resulting in buy-in for all parties. This is a critical component for students whose behavior is aimed at gaining power or control, a specialized form of attention-seeking behavior and for those who often undermine other systems. Formalizing contracts in writing also serves to increase the likelihood of both parties exhibiting the behaviors specified. Further, they are simple to implement, an important consideration in a busy classroom.

Research Support

A behavior contract is a "contingent relationship between the completion of a specified behavior and access to, or delivery of, a specified reward" (Cooper et al., 2020, p. 672). Bowman-Perrott et al. (2015) conducted a meta-analysis of behavior contracts and found contracts to be beneficial as both academic and behavioral interventions across grade level, gender, and disability status. Interestingly, they found contracting to be more effective in reducing inappropriate behaviors than increasing appropriate behaviors. Behavior contracts can be personal, teacher-driven, or a combined effort between teachers and the children whose behavior they are attempting to change (Edgemon et al., 2021).

How to Implement the Intervention

The most important step in developing a behavior contract is to explicitly identify the target behavior(s) using operationalized definitions which helps to avoid disagreements later. These are stated in positive terms and focused on what the student should do. Next, list the steps that adults will enact to support the student (e.g., reminders or prompts). After that, identify the reinforcer(s) earned contingent on completion of the target behavior, followed by the criteria and timeline for receiving the reinforcer. For students with less behavioral expertise, it is better to provide reinforcement once the behavior occurs rather than providing a stringent time period. Once all terms are agreed upon, all parts of the contract are in clear language that everyone can understand. All parties involved (e.g. student, parents, paraprofessionals, administrators) sign the contract and keep it in an accessible location. If a separate recording document is included (e.g., daily behavior report card), it should be kept where it can be seen. At the end of each time period identified in the contract, review the contingencies and deliver the earned reinforcer if conditions were met. The contract is a fluid document, and can be continued, modified, or terminated. Textbox 11.1 provides a behavior contract template.

TEXTBOX 11.1.
BEHAVIOR CONTRACT TEMPLATE

Behavior Contract

Date _____

Goal Behavior

I, _____ am working on _____.
     (student name)   (behavior)

This looks like:

(operationally define behavior here)

Reward

I will receive this reward for meeting my goal:

(identify student-selected reward here)

Review

We will review this behavior contract on this date:

(date contract will be reviewed, can be on a specific date or at time intervals—days, weeks)

_____   _____
    Student Signature   Adult Signature

Daily Behavior Report Cards

Description of the Intervention

Daily behavior report cards (DBRC), also known as direct behavior rating (DBR), serve as both an intervention and a data collection tool. Often, these *point sheets* are used in conjunction with another intervention, like CICO, but offer flexibility to use independently or as part of a multicomponent reinforcement system. DBRCs prompt the teacher to provide frequent, specific behavior feedback to the student (and other stakeholders) on one or more target behaviors. Unlike behavior contracting, the DBRC is intended to document a student's behavior on one school day, but it can also be used for a single activity, class, or throughout the day.

True of any intervention, implementation fidelity is key to successfully using DBRC. Implementation, or treatment fidelity, refers to the extent to which an intervention is implemented as planned (Gresham, 2013). Reviewing the goals of desired behavior at the beginning of the rating period and providing behavior-specific praise and instructional feedback at the conclusion of the period is crucial and cannot be rushed or omitted. With minor adaptations, DBRC can be used effectively across grade and ability levels.

Research Support

The use of DBRC is well-supported in the literature. A randomized controlled trial study by Fabiano and colleagues (2010) was deemed to meet standards of What Works Clearinghouse (WWC) without reservations as an effective practice. WWC, funded by the US Department of Education, evaluates instructional practices and rates their effectiveness based on their ability to improve student outcomes. A meta-analysis study by Vannest et al. (2010) found DBRC to be effective for improving behavior. The elements of DBRC (timely feedback, specific praise, home-school communication) have individual research support as well. While the use of a DBRC as a behavior-monitoring tool has research support, it is recommended as a supplement with other interventions instead of being used as a stand-alone method (Riley-Tillman et al., 2007). Combining DBRC with a robust reinforcement system offers multiplied benefit.

How to Implement the Skill

After identifying which behavior(s) will be rated daily, operational definitions and examples are listed on a paper or electronic form along with specific rating intervals (e.g., hourly, by content area). The form, which will be carried by the student, includes a rating scale that resembles a Likert scale and uses numbers (e.g., 1–5), response anchors (e.g., not at all, sometimes), or pictures (happy/sad faces). The behavior should be stated in positive terms. For example, "Jordan will respect peers by calling peers their real name only," instead of "Jordan will not name-call peers."

After a set time period (e.g., interval or class), the student seeks the teacher's input on the form. The teacher rates the student's performance on the behavior according to the operationalized definition and rating scale, then provides specific praise and constructive feedback to the student. As with any system, the procedures must be taught to and practiced with the student, and modifications may be needed. For example, a student who struggles to remember to request input may need prompting which can be faded later. Points can be graphed so stakeholders can easily see progress. Data should be reviewed often (at least weekly) and the intervention adjusted as necessary.

Over time, self-management strategies can be built into this system (Chafouleas et al., 2012). To accomplish this, the student and teacher rate the student individually and compare scores. A bonus could be awarded for similarity. Later, the student self-rates and the DBRC is intermittently checked for continued reliability. Sharing the DBRC with caregivers, noting positives as well, is an optional but important component. Table 11.2 provides two examples of a DBRC, one for elementary and one for secondary.

Table 11.2. Daily Behavior Report Card Examples

Elementary Example		Secondary Example	
Time	Rating	Class	Rating
8–9 am	☺ ☻ ☹	Period 1	1 2 3 4 5
9–10 am	☺ ☻ ☹	Period 2	1 2 3 4 5
10–11 am	☺ ☻ ☹	Period 3	1 2 3 4 5
11 am–12 pm	☺ ☻ ☹	Period 4	1 2 3 4 5
12–1 pm	☺ ☻ ☹	Period 5	1 2 3 4 5
1–2 pm	☺ ☻ ☹	Period 6	1 2 3 4 5
2–3 pm	☺ ☻ ☹	Period 7	1 2 3 4 5

FBA/BIP

A functional behavioral assessment (FBA) is not an intervention on its own. Rather, it is a systematic problem-solving process used to create interventions. The FBA process addresses misbehavior by identifying its causes (antecedents) and maintaining variables (consequences) for the challenging behavior. Only once the function, or purpose, served by the behavior is identified can effective interventions be implemented. The interventions ultimately derived from this process are referred to as FBA-based interventions and are effective interventions for problem behavior and school engagement according to WWC. These interventions comprise the behavior intervention plan (BIP). The FBA process to develop function-based interventions is described in this section.

Description of the Intervention

Challenging behavior occurs for a specific reason and in a consistent pattern. Patterns of behavior can be predicted to pinpoint when, where, and under what circumstances the behavior will occur (Sugai et al., 2000). Knowing this information is necessary and valuable in developing an effective intervention. All behavior serves a purpose and meets a student's need, regardless of it being appropriate or inappropriate. A functional behavioral assessment (FBA) uses various forms of data (i.e., direct, indirect) to identify the pattern and reason the behavior occurs (Scheuermann et al., 2022), and helps to inform the behavior intervention plan (BIP).

Behavior occurs for the purpose of getting something the student desires (i.e., access to tangibles, attention, or sensory) or avoiding something the student finds unpleasant (i.e., escape). Common classroom functions of behavior include getting the teacher or a peer's attention, gaining a sense of status, power, or control (a particular form of attention-seeking), or getting some tangible item. Additional applications of escape include avoiding a task or demand, a particular activity, or certain person(s). Interventions driven by FBA data are more likely to be effective than those developed by trial and error (Scheuermann et al., 2022).

Research Support

Discussions about the functional relationship of behavior can be found in the writings of Ivan Pavlov, B. F. Skinner, and other early behavioral psychologists (Sugai et al., 2000) who explained that behavior occurs in a predictable manner and is "related directly and functionally to environmental events" (p. 149). More recent school applications found FBA-based interventions to have a positive effect on behavior change across grade levels and disability status (Losinski et al., 2015). According to the Collaboration for Effective Educator Development, Accountability, and Reform (CEEDAR) Center—a technical assistance center that supports efforts by state education agencies, school districts, and higher education institutions in instructing educators to successfully educate students with disabilities—conducting functional behavioral assessments to develop students' behavior support plans is a high-leverage practice and a critical EBP that has been shown to improve student outcomes (Westing, 2015).

How to Implement the Intervention

The first step in conducting a functional assessment of behavior is to gather data from a wide variety of sources, which can be classified into indirect observation, such as interviews, records reviews (i.e., rating scales and disciplinary referrals), and direct observation of the student in places where the behavior is both likely and less likely to occur. Next, the team analyzes all sources of data to identify patterns in the data, including when the behavior was more likely to occur, events that happened prior to the behavior, what happened immediately after the behavior, and whether or not the behavior continued. The final step of the FBA is to formulate a hypothesis about the conditions under which the behavior occurs.

The next phase in the process is to use the hypothesized behavior function to develop a behavior support plan (i.e., positive behavior support plan). Interventions that address the antecedent, or trigger, for the behavior are addressed. For example, if the student exhibits behaviors when seated near certain students, a change of seating should change behavior. If longer academic tasks trigger misbehavior, breaking the assignment into smaller tasks is appropriate.

Following antecedent and environmental changes, the behavior support plan identifies an acceptable replacement behavior for the student and how this will be taught, reinforced, and monitored. The expected behavior should be a part of the student's behavioral repertoire, easily done, and meet the same function as the challenging behavior. The final part of a behavior support plan is to identify reinforcement that is contingent upon desired behavior. Desired reinforcers are identified during the data-gathering process of the FBA.

The following example puts all steps of the FBA/BIP process together: A student disturbs their class by yelling out in class and making off-topic comments. The FBA process determines the function to be that of obtaining the teacher's attention. Knowing the function, the teacher utilizes function-based interventions and seats the student nearby so that the teacher can deliver higher rates of noncontingent attention (antecedent strategy). The teacher tells the student to raise a hand to request teacher attention (replacement behavior) and immediately calls on the student (reinforcement) when the replacement behavior is displayed. As the teacher observes and records behavioral improvements (direct observation, data monitoring), the teacher will begin thinning or fading the immediacy of the reinforcement.

RELEVANT EDUCATIONAL POLICY

There are specific sections of special education policy that provide safeguards and support for students who can benefit from intensive behavior support. Early in the history of special education policy, the Education for All Handicapped Children Act

(Public Law 94-142) was enacted in 1975. In 1990 changes were made to the policy and renamed the act to the Individuals with Disabilities Education Act (IDEA), and was reauthorized in 2004. Within IDEA, section 300.530 (2017) has specific provisions in place for students with behavioral needs to protect them and ensure they have access to an equitable education. Signed into order in 2015, the Every Student Succeeds Act (ESSA) focused on ensuring equity within the educational system for students with disabilities and students who are considered high-risk.

Section 300.530 of IDEA (2004) states that students have a right to a free appropriate public education (FAPE), no matter their behavior. Subcode (b) states that a student who has been identified as having a disability cannot be removed through suspension for more than ten consecutive days, as the student's least restrictive environment (LRE) would be changed. In addition, a student with a disability cannot be removed through suspension for more than a total of ten days per school year, when instances of suspension are due to separate occurrences of behavior. If a student's placement is being changed past ten consecutive days due to a suspension, the student can have a change in placement and be suspended longer than ten days upon holding a manifestation determination. The same team that creates the student's Individualized Education Plan (IEP) meets and determines if the behavior the student is being suspended for has a direct correlation to their diagnosed disability. If the IEP team determines that the behavior is not a manifestation of the student's disability, then the student may be disciplined in the same manner as a peer who does not have a disability. Subsection (d)(i) requires the student to continue receiving general and special services throughout the suspension. This alternative placement is determined by the IEP team and put into place to ensure the student continues to receive an education (IDEA, 2004).

In addition, subsection (d)(ii) states that an FBA should be performed to ensure that appropriate provisions are put into place to aid the student in managing behaviors while at school. Upon the completion of a FBA, the IEP team must create a BIP. A BIP contains goals, interventions, accommodations, and modifications that have been created based on the data collected from the FBA. The goal of the FBA and BIP process is to aid the student in decreasing the occurrences or intensity of an inappropriate behavior and increase the occurrences of expected behavior. For example, if a student was suspended due to physical altercations with other students, the team may determine through an FBA that the student should take frequent breaks to a sensory lab when feelings of anger or distress occur. With these provisions in place, educators, schools, and families can ensure that students who need intensive behavior support are guaranteed those supports and are not discriminated against due to their behavior.

FOUNDATIONAL LEARNING THEORY

Constructivism and behaviorism are two of the learning theories that are used throughout education. Both theories are based on the premise that student knowledge is built upon prior learning or experiences. The term knowledge encompasses not only academic concepts but functional skills that become behavior. In terms of behavior, all behavior is shaped by the contingencies that surround it. In terms of the two learning theories, new behaviors are considered new knowledge and students learn and use them based on prior knowledge or experiences. A similar premise is used in both theories, but there are also noticeable differences.

Constructivism is an educational learning theory based on the premise that student knowledge is built upon prior knowledge (Bächtold, 2013). The theory evolved in the 1980s and is seen by many as an explanation as to how students construct knowledge, not how educators are supposed to teach. Based on this theory students are provided information through instruction and will build connections from their prior knowledge to the new knowledge. By building on prior knowledge, it is understood that each student will interpret and use the new information in a different manner. In addition, there are three different versions of constructivism: cognitive, social, and radical. With cognitive constructivism the ability to interpret new information is based on one's cognitive ability (Powell & Kalina, 2009). In a sense, cognitive development enables certain pieces of information to be learned. If a student has not reached a certain stage of development, then some information cannot be learned to its fullest extent. Social constructivism is based on the idea that students learn new knowledge from social interactions and from interacting with the world around them (Powell & Kalina, 2009). This theory was coined by Lev Vygotsky and is commonly used throughout early childhood education. Lastly, radical constructivism is based on the idea that students only interpret knowledge and that their past experiences aid in creating those interpretations (Von Glasersfeld, 2013). All three can be seen as useful when interpreting how students are retaining and using the new information taught to them.

Behavior analysis is the study of the science of behavior, a philosophy that has three major branches: behaviorism, experimental analysis of behavior, and applied behavior analysis (Cooper et al., 2020). Behaviorism began in the early 1900s with John B. Watson, well-known in the field of psychology. Watsonian behaviorism is founded in the principle of environmental stimulus that evokes a response. An example would be if a bright light (environmental stimulus) flashes in front of your eye, then you blink (response). This relationship is often shown as S-R, with the S standing for stimulus and the R standing for response. B. F. Skinner opened a new world for behavior analysis with the creation of the experimental analysis of behavior branch in the 1930s. Skinner discovered that Watsonian behaviorism could not explain all behavior and therefore coined the terms respondent and operant behavior (Moxley, 1996). Respondent behavior was described by Watson with the S-R relationship. Operant behavior is different as the initial stimulus is not what drives the behavior, it is the stimulus that comes after the response. This relationship is shown as S-R-S, otherwise known as the three-term contingency (Cooper et al., 2020). The last branch of behavior analysis is applied behavior analysis, the implementation and application of behaviorism in applied settings. For example, within a second grade classroom, a student hears the teacher ask a question (S), the student raises their hand (R), and the teacher reinforces the behavior by praising them for raising their hand (S). The behavior of hand raising is reinforced by the teacher's verbal praise and therefore has a higher chance of occurring again.

GUIDING RESEARCH

All intensive behavior supports discussed in the chapter are considered EBPs. Specifically, for an intervention to be considered evidence-based, it must have several high-quality, rigorous, and experimental studies to support its use (Cook et al., 2019). In addition, the study implementing the intervention must meet certain quality indicators to ensure the fidelity of implementation. For example, PBIS was discussed earlier in the chapter and has been widely researched and supported throughout a multitude of settings and populations. The system has tiers of interventions that can be used to guide an educator through the decision-making process of behavior interventions. Each tier has EBPs that are thoroughly supported with rigorous research. Although the use of EBPs is highly suggested in education, these resources are not readily available to educators. Oftentimes, educators lean toward social media sites or websites such as Teacher Pay Teachers, many of which have not yet been empirically validated (Hunter & Hall, 2018; Sawyer et al., 2020). In addition, studies on interventions that are consequence-based and empirically supported, such as group contingencies, are published in smaller numbers than antecedent-based strategies, like precorrection (Hott et al., 2019).

PROFESSIONAL STANDARDS

Professional organizations have established standards for those who work with students with disabilities and/or behavioral needs. For example, the Council for Exceptional Children (CEC) has put forth several different sets of standards that educators can use as a guideline to ensure professional behavior and that students receive an equitable education. In this section we will discuss two separate sets of standards created and published by the CEC, the Code of Ethics and Multi-Tiered Systems of Support. Both are vital to the implementation of intensive behavioral support and the education of students with disabilities. These sets of standards and more can be found in table 11.3.

The Code of Ethics was published by the CEC in 2015. One of the ethical standards is to uphold the inclusion of students with disabilities. Inclusion is an important part of intensive behavior support, as the end goal should always be natural levels of reinforcement and the student being placed in their LRE. Another standard is for educators to use EBPs, as well as utilizing empirically validated evidence to make instruction- and behavior-related decisions. In addition, professionals within education must ensure that they do not partake in or tolerate any practices that could cause harm to an individual. By using EBPs and ensuring that

Table 11.3. Standards and Resources for Educator Conduct and Intervention Implementation

Source	Link
Council for Exceptional Children: Field and Clinical Experience Standards	https://exceptionalchildren.org/sites/default/files/2021-03/K12%20Initial%20Standards%20and%20Components.pdf
Council for Exceptional Children: Multi-Tiered System of Supports: The Integral Role of Special Education and Special Educators	https://exceptionalchildren.org/sites/default/files/2021-11/mtss_position__112021.pdf
Council for Exceptional Children: Code of Ethics	https://exceptionalchildren.org/sites/default/files/2020-07/Code%20of%20Ethics.pdf
Department of Education: Supporting Child and Student Social, Emotional, Behavioral, and Mental Health Needs	https://www2.ed.gov/documents/students/supporting-child-student-social-emotional-behavioral-mental-health.pdf

all interventions are faded to a natural level of reinforcement, one can appropriately use intensive behavior supports.

In November 2021, the CEC published a position statement on the use of MTSS and how educators play a role in those systems. The document sets standards for educators when making decisions pertaining to the education of students with disabilities. An example would be to ensure that the universal screening measures are being used for academics and behavior, which will drive instruction and interventions. Educators are also encouraged to use a multi-tiered system and data to guide decision-making. Universal screening is a Tier 1 support, while most intensive behavior support and response to intervention practices are considered Tier 2 or Tier 3. All three tiers are vital to educators and should be used appropriately to drive decision-making.

FORMATIVE AND SUMMATIVE ASSESSMENT

In general, the term assessment stands for any activity or task that is used to gather information that will be used for feedback and future direction (Black & Wiliam, 1998). Assessments are most often associated with making academic decisions using assignments, quizzes, and high-stakes testing. Although this is often the case, assessments can also be used to guide decisions made about behavioral interventions. Formative and summative assessments are used throughout the school year to aid in the decision-making process. When using formative and summative assessments, educators need to be thoughtful when deciding what assessments to use and what they plan to use the information for (Dixson & Worrell, 2016).

In the behavioral realm, assessments are administered at each tier based on student need. For example, universal screenings (i.e., Tier 1) that can be administered to students to identify risk of emotional or behavioral (i.e., antisocial) disabilities are the Student Risk Screening Scale and the Systematic Screening for Behavior Disorders (Lane et al., 2009). As student need increases, so does the need for assessments to identify appropriate interventions and supports. Examples include the *Behavior Assessment System for Children, 2nd edition (BASC-2): Behavioral and Emotional Screening System (BESS)* (Kamphaus & Reynolds, 2007), a behavior scale provided to individuals close to students receiving Tier 2 and 3 supports, or as part of the FBA process. It is important to use assessments as part of a holistic process that considers all factors of a student's school and home settings to ensure that appropriate supports and interventions are put into place.

CONCLUSION

Supporting students with emotional and behavioral needs is a multicomponent process that takes time and energy from multiple parties who must work together. The school team can help to facilitate this process by coordinating efforts, utilizing evidence-based interventions, and collecting data to make informed decisions. Keeping the students in mind at all points in the process will ensure student success.

REFERENCES

Allen, G. E., Common, E. A., Germer, K. A., Lane, K. L., Buckman, M. M., Oakes, W. P., & Menzies, H. M. (2020). A systematic review of the evidence base for active supervision in pre-K–12 settings. *Behavioral Disorders, 45*(3), 167–182. https://doi.org/10.1177/0198742919837646

Archer, A. L., & Hughes, C. A. (2010). *Explicit instruction: Effective and efficient teaching*. Guilford.

Axelrod, M. I., & Zank, A. J. (2012). Increasing classroom compliance: Using a high-probability command sequence with noncompliant students. *Journal of Behavioral Education, 21*, 119–33. https://doi.org/10.1007/s10864-011-9145-6

Bächtold, M. (2013). What do students "construct" according to constructivism in science education? *Research in Science Education, 43*, 2477–96. https://doi.org/10.1007/s11165-013-9369-7

Barrish, H. H., Saunders, M., & Wolf, M. M. (1969). Good behavior game: Effects of individual contingencies for group consequences on disruptive behavior in a classroom. *Journal of Applied Behavior Analysis, 2*(2), 119–24. https://doi.org/10.1901/jaba.1969.2-119

Black, P., & Wiliam, D. (1998). Inside the black box: Raising standards through classroom assessment. *Phi Delta Kappan, 92*(1), 81–90. https://doi.org/10.1177/003172171009200119

Bowman-Perrott, L., Burke, M. D., de Marin, S., Zhang, N., & Davis, H. (2015). A meta-analysis of single-case research on behavior contracts: Effects on behavioral and academic outcomes among children and youth. *Behavior Modification, 39*(2), 247–69. https://doi.org/10.1177/0145445514551383

Bross, L. A., Common, E. A., Oakes, W. P., Lane, K. L., Menzies, H. M., & Ennis, R. P. (2018). High-probability request sequence: An effective, efficient low-intensity strategy to support student success. *Beyond Behavior, 27*(3), 140–5.

Chafouleas, S. M., Sanetti, L. M. H., Jaffery, R., & Fallon, L. (2012). An evaluation of a classwide intervention package involving self-management and a group contingency on behavior of middle school students. *Journal of Behavioral Education, 21*, 34–57. https://doi.org/doi:10.1007/s10864-011-9135-8

Chow, J. C., & Gilmour, A. F. (2016). Designing and implementing group contingencies in the classroom: A teacher's guide. *TEACHING Exceptional Children, 48*(3), 137–43. https://doi.org/10.1177/0040059915618197

Colvin, G., & Scott, T. M. (2015). *Managing the cycle of acting-out behavior in the classroom* (2nd ed.). Corwin.

Comprehensive, Integrated, Three-Tiered Model of Prevention (Ci3T). (2022). *Operationally defining behavior: Target and replacement behaviors*. Retrieved April 5, 2022 from https://www.ci3t.org/wp-content/uploads/2016/08/FABI_Operationally_Defining_Behavior.pdf

Cook, B. G., Collins, L. W., Cook, S. C., & Cook, L. (2019). Evidence-based reviews: How evidence-based practices are systematically identified. *Learning Disabilities Research & Practice, 35*(1), 6–13. https://doi.org/10.1111/ldrp.12213

Cooper, J. O., Heron, T. E., & Heward, W. L. (2020). *Applied behavior analysis* (3rd ed.). Pearson.

Council for Exceptional Children. (2015a). *Code of ethics*. https://exceptionalchildren.org/sites/default/files/2020-07/Code%20of%20Ethics.pdf

Council for Exceptional Children. (2015b). *What every special educator must know: Professional ethics and standards*. https://exceptionalchildren.org/sites/default/files/2021-03/K12%20Initial%20Standards%20and%20Components.pdf

Council for Exceptional Children. (2021). *Position statement: Multi-tiered system of supports: The integral role of special education and special educators*. https://exceptionalchildren.org/sites/default/files/2021-11/mtss_position_112021.pdf

Dixson, D. D., & Worrell, F. C. (2016). Formative and summative assessment in the classroom. *Theory Into Practice*, 55(2), 153–59. https://doi.org/10.1080/00405841.2016.1148989

Drevon, D. D., Hixson, M. D., Wyse, R. D., & Rigney, A. M. (2019). A meta-analytic review of the evidence for check-in check-out. *Psychology in the Schools*, 56(3), 393–412. https://doi.org/10.1002/pits.22195

Durlak, J. A., Weissberg, R. P., Dymnicki, A. B., Taylor, R. D., & Schellinger, K. B. (2011). The impact of enhancing students' social and emotional learning: A meta-analysis of school-based universal interventions. *Child Development*, 82(1), 405–32. https://doi.org/10.1111/j.1467-8624.2010.01564.x

Edgemon, A. K., Rapp, J. T., Coon, J. C., Cruz-Khalili, A., Brogan, K. M., & Richling, S. M. (2021). Using behavior contracts to improve behavior of children and adolescents in multiple settings. *Behavioral Interventions*, 36(1), 271–88.

Fabiano, G. A., Vujnovic, R. K., Pelham, W. E., Waschbusch, D. A., Massetti, G. M., Pariseau, M. E., Naylor, J., Yu, J., Robins, M., Carnefix, T., Greiner, A. R., & Volker, M. (2010). Enhancing the effectiveness of special education programming for children with attention deficit hyperactivity disorder using a daily report card. *School Psychology Review*, 39(2), 219–39. https://doi.org/10.1080/02796015.2010.12087775

Ficarra, L., & Quinn, K. (2014). Teachers' facility with evidence-based classroom management practices: An investigation of teachers' preparation programmes and in-service conditions. *Journal of Teacher Education for Sustainability*, 16(2), 71–87. https://doi.org/10.2478/jtes-2014-0012

Gage, N. A., Scott, T., Hirn, R., & MacSuga-Gage, A. S. (2018). The relationship between teachers' implementation of classroom management practices and student behavior in Elementary School. *Behavioral Disorders*, 43(2), 302–15. https://doi.org/10.1177/0198742917714809

Goldstein, A. P. (1973). *Structured learning therapy: Toward a psychotherapy for the poor*. Academic.

Goldstein, A. P., & McGinnis, E. (1997). *Skillstreaming the adolescent: New strategies and perspectives for teaching prosocial skills*. Research.

Greenwood, C. R., Horton, B. T., & Utley, C. A. (2002). Academic engagement: Current perspectives on research and practice. *School Psychology Review*, 31(3), 328–49.

Gresham, F. M. (2013). Treatment integrity within a three-tiered model. In H. M. Walker & F. M. Gresham (Eds.), *Handbook of evidence-based practices for emotional and behavioral disorders: Applications in schools*. Guilford.

Hott, B. L., Berkeley, S., Reid, C. C., & Raymond, L. (2019). An analysis of special education practitioner journals: A focus on behavior. *Exceptionality*, 28(5), 333–48. https://doi.org/10.1080/09362835.2019.1579724

Hott, B., Randolph, K. M., Josephson, J., & Heiniger, S. (2021). Implementing electronic check-in/check-out to reduce challenging school bus behavior. *Journal of Special Education Technology*, 36(3), 152–61. https://doi.org/10.1177/0162643421100446

Hunter, L. J., & Hall, C. M. (2018). A survey of K–12 teachers' utilization of social networks as a professional resource. *Education and Information Technologies, 23*, 633–58. https://doi.org/10.1007/s10639-017-9627-9

Individuals with Disabilities Education Act (IDEA), 20 U.S.C. § 1400 (2004).

Kamphaus, R. W., & Reynolds, C. R. (2007). *Behavioral assessment system for children, 2nd edition (BASC-2): Behavioral and emotional screening system (BESS): Manual*. Pearson.

Lane, K. L., Oakes, W. P., Lusk, M. E., Cantwell, E. D., & Schatschneider, C. (2016). Screening for intensive intervention needs in secondary schools. *Journal of Emotional and Behavioral Disorders, 24*(3), 159–72. https://doi.org/10.1177/1063426615618624

Lane, K. L., Little, M. A., Casey, A. M., Lambert, W., Wehby, J., Weisenbach, J. L., & Phillips, A. (2009). A comparison of systematic screening tools for emotional and behavioral disorders. *Journal of Emotional and Behavioral Disorders, 17*(2), 93–105. https://doi.org/10.1177/1063426608326203

Lee, D. L., Belfiore, P. J., & Budin, S. G. (2008). Creating a momentum of school success. *TEACHING Exceptional Children, 40*(3), 65–70. https://doi.org/10.1177/004005990804000307

Lee, D. L., Belfiore, P. J., Scheeler, M. C., Hua, Y., & Smith, R. (2004). Behavioral momentum in academics: Using embedded high-*p* sequences to increase academic productivity. *Psychology in the Schools, 41*(7), 789–801. https://doi.org/10.1002/pits.20014

Litow, L., & Pumroy, D. K. (1975). A brief review of classroom group-oriented contingencies. *Journal of Applied Behavior Analysis, 8*(3), 341–47.

Losinski, M., Maag, J. W., Katsiyannis, A., & Ryan, J. B. (2015). The use of structural behavioral assessment to develop interventions for secondary students exhibiting challenging behaviors. *Education and Treatment of Children, 38*(2), 149–74. https://doi.org/doi:10.1353/etc.2015.0006

Maggin, D. M., Zurheide, J., Pickett, K. C., & Baillie, S. J. (2015). A systematic evidence review of the check-in/check-out program for reducing student challenging behaviors. *Journal of Positive Behavior Interventions, 17*(4), 197–208. https://psycnet.apa.org/record/2015-40173-002

Menzies, H. M., Lane, K. L., & Lee, J. M. (2009). Self-Monitoring strategies for use in the classroom: A promising practice to support productive behavior for students with emotional or behavioral disorders. *Beyond Behavior, 18*(2), 27–35.

Metcalf, T. (2012). What's your plan? Accurate decision making within a multi-tier system of supports: Critical areas in Tier 1. RTI Action Network. National Center for Learning Disabilities.

Mitchell, B. S., Adamson, R., & McKenna, J. W. (2017). Curbing our enthusiasm: An analysis of the check-in/check-out literature using the Council for Exceptional Children's evidence-based practice standards. *Behavior Modification, 41*(3), 343–67.

Moore Partin, T. C., Robertson, R. E., Maggin, D. M., Oliver, R. M., & Wehby, J. H. (2010). Using teacher praise and opportunities to respond to promote appropriate student behavior. *Preventing School Failure, 54*(3), 172–78. https://doi.org/10.1080/10459880903493179

Moreno, G., & Bullock, L. M. (2011). Principles of positive behaviour supports: Using the FBA as a problem-solving approach to address challenging behaviours beyond special populations. *Emotional and Behavioural Difficulties, 16*(2), 117–27. https://doi.org/10.1080/13632752.2011.569394

Moxley, R. A. (1996). The import of Skinner's three-term contingency. *Behavior and Philosophy, 24*(2) 145–67.

Pokorski, E. A. (2019). Group contingencies to improve classwide behavior of young children. *TEACHING Exceptional Children, 51*(5), 340–49.

Powell, K. C., & Kalina, C. (2009). Cognitive and social constructivism: Developing tools for an effective classroom. *Education, 130*(2), 241–50.

Riley-Tillman, T. C., Chafouleas, S. M., & Briesch, A. M. (2007). A school practitioner's guide to using daily behavior report cards to monitor student behavior. *Psychology in the Schools, 44*(1), 77–89. https://doi.org/10.1002/pits.20207

Sawyer, A. G., Dick, L. K., & Sutherland, P. (2020). Online mathematics teacherpreneurs developers on Teachers Pay Teachers: Who are they and why are they popular? *Education Sciences, 10*(9), 248. https://doi.org/10.3390/educsci10090248

Scheuermann, B., Billingsley, G., & Hall, J. (2022). *Positive behavioral supports for the classroom* (4th ed.). Pearson.

Sugai, G., & Horner, R. H. (2002). Introduction to the special series on positive behavior support in schools. *Journal of Emotional and Behavioral Disorders, 10*(3), 130–5. https://journals.sagepub.com/doi/10.1177/10634266020100030101 Sugai, G., Lewis-Palmer, T., & Hagan-Burke, S. (2000). Overview of the functional behavioral assessment process. *Exceptionality, 8*(3), 149–60. https://doi.org/10.1207/S15327035EX0803_2

US Department of Education. (n.d.) Every Student Succeeds Act. https://www.ed.gov/essa?src=rn

US Department of Education, Office of Special Education and Rehabilitative Services (2021). *Supporting child and student social, emotional, behavioral, and mental health needs.* https://www2.ed.gov/documents/students/supporting-child-student-social-emotional-behavioral-mental-health.pdf

Vannest, K. J., Davis, J. L., Davis, C. R., Mason, B. A., & Burke, M. D. (2010). Effective intervention for behavior with a daily behavior report card: A meta-analysis. *School Psychology Review, 39*(4), 654–72. https://doi.org/10.1080/02796015.2010.12087748

Von Glasersfeld, E. (2013). *Radical constructivism*. Routledge.

Westing, D. L. (2015). *Evidence-based practices for improving challenging behaviors of students with severe disabilities* (Document No. IC-14). CEEDAR Center. https://ceedar.education.ufl.edu/wp-content/uploads/2015/11/EBPs-for-improving-challenging-behavior-of-SWD.pdf Wills, H. P., Iwaszuk, W. M., Kamps, D., & Shumate, E. (2014). CW-FIT: Group contingency effects across the day. *Education and Treatment of Children, 37*(2), 191–210. https://doi.org/10.1353/etc.2014.0016

Wolfe, K., Pyle, D., Charlton, C. T., Sabey, C. V., Lund, E. M., & Ross, S. W. (2016). A systematic review of the empirical support for check-in check-out. *Journal of Positive Behavior Interventions, 18*(2), 74–88. https://doi.org/10.1177/1098300715595957

12

Good Study Strategies

B. Keith Ben-Hanania Lenz

FOR THE PURPOSE OF THIS CHAPTER, studying is defined as the intentional effort one directs to understand, remember, and express understanding of information in order to learn and then demonstrate competence. Studying goes beyond having the skills required for initially acquiring information (i.e., word identification, identifying main idea and details, writing sentences and paragraphs, identifying a problem, etc.). Study is more focused on targeting information and then intentionally making a commitment to learn that information so that it can be used to complete a task. Such tasks might include taking a test, making a presentation, writing a response or report, or applying information to complete a task.

For example, you might have read the chapters in this book because you chose (or were assigned) those chapters to read, but the next step in using the information in them would be to intentionally engage in study activities that connect the newly acquired information to what you already know. Selecting strategies that assist you in meaningfully organizing information into categories will allow you to retrieve the information to demonstrate that you can recall, express, and apply it when you need it (i.e., at the request of your teacher and for personal use). Studying implies that you are motivated to intentionally devote energy that will increase the likelihood that you can retrieve what you have learned in the future.

Students who are asked to read a passage and answer a set of comprehension questions immediately (short-term memory) are more likely to answer the questions correctly than when they are asked the next day (longer-term memory); students are even less likely to answer the questions correctly after several weeks, months, or years have passed (long-term memory). A student's ability to answer the questions may be tied to the student's understanding of the recall expectations for the test and the types of remembering strategies that they choose to use. While the passage reading example may or may not have required students to study the passage in order to be ready for a test, the point of the example is to illustrate the importance of a learner understanding and assessing the task, assessing whether or not they considered using different strategies to get ready for the test, asking questions about the test they might have to take, and then deciding how they will approach the task and the test.

The level of understanding achieved from studying information is directly related to the level of intentional energy that is invested in using *good* study strategies.

Good is emphasized because some study strategies are not as effective and efficient as others. For example, if I gave you a list of five fruits to remember to bring to work tomorrow (e.g., apple, orange, banana, peach, pear), and you were not able to write them down, you might simply repeat (i.e., rehearse) the list a few times, because that is a simple strategy to use for most people for this task. Investing energy in creating a complex mnemonic device would be an inefficient strategy for this task for most people. However, if the list of fruits were longer and included more unfamiliar types of fruits, simply repeating that list over a few times might be both ineffective and inefficient.

WHAT SHOULD BE STUDIED?

The elephant in the room in any discussion of studying is that we cannot possibly learn and remember all the information about a topic, or even the information presented in the textbook/material/media, and remember it. To make the elephant even bigger, the task of studying is further complicated by what the teacher is asked/required to teach, what they choose to teach, how they teach it, how much time they have to teach it, and how they choose to assess it. A term that has long been associated with information technology that has also been applied to education is the GIGO (garbage in, garbage out) principle (Stenson, 2016). Originally, GIGO was used to convey the idea that if we put bad information into computer models, the information we get back will be bad. In education, the idea translates to the notion that if we teach and assign bad/not useful information for study and then assess bad/not useful or less-important information, the result will be that students will not learn what is culturally critical and, ultimately, learners will develop poor insights, make poor decisions, and be unprepared for life. Efforts to establish standards and to improve what and how we assess what is taught, as well as what we expose students to when we don't engage in direct instruction, are designed to avoid GIGO. However, the teacher is largely responsible for determining what students should study and how it will be assessed. So, the *quality* of what we want students to study is critical.

TEACHING STUDENTS WITH POOR STUDY STRATEGIES

The literature on students with disabilities and on other struggling learners has long pointed out the problems that these students have with studying. In addition, discussions of factors influencing studying and how to implement interventions designed to help students develop good study strategies represent an important consideration in the delivery of a multi-tiered system of support (e.g., Bryant et al., 2017; Hoover & Patton, 2007). There are two validated models that have been used to guide effective strategy instruction. The self-regulated strategy development (SRSD) instructional model was developed to improve written expression (Harris & Graham, 2018), and (b) the Strategic Instruction Model (SIM™; Schumaker & Deshler, 1988) was originally designed to address the instructional needs of adolescents with disabilities and other struggling learners.

It is striking that the instructional approaches used to teach learning strategies in both models are very similar. The instructional steps for both models are summarized in modules available from the IRIS Center at Peabody–Vanderbilt University (IRIS Center, 2013) and in *High Leverage Practices for Inclusive Classrooms* (McLeskey et al., 2022).

Another consideration in teaching study strategies is the nature of the student's disability. Therefore, decisions about teaching study strategies must be made in conjunction with other areas of strategy instruction (e.g., word identification, comprehension, written expression, test-taking, social skills, etc.), instructional accommodations, and curriculum modifications. If a student has a disability acquiring information from print, listening to presentations, or visually processing what they are shown, they will need supports and accommodations. Students must be able to gain information in a way that allows them to store that information in short-term memory in order for them to study the information for storage in long-term memory, and then be able to express what they know and demonstrate competence on tests. Study includes the strategies that learners use after the acquisition of knowledge and before they are asked to demonstrate/express that knowledge.

The shift from teaching acquisition strategies to teaching study strategies includes teaching *storage strategies* and *retrieval strategies*. Storage strategies involve teaching students how to: (a) distinguish important from less-important information, (b) note/write/record the differentiation of important from less-important information, (c) analyze and organize important information according to relationships between and among information and the learner's background knowledge (e.g., linear, hierarchical, comparative, causal, analogical, inferential, etc.), and finally (d) confirm the accuracy of what they have recorded. Retrieval strategies involve teaching students how to: (a) select appropriate remembering strategies and include the use of rehearsal, elaboration, and mnemonic devices; (b) transform information into remembering systems that are meaningful and accurate; and (c) select and use various forms of review, practice using remembering systems and using information (independently and with others), and self-testing. Retrieval strategies are used to build fluency and students' confidence in their ability to recall information to successfully meet testing demands. During this stage in the process, the teacher guides students in following the steps of good study strategies through the use of ongoing teaching routines that use direct, explicit instruction. As students gain knowledge of basic information-acquisition strategies, the teacher can shift the emphasis from guiding study to instructing students in how to study independently.

Finally, it can be argued that if a student uses poor acquisition, storage, and retrieval strategies to gain and remember information for personal use, there is little use in teaching test-taking strategies or providing accommodations for taking tests to demonstrate what has been learned. Although test-taking strategies and testing accommodations have received a lot of attention as part of the instructional plans for students with disabilities, this attention is only warranted if there is evidence that the student has both good acquisition and study strategies, or that there are supports in place that ensure that it is reasonable to expect that students know and can remember the information so that they can express what they know and demonstrate competence. These considerations must be reflected in the design of educational services, the provision of a multi-tiered system of supports, the implementation of progress monitoring, and the development of individual educational plans.

In addition to the instructional methodology used to teach study strategies, and considerations related to decisions made related to the nature of a student's disability, we also know that good study strategies:

1. teach students to be more *intentional*,
2. require *intensive* instruction,
3. provide *thorough* information about strategy knowledge and performance,
4. provide instruction in *contextually appropriate* information about strategy use when presented with different demands, and
5. promote generalization by the way they are designed and linked to other strategies.

Including these features in the instructional process will increase the likelihood that more students will be successful learning and using good strategies. The following section describes how these features should be incorporated into the design of study strategy instruction.

FEATURES OF GOOD STUDY STRATEGIES

Good learning strategies prompt learners to be *intentional* by including information in the steps of the strategy that inform the learner about the general and specific characteristics of situations that signal that a specific strategy or set of strategies should be considered to complete the task efficiently and effectively. In addition to specific learning situations, such as in a math or science class, intentionality is also characterized by language cues, such as "When you see this . . ." or "In situations where you are given an illustration along with the test, you should. . . ." Intentionality is also indicated by language cues or phrases that signal, for example, "do this first and, as you do this" or "consider two factors before you make a decision and move to the next step." Finally, teaching intentionality means observing when the student does not recognize that a strategy is needed, stopping the student and teaching them to see the cues associated with the need for a strategy, and teaching them to select an appropriate strategy for the situation.

Strategy instruction is *intensive* if it provides a sufficient level of detail about the new strategy that matches the level of strategic background knowledge possessed by the learner. For example, a general set of steps to guide the study of a topic may need to be either condensed or expanded if the learner already has some knowledge of the topic or is already using some successful tactics in the way they study. Likewise, if the study topic assumes background knowledge that the learner does not possess, the steps may need to be modified. Therefore, the strategies employed in study should be personalized for the appropriate level of intensity to maximize each individual student's success. This requires teachers to have knowledge of a variety of ways to study that might be suggested for different learners.

Good learning strategies should address features of the steps that relate to those areas of learning that both promote and inhibit learning. That is, the strategy should be *thorough*. In addition to the steps of a strategy being sufficiently detailed and personalized, they should address the behavioral, cognitive, social, emotional, and metacognitive elements associated with completing the task. Behavioral features address what the learner should be observed doing (e.g., "Start by looking at each page of the chapter."). Cognitive features of the strategy address an unobserved process that should be used (e.g., "Identify each chapter subheading, paraphrase what you think that subheading is about, and turn the subheading into a question that you want to answer when you read that section."). Social features address appropriate interactions that may be needed or considered as part of study (e.g., "When you ask for help, remember . . ."). Emotional features address how to handle anxiety or fears that may emerge as you study (e.g., "Before you begin, remember to take three deep breaths and breathe out slowly."). Metacognitive features address the unobserved reflections related to your progress implementing the other features of a good strategy (e.g., "Ask yourself, 'Did taking three deep breaths work or do I need to take more deep breaths or find another way to relax?'").

Good study strategies are *contextually appropriate*. The way information should be studied varies across disciplines and conditions where information is obtained (e.g., academic versus recreational, face-to-face versus online, listening versus reading requirements, expository versus narrative text, etc.), and with the personalities/characteristics of both the people associated with learning and study conditions and the materials that they use. Elements in study strategies that must be changed to meet contextual demands should be identified and practiced.

While good study strategies should be contextually appropriate, instruction should forecast use of the strategy beyond the immediate context so that it is *generalizable*. To a large degree, the study strategy should be designed so that a good share of the steps build on, repeat, or are similar to other strategies that the learner already knows. Repeating appropriate features makes learning new ways to study at different stages of study easier. For example, repeatedly incorporating the prompt to self-test with flash cards, turn headings into questions, paraphrase what the passage was about, or create lists to remember as part of study will help a learner use these study habits across learning conditions. Study strategies that are applicable across disciplines, settings, people, materials, and performance tasks make them more *generalizable*.

APPROACHES TO TEACHING GOOD STUDY STRATEGIES

Study strategies are learned by what the teacher does both implicitly and explicitly. *Implicit* knowledge is implied, may be suggested, or may be hinted at but is not actually stated or explained. Individuals who are fluent with regard to a topic often have a lot of implicit knowledge but forget to "surface" the insights they subconsciously use as they present information to others. Experts may assume that this implicit knowledge is common knowledge.

Explicit knowledge is information that is described in a manner that leaves nothing in doubt and needs no further explanation or interpretation. When the goal is to be more explicit, the number of details provided in the explanation increases. When we are trying to be more explicit, we are intentionally trying to surface our implicit knowledge to provide critical insights about what we know.

One caution when providing very explicit instruction to struggling learners is that this type of instruction can become tedious and overwhelming if all the information is provided at once. To avoid this, two approaches to introducing study strategies should be considered.

The first approach is to take class time to lead students through the study process using evidence-based practices that are linked to successful independent study.

When students do not have the strategies to study independently (and there is no time to teach good study strategies), the teacher accommodates for this strategy deficit by leading students through the study process. This becomes an instructional accommodation which, when used as a classwide teaching routine, provides a group accommodation that is likely to be in the best interest of every student in the class due to varying levels of strategy knowledge related to studying. This moves the practice of supporting studying to instruction that is *universally designed for learning*. Surfacing "how to study" as an ongoing, classwide activity requires that the teacher establish effective teaching routines that model the use of steps related to good study as a way to provide guided study support. The following is an example of a teacher setting up information in science that needs to be learned for a test:

> The first thing we need to do is take a look at the information and organize or format it so that it is a form that is easy to learn. Let's see . . . This information can be put into the form of a list. The title of the list is "Vertebrates." *(The teacher displays "Vertebrates" on the board and underlines it.)* What items should we put in this list? *[Fishes; Amphibians; Reptiles; Birds; and Mammals.] (The teacher writes these words in list form under "Vertebrates.")* Great. This is how we're going to make lists in this class, with underlined heading and items underneath. Please write this list in your notes. The list format is one format we will use in this class. There are other formats that we will explore as well. (Schumacher et al., 1998, p. 15)

When the teacher routinely describes, models, prompts students to record the study device, and provides feedback related to how well students set up and record information as part of an ongoing instructional routine, they are making an implicit expectation about studying more explicit. When the process is repeated, students are taught that the study strategies that are being modeled are good practices to use in independent study. However, after students have been exposed to the study routine over time, the teacher should move to more explicit instruction in the strategy. The following example demonstrates a teacher doing this:

> We have just created a list with a heading to organize information that you will study. We have been doing this together, but you need to learn how to do this on your own. Let's stop and look at how we created a list and identified a heading. I want you to take notes about what I am going to describe for you. I will also display each step, so you copy them into your notes. I want you to know these steps so that you can create your own lists to study.
>
> Studying requires you to organize information, and one way to organize information is to identify lists of important information. Where do you think you can find the list that you need to remember? *[Display "Places to find lists," and write the students' responses under the heading. The list of places should include at least the following: textbooks, study guides, classroom displays, and student notes from presentations.]* These are all places you will find lists. You need to find lists of important information so that you can decide which ways are best to remember the different types of information in your lists.
>
> We're now going to learn a quick and simple strategy for making and remembering lists so that you can use that information. The remembering system, which is called a mnemonic device, is called "LISTS." (Nagel et al., 1986, p. 26)

The teacher's instructions begin to surface their own knowledge of how to create lists in order to prepare their students to use more specific study strategies (i.e., the selection of appropriate remembering strategies). However, this approach assumes that the teacher is willing to surface the study strategy as they teach and is able to include the time necessary to teach students how to use it as part of the course content. In addition, this approach does not address the degree of success that students will have in generalizing the study strategies to other courses.

The second approach is to explicitly teach effective study strategies that students can use to meet the demands presented across a variety of disciplines, and then to teach them insights about how to adapt these strategies to meet the varying demands of different disciplines and classroom settings. This second approach is often used in special education, because it does not require close collaboration with general education teachers as to how instruction in study strategies might be integrated into their course instruction. However, regardless of who is teaching study strategies, it is important that the teacher inform students about how strategies apply to specific disciplinary content. For example, in the procedures developed for *strategic tutoring* (e.g., Hock et al., 2000), the goal of instruction is to directly link good strategies that the student is currently using to study to a set of additional good strategies that will improve study outcomes in a specific course.

While practices associated with *disciplinary literacy* (e.g., Shanahan & Shanahan, 2012) are aligned with integrating how to acquire disciplinary knowledge, disciplinary literacy practices often target students who are already fairly strategic in learning content; disciplinary literacy introduces thinking processes for deeper investigation of content-area knowledge. Students who are less strategic often do not have the foundational and intermediate strategies required for disciplinary literacy. As a result, opportunities for students with disabilities to learn good study strategies to apply in their content-area courses to access and master critical information are often required within a multi-tiered system of supports (Faggella-Luby et al., 2012). The steps for direct instruction in strategies are summarized in modules available from the IRIS Center at Peabody–Vanderbilt University (IRIS Center, 2013) and in *High Leverage Practices for Inclusive Classrooms* (McLeskey et al., 2022).

GOOD WAYS TO STUDY

Efforts to understand, remember, and express understanding of information and to demonstrate competence may involve different strategies at different stages of study. In addition, it is impossible to teach every way to study; there are a variety of effective study strategies appropriate for different stages of study. As we teach, we need to adopt a mindset that, at every stage of learning, we need to decide what information is most critical to know, how that information is best organized for understanding so that it can be processed and held in short-term memory, and how we can help students link that information to what they already know so that they can recall it later. This is when good study must become more intentional. The two groups of good study strategies that contribute to this intentionality include *storage strategies* and *retrieval strategies*.

Organizing Information to Structure Study

It's difficult to organize information that you don't understand. Organization requires a learner to identify patterns in information. The ability to identify patterns is dependent on the learner's background knowledge and their capacity to make associations with what is already known, and then to link new information to prior knowledge in meaningful ways. As a result, how a teacher, media, or textbook initially presents, provides learning experiences, and makes assignments that engage students in learning information defines what and how a student studies. The first set of study strategies revolves around teaching students to recognize and compensate for how the information they receive is organized, so that they develop a set of information *storage strategies* that they can use to respond to the different ways information is presented.

Listening and Note-Taking

What is recorded in notes for study is influenced by the ability of a learner to use cues that signal: (a) level of importance (e.g., very important, moderately important, less important); (b) structure (e.g., hierarchical, linear); (c) relationships (e.g., causal, comparative, analogical, inferential); (d) links to background knowledge; and (e) links to the way information will be assessed (i.e., "What do I know about the way my knowledge will be assessed?"). In addition, *how* a learner records information for study (e.g., use of abbreviations, note-taking systems, completeness, efficiency, etc.) (Seigel, 2018) also influences the quality of what is studied.

Suggestions for teaching students different tactics for improving the quality of their notes can be found in the literature (e.g., Bryant et al., 2017; IRIS Center, 2013). Instruction in good listening and note-taking requires teaching students the prerequisites for note-taking, which includes how to listen for signals related to what to record in their notes. Berry, Deshler, and Schumaker (2011) demonstrated that teaching a set of integrated strategies to create a listening/note-taking system improved note-taking for college students with learning disabilities as well as students without learning disabilities. *The Listening and Note-Taking Strategy* (Berry et al., 2011) is comprised of four lessons. The first lesson teaches students a strategy for how to listen as class begins and includes teaching students how to recognize different types of cues that signal attention, importance, structure, and relationships to guide what information to note. These cues include identifying the mannerisms of the presenter, introductory cues, big idea questions, sequential cues, and summarizing cues, as well as verbal cues to show emphasis based on repeating, to draw attention to specific information, and to clarify.

The second and third lessons focus on teaching students what and how to note information. The steps include teaching students how to quickly record information by using key words, synonyms, abbreviations, and symbols. This process also includes reviewing notes to highlight key words and cross out mistakes. Students are then taught the "T" method for organizing how they note information; students are taught that all topics and main ideas identified in the presentation are placed on the left side of the "T" and all supporting information is placed on the right side.

Another dimension of collecting and organizing information for study is related to assignment completion. Beyond the information provided by teachers, in textbooks, and by the use of media, another source for identifying what should be important to study is represented in the assignments given by teachers. When teachers create high-quality assignments designed with the test in mind, successful completion of these can provide students with valuable materials to study when preparing for tests. High-quality assignments should forecast the types of thinking and the types of relationships between and among content elements that teachers plan to evaluate on outcome measures. Assignments should provide opportunities for students to practice demonstrating their ability to see and show understanding of relationships. However, assignment completion has often been a challenge for many students who have difficulty organizing information.

Hughes, Ruhl, Deshler, and Schumaker (1995) developed and evaluated a system for teaching students how to record and track assignments, divide assignments into major parts, plan how and when to complete the parts of assignments, review assignments to ensure their completeness and quality, and turn assignments in on time. As part of evaluating the assignment completion process, Hughes et al., 1995) found that an important element of being prepared for academic tests was how students recorded information about assignments in planners. Noting the inconsistent way that typical school "planners" were structured to record assignment information from teachers, the authors designed a planner to allow students to record more detailed information about assignments with prompts for them to develop plans related to completing high-quality assignments, setting assignment completion goals, and turning assignments in on time. Hughes, Ruhl, Schumaker, and Deshler (2002) conducted research on students with learning disabilities who were completing half of their assignments in their general education classes. Student assignment completion increased from 58% during baseline to 70% completion during the maintenance phase of the intervention period. In addition, the grade point average in targeted general education classrooms improved.

Building on the importance of assignments, Rademacher, Deshler, Schumaker, and Lenz (2011) created and evaluated instructional guidelines for teachers to develop high-quality assignments, teach students how to record them, and model how to use an assignment completion quality checking system when working independently. Rademacher et al. (2011) also used the same planner designed by Hughes et al. to guide students in how to record more detailed assignments and to plan assignment completion. Student satisfaction with assignments increased compared to students who did not receive the intervention (Rademacher, 1993).

The ability to identify relationships within and between sets of information is a major prerequisite for organizing information for study. Scanlon, Schumaker, and Deshler (1996) investigated the effect of teaching both students with and without learning disabilities to develop a graphic organizer depicting the relationships (i.e., comparative, causal/sequential, descriptive, problem/solution), explain the organizer to others, and then use the organizer to study for tests. Both students with and without learning disabilities outperformed students on outcome tests compared to students who did not receive the intervention (Scanlon et al., 2004).

Structuring Good Study

Berry et al. (2011) added instruction in the fourth lesson of *The Listening and Note-Taking Strategy* in which students are taught a set of good study strategies, including: (a) how to gather information that they might have missed by asking for information, when to ask, and how to ask (i.e., the use of appropriate social skills); (b) a process for rereading and highlighting lists, important terms/relationships, definitions, and connections to supporting details; (c) a self-testing process that involves using topics, main ideas, and details in their notes to ask and answer questions; (d) a strategy for drawing diagrams to represent relationships (e.g., descriptive, causal/sequential, comparative, etc.) signaled as important in their notes to leverage the effective use of visual organizers; and (e) using positive self-talk throughout the entire process of approaching learning in the class, taking notes, studying, and taking tests.

An important element of the self-test process involved in studying includes identifying and organizing information, creating good lists, and determining how to remember information for personal use, which includes performing well on tests. For example, teaching strategies for remembering information should be paired with instruction in targeting, organizing, preparing information that must be remembered, selecting the most effective and efficient approach for remembering, and then setting up both individual and group self-testing activities. Nagel, Schumaker, and Deshler (1986) developed and evaluated a systematic set of study strategies specifically designed to address the poor study habits of students with disabilities. In addition, this intervention included detailed instructions for teachers to implement a progress monitoring system to gauge student improvement in learning and implementing good study practices across classrooms.

Nagel et al. organized their approach to good study into five stages of instruction, including: (a) assessment of a student's ability to construct lists of information targeted for learning and their ability to recall the information in lists; (b) detailed instruction in five steps to create a mnemonic device using the first-letter mnemonic technique (see figure 12.1) and, keeping the knowledge of how to use the first-letter mnemonic device technique in mind, how to use cues in information to create lists of high-quality, appropriately chunked, to-be-remembered information; (c) demonstration of how to match the listed information to the best mnemonic device; (d) description of method for transferring the information packaged in the mnemonic device to an index card that can be used in study; and (e) explanation of how to use the index card to self-test knowledge of the information and what that information means.

STEPS FOR MAKING AND MASTERING LISTS

Step 1: **L**ook for clues (i.e., use signals of importance/relationships to chunk types of information to create informative headings).

Step 2: **I**nvestigate the items (i.e., a process for chunking lists of information and checking the quality and format of list items so that they are suitable for creating mnemonics).

Step 3: **S**elect a mnemonic device using "FIRST."

Step 4: **T**ransfer the information to a card (i.e., create and organize study cards for study).

Step 5: **S**elf-test (i.e., a process for self- and partner-testing with flash cards).

STEPS FOR MAKING AND MASTERING LISTS USING "FIRST"

Step 1: **F**orm a word (with the first letters of the words).

Step 2: **I**nsert a letter (when inserting a letter will create a memorable word).

Step 3: **R**earrange the letters (to form a word if order is not important).

Step 4: **S**hape a sentence (using the first word of each item in the list).

Step 5: **T**ry combinations (create a remembering system by combining the information learned in "FIRST" steps 1–4).

Figure 12.1 Example of an Integrated System of Strategies: The FIRST-Letter Mnemonic Strategy Intervention

Note: The instructional details that the teacher uses with a student to describe, model, practice, give feedback, generalize across classes, and monitor progress are included in the manual used to implement this intervention with fidelity. The steps presented above are only the mnemonic devices used in the remembering system to help the student recall a larger set of cognitive, metacognitive, social, and emotional information prompts related to success in studying.

Source: Nagel et al. (1986). Used with permission.

The intervention developed by Nagel et al. (1986) was designed to be taught directly, with its use then transferred to a general education classroom via collaborative co-teaching arrangements to ensure generalization of the strategy to different content areas to meet the study demands of those settings. Similar interventions have been designed and empirically validated to address the process of remembering different types of information, such as pairs or grouping of information (e.g., *The Paired Associates Strategy* [Bulgren & Schumaker, 1996]) and vocabulary (e.g., *The LINCS Vocabulary Strategy* [Ellis, 2000] and *The Vocabulary LINCING Routine* [Ellis, 2001]). These interventions used a validated instructional methodology that ensured the use of direct, explicit instruction, practice, and feedback to promote learning for students with disabilities.

Another approach to promoting the use of good strategies for studying information was developed (Schumaker et al., 1998) and evaluated (Bulgren et al., 1994, 1997) to present design-and-use strategies for remembering as a collaborative instructional routine that a general education teacher could embed in their teaching as a part of ongoing content-area instruction. In this teaching routine, instruction is provided to an entire class on different types of recall devices (see textbox 12.1). Each device is described along with how and when it should be used. A "glossary" of recall devices is created for the class to reference on an ongoing basis.

TEXTBOX 12.1. THE "GLOSSARY" OF RECALL DEVICES INTRODUCED IN THE RECALL ENHANCEMENT ROUTINE

Picture Devices
- Snapshot
- Movie
- Story
- Relating
- Symbol

Keyword Devices
- Boxing
- Reminding

First-Letter
- Acronym
- Sentence

Series
- Pegword
- Location

Other
- Rhyming
- Coding

Source: Schumaker et al. (1998). Used with permission.

Once students are aware of the different types of devices that can be used to remember information, the teacher continues providing content-area instruction. When the teacher determines that there is a significant body of information that needs to be remembered, the teacher guides the class in creating a remembering system for that information. The routine involves: (a) formatting the information for recall, (b) analyzing the type of information and selecting an appropriate recall device from the "glossary," (c) creating a recall device for that information, (d) developing a narrative that links the device to their prior knowledge, (e) creating a set of questions to use for self-testing, and (f) developing a plan related to how they will use the device to study. Textbox 12.2 presents a worksheet that shows how a teacher would guide students in developing a recall device for study. This example incorporates many of the elements associated with developing a remembering system that can be used to retrieve information for performance tasks and personal use.

TEXTBOX 12.2. THE FACTOR WORKSHEET USED IN THE RECALL ENHANCEMENT ROUTINE

Recall Device Sheet

Format the Information (Type of information: List, Pair, Trio, Definition, or Other)
   Classes of Fishes
      Boney
      Jawless
      Cartilage

Analyze the Information and Select a Device
   Type of Memory Device: *Boxina*

Create the Recall Device

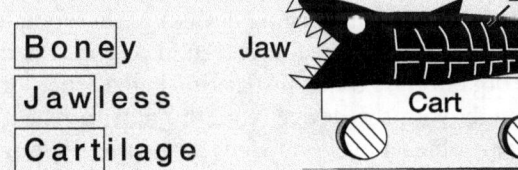

Tie It Together

   My husband went fishing and caught a huge shark, a type of fish. He had a big jaw, and we could see his bones. I wanted to show him to all of my students, so I took him to class on a cart. He was too heavy for me to carry. I got the words "jaw," "bone," and "cart" by looking for the little words found in the three items in our list. Be sure to remember the longer words for each of these short words.

Organize Some Questions
   What are the three classes of fishes?
   Describe the three classes of fishes.
   Compare and contrast the three classes of fishes.

Review Plan
   Partners will study together on Sept. 15

Note: From Schumaker et al. (1998). Used with permission.

224　Chapter 12: Good Study Strategies

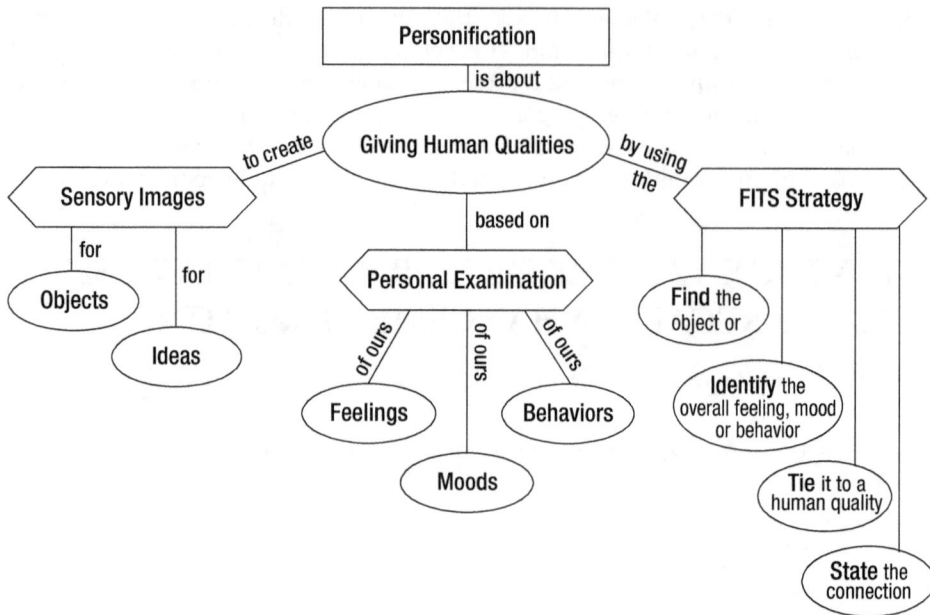

Figure 12.2　Curriculum Map of Figurative Language: Personification
Source: Lenz et al. (2008). Used by permission.

Many of the study strategies related to storage and retrieval suggest the use of flash cards for self-testing. In addition to the use of flash cards, self-questioning, rehearsal, and self-testing, some study interventions have included the use of graphic organizers to organize and prepare for tests. When teaching devices, such as graphic organizers, are used with students and students are also involved in co-constructing the information recorded in graphic organizers, explicit instruction in the procedural steps related to how and when to study with the device (e.g., prompts to rehearse and self-test) should be included as part of teaching good study strategies. As shown in figure 12.1, the last step in the strategy is to self-test.

For example, *The ORDER Routine* (Scanlon et al., 2004) incorporated the study of graphic organizers as part of self-testing. In another study, Lenz, Adams, Bulgren, Pouliot, and Laraux (2007) compared repeated information, guiding questions, and curriculum maps as ways to review information for tests. The results indicated that the test performance of students with learning disabilities on content tests was significantly greater when students reviewed information using questions based on the structure and line labels included in graphic curriculum maps over the use of only guiding questions or repetition. Figure 12.2 depicts one of the curriculum maps used in the intervention.

A question was posed for each shape with the corresponding answer found beneath it. Students were taught to use the map to generate questions and formulate answers as part of their review. The following example provides a possible question/answer chain prompted by the curriculum map.

Question: What is this lesson about?

Answer: Personification.

Question: What is personification?

Answer: Personification is about giving human qualities to something.

Question: How do we give human qualities to something?

Answer: We create a sensory image for an object or idea.

Question: What is giving human qualities based on?

Answer: We use personal examination of our own human feelings, moods, or behaviors.

Question: How do we use personification to give human qualities to objects or ideas?

Answer: We find an object/idea. Then we identify the overall feeling or behavior. Next, we tie the object or idea to the human quality.

Question: What is an example of an object that might be personified in a story?

Answer: Tree.

Question: What feeling, mood, or behavior could you tie to a tree?

Answer: A tree might be "crying."

Question: What could be the connection between a tree and crying?

Answer: A tree might be sad because it was going to be cut down. The tree could be described as crying.

Another important element that is often overlooked in teaching students how to study is their knowledge and use of social skills required to engage in collaborative study and self-testing. A set of interventions designed to promote collaborative study was developed by Sue Vernon and her colleagues at the University of Kansas. The social/emotional interventions developed by Vernon et al. represent the emphasis on teaching and practicing social skills in the context of authentic academic tasks where students are expected to collaborate around learning rather than social skills being taught as a separate curriculum. Table 12.1 lists interventions that were designed to teach students how to collaborate in ways that influence good study.

The Overall Study Plan

In addition, taking advantage of resources that can improve or make the process of studying better should be part of the study process. For example, opportunities for using technology to provide multiple ways to represent information, locating both print and online open education resources (OERs) that clarify information that is still misunderstood, using resources that show how information is organized, seeking out different opportunities for practice, creating different types of self-testing opportunities, and promoting collaboration that depends on the use of good strategies are also part of learning how to engage in good study under different conditions. These opportunities can be used to support the design of an overall study plan.

Table 12.1. Interventions to Promote Collaborative Study

Collaborative Skill	Focus of Intervention
Talking Together	Teaching students how to collaborate respectfully and responsibly during study by taking turns, giving others a chance to speak and be heard, showing kindness.
Basic Social Skills for Cooperation: *The SCORE Skills*	Teaching students how to share ideas, compliment others, offer help and encouragement, recommend changes, exercise self-control.
Following Instructions Together	Teaching students how to help each other follow oral and written instructions and complete assignments
Organizing Together	Teaching students how create an organized learning environment with partners to learn and apply organizational strategies such as calendars, notebooks, desks, lockers, and backpacks.
Taking Notes Together	Teaching students how to work with a partner to recording information quickly when listening to presentation, reading assignments, and using media.
The Teamwork Strategy	Teaching students how to work in a small group to analyze and break up assignments, equitably assign tasks to group members, ask and offer help, ask and give feedback, assemble assignment parts to a final product, and evaluate the group process and collaborative skills.
Thinking Together: *The THINK Strategy*	Teaching students how to work together to solve problems in different content areas to identify and analyze problems, investigate the problem, brainstorm solutions and their pros and cons, decide on a solution, develop implementation plan, evaluate the collaborative process.
Learning Together: *The LEARN Strategy*	Teaching students how to work with a partner to study and learn together by deciding what is important to learn, identifying key words and phrases, creating lists and developing mnemonic devices, self-testing together, and evaluating the collaborative process.
Building a Decision Together: *The BUILD Strategy*	Teaching students how to arrive at a decision by working with partners to examine an issue, gather facts, examine consequences of different decisions, identify compromises, review information to conduct a team vote, and evaluate the collaborative process.

Source: Vernon et al. (1993–2002).

PROGRESS MONITORING AND STUDYING

Evaluating and demonstrating the progress of a student learning a study strategy is based on several measurement factors. First, the teacher must identify measurable elements of the student's knowledge and use of the study process and how each element should be scored. For many of the interventions described in this chapter, a measurement system is included in the intervention materials. Often a checklist is created and used to evaluate a student's baseline performance and progress after the study intervention is introduced. For example, if the study strategy taught relates to the quality of steps needed for creating good lists needed for study, such as those incorporated in the "LIST" steps in the FIRST-Letter Mnemonic Strategy (see figure 12.1), two measures are needed. One measure evaluates the strategy for creating lists that the student uses during both baseline and the intervention period; another measure evaluates the student's test performance during baseline and then after the study intervention is introduced. The strategy knowledge and use measure (i.e., the process measure) might include the checklist elements and scoring format based on the steps of a strategy for creating good lists for studying (see table 12.2).

The second measure focuses on how well the strategy for creating good lists affects the student's test performance (i.e., the content measure). For example, a passage from a content-area textbook is selected that contains information that could be used to create lists. The student is told that they have 30 minutes to read the passage, take notes to study, and to study for a test that they will take the following day.

Table 12.2. Scoring Lists for Studying

Points	Strategy Performance	Examples of Informative and Corrective Feedback
1	The heading of the list summarizes an information grouping in the passage.	Your heading is from the passage and is general so it cannot be confused with a list item.
1	The heading is designated as a heading by being separated from the list.	Your heading is correct, and you underlined it, so you can tell it is the heading.
0	The heading is short.	You have the right idea for a heading, but you should try to use fewer words.
1	The heading must be accurate.	Your heading accurately describes the items in your list.
0	The heading is limited so that it covers seven or fewer list items.	You have good items, but there are 12 items in your list. Can you organize it into two lists to study?
0	Each item in the list is related to the heading.	One of your items does not fit with your heading. It goes in another list.
1	Each item is short.	Each item you list is short and will be easy to remember.
0	Each item is accurate according to the passage.	Two of your list items are misspelled.
0	Each item must be useful/meaningful to understanding the passage.	One of your list items on the parts of digestive system is "How it works." Another list with items about how the digestive system works would be more useful.
0	Each item must be unique (not repetitive).	Two of the items on your list are the same.
Total Points 4/10		
Percentage 40%		

Scoring guidelines: Score "0" if the student does not perform the step correctly or if there is no response, and student should be provided informative and corrective feedback.* Score "1" point if the student performed the step correctly.

*During baseline, informative and corrective feedback is not provided since the purpose of the baseline phase is to measure the student's approach to studying.

Note: Adapted from Nagel et al. (1986). Used with permission.

Chapter 12: Good Study Strategies

At the end of 30 minutes, the passage and study notes are removed. The following day a test over the information is given. The testing process is constructed similarly for each passage. Since passages are selected that include an identifiable list, the question prompt is based on the heading of the list identified by the teacher. For example, the following test questions might serve as study prompts:

What are the parts of the digestive system?
What are the types of blood vessels?
What are defenses against diseases?
What did the author do to make you sympathetic to the villain?
How does an author build the plot of a novel?
How do you solve a multistep equation?

The student's score is the percentage of correct items generated by the student compared to the total number of items listed in the passage. Both the process score and the content score are placed on a graph. In the graph presented in figure 12.3, the teacher collected data across several days to assess the quality of the student's approach to study (i.e., the process used) and the effects of the approach to study (i.e., the content learned). In figure 12.3, baseline data showed that the student's process and content scores were at or below 10% of the total points possible. During the first intervention phase, the student was taught how to create lists and then was given opportunities to demonstrate the listing strategy and was given feedback to improve the quality of their lists. Data showed that the student learned to make good lists, and some increase was seen in content test scores (i.e., content test scores increased from about 10% to about 40% of the possible points).

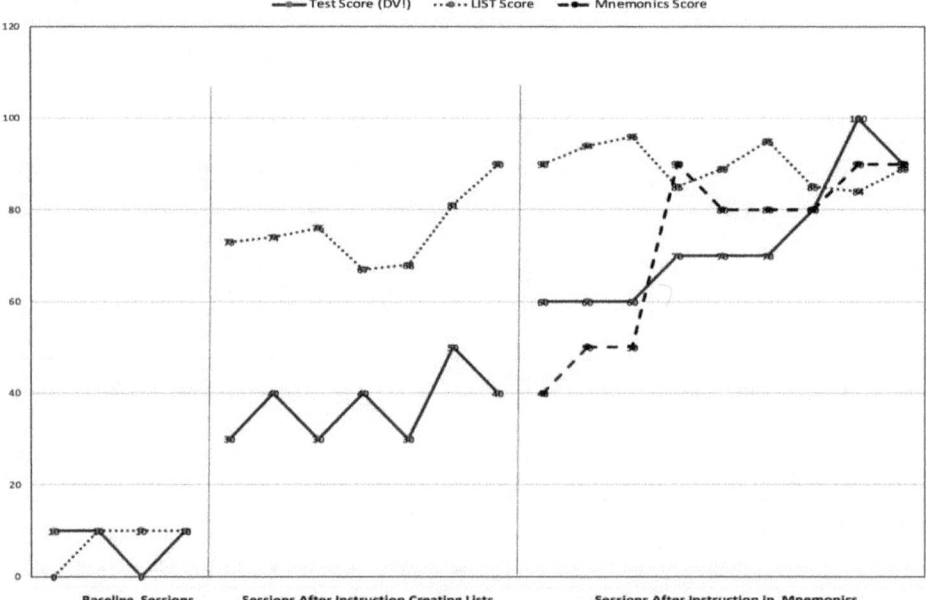

Figure 12.3 Progress Monitoring for Learning a Study Strategy

While an increase in a student's test scores is encouraging, the test scores earned were mostly below a 50% level. A score of 50% of the points possible on a test would be considered an "F" on a typical grading scale. Since the goal of instruction in good study strategies is to teach the student how to earn grades at a passing level or above, a grade of an "F" on a test is not going to convince a student or their teachers that the effort invested in learning a strategy for listing and organizing information was worth it. To meet the goal of earning passing grades, additional study interventions and measures should be introduced.

In textbox 12.1, the teacher analyzed the data and concluded that while the student had improved how they were identifying and organizing the information for study, an intervention focused on teaching them how to study the listed information and to conduct self-testing to prepare for the test was needed. The graph shows the effects of teaching the student a first-letter mnemonic intervention to improve test scores. The graph shows that the student maintained their use of a strategy to create good lists and that they learned how to create good mnemonics from those lists as well. As a result, the student's scores on the tests increased to grades that would be judged as passing.

While this progress monitoring example demonstrates the effectiveness of the study interventions introduced, the interventions and measures only addressed the use of some strategies, and those strategies only addressed a specific type of knowledge and testing demand. Additional study interventions with supports and measures that reflect the types of testing demands that students must face will be need to be incorporated as part of an overall plan to teach good study strategies to a student. As these study interventions are introduced, both the student's ability to apply the strategy as well as how the strategy influences content-learning outcomes should be included in progress monitoring efforts.

CONCLUSION

Our knowledge about what are good study strategies and how to teach them has grown significantly from the days in which instruction in study skills was included as a short unit in a middle school language arts class. Once characterized as habits to develop and general suggestions to guide study, research on how information is processed has helped us better define what must be taught about good studying. Good study involves the application of a set of integrated cognitive and metacognitive activities that evolve through the acquisition, storage, retrieval, and expression of knowledge. It is further shaped by our reading, writing, and listening abilities as well as the learning and performance demands of different settings, our motivation to learn, and social and emotional factors unique to each learner. We also know much more about the pedagogy required to ensure that students acquire and generalize good strategies for personal use. The body of knowledge that we now have about good study, especially for students who struggle with learning, should be used to offer a coherent curriculum that will increase the learning of information that is critical for student success.

REFERENCES

Berry, G., Deshler, D., & Schumaker, J. (2011). *The listening & note-taking strategy*. Edge Enterprises.

Bjorklund, D. F., & Douglas, R. N. (1997). The development of memory strategies. In N. Cowan (Ed.), *The development of memory in childhood* (pp. 201–46). Psychology.

Bryant, D. P., Bryant, B. R., & Smith, D. D. (2017). *Teaching students with special needs in inclusive classrooms*. Sage.

Bulgren, J. A., & Schumaker, J. B. (1996). *The Paired Associates Strategy*. Edge Enterprises.

Bulgren, J. A., Deshler, D. D., & Schumaker, J. B. (1997). Use of a recall enhancement routine and strategies in inclusive secondary classes. *Learning Disabilities Research & Practice, 12*(4), 198–208.

Bulgren, J. A., Schumaker, J. B., & Deshler, D. D. (1994). The effects of a recall enhancement routine on the test performance of secondary students with and without learning disabilities. *Learning Disabilities Research & Practice, 9*(1), 2–11.

Ellis, E. (2000). *The LINCS vocabulary strategy*. Edge Enterprises.

Ellis, E. (2001). *The vocabulary LINCING routine*. Edge Enterprises.

Faggella-Luby, M., Graner, P., Deshler, D, and Drew, S. (2012). Building a house on sand: Why disciplinary literacy is not sufficient to replace general strategies for adolescent learners who struggle. *Topics in Language Disorders, 32*(1), 69–84.

Harris, K. R., & Graham, S. (2018). Self-regulated strategy development: Theoretical bases, critical instructional elements, and future research. In R. Fidalgo, K. R. Harris, & M. Braaksma (Eds.), *Design principles for teaching effective writing: Theoretical and empirical grounded principles* (pp. 119–51). Brill.

Hock, M., Deshler, D., & Schumaker, J. (2000). *Strategic tutoring*. Edge Enterprises.

Hoover, J. J., & Patton, J. R. (2007). *Teaching study skills to students with learning problems: A teacher's guide for meeting diverse needs*. Pro Ed.

Hughes, C. A., Ruhl, K. L., Deshler, D. D., & Schumaker, J. B. (1995). *The assignment completion strategy*. Edge Enterprises.

Hughes, C. A., Ruhl, K. L., Schumaker, J. B., & Deshler, D. D. (2002). Effects of instruction in an assignment completion strategy on the homework performance of students with learning disabilities in general education classes. *Learning Disabilities Research & Practice, 17*(1), 1–18.

IRIS Center. (2013). *Study skills strategies (part 1): Foundations for effectively teaching study skills*. https://iris.peabody.vanderbilt.edu/module/ss1/

IRIS Center. (2013). *Study skills strategies (part 2): Strategies that improve students' academic performance*. https://iris.peabody.vanderbilt.edu/module/ss2/

Lenz, B. K., Adams, G. L., Bulgren, J. A., Pouliot, N., & Laraux, M. (2007). Effects of curriculum maps and guiding questions on the test performance of adolescents with learning disabilities. *Learning Disability Quarterly, 30*(4), 235–44.

McLeskey, J., Maheady, L., Billingsley, B., Brownell, M., & Lewis , T. (2022). *High leverage practices for inclusive classrooms* (2nd ed). Routledge.

Nagel, D., Schumaker, J., & Deshler, D. (1986). *The FIRST-letter mnemonic strategy*. Lawrence, KS: Edge Enterprises.

Rademacher, J. (1993). *The development and validation of a classroom assignment routine for mainstream settings* [Unpublished doctoral dissertation]. University of Kansas.

Rademacher, J. A., Deshler, D. D., Schumaker, J. B., & Lenz, B. K. (2011). *The quality assignment routine*. Lawrence, KS: Edge Enterprises.

Scanlon, D., Schumaker, J. B., & Deshler, D. D. (1996). Can a strategy be taught and learned in secondary inclusive classrooms? *Learning Disabilities Research and Practice, 11*(1), 41–57.

Scanlon, D., Schumaker, J. B., & Deshler, D. D. (2004). *The ORDER routine*. Edge Enterprises.

Schumacher, J., Bulgren, J., Deshler, D. & Lenz, B. K. (1998). *The recall enhancement routine*. University of Kansas.

Schumaker, J. B., & Deshler, D. D. (1988). Implementing the regular education initiative in secondary schools: A different ball game. *Journal of Learning Disabilities, 21*(1), 36–42.

Schumaker, J. B., & Fisher, J. B. (2021). 35 years on the road from research to practice: A review of studies on four content enhancement routines for inclusive subject-area classes, part I. *Learning Disabilities Research & Practice, 36*(3), 258–72. https://doi.org/10.1111/ldrp.12258

Schumaker, J. B., & Fisher, J. B. (2021). 35 years on the road from research to practice: A review of studies on four content enhancement routines for inclusive subject-area classes, part II. *Learning Disabilities Research & Practice, 36*(3), 258–72. https://doi.org/10.1111/ldrp.12259

Seigel, J. (2018). Did you take "good" notes? On methods for evaluating student notetaking performance. *Journal of English for Academic Purposes, 35*, 85–92.

Shanahan, T., & Shanahan, C. (2012). What is disciplinary literacy and why does it matter? *Topics in Language Disorders, 32*(1), 7–18.

Stenson, R. (2016, March 14). Is this the first time anyone printed, "garbage in, garbage out"? Atlas Obscura. https://www.atlasobscura.com/articles/is-this-the-first-time-anyone-printed-garbage-in-garbage-out

Vernon, S., Deshler, D., & Schumaker, J. (1993). *The teamwork strategy*. Edge Enterprises.

Vernon, S., Deshler, D., & Schumaker, J. (1999). *The THINK strategy*. Edge Enterprises.

Vernon, S., Deshler, D., & Schumaker, J. (2000). *Talking together*. Edge Enterprises.

Vernon, S., Deshler, D., & Schumaker, J. (2002). *Organizing together*. Edge Enterprises.

Vernon, S., Schumaker, J., & Deshler, D. (1996). *The SCORE skills*. Edge Enterprises.

Vernon, S., Schumaker, J., & Deshler, D. (1999a). *The BUILD strategy*. Edge Enterprises.

Vernon, S., Schumaker, J., & Deshler, D. (1999b). *The LEARN strategy*. Edge Enterprises.

Vernon, S., Schumaker, J., & Deshler, D. (2001). *Following instructions together*. Edge Enterprises.

Vernon, S., Schumaker, J., & Deshler, D. (2002). *Taking notes together*. Edge Enterprises.

13

Additional Resources

Julie Atwood and Jacquelyn Purser

IT IS AN INTERESTING TIME TO BE AN EDUCATOR. Resources like Pinterest and Teachers Pay Teachers can be a great way for teachers to share information, visuals, forms, and resources. However, educators need to look at what is being found online with a critical eye. It can be difficult to sift through all of the information out there and home in on what is truly evidence-based. Using evidence-based practices is key to student success, and using intervention without a clear evidence base can have significant repercussions. At best, students don't get the most up-to-date or effective intervention. At worst, real harm can occur.

How do teachers know what is evidence-based? The guidelines can be unclear to those who are not well versed in the standards of scientific research, and they are not always consistent from source to source. For example, the Every Student Succeeds Act (ESSA) states that for an intervention to be evidence-based, it must show a statistically significant effect on the improvement of student outcomes. This should be based on either strong evidence from one well-designed and implemented experimental study, moderate evidence from one well-designed and implemented quasi-experimental study, promising evidence from one well-designed and implemented correlational study, or demonstrates a rationale based on high-quality research findings (ESEA, 2012). The National Professional Development Center on Autism Spectrum Disorders indicates that five single-subject designs or two randomized designs or a combination of evidence are necessary to demonstrate that an intervention or practice is "evidence-based" (NPDC, 2016). Without training and support educators may struggle to identify evidence-based programs, resources, and materials. Below are a few of our favorite, evidence-based resources recommended by the authors of this text.

Table 13.1. Further Resources, Organized by Subject

	Resource	Link	Description
Reading	Anita Archer Video Examples: Explicit Vocabulary Instruction Routine	www.explicitinstruction.org	This site provides videos illustrating explicit vocabulary instruction.
	Evidence Based Intervention Network	https://education.missouri.edu/ebi/interventions/	The Evidence Based Intervention Network is housed within the University of Missouri's College of Education & Human Development. EBIN provides resources for the implementation of evidence-based interventions in a classroom setting. Reading Interventions (EBIN, 2022).
	Improving Adolescent Literacy: Effective Classroom and Intervention Practices	https://ies.ed.gov/ncee/wwc/docs/practiceguide/adlit_pg_082608.pdf	This Institute of Education Sciences Practice Guide includes evidence-based strategies to enhance adolescent literacy instruction and intervention.
	IRIS Center Trainings	https://iris.peabody.vanderbilt.edu/resources/iris-resource-locator/	Interactive online trainings related to literacy, reading, and writing (IRIS Center, 2022).
	National Center on Intensive Intervention: Intensive Intervention in Reading Course Content Training Modules	https://intensiveintervention.org/training/course-content/intensive-intervention-reading	The National Center on Intensive Intervention at the American Institutes for Research website includes several modules focused on intensive intervention in reading.
	Project EXPERT: DBI Training Video Repository	http://tinyurl.com/EXPERTModules	Developed by Dr. Jessica Toste and colleagues, the EXPERT DBI videos provide mini trainings on targeted reading topics.
Mathematics	Center on Instruction	https://www.centeroninstruction.org/topic.cfm?k=ST	The Center on Instruction offers materials and resources on mathematics and science instruction and assessment that help educators improve academic outcomes for all students in these content areas (Center on Instruction, n.d.).

(continued)

Table 13.1. *Continued*

	Resource	Link	Description
Mathematics	Evidence Based Intervention Network	https://education.missouri.edu/ebi/interventions/	Math Interventions (EBIN, 2022).
	National Library of Manipulatives	http://nlvm.usu.edu/en/nav/vlibrary.html	The NLVM is a National Science Foundation (NSF) supported project that began in 1999 to develop a library of uniquely interactive, Web-based virtual manipulatives or concept tutorials for mathematics instruction (K–12 emphasis) (Utah State University, 2022).
	Teaching Strategies for Improving Algebra Knowledge in Middle and High School Students	https://ies.ed.gov/ncee/wwc/PracticeGuide/20	This Institute of Education Sciences Practice Guide includes evidence-based strategies to enhance algebra instruction.
	Virginia Department of Education's Training and Technical Assistance Center	https://ttac.odu.edu/curriculum-and-instruction/math/from-research-to-practice-check-out-these-user-friendly-math-resources/	Resource for teachers that has condensed evidence-based math best practices into a ready-to-use guide (TTAC, 2022).
Writing	National Council of Teachers of English	https://ncte.org/resources/	A collection of books, materials, websites, and resources for English teachers.
	Read Write Think	https://www.readwritethink.org/	Resources by grade and professional development for teachers (NCTE, 2022).
Science	National Science Teaching Association	https://www.nsta.org/overview	The NSTA is a community of science educators and professionals providing resources and best practices in science and STEM (NSTA, 2022).
	Research and Practice Collaboratory	http://researchandpractice.org/whyrp/	The Research and Practice Collaboratory presents resources and research in STEM for educators. This organization emphasizes a collaborative approach to engage educators in the research available (Research and Practice Collaboratory, n.d.).

	Resource	Link	Description
History/Social Studies	American Historical Association	https://www.historians.org/teaching-and-learning	The American Historical Association creates and provides resources to educators of all grade levels. The AHA incorporates a variety of historical topics including world and US history (AHA, 2022).
	Library of Congress	https://www.loc.gov/programs/teachers/about-this-program/	The Library of Congress provides professional development and classroom resources for educators (Library of Congress, n.d.).
	National Archives	https://www.archives.gov/education	The National Archives provides a variety of primary sources and other resources for educators including professional development and National History Day information (National Achieves, 2022).
	Smithsonian Learning Lab	https://learninglab.si.edu	The Smithsonian Learning Lab provides content and education from the museum and research complex in an accessible and interactive platform for educators. Activities are adaptable and easy to combine with your own lessons (Smithsonian, n.d.).
Behavior	Center on PBIS	https://www.pbis.org	The Center on PBIS provides resources that help establish, maintain, and improve tiered intervention systems in educational settings (Center on PBIS, 2022).
	Evidence Based Intervention Network	https://education.missouri.edu/ebi/	Behavior Interventions (EBIN, 2022).

(*continued*)

Table 13.1. *Continued*

	Resource	Link	Description
Behavior	Intervention Central	https://www.interventioncentral.org/behavioral-intervention-modification	Intervention Central provides an overview of Response to Intervention (RtI) and behavioral interventions (Intervention Central, n.d.).
	National Center on Intensive Intervention	https://intensiveintervention.org/implementation-intervention/behavior-strategies	The National Center on Intensive Intervention (NCII) is funded by the US Department of Education's OSEP. NCII works to build knowledge and resources for local stakeholders implementing intervention for students with behavioral and other needs (NCII, n.d.).
	What Works Clearinghouse	https://ies.ed.gov/ncee/wwc/FWW/Results?filters=,Behavior	What Works Clearinghouse was established in 2002 as an investment within the US Department of Education and provides evidence-based programs, practices, etc. (IES/WWC, n.d.).

REFERENCES

Education Act, SA 2012, c E-0.3. Elementary and Secondary Education Act (ESEA). National Professional Development Center on Autism Spectrum Disorder. (2016). Evidence-based practices. https://autismpdc.fpg.unc.edu/evidence-based-practices

References

Achieve the Core (2016). CCSS Instructional Practice Guide. https://achievethecore.org/page/1119/instructional-practice-guide

ACT. (2005). *Crisis at the core: Preparing all students for college and work*. Iowa City, IA: ACT, Inc. https://www.act.org/content/dam/act/unsecured/documents/crisis_report.pdf

Adelman, C. (2006). *The toolbox revisited: Paths to degree completion from high school through college.* US Department of Education.

Al Otaiba, S., & Fuchs, D. (2006). Who are the young children for whom best practices in reading are ineffective? An experimental and longitudinal study. *Journal of Learning Disabilities, 39*(5), 414–31.

Aleixandre, M. P. J., & Crujeiras, B. (2017). Epistemic practices and scientific practices in science education. In K. S. Taber & B. B. Akpan (Eds.), *Science education: An international course companion* (pp. 69–80). Brill Sense.

Allen, G. E., Common, E. A., Germer, K. A., Lane, K. L., Buckman, M. M., Oakes, W. P., & Menzies, H. M. (2020). A systematic review of the evidence base for active supervision in pre-K–12 settings. *Behavioral Disorders, 45*(3), 167–182. https://doi.org/10.1177/0198742919837646

Allsopp, D. H. (1997). Using classwide peer tutoring to teach beginning algebra problem-solving skills in heterogeneous classrooms. *Remedial and Special Education, 18*(6), 367–79.

Allsopp, D. H., Lovin, L. H., & van Ingen, S. (2018). *Teaching mathematics meaningfully. Solutions for reaching struggling learners* (2nd ed.). Paul H. Brookes.

Aloe, A. M., Amo, L. C., & Shanahan, M. E. (2014). Classroom management self-efficacy and burnout: A multivariate meta-analysis. *Educational Psychology Review, 26*(1), 101–26.

Alter, P., & Haydon, T. (2017). Characteristics of effective classroom rules: A review of the literature. *Teacher Education and Special Education, 40*(2), 114–27. https://doi.org/10.1177/0888406417700962

American Diploma Project. (2004) *Ready or not: Creating a high school diploma that counts*. Washington, DC: Achieve, Inc. https://files.eric.ed.gov/fulltext/ED494733.pdf

American Institutes for Research (2022). Center on Multi-Tiered Systems of Support. https://www.air.org/centers/center-multi-tiered-system-supports-mtss-center

Applebee, A. N., & Langer, J. A. (2009). EJ Extra: What is happening in the teaching of writing? *English Journal, 98*(5), 18–28.

Archer, A. L., Gleason, M. M., & Vachon, V. L. (2003). Decoding and fluency: Foundation skills for struggling older readers. *Learning Disability Quarterly*, 26(2), 89–101. https://doi.org/10.2307/1593592

Archer, A. L., & Hughes, C. A. (2011). *Explicit instruction: Effective and efficient teaching*. Guilford.

Asaro-Saddler, K., Muir-Knox, H., & Meredith, H. (2018). The effects of a summary writing strategy on the literacy skills of adolescents with disabilities. *Exceptionality*, 26(2), 106–18. https://doi.org/10.1080/09362835.2017.1283626

Axelrod, M. I., & Zank, A. J. (2012). Increasing classroom compliance: Using a high-probability command sequence with noncompliant students. *Journal of Behavioral Education*, 21, 119–33. https://doi.org/10.1007/s10864-011-9145-6

Bächtold, M. (2013). What do students "construct" according to constructivism in science education? *Research in Science Education*, 43, 2477–96. https://doi.org/10.1007/s11165-013-9369-7

Ball, A. (2006). Teaching writing in culturally diverse classrooms. In C. MacArthur, S. Graham, & J. Fitzgerald (Eds.), *Handbook of writing research* (pp. 293–310). New York: Guilford.

Bandura, A. (1986). *Social foundations of thought and action: A social cognitive theory*. Prentice Hall.

Barnes, M. A., Ahmed, Y., Barth, A., & Francis, D. J. (2015). The relation of knowledge-text integration processes and reading comprehension in 7th- to 12th-grade students. *Scientific Studies of Reading*, 19(4), 253–72. https://doi:10.1080/10888438.2015.1022650

Baroody, A. J., Feil, Y., & Johnson, A. R. (2007). An alternative reconceptualization of procedural and conceptual knowledge. *Journal for Research in Mathematics Education*, 38(2), 115–31.

Barrish, H. H., Saunders, M., & Wolf, M. M. (1969). Good behavior game: Effects of individual contingencies for group consequences on disruptive behavior in a classroom. *Journal of Applied Behavior Analysis*, 2(2), 119–24. https://doi.org/10.1901/jaba.1969.2-119

Basham, J. D., & Marino, M. T. (2013). Understanding STEM education and supporting students through Universal Design for Learning. *TEACHING Exceptional Children*, 45(4), 8–15. https://doi.org/10.1177/004005991304500401

Bate, J. (2020, March 4). *The growing popularity of podcasts*. PPL PRS United for Music. https://pplprs.co.uk/popularity-of-podcasts

Bazerman, C. (2000 [1988]). *Shaping written knowledge: The genre and activity of the experimental article in science*. WAC Clearinghouse. (Originally published in 1988 by University of Wisconsin Press).

Bazerman, C., Bonini, A., & Figueiredo, D. (Eds.). (2009). *Genre in a changing world*. Parlor.

Bazerman, C., & Prior, P. (2005). Participating in emergent socio-literate worlds: Genre, disciplinarity, interdisciplinarity. In R. Beach, J. Green, M. Kamil, & T. Shanahan (Eds.), *Multidisciplinary perspectives on literacy research* (2nd ed., pp. 133–78). Hampton.

Beaufort, A. (1999). *Writing in the real world: Making the transition from school to work*. Teachers College Press.

Bell, R. L., Smetana, L., & Binns, I. C. (2005). Simplifying inquiry instruction. *Science Teacher*, 72(7), 30–33.

Bellezza, F. S. (1981). Mnemonic devices: Classification, characteristics, and criteria. *Review of Educational Research, 51*(2), 247–75. https://www.jstor.org/stable/1170198

Benedek-Wood, E., Mason, L. H., Wood, P. H., Hoffman, K. E., & McGuire, A. (2014). An experimental examination of quick writing in the middle school science classroom. *Learning Disabilities: A Contemporary Journal, 12*(1), 69–92.

Bergsmann, E. M., Van De Schoot, R., Schober, B., Finsterwald, M., & Spiel, C. (2013). The effect of classroom structure on verbal and physical aggression among peers: A short-term longitudinal study. *Journal of School Psychology, 51*(2), 159–74. https://doi.org/10.1016/j.jsp.2012.10.003

Berry, G., Deshler, D., & Schumaker, J. (2011). *The listening & note-taking strategy*. Edge Enterprises.

Biggs, J., & Collis, K. (1982). *Evaluating the quality of learning: The SOLO taxonomy*. Academic.

Billingsley, G. M., McKenzie, J. M., & Scheuermann, B. K. (2020). The effects of a structured classroom management system in Secondary Resource Classrooms. *Exceptionality, 28*(5), 317–32. https://doi.org/10.1080/09362835.2018.1522257

Bjorklund, D. F., & Douglas, R. N. (1997). The development of memory strategies. In N. Cowan (Ed.), *The development of memory in childhood* (pp. 201–46). Psychology.

Black, P., & Wiliam, D. (1998). Inside the black box: Raising standards through classroom assessment. *Phi Delta Kappan, 92*(1), 81–90. https://doi.org/10.1177/003172171009200119

Bley, N. S., & Thorton, C. A. (2001). *Teaching mathematics to students with learning disabilities* (4th ed.). PRO-ED.

Boaler, J. (2019). *Limitless mind: Learn, lead, and live without barriers*. HarperOne.

Boardman, A. G., Roberts, G., Vaughn, S., Wexler, J., Murray, C. S., & Kosanovich, M. (2008). *Effective instruction for adolescent struggling readers: A practice brief*. RMC Research Corporation, Center on Instruction. https://files.eric.ed.gov/fulltext/ED521836.pdf

Boon, R. T., Fore III, C., Ayres, K., & Spencer, V. G. (2005). The effects of cognitive organizers to facilitate content-area learning for students with mild disabilities: A pilot study. *Journal of Instructional Psychology, 32*(2), 101–17. https://eric.ed.gov/?id=EJ774145

Boscolo, P., & Ascorti, K. (2004). Effects of collaborative revision on children's ability to write understandable narrative texts. In L. Allal, L. Chanquoy, & P. Largy (Eds.), *Revision: Cognitive and instructional processes* (pp. 157–70). Kluwer.

Bouck, E. C., Park, J., Satsangi, R., Cwiakala, K., & Levy, K. (2019). Using virtual-abstract instructional sequence to support acquisition of algebra. *Journal of Special Education Technology, 34*(4), 253–68.

Bouck, E. C., & Sprick, J. (2019). The virtual-representational-abstract framework to support students with disabilities in mathematics. *Intervention in School and Clinic, 54*(3), 173–80.

Bowman-Perrott, L., Burke, M. D., de Marin, S., Zhang, N., & Davis, H. (2015). A Meta-analysis of single-case research on behavior contracts: Effects on behavioral and academic outcomes among children and youth. *Behavior Modification, 39*(2), 247–69. https://doi.org/10.1177/0145445514551383

Bowman-Perrott, L., Burke, M. D., de Marin, S., Zhang, N., & Davis, H. (2015). A meta-analysis of single-case research on behavior contracts: Effects on behavioral and academic outcomes among children and youth. *Behavior Modification, 39*(2), 247–69. https://doi.org/10.1177/0145445514551383

Bowman-Perrott, L., Davis, H., Vannest, K., Williams, L., Greenwood, C., & Parker, R. (2013). Academic benefits of peer tutoring: A meta-analytic review of single-case research. *School Psychology Review, 42*(1), 39–55. https://doi.org/10.1080/02796015.2013.12087490

Brandt, D. (2001). *Literacy in American lives*. Cambridge University Press.

Brooks, D. (1985). The teacher's communicative competence: The first day of school. *Theory into Practice, 24*, 63–70.

Brophy, J. (1986). Teacher influences on student achievement. *American Psychologist, 41*(10), 1069–77.

Brophy, J. (2006). Observational research on generic aspects of classroom teaching. In P. A. Alexander & P. H. Winne (Eds.), *Handbook of educational psychology* (2nd ed., pp. 755–80). Erlbaum.

Brophy, J., & Good, T. (1986). Teacher behavior and student achievement. In M. C. Wittrock (Ed.), *Handbook of research on teaching* (3rd ed., pp. 328–75). Macmillan.

Bross, L. A., Common, E. A., Oakes, W. P., Lane, K. L., Menzies, H. M., & Ennis, R. P. (2018). High-probability request sequence: An effective, efficient low-intensity strategy to support student success. *Beyond Behavior, 27*(3), 140–5.

Bryant, D. P., Bryant, B. R., & Smith, D. D. (2017). *Teaching students with special needs in inclusive classrooms*. Sage.

Bulgren, J., Deshler, D. D., & Lenz, B. K. (2007). Engaging adolescents with LD in higher order thinking about history concepts using integrated content enhancement routines. *Journal of Learning Disabilities, 40*(2), 121–33. https://doi.org/10.1177%2F00222194070400020301

Bulgren, J. A. (2006). Integrated content enhancement routines: Responding to the needs of adolescents with disabilities in rigorous inclusive secondary content classes. *TEACHING Exceptional Children, 38*(6), 54–58.

Bulgren, J. A. (2014). *Teaching cause and effect*. University of Kansas Center for Research on Learning.

Bulgren, J. A. (2018). *Teaching decision-making*. University of Kansas Center for Research on Learning.

Bulgren, J. A. (2020). *Cross-curricular argumentation*. University of Kansas Center for Research on Learning.

Bulgren, J. A., Deshler, D. D., & Schumaker, J. B. (1997). Use of a recall enhancement routine and strategies in inclusive secondary classes. *Learning Disabilities Research & Practice, 12*(4), 198–208.

Bulgren, J. A., Lenz, B. K., Deshler, D. D., & Schumaker, J. B. (2001). *The question exploration routine*. Edge Enterprises.

Bulgren, J. A., Lenz, K., Schumaker, J. B., & Deshler, D. D. (1995). *Concept comparison routine*. Edge Enterprises.

Bulgren, J. A., Marquis, J. G., Lenz, B. K., Deshler, D. D., & Schumaker, J. B. (2011). The effectiveness of the question-exploration routine for enhancing the content learning of secondary students. *Journal of Educational Psychology, 103*(3), 578–93.

Bulgren, J. A., Marquis, J. G., Lenz, B. K., Schumaker, J. B., & Deshler, D. D. (2009). Effectiveness of question exploration to enhance students' written expression of content knowledge and comprehension. *Reading & Writing Quarterly, 25*(4), 271–89.

Bulgren, J. A., & Schumaker, J. B. (1996). *The Paired Associates Strategy*. Edge Enterprises.

Bulgren, J. A., Schumaker, J. B., & Deshler, D. D. (1994). The effects of a recall enhancement routine on the test performance of secondary students with and without learning disabilities. *Learning Disabilities Research & Practice, 9*(1), 2–11.

Burke, L., Poll, G., & Fiene, J. (2017). Response to an expository writing strategy across middle school RtI tiers. *Learning Disabilities: A Contemporary Journal, 15*(1), 85–101.

Caccamise, D., Franzke, M., Eckhoff, A., Kintsch, E., & Kintsch, W. (2007). Guided practice in technology-based summary writing. In D. S. McNamara (Ed.), *Reading comprehension strategies: Theories, interventions, and technologies* (pp. 375–96). Erlbaum.

Cain, K., & Oakhill, J. V. (2009). Reading comprehension development from 8 to 14 years: The contribution of component skills and processes. In R. K. Wagner, C. Schatschneider, & C. Phythian-Sence (Eds.), *Beyond decoding: The behavioral and biological foundations of reading comprehension* (pp. 143–75). Guilford.

Cariveau, T., La Cruz Montilla, A., Gonzalez, E., & Ball, S. (2019). A review of error correction procedures during instruction for children with developmental disabilities. *Journal of Applied Behavior Analysis, 52*(2), 574–79. https://doi.org/10.1002/jaba.524

Carlisle, J. F., & Goodwin, A. (2013). Morphemes matter: How morphological knowledge contributes to reading and writing. In C. A. Stone, E. R. Silliman, B. J. Ehren, & G. P. Wallach (Eds.), *Handbook of language and literacy: Development and disorders* (2nd ed., pp. 265–82). Guilford.

Carnahan, C. R., & Williamson, P. S. (2013). Does compare-contrast text structure help students with autism spectrum disorder comprehend science text? *Exceptional Children, 79*(3), 347–63. https://doi.org/10.1177/001440291307900302

Carnahan, C. R., Williamson, P., Birri, N., Swoboda, C., & Snyder, K. K. (2016). Increasing comprehension of expository science text for students with autism spectrum disorder. *Focus on Autism and Other Developmental Disabilities, 31*(3), 208–20. https://doi:10.1177/1088357615610539

Carter, E. W., Asmus, J. M., & Moss, C. K. (2014). Peer support interventions to support inclusive schools. In J. McLeskey, F. Spooner, B. Algozzine, & N. L. Waldron (Eds.), *Handbook of effective inclusive schools: Research and practice* (pp. 387–404). Routledge.

CAST. (2018). *Universal Design for Learning Guidelines* version 2.2. http://udlguidelines.cast.org

Castles, A., & Nation, K. (2022). Learning to read words. In M. J. Snowling, C. A. Hulme, & K. Nation (Eds.), *The science of reading: A handbook* (2nd ed., pp. 165–80). Wiley-Blackwell.

Castles, A., Rastle, K., & Nation, K. (2018). Ending the reading wars: Reading acquisition from novice to expert. *Psychological Science in the Public Interest, 19*(1), 5–51. https://doi.org/10.1177/1529100618772271

Catts, H., Hogan, T., & Adolf, S. (2005). Developmental changes in reading and reading disabilities. In H. Catts & A. Kamhi (Eds.), *Connections between language and reading disabilities*. Erlbaum.

Center for Responsive Schools. (n.d.). Responsive Classroom® and PBIS: Can schools use them together? https://www.responsiveclassroom.org/sites/default/files/pdf_files/RC_PBIS_white_paper.pdf

Chafouleas, S. M., Sanetti, L. M. H., Jaffery, R., & Fallon, L. (2012). An evaluation of a classwide intervention package involving self-management and a group contingency on behavior of middle school students. *Journal of Behavioral Education, 21*, 34–57. https://doi.org/doi:10.1007/s10864-011-9135-8

Chalk, J. C., Hagan-Burke, S., & Burke, M. D. (2005). The effects of self-regulated strategy development on the writing process for high school students with learning disabilities. *Learning Disability Quarterly, 28*(1), 75–87. https://doi.org/10.2307/4126974

Chall, J. S., & Jacobs, V. A. (1983). Writing and reading in the elementary grades: Developmental trends among low SES children. *Language Arts, 60*(5), 617–26.

Chard, D. J., Vaughn, S., & Tyler, B-J. (2002). A synthesis of research on effective interventions for building reading fluency with elementary students with learning disabilities. *Journal of Learning Disabilities, 35*(5), 386–406.

Chow, J. C., & Gilmour, A. F. (2016). Designing and implementing group contingencies in the classroom: A teacher's guide. *TEACHING Exceptional Children, 48*(3), 137–43. https://doi.org/10.1177/0040059915618197

Ciullo, S., Collins, A., Wissinger, D. R., McKenna, J. W., Lo, Y-L., & Osman, D. (2020). Students with learning disabilities in the social studies: A meta-analysis of intervention research. *Exceptional Children, 86*(4), 393–412. https://doi.org/10.1177%2F0014402919893932

Ciullo, S., Lembke, E. S., Carlisle, A., Thomas, C. N., Goodwin, M., & Judd, L. (2016). Implementation of evidence-based literacy practices in middle school response to intervention: An observation study. *Learning Disability Quarterly, 39*(1), 44–57. https://doi.org/10.1177/0731948714566120

Clough, M. P. (2011). Teaching and assessing the nature of science: How to effectively incorporate the nature of science in your classroom. *Science Teacher 78*(6), 56–60.

Colvin, G., & Scott, T. M. (2015). *Managing the cycle of acting-out behavior in the classroom* (2nd ed.). Corwin.

Common Core State Standards Initiative. (2010). National Governors Association Center for Best Practices and Council of Chief State School Officers.

Common Core State Standards. (2010). ELA: National Governors Association Center for Best Practices & Council of Chief State School Officers. Washington, DC: Authors.

Common, E. A., Lane, K. L., Cantwell, E. D., Brunsting, N. C., Oakes, W. P., Germer, K. A., & Bross, L. A. (2020). Teacher-delivered strategies to increase students' opportunities to respond: A systematic methodological review. *Behavioral Disorders, 45*(2), 67–84. https://doi.org/10.1177/0198742919828310

Comprehensive, Integrated, Three-Tiered Model of Prevention (Ci3T). (2022). *Operationally defining behavior: Target and replacement behaviors*. Retrieved April 5, 2022 from https://www.ci3t.org/wp-content/uploads/2016/08/FABI_Operationally_Defining_Behavior.pdf

Connor, C. M., Alberto, P. A., Compton, D. L., & O'Connor, R. E. (2014). *Improving reading outcomes for students with or at risk for reading disabilities: A synthesis of the contributions from the Institute of Education Sciences Research Centers* (NCSER 2014-3000). National Center for Special Education Research, Institute of Education Sciences, US Department of Education.

Cook, B. G., Buysse, V., Klingner, J., Landrum, T. J., McWilliam, R. A., Tankersley, M., & Test, D. W. (2015). CEC's standards for classifying the evidence base of practices in special education. *Remedial and Special Education, 36*(4), 220–34. http://doi.org/10.1177/0741932514557271

Cook, B. G., Collins, L. W., Cook, S. C., & Cook, L. (2019). Evidence-based reviews: How evidence-based practices are systematically identified. *Learning Disabilities Research & Practice, 35*(1), 6–13. https://doi.org/10.1111/ldrp.12213

Cook, B. G., & Odom, S. L. (2013). Evidence-based practices and implementation science in special education. *Exceptional Children, 79*(3), 135–44. https://doi.org/10.1177/001440291307900201

Cook, B. G., Tankersley, M., & Landrum, T. J. (2009). Determining evidence-based practices in special education. *Exceptional Children, 75*(3), 365–83. https://doi.org/10.1177%2F001440290907500306

Cooper, J. O., Heron, T. E., & Heward, W. L. (2020). *Applied behavior analysis* (3rd ed.). Pearson.

Council for Exceptional Children. (2014). Council for exceptional children: Standards for evidence-based practices in special education. *TEACHING Exceptional Children, 46*(6), 206. http://doi.org/10.1177/0040059914531389

Council for Exceptional Children. (2015a). *Code of ethics.* https://exceptionalchildren.org/sites/default/files/2020-07/Code%20of%20Ethics.pdf

Council for Exceptional Children. (2015b). *What every special educator must know: Professional ethics and standards.* https://exceptionalchildren.org/sites/default/files/2021-03/K12%20Initial%20Standards%20and%20Components.pdf

Council for Exceptional Children. (2021). *Position statement: Multi-tiered system of supports: The integral role of special education and special educators.* https://exceptionalchildren.org/sites/default/files/2021-11/mtss_position__112021.pdf

Council for Exceptional Children. (2021). *Initial practice-based professional preparation standards for special educators.* https://exceptionalchildren.org/standards/initial-practice-based-professional-preparation-standards-special-educators

Council of Chief State School Officers (CCSSO). (2010). *Common core state standards for mathematics.* Common Core State Standards Initiative. https://learning.ccsso.org/wp-content/uploads/2022/11/Math_Standards1.pdf

Council of Chief State School Officers (CCSSO). (2020). *Common core state standards for English language arts.* Common Core State Standards Initiative. https://learning.ccsso.org/wp-content/uploads/2022/11/ELA_Standards1.pdf

Crabtree, T., Alber-Morgan, S. R., & Konrad, M. (2010). The effects of self-monitoring of story elements on the reading comprehension of high school seniors with learning disabilities. *Education & Treatment of Children, 33*(2), 187–203.

Cuenca, A. (2020). Proposing core practices for social studies teacher education: A qualitative content analysis of inquiry-based lessons. *Journal of Teacher Education, 72*(3), 298–313. https://doi.org/10.1177/0022487120948046

Cunningham, A. E., & Stanovich, K. E. (1991). Tracking the unique effects of print exposure in children: Associations with vocabulary, general knowledge, and spelling. *Journal of Educational Psychology, 83*(2), 264–74.

Darch, C., & Eaves, R. C. (1986). Visual displays to increase comprehension of high school learning-disabled students. *Journal of Special Education, 20*(3), 309–18. https://doi.org/10.1177/002246698602000305

Datchuk, S. M. (2017). A direct instruction and precision teaching intervention to improve the sentence construction of middle school students with writing difficulties. *Journal of Special Education, 51*(2), 62–71. https://doi.org/10.1177/0022466916665588

Datchuk, S. M., & Kubina, R. M. (2017). A writing intervention to teach simple sentences and descriptive paragraphs to adolescents with writing difficulties. *Education and Treatment of Children, 40*(3), 303–26.

Datchuk, S. M., & Rogers, D. B. (2019). Text writing within simple sentences: A writing fluency intervention for students with high-incidence disabilities. *Learning Disabilities Research & Practice, 34*(1), 23–34. https://doi.org/10.1111/ldrp.12185

de Jong, T., & Ferguson-Hessler, M. G. M. (1996). Types and qualities of knowledge. *Educational Psychologist, 31*(2), 105–13.

De La Paz, S. (1999). Self-regulated strategy instruction in regular education settings: Improving outcomes for students with and without learning disabilities. *Learning Disabilities Research and Practice, 14*(2), 92–106.

De La Paz, S., Monte-Sano, C., Felton, M., Croninger, R., Jackson, C., & Piantedosi, K. W. (2017). A historical writing apprenticeship for adolescents: Integrating disciplinary learning with cognitive strategies. *Reading Research Quarterly, 52*(1), 31–52. https://doi.org/10.1002/rrq.147

De La Paz, S., & Wissinger, D. R. (2016). Improving the historical knowledge and writing of students with or at risk for LD. *Journal of Learning Disabilities, 5*(6), 658–671. https://doi.org/10.1177/0022219416659444

Dean., D. (2008). *Genre theory: Teaching, writing, and being.* National Council of Teachers of English.

DeJager, B., Houlihan, D., Filter, K. J., Mackie, P. F., & Klein, L. (2020). Comparing the effectiveness and ease of implementation of token economy, response cost, and a combination condition in rural elementary school classrooms. *Journal of Rural Mental Health, 44*(1), 39–46.

Deno, S. L. (1985). Curriculum-based measurement: The emerging alternative. *Exceptional Children, 52*(3), 219–32.

Denton, C. A., Vaughn, S., Wexler, J., Bryan, D., & Reed, D. (2012). *Effective instruction for middle school students with reading difficulties: The reading teacher's sourcebook.* Brookes.

DeWalt, D. A., & Pignone, M. P. (2005). The role of literacy in health and health care. *American Family Physician, 72*(3), 387–8.

Dewey, J. (1916). *Democracy and education.* Macmillan.

Dewey, J. (1959). *The school and society.* University of Chicago Press.

Dexter, D. D., Park, Y. J., & Hughes, C. A. (2011). A meta-analytic review of graphic organizers and science instruction for adolescents with learning disabilities: Implications for the intermediate and secondary science classroom. *Learning Disabilities Research & Practice, 26*(4), 204–13. https://doi.org/10.1111/j.1540-5826.2011.00341.x

DiSalvo, C. A., & Oswald, D. P. (2002). Peer-mediated interventions to increase the social interaction of children with autism: Consideration of peer expectancies. *Focus on Autism and Other Developmental Disabilities, 17*(4), 198–207. https://doi.org/10.1177/10883576020170040201

Dixson, D. D., & Worrell, F. C. (2016). Formative and summative assessment in the classroom. *Theory Into Practice, 55*(2), 153–59. https://doi.org/10.1080/00405841.2016.1148989

Drevon, D. D., Hixson, M. D., Wyse, R. D., & Rigney, A. M. (2019). A meta-analytic review of the evidence for check-in check-out. *Psychology in the Schools, 56*(3), 393–412. https://doi.org/10.1002/pits.22195

Durlak, J. A., Weissberg, R. P., Dymnicki, A. B., Taylor, R. D., & Schellinger, K. B. (2011). The impact of enhancing students' social and emotional learning: A meta-analysis of school-based universal interventions. *Child Development, 82*(1), 405–32. https://doi.org/10.1111/j.1467-8624.2010.01564.x

Early, J. S. (2019). A case for teaching biography-driven writing in ELA classrooms. *English Journal, 108*(3), 89–94.

Early, J. S. (2017). Escribiendo juntos: Toward a collaborative model of multiliterate family literacy in English only and anti-immigrant contexts. *Research in the Teaching of English, 52*(2), 156–80.

Early, J. S. (2010). "Mi hija, you should be a writer": The role of parental support and learning to write. *Bilingual Research Journal, 33*(3), 277–91.

Early, J. S. (2022). *Next generation genres: Teaching writing for civic and academic engagement*. Norton.

Early, J. S., & Saidy, C. (2018). *Creating literacy communities as pathways to success: Equity and access for Latina students*. Routledge.

Edelsky, C. (1986). *Writing in a bilingual program: Habia una vez*. Ablex. https://eric.ed.gov/?id=ED305192

Edgemon, A. K., Rapp, J. T., Coon, J. C., Cruz-Khalili, A., Brogan, K. M., & Richling, S. M. (2021). Using behavior contracts to improve behavior of children and adolescents in multiple settings. *Behavioral Interventions, 36*(1), 271–88.

Education Act, SA 2012, c E-0.3. Elementary and Secondary Education Act (ESEA).

Eissa, M. A. (2009). The effectiveness of a program based on self-regulated strategy development on the writing skills of writing-disabled secondary school students. *Electronic Journal of Research in Educational Psychology, 7*(1), 5–24.

Ellis, E. (2000). *The LINCS vocabulary strategy*. Edge Enterprises.

Ellis, E. (2001). *The vocabulary LINCING routine*. Edge Enterprises.

Engelmann, S. (1980). *Direct instruction*. Educational Technology.

Engelmann, S., & Carnine, D. (1982). *Theory of instruction: Principles and applications*. Irvington.

Ennis, R. P., Royer, D. J., Lane, K. L., & Dunlap, K. D. (2020). The impact of coaching on teacher-delivered behavior-specific praise in pre-K–12 settings: A systematic review. *Behavioral Disorders, 45*(3), 148–66. https://doi.org/10.1177/0198742919839221

Everett, G. E., Hupp, S. D. A., & Olmi, D. J. (2010). Time-out with parents: A descriptive analysis of 30 years of research. *Education and Treatment of Children, 33*(2), 235–59.

Evertson, C. M., & Weinstein C. S. (Eds.). (2006). *Handbook of classroom management: Research, practice, and contemporary issues*. Erlbaum.

Every Student Succeeds Act, 20 U.S.C. § 6301 (2015). https://www.congress.gov/114/plaws/publ95/PLAW-114publ95.pdf

Fabiano, G. A., Vujnovic, R. K., Pelham, W. E., Waschbusch, D. A., Massetti, G. M., Pariseau, M. E., Naylor, J., Yu, J., Robins, M., Carnefix, T., Greiner, A. R., & Volker, M. (2010). Enhancing the effectiveness of special education programming for children with attention deficit hyperactivity disorder using a daily report card. *School Psychology Review, 39*(2), 219–39. https://doi.org/10.1080/02796015.2010.12087775

Faggella-Luby, M., Graner, P., Deshler, D, and Drew, S. (2012). Building a house on sand: Why disciplinary literacy is not sufficient to replace general strategies for adolescent learners who struggle. *Topics in Language Disorders, 32*(1), 69–84.

Faltis, C., & Wolfe, P. M. (1999). *So much to say: Adolescents, bilingualism, and ESL in the secondary school*. Teachers College Press.

Ferretti, R. P., & Okolo, C. M. (1996). Authenticity in learning: Multimedia design projects in the social studies for students with disabilities. *Journal of Learning Disabilities, 29*(5), 450–60. https://doi.org/10.1177%2F002221949602900501

Ficarra, L., & Quinn, K. (2014). Teachers' facility with evidence-based classroom management practices: An investigation of teachers' preparation programmes and in-service conditions. *Journal of Teacher Education for Sustainability, 16*(2), 71–87. https://doi.org/10.2478/jtes-2014-0012

Filderman, M. J., Austin, C. R., Boucher, A. N., O'Donnell, K., & Swanson, E. A. (2021). A meta-analysis of the effects of reading comprehension interventions on reading comprehension outcomes of struggling readers in third through 12th grades. *Exceptional Children, 88*(2), 163–84. https://doi.org/10.1177/00144029211050860

Filderman, M. J., & Toste, J. R. (2018). Decisions, decisions, decisions: Using data to make instructional decisions for struggling readers. *TEACHING Exceptional Children, 50*(3), 130–40.

Filderman, M. J., Toste, J. R., Didion, L. A., Peng, P., & Clemens, N. H. (2018). Data-based decision making in reading interventions: A synthesis and meta-analysis of the effects for struggling readers. *Journal of Special Education, 52*(3), 174–87. https://doi.org/10.1177/0022466918790001

Foegen, A. (2008). Algebra progress monitoring and intervention for students with learning disabilities. *Learning Disabilities Quarterly, 31*(2), 65–78.

Foorman, B., Beyler, N., Borradaile, K., Coyne, M., Denton, C. A., Dimino, J., Furgeson, J., Hayes, L., Henke, J., Justice, L., Keating, B., Lewis, W., Sattar, S., Streke, A., Wagner, R., & Wissel, S. (2016). *Foundational skills to support reading for understanding in kindergarten through 3rd grade* (NCEE 2016-4008). National Center for Education Evaluation and Regional Assistance (NCEE), Institute of Education Sciences, US Department of Education. Retrieved from the NCEE website: https://ies.ed.gov/ncee/wwc/practiceguide/21

Foorman, B. R., Wu, Y-C., Quinn, J. M., & Petscher, Y. (2020). How do latent decoding and language predict latent reading comprehension: Across two years in grades 5, 7, and 9? *Reading and Writing, 33*(9), 2281–2309.

Foxworth, L. L., Mason, L. H., & Hughes, C. A. (2017). Improving narrative writing skills of secondary students with disabilities using strategy instruction. *Exceptionality, 25*(4), 217–34. http://doi.org/10.1080/09362835.2016.1196452

Francis, D. J., Shaywitz, S. E., Stuebing, K. K., Shaywitz, B. A., & Fletcher, J. M. (1996). Developmental lag versus deficit models of reading disability: A longitudinal, individual growth curves analysis. *Journal of Educational Psychology*, 88(1), 3–17.

Freeman, J., Simonsen, B., Briere, D. E., & MacSuga-Gage, A. S. (2014). Pre-service teacher training in classroom management: A review of state accreditation policy and teacher preparation programs. *Teacher Education and Special Education*, 37(2), 106–20. https://doi.org/10.1177/0888406413507002

Fuchs, D., & Fuchs, L. S. (2016). Responsiveness-to-intervention: A "systems" approach to instructional adaptation. *Theory Into Practice*, 55(3), 225–33.

Fuchs, D., Fuchs, L. S., & Vaughn, S. (2014). What is intensive instruction and why is it important? *TEACHING Exceptional Children*, 46(4), 13–18.

Fuchs, L. S., Fuchs, D., & Compton, D. L. (2010). Rethinking response to intervention at middle and high school. *School Psychology Review*, 39(1), 22–28.

Fuchs, L. S., Fuchs, D., Hamlett, C. L., & Stecker, P. M. (2021). Bringing data-based individualization to scale: A call for the next-generation technology of teacher supports. *Journal of Learning Disabilities*, 54(5), 319–33.

Fuchs, L. S., Fuchs, D., & Malone, A. S. (2017). The taxonomy of intervention intensity. *TEACHING Exceptional Children*, 50(4), 35–43. https://doi.org/10.1177/0040059918758166

Fuchs, L. S., Newman-Gonchar, R., Schumacher, R., Dougherty, B., Bucka, N., Karp, K. S., Woodward, J., Clarke, B., Jordan, N. C., Gersten, R., Jayanthi, M., Keating, B., & Morgan, S. (2021). *Assisting students struggling with mathematics: Intervention in the elementary grades* (WWC 2021006). National Center for Education Evaluation and Regional Assistance (NCEE), Institute of Education Sciences, US Department of Education. http://whatworks.ed.gov/

Gage, N. A., Haydon, T., MacSuga-Gage, A. S., Flowers, E., & Erdy, L. (2020). An evidence-based review and meta-analysis of active supervision. *Behavioral Disorders*, 45(2), 117–28. https://doi.org/10.1177/0198742919851021

Gage, N. A., & McDaniel, S. (2012). Creating smarter classrooms: Data-based decision making for effective classroom management. *Beyond Behavior*, 22(1), 48–55. https://doi.org/10.1177/107429561202200108

Gage, N. A., Scott, T., Hirn, R., & MacSuga-Gage, A. S. (2017). The relationship between teachers' implementation of classroom management practices and student behavior in elementary school. *Behavioral Disorders*, 43(2), 302–15. https://doi.org/10.1177/0198742917714809

Gagnon, J. C., & Maccini, P. (2001). Preparing students with disabilities for algebra. *TEACHING Exceptional Children*, 34(1), 8–15.

Garwood, J. D. (2018). Literacy interventions for secondary students formally identified with emotional and behavioral disorders: Trends and gaps in the research. *Journal of Behavioral Education*, 27, 23–52. http://doi.org/10.1007/s10864-017-9278-3

Geary, D. C. (2004). Mathematics and learning disabilities. *Journal of Learning Disabilities*, 37(1), 4–15.

Geary, D. C. (2011). Consequences, characteristics, and causes of mathematical learning disabilities and persistent low achievement in mathematics. *Journal of Developmental and Behavioral Pediatrics*, 32(3), 250–63. DOI:10.1097/DBP.0b013e318209edef

Geres-Smith, R., Mercer, S. H., Archambault, C., & Bartfai, J. M. (2019). A preliminary component analysis of self-regulated strategy development for persuasive writing in grades 5 to 7 in British Columbia. *Canadian Journal of School Psychology, 34*(1), 38–55. https://doi.org/10.1177/0829573517739085

Germán, L. E. (2021). *Textured teaching: A framework for culturally sustaining practices*. Heinemann.

Gersten, R., Baker, S. K., Smith-Johnson, J., Dimino, J., & Peterson, A. (2006). Eyes on the prize: Teaching complex historical content to middle school students with learning disabilities. *Exceptional Children, 72*(3), 264–80. https://doi.org/10.1177%2F001440290607200301

Gersten, R., Beckmann, S., Clarke, B., Foegen, A., Marsh, L., Star, J. R., & Witzel, B. (2009). *Assisting students struggling with mathematics: Response to intervention (RtI) for elementary and middle schools* (NCEE 2009-4060). National Center for Education Evaluation and Regional Assistance, Institute of Education Sciences, US Department of Education. https://ies.ed.gov/ncee/wwc/Docs/PracticeGuide/rti_math_pg_042109.pdf

Gersten, R., Chard, D. J., Jayanthi, M., Baker, S. K., Morphy, P., Flojo, J. (2009). *A meta-analysis of mathematical instructional interventions for students with learning disabilities: Technical report*. Instructional Research Group.

Gersten, R., Fuchs, L. S., Compton, D., Coyne, M., Greenwood, C., & Innocenti, M. S. (2005). Quality indicators for group experimental and quasi-experimental research in special education. *Exceptional Children, 71*(2), 149–164. https://doi.org/10.1177%2F001440290507100202

Gersten, R., Jordan, N. C., & Flojo, R. (2005). Early identification and interventions for students with mathematics difficulties. *Journal of Learning Disabilities, 38*(4), 293–304.

Gersten, R., Newman-Gonchar, R., Haymond, K. S., & Dimino, J. (2017). What is the evidence base to support reading interventions for improving student outcomes in grades 1–3? (REL 2017-271). *Regional Educational Laboratory Southeast*.

Gilmour, A. F., Fuchs, D., & Wehby, J. H. (2019). Are students with disabilities accessing the curriculum? A meta-analysis of the reading achievement gap between students with and without disabilities. *Exceptional Children, 85*(3), 329–46. https://doi.org/10.1177/0014402918795830

Goldstein, A. P. (1973). *Structured learning therapy: Toward a psychotherapy for the poor*. Academic.

Goldstein, A. P., & McGinnis, E. (1997). *Skillstreaming the adolescent: New strategies and perspectives for teaching prosocial skills*. Research.

Gough, P. B., & Tunmer, W. E. (1986). Decoding, reading, and reading disability. *Remedial and Special Education, 7*(1), 6–10. https://doi.org/10.1177/074193258600700104

Grabill, J. T., & Hicks, T. (2005). Multiliteracies meet methods: The case for digital writing in English education. *English Education, 37*(4), 301–11. http://www.jstor.org/stable/40173204

Graham, S. (2019). Changing how writing is taught. *Review of Research in Education, 43*(1), 277–303. https://doi.org/10.3102/0091732X18821125

Graham, S., Bañales, G., Ahumada, S., Muñoz, P., Alvarez, P., & Harris, K. R. (2020). Writing strategies interventions. In D. L. Dinsmore, L. K. Fryer, & M. M. Parkinson (Eds.), *Handbook of strategies and strategic processing* (pp. 141–58). Routledge.

Graham, S., Bruch, J., Fitzgerald, J., Friedrich, L., Furgeson, J., Greene, K., Kim, J., Lyskawa, J., Olson, C. B., & Smither Wulsin, C. (2016). Teaching secondary students to write effectively (NCEE 2017-4002). National Center for Education Evaluation and Regional Assistance (NCEE), Institute of Education Sciences, US Department of Education. Retrieved from the NCEE website: http://whatworks.ed.gov

Graham, S., & Harris, K. R. (2018). Evidence-based writing practices: A meta-analysis of existing meta-analyses. In M. Braaksma, K. R. Harris, & R. Fidalgo (Eds.). *Design principles for teaching effective writing: Theoretical and empirical grounded principles* (pp. 13–37). Brill Academic.

Graham, S., Hebert, M., & Harris, K. R. (2015). Formative assessment and writing: A meta-analysis. *Elementary School Journal, 115*(4), 523–47. https://doi.org/10.1086/681947

Grant, S. G. (2013). From Inquiry Arc to instructional practice: The potential of the C3 Framework. *Social Education, 77*(6), 322–26.

Grant, S. G., Lee, J., & Swan, K. (2015). *The inquiry design model.* http://www.c3teachers.org/wp-content/uploads/2014/10/IDM_Assumptions_C3-Brief.pdf

Greenwood, C. R., Horton, B. T., & Utley, C. A. (2002). Academic engagement: Current perspectives on research and practice. *School Psychology Review, 31*(3), 328–49.

Gresham, F. M. (2013). Treatment integrity within a three-tiered model. In H. M. Walker & F. M. Gresham (Eds.), *Handbook of evidence-based practices for emotional and behavioral disorders: Applications in schools.* Guilford.

Guerra, J. (2008). Cultivating transcultural citizenship: A writing across communities model. *Language Arts, 85*(4), 296–304.

Gurganus, S. P. (2007). *Math instruction for students with learning problems.* Pearson Education.

Hall, C., Kent, S. C., McCulley, L., Davis, A., & Wanzek, J. (2013). A new look at mnemonics and graphic organizers in the secondary social studies classroom. *TEACHING Exceptional Children, 46*(1), 47–55. https://doi.org/10.1177/004005991304600106

Harper, G. F., & Maheady, L. (2007). Peer-mediated teaching and students with learning disabilities. *Intervention in School and Clinic, 43*(2), 101–7. https://doi.org/10.1177/10534512070430020101

Harris, K. R., & Graham, S. (2018). Self-regulated strategy development: Theoretical bases, critical instructional elements, and future research. In M. Braaksma, K. R. Harris, & R. Fidalgo (Eds.). *Design principles for teaching effective writing: Theoretical and empirical principles* (Studies in Writing, vol. 34, pp. 119–51). Brill Academic. https://doi.org/10.1163/9789004270480_007

Harris, M. L., Schumaker, J. B., & Deshler, D. D. (2011). The effects of strategic morphological analysis instruction on the vocabulary performance of secondary students with and without disabilities. *Learning Disability Quarterly, 34*(1), 17–33.

Harris, R. (2000). *WebQuester: A guidebook to the Web.* McGraw-Hill.

Haydon, T., Mancil, G. R., Kroeger, S. D., McLeskey, J., & Lin, W. Y. J. (2011). A review of the effectiveness of guided notes for students who struggle learning academic content. *Preventing School Failure: Alternative Education for Children and Youth, 55*(4), 226–31.

Hayes, J. R., & Nash, J. G. (1996). On the nature of planning in writing. In C. M. Levy & S. Ransdell (Eds.), *The science of writing: Theories, methods, individual differences, and applications* (pp. 29–55). Lawrence Erlbaum.

Herrera, S., Truckenmiller, A. J., & Foorman, B. R. (2016). *Summary of 20 years of research on the effectiveness of adolescent literacy programs and practices*. REL 2016-178. Regional Educational Laboratory Southeast.

Hock, M., Deshler, D., & Schumaker, J. (2000). *Strategic tutoring*. Edge Enterprises.

Hoffer, T. B., Venkataraman, L., Hedberg, E. C., & Shagle, S. (2007). Final report on the National Survey of Algebra Teachers for the National Math Panel: NORC at the University of Chicago.

Honig, B., Diamond, L., Gutlohn, L., Fertig, B., Daniel, H., Zemelman, S., & Steineke, N. (2018). *Teaching reading sourcebook* (3rd ed.). Arena.

Hoover, J. J., & Patton, J. R. (2007). *Teaching study skills to students with learning problems: A teacher's guide for meeting diverse needs*. Pro Ed.

Hoover, T. M., Kubina, R. M., & Mason, L. H. (2012). Effects of self-regulated strategy development for POW+TREE on high school students with learning disabilities. *Exceptionality: A Special Education Journal, 20*(1), 20–38. https://doi.org/10.1080/09362835.2012.640903

Hoover, W. A., & Gough, P. B. (1990). The simple view of reading. *Reading and Writing: An Interdisciplinary Journal, 2*(2), 127–60.

Hoover, W. A., & Tunmer, W. E. (2018). The simple view of reading: Three assessments of its adequacy. *Remedial and Special Education, 39*(5), 304–12. https://doi.org/10.1177/0741932518773154

Horner, R. H., Carr, E. G., Halle, J., McGee, G., Odom, S., & Wolery, M. (2005). The use of single-subject research to identify evidence-based practice in special education. *Exceptional Children, 71*(2), 165–79. https://doi.org/10.1177/001440290507100203

Hosp, M. K., Hosp, J. L., & Howell, K. W. (2016). *The ABCs of CBM: A practical guide to curriculum-based measurement*. Guilford.

Hosp, M. K., Hosp, J. L., & Howell, K. W. (2016). *The ABCs of CBM* (2nd ed.). Guilford.

Hott, B., Randolph, K. M., Josephson, J., & Heiniger, S. (2021). Implementing electronic check-in/check-out to reduce challenging school bus behavior. *Journal of Special Education Technology, 36*(3), 152–61. https://doi.org/10.1177/01626434211004446

Hott, B. L., Berkeley, S., Reid, C. C., & Raymond, L. (2019). An analysis of special education practitioner journals: A focus on behavior. *Exceptionality, 28*(5), 333–48. https://doi.org/10.1080/09362835.2019.1579724

Hudson, M. E., Browder, D. M., & Jimenez, B. A. (2014). Effects of a peer-delivered system of least prompts intervention and adapted science read-alouds on listening comprehension for participants with moderate intellectual disability. *Education and Training in Autism and Developmental Disabilities, 49*(1), 60–77. https://www.jstor.org/stable/23880655

Hudson, P., Miller, S. P., & Butler, F. (2006). Adapting and merging explicit instruction within reform based mathematics classrooms. *American Secondary Education, 35*(1), 19–32.

Hue, M. T. (2022). Inclusive education: Equal opportunities for all. In K. J. Kennedy, M. Pavlova, & J. C-K. Lee (Eds.), *Soft skills and hard values* (pp. 93–111). Routledge.

Hughes, C. A., Morris, J. R., Therrien, W. J., & Benson, S. K. (2017). Explicit instruction: Historical contemporary contexts. *Learning Disabilities Research & Practice*, *32*(3), 140–48.

Hughes, C. A., Ruhl, K. L., Deshler, D. D., & Schumaker, J. B. (1995). *The assignment completion strategy*. Edge Enterprises.

Hughes, C. A., Ruhl, K. L., Schumaker, J. B., & Deshler, D. D. (2002). Effects of instruction in an assignment completion strategy on the homework performance of students with learning disabilities in general education classes. *Learning Disabilities Research & Practice, 17*(1), 1–18.

Hull, G. A., & Schultz, K. (2002). *School's out! Bridging out-of-school literacies with classroom practice*. Teachers College Press.

Hunter, L. J., & Hall, C. M. (2018). A survey of K–12 teachers' utilization of social networks as a professional resource. *Education and Information Technologies, 23*, 633–58. https://doi.org/10.1007/s10639-017-9627-9

Hussar, B., Zhang, J., Hein, S., Wang, K., Roberts, A., Cui, J., Smith, M., Bullock, F., Barmer, A., & Dilig, R. (2020). *The condition of education 2020* (NCES 2020-144). US Department of Education: National Center for Education Statistics. https://nces.ed.gov/pubsearch/pubsinfo.asp?pubid=2020144

Huston-Stein, A., Friedrich-Cofer, L., & Susman, E. J. (1977). The relation of classroom structure to social behavior, imaginative play, and self-regulation of economically disadvantaged children. *Child Development, 48*(3), 908–16.

Impecoven-Lind, L. S., & Foegen, A. (2010). Teaching algebra to students with learning disabilities. *Intervention in School and Clinic, 46*(1), 31–37.

Individuals with Disabilities Education Act (IDEA), 20 U.S.C. § 1400 (2004).

International Literacy Association. (2020). *Research advisory: Teaching writing to improve reading skills.* https://www.literacyworldwide.org/docs/default-source/where-we-stand/ila-teaching-writing-to-improve-reading-skills.pdf

IRIS Center. (2013). *Study skills strategies (part 1): Foundations for effectively teaching study skills.* https://iris.peabody.vanderbilt.edu/module/ss1/

IRIS Center. (2013). *Study skills strategies (part 2): Strategies that improve students' academic performance.* https://iris.peabody.vanderbilt.edu/module/ss2/

IRIS Center. (2020). Graphic organizers. https://iris.peabody.vanderbilt.edu/module/ss2/cresource/q1/p02/

Jameson, J. M., McDonnell, J., Polychronis, S., Riesen, T., & Taylor, S. J. (2008). Embedded, constant time delay instruction by peers without disabilities in general education classrooms. *Intellectual and Developmental Disabilities, 46*(5), 346–63. https://doi.org/10.1352/2008.46:346-363

Jane Schaffer Academic Writing Program. (n.d.). *Writing is about thinking.* Louis Educational Concepts. https://janeschaffer.com/

Jang, H., Reeve, J., & Deci, E. L. (2010). Engaging students in learning activities: It is not autonomy support or structure but autonomy support and structure. *Journal of Educational Psychology, 102*(3), 588–600. https://doi.org/10.1037/a0019682

Jimenez, B. A., Browder, D. M., Spooner, F., & Dibiase, W. (2012). Inclusive inquiry science using peer-mediated embedded instruction for students with moderate intellectual disability. *Exceptional Children, 78*(3), 301–17. https://doi.org/10.1177%2F001440291207800303

Jitendra, A. K., & Gajria, M. (2011). Reading comprehension instruction for students with learning disabilities. *Focus on Exceptional Children, 43*(8), 1–16. https://doi.org/10.17161/foec.v43i8.6690

Johns, A. M. (2001). *Genre in the classroom: Multiple perspectives*. Routledge.

Jung, P. G., McMaster, K. L., Kunkel, A. K., Shin, J., & Stecker, P. M. (2018). Effects of data-based individualization for students with intensive learning needs: A meta-analysis. *Learning Disabilities Research and Practice, 33*(3), 144–55.

Kamil, M. L., Borman, G. D., Dole, J., Kral, C. C., Salinger, T., & Torgesen, J. (2008). *Improving adolescent literacy: Effective classroom and intervention practices*. IES Practice Guide. NCEE 2008-4027. National Center for Education Evaluation and Regional Assistance. https://ies.ed.gov/ncee/wwc/docs/practiceguide/adlit_pg_082608.pdf

Kamphaus, R. W., & Reynolds, C. R. (2007). *Behavioral assessment system for children, 2nd edition (BASC-2): Behavioral and emotional screening system (BESS): Manual*. Pearson.

Kamps, D., Wills, H., Heitzman-Powell, L., Laylin, J., Szoke, C., Petrillo, T., & Culey, A. (2011). Classwide function-related intervention teams: Effects of group contingency programs in urban classrooms. *Journal of Positive Behavior Interventions, 13*(3), 154–76. https://doi:10.1177/1098300711398935

Kamps, D. M., Greenwood, C., Arreaga-Mayer, C., Veerkamp, M. B., Utley, C., Tapia, Y., Bowman-Perrott, L., & Bannister, H. (2008). The efficacy of classwide peer tutoring in middle schools. *Education and Treatment of Children, 31*(2), 119–52.

Kearns, D. M., Steacy, L. M., Compton, D. L., Gilbert, J. K., Goodwin, A. P., Cho, E., Lindstrom, E. R., & Collins, A. A. (2016). Modeling polymorphemic word recognition: Exploring differences among children with early-emerging and late-emerging word reading difficulty. *Journal of Learning Disabilities, 49*(4), 368–94.

Kennedy, M. J., Cook, L., Cook, B., Brownell, M. T., & Holdheide, L. (2020). Special video: Clarifying the relationship between HLPs and EBPs. Council for Exceptional Children. https://highleveragepractices.org/clarifying-relationship-between-hlps-and-ebps

King-Sears, M. E., Mercer, C. D., & Sindelar, P. T. (1992). Toward independence with keyword mnemonics: A strategy for science vocabulary instruction. *Remedial and Special Education, 13*(5), 22–33. https://doi.org/10.1177/074193259201300505

Klassen, R. M., & Chiu, M. M. (2010). Effects on teachers' self-efficacy and job satisfaction: Teacher gender, years of experience, and job stress. *Journal of Educational Psychology, 102*(3), 741–69.

Klauda, S. L., Wigfield, A., & Cambria, J. (2012). Struggling readers' information text comprehension and motivation in early adolescence. In J. T. Guthrie, A. Wigfield, & S. L. Klauda (Eds.), *Adolescents' engagement in academic literacy* (pp. 295–351). College Park: University of Maryland.

Klein, P. D., Haug, K. N., & Bildfell, A. (2019). Writing to learn. In S. Graham, C. A. MacArthur, & M. Hebert (Eds.), *Best practices in writing instruction* (3rd ed., pp. 162–184). Guilford.

Kokotsaki, D., Menzies, V., & Wiggins, A. (2016). Project-based learning: A review of the literature. *Improving schools, 19*(3), 267–77.

Konrad, M., & Test, D. W. (2007). Effects of GO 4 IT . . . NOW! strategy instruction on the written IEP goal articulation and paragraph-writing skills of middle school students with disabilities. *Remedial and Special Education, 28*(5), 277–91. https://doi.org/10.1177/07419325070280050301

Korpershoek, H., Harms, T., de Boer, H., van Kuijk, M., & Doolaard, S. (2016). A meta-analysis of the effects of classroom management strategies and classroom management programs on students' academic, behavioral, emotional, and motivational outcomes. *Review of Educational Research, 86*(3), 643–80.

Kortering, L. J., deBettencourt, L. U., & Braziel, P. M. (2005). Improving performance in high school algebra: What students with learning disabilities are saying. *Learning Disability Quarterly, 28*, 191–203.

KQED Teach. (2023). *Bring media literacy and media making to your teaching.* KQED Teach. https://teach.kqed.org

Krajcik, J. S., Czerniak, C., & Berger, C. (1999). Teaching children science: A project-based approach. McGraw-Hill.

Kunsch, C. A., Jitendra, A. K., & Sood, S. (2007). The effects of peer-mediated instruction in mathematics for students with learning problems: A research synthesis. *Learning Disabilities Research & Practice, 22*(1), 1–12.

Kwok, A. (2019). Classroom management actions of beginning urban teachers. *Urban Education, 54*(3), 339–67.

Lane, K. L., Little, M. A., Casey, A. M., Lambert, W., Wehby, J., Weisenbach, J. L., & Phillips, A. (2009). A comparison of systematic screening tools for emotional and behavioral disorders. *Journal of Emotional and Behavioral Disorders, 17*(2), 93–105. https://doi.org/10.1177/1063426608326203

Lane, K. L., Oakes, W. P., Lusk, M. E., Cantwell, E. D., & Schatschneider, C. (2016). Screening for intensive intervention needs in secondary schools. *Journal of Emotional and Behavioral Disorders, 24*(3), 159–72. https://doi.org/10.1177/1063426615618624

Lederman, N. G. (2007). Nature of science: Past, present, and future. In S. K. Abell & N. G. Lederman (Eds.), *Handbook of research on science education* (pp. 831–80). Lawrence Erlbaum.

Lee, A., & Gage, N. A. (2020). Updating and expanding systematic reviews and meta-analyses on the effects of school-wide positive behavior interventions and supports. *Psychology in the Schools, 57*(5), 783–804. https://doi.org/10.1002/pits.22336

Lee, D. L., Belfiore, P. J., & Budin, S. G. (2008). Creating a momentum of school success. *TEACHING Exceptional Children, 40*(3), 65–70. https://doi.org/10.1177/004005990804000307

Lee, D. L., Belfiore, P. J., Scheeler, M. C., Hua, Y., & Smith, R. (2004). Behavioral momentum in academics: Using embedded high-p sequences to increase academic productivity. *Psychology in the Schools, 41*(7), 789–801. https://doi.org/10.1002/pits.20014

Lembke, E. S., Strickland, T. K., & Powell, S. R. (2016). Monitoring student progress to determine instructional effectiveness. In B. Witzel (Ed.) *Bridging the gap between arithmetic & algebra.* Council for Exceptional Children.

Lenz, B. K., Adams, G. L., Bulgren, J. A., Pouliot, N., & Laraux, M. (2007). Effects of curriculum maps and guiding questions on the test performance of adolescents with learning disabilities. *Learning Disability Quarterly, 30*(4), 235–44.

Lenz, B. K., Bulgren, J. A., Kissam, B. R. , & Taymans, J. (2004). SMARTER planning for academic diversity. In B. K. Lenz, D. D. Deshler, with B. R. Kissam (Eds.),

Teaching content to all: Evidence-based inclusive practices in middle and secondary schools (pp. 47–77). Pearson.

Lervåg, A., & Melby-Lervåg, M. (2022). Early prediction of learning outcomes in reading. In M. Skeide (Ed.), *The Cambridge Handbook of Dyslexia and Dyscalculia* (Cambridge Handbooks in Psychology, pp. 305–17). Cambridge: Cambridge University Press. https://doi.org/10.1017/9781108973595.024

Letendre, W. (1993). Mnemonic instruction with regular and special education students in social studies. *Southern Social Studies Journal, 18*(2), 25–37.

Litow, L., & Pumroy, D. K. (1975). A brief review of classroom group-oriented contingencies. *Journal of Applied Behavior Analysis, 8*(3), 341–47.

Lombardo, C. (2019). *8 student-made podcasts that made us smile*. NPR. https://www.npr.org/2019/06/08/729605772/eight-student-made-podcasts-that-made-us-smile

Lonigan, C. J., Burgess, S. R., & Schatschneider, C. (2018). Examining the simple view of reading with elementary school children: Still simple after all these years. *Remedial and Special Education, 39*(5), 260–73. https://doi:10.1177/0741932518764833

Losinski, M., Maag, J. W., Katsiyannis, A., & Ryan, J. B. (2015). The use of structural behavioral assessment to develop interventions for secondary students exhibiting challenging behaviors. *Education and Treatment of Children, 38*(2), 149–74. https://doi.org/doi:10.1353/etc.2015.0006

Lovett, M. W., Lacerenza, L., Borden, S. L., Frijters, J. C., Steinbach, K. A., & De Palma, M. (2000). Components of effective remediation for developmental reading disabilities: Combining phonological and strategy-based instruction to improve outcomes. *Journal of Educational Psychology, 92*(2), 263–83.

Lowrey, K. A., Hollingshead, A., Howery, K., & Bishop, J. B. (2017). More than one way: Stories of UDL and inclusive classrooms. *Research and Practice for Persons with Severe Disabilities, 42*(4), 225–242. https://doi.org/10.1177/1540796917711668

Lubin, J., & Polloway, E. A. (2016). Mnemonic instruction in science and social studies for students with learning problems: A review. *Learning Disabilities: A Contemporary Journal, 14*(2), 207–24. http://files.eric.ed.gov/fulltext/EJ1118431.pdf

MacArthur, C. A., & Graham, S. (2016). Writing research from a cognitive perspective. In C. A. MacArthur, S. Graham, & J. Fitzgerald (Eds.), *Handbook of writing research* (pp. 24–40). Guilford.

MacArthur, C. A., & Philippakos, Z. (2010). Instruction in a strategy for compare-contrast writing. *Exceptional Children, 76*(4), 438–56. https://doi.org/10.1177/001440291007600404

Maccini, P., & Gagnon, J. C. (2002). Perceptions and application of NCTM standards by special and general education teachers. *Exceptional Children, 68*(3), 325–44.

Maccini, P., Strickland, T., Gagnon, J. C., & Malmgren, K. (2008). Accessing the general education math curriculum for secondary students with high-incidence disabilities. *Focus on Exceptional Children, 40*(8), 1–32.

MacSuga-Gage, A. S., & Simonsen, B. (2015). Examining the effects of teacher-directed opportunities to respond on student outcomes: A systematic review of the literature. *Education and Treatment of Children, 38*(2), 211–39.

Maggin, D. M., Chafouleas, S. M., Goddard, K. M., & Johnson, A. H. (2011). A systematic evaluation of token economies as a classroom management tool for students with challenging behavior. *Journal of School Psychology, 49*(5), 529–54. https://doi.org/10.1016/j.jsp.2011.05.001

Maggin, D. M., Zurheide, J., Pickett, K. C., & Baillie, S. J. (2015). A systematic evidence review of the check-in/check-out program for reducing student challenging behaviors. *Journal of Positive Behavior Interventions, 17*(4), 197–208. https://psycnet.apa.org/record/2015-40173-002

Maheady, L., Harper, G. F., & Mallette, B. (2001). Peer-mediated instruction and interventions and students with mild disabilities. *Remedial and Special Education, 22*(1), 4–14. https://doi.org/10.1177/074193250102200102

Majeika, C. E., Wilkinson, S., & Kumm, S. (2020). Supporting student behavior through behavioral contracting. *TEACHING Exceptional Children, 53*(2), 132–39. https://doi.org/10.1177/0040059920952475

Malatesha Joshi, R. (2005). Vocabulary: A critical component of comprehension. *Reading & Writing Quarterly, 21*(3), 209–19.

Mason, L. H., Kubina Jr., R. M., Kostewicz, D. E., Cramer, A. M., & Datchuk, S. (2013). Improving quick writing performance of middle-school struggling learners. *Contemporary Educational Psychology, 38*(3), 236–46. https://doi.org/10.1016/j.cedpsych.2013.04.002

Mastropieri, M. A., & Scruggs, T. E. (1989). Mnemonic social studies instruction: Classroom applications. *Remedial and Special Education, 10*(3), 40–46. https://doi.org/10.1177/074193258901000308

Mastropieri, M. A., & Scruggs, T. E. (1992). Science for students with disabilities. *Review of Educational Research, 62*(4), 377–411. https://doiorg/10.3102/00346543062004377

Mastropieri, M. A., & Scruggs, T. E. (1998). Enhancing school success with mnemonic strategies. *Intervention in School and Clinic, 33*(4), 201–8. https://doi.org/10.1177%2F105345129803300402

Mastropieri, M. A., Scruggs, T. E., Bakken, J. P., & Brigham, F. J. (1992). A complex mnemonic strategy for teaching states and their capitals: Comparing forward and backward associations. *Learning Disabilities Research & Practice, 7*(2), 96–103.

Mastropieri, M. A., Scruggs, T. E., & Levin, J. R. (1986). Direct vs. mnemonic instruction: Relative benefits for exceptional learners. *Journal of Special Education, 20*(3), 299–308. https://doi.org/10.1177/002246698602000304

Mastropieri, M. A., Scruggs, T. E., Levin, J. R., Gaffney, J., & McLoone, B. (1985). Mnemonic vocabulary instruction for learning disabled students. *Learning Disability Quarterly, 8*(1), 57–63. https://doi.org/10.2307/1510908

Mastropieri, M. A., Scruggs, T. E., Norland, J. J., Berkeley, S., McDuffie, K., Tornquist, E. H., & Connors, N. (2006). Differentiated curriculum enhancement in inclusive middle school science: Effects on classroom and high-stakes tests. *Journal of Special Education, 40*(3), 130–7. https://doi.org/10.1177/00224669060400030101

Mastropieri, M. A., Scruggs, T. E., & Whedon, C. (1997). Using mnemonic strategies to teach information about US presidents: A classroom-based investigation. *Learning Disability Quarterly, 20*(1), 13–21. https://doi.org/10.2307/1511089

Mastropieri, M.A., Scruggs, T.E, Whittaker, M.E.S., & Bakken, J.P. (1994). Applications of mnemonic strategies with students with mild mental disabilities. *Remedial and Special Education, 15*(1), 34–43. https://doi.org/10.1177/074193259401500106

Mazzocco, M. M. M. (2007). Defining and differentiating mathematical learning disabilities and difficulties. In D. B. Berch & M. M. M. Mazzocco (Eds.), *Why is* math so hard for some children? The nature and origins of mathematical learning difficulties and disabilities (pp. 29–48). Paul H. Brookes.

McCarthy, C. B. (2005). Effects of thematic-based, hands-on science teaching versus a textbook approach for students with disabilities. *Journal of Research in Science Teaching, 42*(3), 245–63. https://doi.org/10.1002/tea.20057

McDuffie, K. A., & Scruggs, T. E. (2008). The contributions of qualitative research to discussions of evidence-based practice in special education. *Intervention in School and Clinic, 44*(2), 91–97. https://doi.org/10.1177/1053451208321564

McKenna, J. W., Shin, M., & Ciullo, S. (2015). Evaluating reading and mathematics instruction for students with learning disabilities: A synthesis of observation research. *Learning Disability Quarterly, 38*(4), 195–207.

McLeskey, J., Barringer, M-D., Billingsley, B., Brownell, M., Jackson, D., Kennedy, M., Lewis, T., Maheady, L., Rodriguez, J., Scheeler, M. C., Winn, J., & Ziegler, D. (2017). *High-leverage practices in special education.* Council for Exceptional Children & CEEDAR Center.

McLeskey, J., Maheady, L., Billingsley, B., Brownell, M., & Lewis, T. (2022). *High leverage practices for inclusive classrooms* (2nd ed). Routledge.

McMaster, K. L., Fuchs, D., Fuchs, L. S., & Compton, D. L. (2005). Responding to nonresponders: An experimental field trial of identification and intervention methods. *Exceptional Children, 71*(4), 445–63.

McNamara, D. S. (2007). *Reading comprehension strategies: Theories, interventions, and technologies.* Taylor & Francis Group.

McNamara, D. S., Floyd, R. G., Best, R., & Louwerse, M. (2004). World knowledge driving young readers' comprehension difficulties. In *Proceedings of the 6th international conference on learning sciences* (pp. 326–33). International Society of the Learning Sciences.

Menzies, H. M., Lane, K. L., & Lee, J. M. (2009). Self-Monitoring strategies for use in the classroom: A promising practice to support productive behavior for students with emotional or behavioral disorders. *Beyond Behavior, 18*(2), 27–35.

Metcalf, T. (2012). What's your plan? Accurate decision making within a multi-tier system of supports: Critical areas in Tier 1. RTI Action Network. National Center for Learning Disabilities.

Miller, B., Doughty, T., & Krockover, G. (2015). Using science inquiry methods to promote self-determination and problem-solving skills for students with moderate intellectual disability. *Education and Training in Autism and Developmental Disabilities, 50*(3), 356–68.

Mitchell, B. S., Adamson, R., & McKenna, J. W. (2017). Curbing our enthusiasm: An analysis of the check-in/check-out literature using the Council for Exceptional Children's evidence-based practice standards. *Behavior Modification, 41*(3), 343–67.

Moore, C., & Shulock, N. (2009). *Student progress toward degree completion: Lessons from the research literature.* Institute for Higher Education Leadership & Policy, California State University.

Moore Partin, T. C., Robertson, R. E., Maggin, D. M., Oliver, R. M., & Wehby, J. H. (2010). Using teacher praise and opportunities to respond to promote appropriate student behavior. *Preventing School Failure, 54*(3), 172–78. https://doi.org/10.1080/10459880903493179

Moreno, G., & Bullock, L. M. (2011). Principles of positive behaviour supports: Using the FBA as a problem-solving approach to address challenging behaviours beyond special populations. *Emotional and Behavioural Difficulties, 16*(2), 117–27. https://doi.org/10.1080/13632752.2011.569394

Morris, V. O. (1966). *Existentialism in education*. Harper and Row.

Moxley, R. A. (1996). The import of Skinner's three-term contingency. *Behavior and Philosophy, 24*(2) 145–67.

Myers, D., Simonsen, B., & Freeman, J. (2020). *Implementing classwide PBIS: A guide to supporting teachers*. Guilford.

Myers, J. A., Brownell, M. T., Griffin, C. C., Hughes, E. M., Witzel, B. S., Gage, N. A., Peyton, D., Acosta, K. & Wang, J. (2021). Mathematics interventions for adolescents with mathematics difficulties: A meta-analysis. *Learning Disabilities Research & Practice, 36*(2), 145–66. https://doi.org/10.1111/ldrp.12244

Nagel, D., Schumaker, J., & Deshler, D. (1986). *The FIRST-letter mnemonic strategy*. Lawrence, KS: Edge Enterprises.

National Assessment Governing Board. (2019). *Reading framework for the 2019 national assessment of educational progress*. US Department of Education. https://www.nagb.gov/content/dam/nagb/en/documents/publications/frameworks/reading/2019-reading-framework.pdf

National Assessment of Education Progress. (2009, July 21). *The nation's report card*. https://www.nationsreportcard.gov/reading_math_grade12_2005/s0206.asp

National Center for Education Statistics. (2003). *The nation's report card: Writing 2002, NCES 2003–529*, by H. R. Persky, M. C. Daane, & Y. Jin. Washington, DC: US Department of Education. Institute of Education Sciences.

National Center for Education Statistics. (2015). *Average mathematics score lower and reading score unchanged*. The Nation's Report Card. https://www.nationsreportcard.gov/reading_math_g12_2015/#

National Center for Education Statistics. (2019). *Explore results for the 2019 NAEP mathematics assessment*. The Nation's Report Card.

National Center for Education Statistics. (2019). *Explore results for the 2019 NAEP reading assessment*. The Nation's Report Card. https://www.nationsreportcard.gov/reading?grade=4

National Center for Education Statistics. (2022). *Students with disabilities: Fast facts*. https://nces.ed.gov/fastfacts/display.asp?id=64

National Center for Education Statistics. (2022). *Reading and mathematics scores decline during COVID-19 pandemic*. The Nation's Report Card. https://www.nationsreportcard.gov/highlights/ltt/2022/

National Center on Intensive Intervention. (2013). *Data-based individualization: A framework for intensive intervention*. American Institutes for Research (AIR). https://intensiveintervention.org/sites/default/files/DBI_Framework.pdf

National Commission on Writing in America's Schools and Colleges. (2003). *The neglected "R": The need for a writing revolution*. College Entrance Examination Board.

National Commission on Writing in America's Schools and Colleges. (2006). *Writing and school reform*. College Board.

National Council for the Social Studies (NCSS). (2013). *College, career, and civic life (C3) framework for social studies state standards*. https://www.socialstudies.org/standards/c3

National Council of Teachers of English. (2005). *Multimodal literacies*. NCTE. https://ncte.org/statement/multimodalliteracies

National Council of Teachers of English. (2011). *Framework for success in postsecondary writing*. NCTE. Distributed by ERIC Clearinghouse. https://files.eric.ed.gov/fulltext/ED516360.pdf

National Council of Teachers of Mathematics. (2000). *Principles and standards for school mathematics*.

National Governors Association Center for Best Practices & Council of Chief State School Officers. (2010). Common core state standards. Washington, DC: Authors.

National Governors Association, Council of Chief State School Officers (NGA CCSSO). (2010). *Common core state standards for English language arts*. Washington, DC: NGA Center for Best Practices and CCSSO.

National Mathematics Advisory Panel. (2008). *Foundations for success: The final report of the National Mathematics Advisory Panel*. US Department of Education.

National Mathematics Advisory Panel. (2008). *Foundations for success: The final report of the national mathematics advisory panel*. US Department of Education. https://files.eric.ed.gov/fulltext/ED500486.pdf

National Professional Development Center on Autism Spectrum Disorder. (2016). Evidence-based practices. https://autismpdc.fpg.unc.edu/evidence-based-practices

National Reading Panel. (2000). *Report of the national reading panel: Teaching children to read: An evidence-based assessment of the scientific research literature on reading and its implications for reading instruction*, Vol. 1. National Institute of Child Health and Human Development.

National Research Council. (2012). *A framework for K–12 science education: Practices, crosscutting concepts, and core ideas*. National Academies.

National Science Teaching Association. (2020). Position statement on nature of science. https://www.nsta.org/nstas-official-positions/nature-science

Neuman, S. B., Kaefer, T., & Pinkham, A. (2014). Building background knowledge. *Reading Teacher*, 68(2), 145–48.

New York Times. (2021, July 1). Winners of our Fourth annual podcast contest. Learning Network. https://www.nytimes.com/2021/07/01/learning/winners-of-our-fourth-annual-podcast-contest.html

NGSS Lead State (2013). The next generation science standards: Executive summary. https://www.nextgenscience.org/sites/default/files/Final%20Release%20NGSS%20Front%20Matter%20-%206.17.13%20Update_0.pdf

Nielsen Company. (2017). Nielsen podcast insights. https://www.nielsen.com/us/en/insights/report/2017/nielsen-podcast-insights-q3-2017

NPR. *This I Believe*. (n.d.). https://www.npr.org/series/4538138/this-i-believe

O'Connor, R. E., & Fuchs, L. S. (2013). Responsiveness to intervention in the elementary grades: Implications for early childhood education. In V. Buysse & E. S. Peisner-Feinberg (Eds.), *Handbook of response to intervention in early childhood* (pp. 41–55). Paul H. Brookes.

Okolo, C. M., & Ferretti, R. (2014). History instruction for students with learning disabilities. In H. L. Swanson, K. Harris, & S. Graham (Eds.), *Handbook of learning disabilities* (2nd ed., pp. 462–86). Guilford.

Oliver, R. M., Wehby, J. H., & Reschly, D. J. (2011). Teacher classroom management practices: Effects on disruptive or aggressive student behavior. *Campbell Systematic Reviews*, 7(1), 1–55.

Olson, C. B., Scarcella, R., & Matuchniak, T. (2013). Best practices in teaching writing to English learners: Reducing constraints to facilitate writing development.

In S. Graham, C. A. MacArthur, & J. Fitzgerald (Eds.), *Best practices in writing instruction* (2nd ed., pp. 381–402). Guilford.

Palincsar, A. S., Collins, K. M., Marano, N. L., & Magnusson, S. J. (2000). Investigating the engagement and learning of students with learning disabilities in guided inquiry science teaching. *Language, Speech, and Hearing Services in Schools, 31*(3), 240–51. https://doi.org/10.1044/0161-1461.3103.240

Paré, A., & Smart, G. (1994). Observing genres in action: Towards a research methodology. In A. Freedman & P. Medway (Eds.), *Genre and the new rhetoric* (pp. 146–54). Routledge. https://doi.org/10.4324/9780203393277

Parker, W. C. (Ed.). (2010). *Social studies today: Research and practice*. Routledge.

Pashler, H., Bain, P., Bottge, B., Graesser, A., Koedinger, K., McDaniel, M., and Metcalfe, J. (2007). *Organizing instruction and study to improve student learning* (NCER 2007-2004). National Center for Education Research, Institute of Education Sciences, US Department of Education. https://files.eric.ed.gov/fulltext/ED498555.pdf

Perfetti, C., & Stafura, J. (2014). Word knowledge in a theory of reading comprehension. *Scientific Studies of Reading, 18*(1), 22–37.

Perfetti, C. A., Landi, N., & Oakhill, J. (2005). The acquisition of reading comprehension skill. In M. J. Snowling & C. Hulme (Eds.), *The science of reading: A handbook* (pp. 227–47). Blackwell.

Perfetti, C. A., Marron, M. A., & Foltz, P. W. (1996). Sources of comprehension failure: Theoretical perspectives and case studies. In C. Cornoldi & J. Oakhill (Eds.), *Reading comprehension difficulties: Processes and interventions* (pp. 137–65). Lawrence Erlbaum.

Petscher, E. S., Rey, C., & Bailey, J. S. (2009). A review of empirical support for differential reinforcement of alternative behavior. *Research in Developmental Disabilities, 30*(3), 409–25. https://doi.org/10.1016/j.ridd.2008.08.008

Pfannenstiel, K. H., Bryant, D. P., Bryant, B. R., & Porterfield, J. A. (2015). Cognitive strategy instruction for teaching word problems to primary-level struggling students. *Intervention in school and clinic, 50*(5), 291–96. https://doi.org/10.1177/1053451214560890

Picciotto, H. (1995). *The algebra lab: Lab gear activities for Algebra 1*. Creative.

Pokorski, E. A. (2019). Group contingencies to improve classwide behavior of young children. *TEACHING Exceptional Children, 51*(5), 340–49.

Polya, G. (1957). *How to solve it. A new aspect of mathematical method* (2nd ed). Princeton University Press.

Pongsakdi, N., Kajamies, A., Veermans, K., Lertola, K., Vaurus, M., & Lehtinen, E. (2020). What makes mathematical word problem solving challenging? Exploring the roles of word problem characteristics, text comprehension, and arithmetic skills. *ZDM Mathematics Education, 52*(1), 33–44. https://link.springer.com/article/10.1007/s11858-019-01118-9

Powell, K. C., & Kalina, C. (2009). Cognitive and social constructivism: Developing tools for an effective classroom. *Education, 130*(2), 241–50.

Prior, P. (2006). A sociocultural theory of writing. In C. A. MacArthur, S. Graham, & J. Fitzgerald (Eds.), *The handbook of writing research* (pp. 54–66). Guilford.

Purcell-Gates, V., Duke, N. K., & Martineau, J. A. (2007). Learning to read and write genre-specific text: Roles of authentic experience and explicit teaching. *Reading Research Quarterly, 42*(1), 8–45. https://doi.org/10.1598/RRQ.42.1.1

Putnam, A. L. (2015). Mnemonics in education: Current research and applications. *Translational Issues in Psychological Science, 1*(2), 130–39. https://doi.org/10.1037/tps0000023

Rademacher, J. (1993). *The development and validation of a classroom assignment routine for mainstream settings* [Unpublished doctoral dissertation]. University of Kansas.

Rademacher, J. A., Deshler, D. D., Schumaker, J. B., & Lenz, B. K. (2011). *The quality assignment routine*. Lawrence, KS: Edge Enterprises.

RAND Reading Study Group: Snow, C. (2002). *Reading for understanding: Toward an R&D program in reading comprehension*. Santa Monica, CA: RAND.

Rashotte, C. A., & Torgesen, J. K. (1985). Repeated reading and reading fluency in learning disabled children. *Reading Research Quarterly, 20*, 180–88.

Ray, A. B. (in press). Writing interventions using SRSD for secondary students with and at-risk for learning disabilities: A review of empirical research. In Xinghua Liu, Michael Hebert, & Rui A. Alves (Eds.), *The Hitchhiker's Guide to Writing Research*. Springer.

Ray, A. B., & Graham, S. (2020). A college entrance essay exam intervention for students with high-incidence disabilities and struggling writers. *Learning Disability Quarterly, 44*(4), 275–87. Advanced online publication. https://doi.org/10.1177/0731948720917761

Ray, A. B., Graham, S., & Liu, X. (2019). Effects SRSD of college entrance essay exam instruction for high school students with disabilities or at-risk for writing difficulties. *Reading and Writing: An Interdisciplinary Journal, 32*(6), 1507–29. https://doi.org/ 10.1007/s11145-018-9900-3

Rayner, K., Foorman, B., Perfetti, C. A., Pesetsky, D., & Seidenberg, M. S. (2001). How psychological science informs the teaching of reading. *Psychological Science in the Public Interest, 2*(2), 31–74.

Reed, D. K. (2008). A synthesis of morphology interventions and effects on reading outcomes for students in grades K–12. *Learning Disabilities Research & Practice, 23*(1), 36–49. https://doi.org/10.1111/j.1540-5826.2007.00261.x

Reed, D. K., Wexler, J., & Vaughn, S. (2012). *RTI for reading at the secondary level: Recommended literacy practices and remaining questions*. Guilford.

Reid, R., Ortiz Lienemann, T., & Hagaman, J. L. (2013). *Strategy instruction for students with learning disabilities* (2nd ed.). Guilford.

Reschly, A. L., Busch, T. W., Betts, J., Deno, S. L., & Long, J. D. (2009). Curriculum-based measurement oral reading as an indicator of reading achievement: A meta-analysis of the correlational evidence. *Journal of School Psychology, 47*(6), 427–69.

Reynolds, A. J., & Ou, S. (2004). Alterable predictors of child well-being in the Chicago longitudinal study. *Children and Youth Services Review, 26*(1), 1–14.

Riccomini, P. J., Morano, S., & Hughes, C. A. (2017). Big ideas in special education: Specially designed instruction, high-leverage practices, explicit instruction, and intensive instruction. *TEACHING Exceptional Children, 50*(1), 20–27.

Rila, A., Estrapala, S., & Bruhn, A. L. (2019). Using technology to increase opportunities to respond. *Beyond Behavior, 28*(1), 36–45. https://doi.org/10.1177/1074295619835207

Riley-Tillman, T. C., Chafouleas, S. M., & Briesch, A. M. (2007). A school practitioner's guide to using daily behavior report cards to monitor student behavior. *Psychology in the Schools, 44*(1), 77–89. https://doi.org/10.1002/pits.20207

Rissman, L. M., Miller, D. H., & Torgesen, J. K. (2009). *Adolescent Literacy Walk-Through for Principals: A Guide for Instructional Leaders*. RMC Research Corporation, Center on Instruction.

Rizzo, K. L., & Taylor, J. C. (2016). Effects of inquiry-based instruction on science achievement for students with disabilities: An analysis of the literature. *Journal of Science Education for Students with Disabilities, 19*(1), 2. http://doi.org/10.14448/jsesd.09.0001

Roberts, B. (2009). Performative social science: A consideration of skills, purpose and context. *Historical Social Research, 34*(1), 307–53.

Rohrer, D., Dedrick, R. F., & Stershic, S. (2015). Interleaved practice improves mathematics learning. *Journal of Educational Psychology, 107*(3), 900–908.

Romig, J. E., Miller, A. A., Therrien, W. J., & Lloyd, J. W. (2020). Meta-analysis of prompt and duration for curriculum-based measurement of written language. *Exceptionality*. Advance online publication. https://doi.org/10.1080/09362835.2020.1743706

Romig, J. E., & Olsen, A. A. (2021). Technical features of slopes for curriculum-based measures of secondary writing. *Reading and Writing Quarterly, 37*(6), 535–51. https://www.tandfonline.com/doi/abs/10.1080/10573569.2020.1860841

Romig, J. E., Therrien, W. J., & Lloyd, J. W. (2017). Meta-analysis of criterion validity for curriculum-based measurement in written language. *Journal of Special Education, 51*(2), 72–82. https://doi.org/10.1177/0022466916670637

Royer, D. J., Lane, K. L., Dunlap, K. D., & Ennis, R. P. (2019). A systematic review of teacher-delivered behavior-specific praise on K–12 student performance. *Remedial and Special Education, 40*(2), 112–128. https://doi.org/10.1177/0741932517751054

Ryan, J. B., Sanders, S., Katsiyannis, A., & Yell, M. L. (2007). Using time-out effectively in the classroom. *TEACHING Exceptional Children, 39*(4), 60–67. https://doi.org/10.1177/004005990703900407

Saddler, B. (2019). Sentence Construction. In S. Graham, C. A. MacArthur, & M. Hebert (Eds.), *Best practices in writing instruction* (3rd ed., pp. 240–60). Guilford.

Saddler, B., Asaro-Saddler, K., Moeyaert, M., & Cuccio-Slichko, J. (2019). Teaching summary writing to students with learning disabilities via strategy instruction. *Reading & Writing Quarterly, 35*(6), 572–86. https://doi.org/10.1080/10573569.2019.1600085

Salahu-Din, D., Persky, H., & Miller, J. (2008). The nation's report card[TM]: Writing 2007. National assessment of educational progress at grades 8 and 12: National, state, and trial urban district results. NCES 2008-468. Distributed by ERIC Clearinghouse.

Santi, K. L., & Reed, D. K. (2015). *Improving reading comprehension of middle and high school students*. Springer International.

Sawyer, A. G., Dick, L. K., & Sutherland, P. (2020). Online mathematics teacherpreneurs developers on Teachers Pay Teachers: Who are they and why are they popular? *Education Sciences, 10*(9), 248. https://doi.org/10.3390/educsci10090248

Scammacca, N. K., Roberts, G., Cho, E., Williams, K. J., Roberts, G., Vaughn, S. R., & Carroll, M. (2016). A century of progress: Reading interventions for students in grades 4–12, 1914–2014. *Review of Educational Research, 86*(3), 756–800. https://doi.org/10.3102/0034654316652942

Scammacca, N. K., Roberts, G., Vaughn, S., Edmonds, M., Wexler, J., Reutebuch, C. K., & Torgesen, J. K. (2007). *Interventions for adolescent struggling readers: A meta-analysis with implications for practice*. RMC Research Corporation, Center on Instruction.

Scammacca, N. K., Roberts, G., Vaughn, S., & Stuebing, K. K. (2015). A meta-analysis of interventions for struggling readers in grades 4–12, 1980–2011. *Journal of Learning Disabilities, 48*(4), 369–90. https://doi.org/10.1177/0022219413504995

Scanlon, D., Schumaker, J. B., & Deshler, D. D. (1996). Can a strategy be taught and learned in secondary inclusive classrooms? *Learning Disabilities Research and Practice, 11*(1), 41–57.

Scanlon, D., Schumaker, J. B., & Deshler, D. D. (2004). *The ORDER routine*. Edge Enterprises.

Scarborough, H. S. (2001). Connecting early language and literacy to later reading (dis)abilities: Evidence, theory, and practice. In S. B. Neuman & D. K. Dickinson (Eds.), *Handbook of early literacy research*. Guilford.

Scheuermann, B., Billingsley, G., & Hall, J. (2022). *Positive behavioral supports for the classroom* (4th ed.). Pearson.

Schreiber, P. A. (1980). On the acquisition of reading fluency. *Journal of Reading Behavior, 12*(3), 177–86.

Schumacher, J., Bulgren, J., Deshler, D. & Lenz, B. K. (1998). *The recall enhancement routine*. University of Kansas.

Schumaker, J. B., & Deshler, D. D. (1988). Implementing the regular education initiative in secondary schools: A different ball game. *Journal of Learning Disabilities, 21*(1), 36–42.

Schumaker, J. B., & Fisher, J. B. (2021). 35 years on the road from research to practice: A review of studies on four content enhancement routines for inclusive subject-area classes, part I. *Learning Disabilities Research & Practice, 36*(3), 258–72. https://doi.org/10.1111/ldrp.12258

Schumaker, J. B., & Fisher, J. B. (2021). 35 years on the road from research to practice: A review of studies on four content enhancement routines for inclusive subject-area classes, part II. *Learning Disabilities Research & Practice, 36*(3), 258–72. https://doi.org/10.1111/ldrp.12259

Schunk, D. (2019). *Learning theories: An educational perspective* (8th ed.). Pearson.

Schwanenflugel, P. J., Hamilton, A. M., Wisenbaker, J. M., Kuhn, M. R., & Stahl, S. A. (2004). Becoming a fluent reader: Reading skill and prosodic features in the oral reading of young readers. *Journal of Educational Psychology, 96*(1), 119–29.

Scruggs, T., Mastropieri, M., Bakken, J., & Brigham, F.J. (1993). Reading versus doing: The relative effects of textbook-based and inquiry-oriented approaches to science learning in special education classrooms. *Journal of Special Education, 27*(1), 1–15. https://doi.org/10.1177/002246699302700101

Scruggs, T. E., & Mastropieri, M. A. (2000). The effectiveness of mnemonic instruction for students with learning and behavior problems: An update and research synthesis. *Journal of Behavioral Education, 10*(2), 163–73. https://psycnet.apa.org/record/2001-11204-006

Scruggs, T. E., Mastropieri, M. A., Berkeley, S., & Graetz, J. E. (2010). Do special education interventions improve learning of secondary content? A meta-analysis. *Remedial and Special Education, 31*(6), 437–49.

Scruggs, T. E., Mastropieri, M. A., & Boon, R. (1998). Science education for students with disabilities: A review of recent research. *Studies in Science Education, 32*(1), 21. https://doi.org/10.1080/03057269808560126

Scruggs, T. E., Mastropieri, M. A., Levin, J. R., & Gaffney, J. S. (1985). Facilitating the acquisition of science facts in learning disabled students. *American Educational Research Journal, 22*(4), 575–586. https://doi.org/10.3102/00028312022004575

Scruggs, T. E., Mastropieri, M. A., & Marshak, L. I. S. A. (2011). Science and social studies. In J. M. Kauffman & D. P. Hallahan, D. P. (Eds.), *Handbook of special education* (pp. 445–55). Routledge.

Scruggs, T. E., Mastropieri, M. A., & Okolo, C. M. (2008). Science and social studies for students with disabilities. *Focus on Exceptional Children, 41*(2), 1–24. https://doi.org/10.17161/foec.v41i2.6835

Scruggs, T. E., Mastropieri, M. A., & Sullivan, G. S. (1994). Promoting relational thinking: Elaborative interrogation for students with mild disabilities. *Exceptional Children, 60*, 45–57. https://www.researchgate.net/scientific-contributions/Thomas-E-Scruggs-35534331/publications/2

Seigel, J. (2018). Did you take "good" notes? On methods for evaluating student notetaking performance. *Journal of English for Academic Purposes, 35*, 85–92.

Shanahan, C., Shanahan, T., & Misischia, C. (2011). Analysis of expert readers in three disciplines: History, mathematics, and chemistry. *Journal of Literacy Research, 43*(4), 393–429. http://doi.org/10.1177/1086296X11424071

Shanahan, T., Callison, K., Carriere, C., Duke, N. K., Pearson, P. D., Schatschneider, C., & Torgesen, J. (2010). *Improving reading comprehension in kindergarten through 3rd grade: IES practice guide* (NCEE 2010-4038). What Works Clearinghouse, National Center for Education Evaluation and Regional Assistance (NCEE), Institute of Education Sciences, US Department of Education.

Shanahan, T., & Shanahan, C. (2012). What is disciplinary literacy and why does it matter? *Topics in Language Disorders, 32*(1), 7–18.

Shin, J., & McMaster, K. (2019). Relations between CBM (oral reading and maze) and reading comprehension on state achievement tests: A meta-analysis. *Journal of School Psychology, 73*, 131–49.

Sierens, E., Vansteenkiste, M., Goossens, L., Soenens, B., & Dochy, F. (2009). The synergistic relationship of perceived autonomy support and structure in the prediction of self-regulated learning. *British Journal of Educational Psychology, 79*(1), 57–68.

Silva, M., & Cain, K. (2015). The relations between lower and higher level comprehension skills and their role in prediction of early reading comprehension. *Journal of Educational Psychology, 107*(2), 321–31.

Simonsen, B., & Myers, D. (2014). *Classwide positive behavior interventions and supports: A guide to proactive classroom management.* Guilford.

Simonsen, B., Fairbanks, S., Briesch, A., Myers, D., & Sugai, G. (2008). Evidence-based practices in classroom management: Considerations for research to practice. *Education and Treatment of Children, 31*(3), 351–80. http://doi.org/10.1353/etc.0.0007

Simonsen, B., Myers, D., & DeLuca, C. (2010). Teaching teachers to use prompts, opportunities to respond, and specific praise. *Teacher Education and Special Education, 33*(4), 300–318. http://doi.org/10.1177/0888406409359905

Skinner, B. F. (1953). Some contributions of an experimental analysis of behavior to psychology as a whole. *American Psychologist, 8*(2), 69–78.

Skinner, E. A., & Belmont, M. J. (1993). Motivation in the classroom: Reciprocal effects of teacher behavior and student engagement across the school year. *Journal of Educational Psychology, 85*(4), 571–81.

Smith, K. (2006). In defense of the five-paragraph essay. *English Journal, 95*(4), 16–17.

Smith, S., Barajas, K., Ellis, B., Moore, C., McCauley, S., & Reichow, B. (2021). A meta-analytic review of randomized controlled trials of the Good Behavior Game. *Behavior Modification, 45*(4), 641–666. https://doi.org/10.1177/0145445519878670

Solis, M., Miciak, J., Vaughn, S., & Fletcher, J. (2014). Why intensive interventions matter: Longitudinal studies of adolescents with reading disabilities and poor reading comprehension. *Learning Disability Quarterly, 37*(4), 218–29. https://doi.org/10.1177/0731948714528806

Spencer, V. G., Simpson, C. G., & Oatis, T. L. (2009). An update on the use of peer tutoring and students with emotional and behavioural disorders. *Exceptionality Education International, 19*(1). https://doi.org/10.5206/eei.v19i1.7634

Spires, H. A., Kerkhoff, S. N., & Graham A. (2016). Disciplinary literacy and inquiry: Teaching for deeper content learning. *Journal of Adolescent and Adult Literacy, 60*(2), 151–61. https://doi.org/10.1002/jaal.577

Stanovich, K. E., & West, R. F. (1989). Exposure to print and orthographic processing. *Reading Research Quarterly, 24*(4), 402–33.

Star, J. R. (2005). Reconceptualizing procedural knowledge. *Journal for Research in Mathematics Education, 36*(4), 404–11.

Star, J. R., Caronongan, P., Foegen, A., Furgeson, J., Keating, B., Larson, M. R., Lyskawa, J., McCallum, W. G., Porath, J., & Zbiek, R. M. (2019 [2015]). Teaching strategies for improving algebra knowledge in middle and high school students (NCEE 2014-4333). National Center for Education Evaluation and Regional Assistance (NCEE), Institute of Education Sciences, US Department of Education. http://whatworks.ed.gov

Stenson, R. (2016, March 14). Is this the first time anyone printed, "garbage in, garbage out"? Atlas Obscura. https://www.atlasobscura.com/articles/is-this-the-first-time-anyone-printed-garbage-in-garbage-out

Stevens, E. A., Vaughn, S., Swanson, E., & Scammacca, N. (2020). Examining the effects of a tier 2 reading comprehension intervention aligned to tier 1 instruction for fourth-grade struggling readers. *Exceptional Children, 86*(4), 430–48.

Stichter, J. P., Stormont, M., Lewis, T. J., & Schultz, T. (2009). Rates of specific antecedent instructional practices and differences between Title I and non-Title I schools. *Journal of Behavioral Education, 18*(4), 331–44.

Stockard, J., Wood, T. W., Coughlin, C., & Khoury, C. R. (2018). The effectiveness of direct instruction curricula: A meta-analysis of a half century of research. *Review of Educational Research, 88*(4), 479–507.

StoryCorps. (2003–2023). https://storycorps.org

Straub, C. L., & Vasquez, E. (2015). Effects of synchronous online writing instruction for students with learning disabilities. *Journal of Special Education Technology, 30*(4), 213–22. https://doi.org/10.1177/0162643415618929

Strickland, T. K. (2017). Using the CRA-I strategy to develop conceptual and procedural knowledge of quadratic expressions. *TEACHING Exceptional Children, 49*(2), 115–25.

Strickland, T. K. (2021). Algebra instruction for students with disabilities in the era of common core. *Intervention in School and Clinic, 57*(5), 306–15. https://doi.org/10.1177%2F10534512211032613

Strickland, T. K., & Maccini, P. (2012). The effects of the concrete-representational-abstract-integration strategy on the ability of students with learning disabilities to multiply linear expressions within area problems. *Remedial and Special Education, 34*(3), 142–53.

Strickland, T. K., & Maccini, P. (2013). Exploration of quadratic expressions through multiple representations for students with mathematics difficulties. *Learning Disabilities: A Multidisciplinary Journal, 19*(2), 61–71.

Sugai, G., & Horner, R. H. (2002). Introduction to the special series on positive behavior support in schools. *Journal of Emotional and Behavioral Disorders, 10*(3), 130–5. https://journals.sagepub.com/doi/10.1177/10634266020100030101 Sugai, G., Lewis-Palmer, T., & Hagan-Burke, S. (2000). Overview of the functional behavioral assessment process. *Exceptionality, 8*(3), 149–60. https://doi.org/10.1207/S15327035EX0803_2

Sundeen, T. H. (2012). Explicit prewriting instruction: Effect on writing quality of adolescents with learning disabilities. *Learning Disabilities: A Multidisciplinary Journal, 18*(1), 23–33.

Sundeen, T. H. (2015). Writing instruction for adolescents in the shadow of the common core state standards. *Journal of Adolescent and Adult Literacy, 59*(2), 197–206. https://doi.org/10.1002/jaal.444

Swanson, E., Stevens, E. A., Scammacca, N. K., Capin, P., Stewart, A. A., & Austin, C. R. (2017). The impact of tier 1 reading instruction on reading outcomes for students in grades 4–12: A meta-analysis. *Reading and Writing, 30*(8), 1639–65.

Swanson, E., & Wexler, J. (2017). Selecting appropriate text for adolescents with disabilities. *TEACHING Exceptional Children, 49*(3), 160–67.

Taylor, J. C., & Hwang, J. (2021). Science, technology, engineering, arts, and mathematics remote instruction for students with disabilities. *Intervention in School and Clinic, 57*(2), 111–18. http://doi.org/10.1177/10534512211001858

Taylor, J. C., Hwang, J., Rizzo, K. L., & Hill, D. A. (2020). Supporting science-related instruction for students with intellectual and developmental disabilities: A review and analysis of research studies. *Science Educator, 27*(2), 102–13. https://eric.ed.gov/?id=EJ1259835

Taylor, J. C., Therrien, W. J., Kaldenberg, E., Watt, S., Chanlen, N., & Hand, B. (2012). Using an inquiry-based teaching approach to improve science outcomes for students with disabilities: Snapshot and longitudinal data. *Journal of Science Education for Students with Disabilities, 15*(1), 27–39. http://doi.org/10.14448/jsesd.04.0003

Taylor, J. C., Tseng, C-M., Murillo, A., Therrien, W., & Hand, B. (2018). Using argument-based science inquiry to improve science achievement for students with disabilities in inclusive classrooms. *Journal of Science Education for Students with Disabilities, 21*(1), 1–14. http://doi.org/10.14448/jsesd.10.0001

Therrien, W. J. (2004). Fluency and comprehension gains as a result of repeated reading: A meta-analysis. *Remedial and Special Education, 25*(4), 252–61.

Therrien, W. J., Taylor, J. C., Hosp, J. L., Kaldenberg, E. R., & Gorsh, J. (2011). Science instruction for students with learning disabilities: A meta-analysis. *Learning Disabilities Research & Practice, 26*(4), 188–203. https://doi.org/10.1111/j.1540-5826.2011.00340.x

Therrien, W. J., Taylor, J. C., Watt, S., & Kaldenberg, E. R. (2014). Science instruction for students with emotional and behavioral disorders. *Remedial and Special Education, 35*(1), 15–27. https://doi.org/10.1177/0741932513503557

Torgesen, J. K. (2004). Lessons learned from research on interventions for students who have difficulty learning to read. In P. McCardle& V. Chhabra (Eds.), *The voice of evidence in reading research* (pp. 355–82). Paul H. Brookes.

Torgesen, J. K., Houston, D. D., Rissman, L. M., Decker, S. M., Roberts, G., Vaughn, S., Wexler, J., Francis, D. J., Rivera, M. O., & Lesaux, N. (2007). *Academic literacy instruction for adolescents: A guidance document from the Center on Instruction.* RMC Research Corporation, Center on Instruction. https://media.carnegie.org/filer_public/a7/9b/a79bee13-b82e-47bd-ab63-9190baa31975/ccny_report_2007_guidance.pdf

Toste, J. R., Capin, P., Williams, K. J., Cho, E., & Vaughn, S. (2019). Replication of an experimental study investigating the efficacy of a multisyllabic word reading intervention with and without motivational beliefs training for struggling readers. *Journal of Learning Disabilities, 52*(1), 45–58.

Toste, J. R., Williams, K. J., & Capin, P. (2017). Reading big words: Instructional practices to promote multisyllabic word reading fluency. *Intervention in School and Clinic, 52*(5), 270–78.

Troia, G. A., & Olinghouse, N. G. (2013). The common core state standards and evidence-based educational practices: The case of writing. *School Psychology Review, 42*(3), 343–57.

Tucker, C. M., Zayco, R. A., Herman, K. C., Reinke, W. M., Trujillo, M., Carraway, K., Wallack, C., & Ivery, P. D. (2002). Teacher and child variables as predictors of academic engagement among low-income African American children. *Psychology in the Schools, 39*(4), 477–88.

United States Congress, 107th, 1st session. (2001). No Child Left Behind Act of 2001: Conference Report to Accompany H.R.1, Report 107–334. US Government Printing Office.

US Department of Education. (n.d.) Every Student Succeeds Act. https://www.ed.gov/essa?src=rn

US Department of Education. (2022, July). *Students with disabilities.* Institute of Education Sciences, National Center for Education Statistics. https://nces.ed.gov/programs/coe/indicator/cgg

US Department of Education, Office for Civil Rights. (2018). *2015–2016 civil rights data collection STEM course taking.* https://www2.ed.gov/about/offices/list/ocr/docs/stem-course-taking.pdf

US Department of Education, Office of Special Education and Rehabilitative Services (2016). *Dear colleague letter on positive behavior interventions in IEPs.* https://sites.ed.gov/idea/files/dcl-on-pbis-in-ieps-08-01-2016.pdf

US Department of Education, Office of Special Education and Rehabilitative Services (2021). *Supporting child and student social, emotional, behavioral, and mental health needs.* https://www2.ed.gov/documents/students/supporting-child-student-social-emotional-behavioral-mental-health.pdf

US Department of Education, Office of Special Education Programs (2016). *Supporting and responding to behavior: Evidence-based classroom strategies for teachers.* https://osepideasthatwork.org/sites/default/files/ClassroomPBIS_508.pdf

Valdés, G. (2001). *Learning and not learning English: Latino students in American schools*. Teachers College Press.

Van Luit, J. E. H., & Toll, S. W. M. (2018). Associative cognitive factors of math problems in students diagnosed with developmental dyscalculia. *Frontiers in Psychology, 9*, 1907. https://doi.org/10.3389/fpsyg.2018.01907

Vannest, K. J., Davis, J. L., Davis, C. R., Mason, B. A., & Burke, M. D. (2010). Effective intervention for behavior with a daily behavior report card: A meta-analysis. *School Psychology Review, 39*(4), 654–72. https://doi.org/10.1080/02796015.2010.12087748

Vaughn, S., & Fletcher, J. M. (2012). Response to intervention with secondary school students with reading difficulties. *Journal of Learning Disabilities, 45*(3), 244–56. https://doi.org/10.1177/0022219412442157

Vaughn, S., & Fletcher, J. M. (2021). Explicit instruction as the essential tool for executing the science of reading. *Reading League Journal, 2*(2), 13–20.

Vaughn, S., Gersten, R., Dimino, J., Taylor, M. J., Newman-Gonchar, R., Krowka, S., Kieffer, M. J., McKeown, M., Reed, D., Sanchez, M., St. Martin, K., Wexler, J., Morgan, S., Yañez, A., & Jayanthi, M. (2022). *Providing reading interventions for students in grades 4–9* (WWC 2022007). National Center for Education Evaluation and Regional Assistance (NCEE), Institute of Education Sciences, US Department of Education. https://ies.ed.gov/ncee/wwc/Docs/PracticeGuide/WWC-practice-guide-reading-intervention-full-text.pdf

Vaughn, S., Kieffer, M. J., McKeown, M., Reed, D. K., Sanchez, M., St. Martin, K., Wexler, J., Jayanthi, M., Gersten, R., Dimino, J., Taylor, M. J., Newman-Gonchar, R., Krowka, S., Haymond, K., Wavell, S., Lyskawa, J., Morgan, S., Keating, B., & Yañez, A. (2022). Providing reading interventions for students in grades 4–9: Educator's practice guide (WWC 2022007). What Works Clearinghouse.

Vaughn, S., Linan-Thompson, S., Kouzekanani, K., Bryant, D. P., Dickson, S., & Blozis, S. A. (2003). Reading instruction grouping for students with reading difficulties. *Remedial and Special Education, 24*(5), 301–15.

Vaughn, S., Roberts, G., Wexler, J., Vaughn, M. G., Fall, A. M., & Schnakenberg, J. B. (2015). High school students with reading comprehension difficulties: Results of a randomized control trial of a two-year reading intervention. *Journal of Learning Disabilities, 48*(5), 546–58. http://dx.doi.org/10.1177/0022219413515511

Vernon, S., Deshler, D., & Schumaker, J. (1993). *The teamwork strategy*. Edge Enterprises.

Vernon, S., Deshler, D., & Schumaker, J. (1999). *The THINK strategy*. Edge Enterprises.

Vernon, S., Deshler, D., & Schumaker, J. (2000). *Talking together*. Edge Enterprises.

Vernon, S., Deshler, D., & Schumaker, J. (2002). *Organizing together*. Edge Enterprises.

Vernon, S., Schumaker, J., & Deshler, D. (1996). *The SCORE skills*. Edge Enterprises.

Vernon, S., Schumaker, J., & Deshler, D. (1999a). *The BUILD strategy*. Edge Enterprises.

Vernon, S., Schumaker, J., & Deshler, D. (1999b). *The LEARN strategy*. Edge Enterprises.

Vernon, S., Schumaker, J., & Deshler, D. (2001). *Following instructions together*. Edge Enterprises.

Vernon, S., Schumaker, J., & Deshler, D. (2002). *Taking notes together*. Edge Enterprises.

Verschaffel, L., Schukajlow, S., Star, J., & Van Dooren, W. (2020). Word problems in mathematics education: A survey. *ZDM, 52*(1), 1–16. https://doi.org/10.1007/s11858-020-01130-4

Von Glasersfeld, E. (2013). *Radical constructivism*. Routledge.

Vygotsky, L. (1978). Interaction between learning and development. *Readings on the Development of Children, 23*(3), 34–41.

Vygotsky, L. S. (1978). *Mind in society: The development of higher psychological processes*. Harvard University Press.

Wagner, M., Marder, C., Blackorby, J., Cameto, R., Newman, L., Levine, P., Davies-Mercer, E., Chorost, M., Garza, N., Guzman, A. M., & Sumi, C. (2003). *The achievements of youth with disabilities during secondary school: A report from the National Longitudinal Transition Study-2 (NLTS2)*. SRI International. https://nlts2.sri.com/reports/2003_11/nlts2_report_2003_11_complete.pdf

Wallace, T. L. B., Sung, H. C., & Williams, J. D. (2014). The defining features of teacher talk within autonomy-supportive classroom management. *Teaching and Teacher Education, 42*, 34–46. https://doi.org/10.1016/j.tate.2014.04.005

Wanzek, J., Wexler, J., Vaughn, S., & Ciullo, S. (2010). Reading interventions for struggling readers in the upper elementary grades: A synthesis of 20 years of research. *Reading and Writing, 23*(8), 889–912.

Wayman, M., Wayman, T., Wallace, H., Wiley, I., Tichá, R., & Espin, C. (2007). Literature synthesis on curriculum-based measurement in reading. *Journal of Special Education, 41*(2), 85–120.

Westing, D. L. (2015). *Evidence-based practices for improving challenging behaviors of students with severe disabilities* (Document No. IC-14). CEEDAR Center. https://ceedar.education.ufl.edu/wp-content/uploads/2015/11/EBPs-for-improving-challenging-behavior-of-SWD.pdf Wills, H. P., Iwaszuk, W. M., Kamps, D., & Shumate, E. (2014). CW-FIT: Group contingency effects across the day. *Education and Treatment of Children, 37*(2), 191–210. https://doi.org/10.1353/etc.2014.0016

Weston, R., Hodges, A., & Davis, T. N. (2018). Differential reinforcement of other behaviors to treat challenging behaviors among children with autism: A systematic and quality review. *Behavior Modification, 42*(4), 584–609. https://doi.org/10.1177/0145445517743487

Wexler, J., Kearns, D. M., Lemons, C. J., Mitchell, M., Clancy, E., Davidson, K. A., Sinclair, A. C., & Wei, Y. (2018). Reading comprehension and co-teaching practices in middle school English language arts classrooms. *Exceptional Children, 84*(4), 384–402. https://doi.org/10.1177/0014402918771543

White, T. G., Power, M. A., & White, S. (1989). Morphological analysis: Implications for teaching and understanding vocabulary growth. *Reading Research Quarterly, 24*(3), 283–304.

Wilcox, B. R., Caballero, M. D., Rehn, D. A., & Pollock, S. J. (2013). Analytic framework for students' use of mathematics in upper-division physics. *Physical Review Special Topics–Physics Education Research, 9*(2), 020119. https://link.aps.org/doi/10.1103/PhysRevSTPER.9.020119

Wiley, M. (2000). The popularity of formulaic writing (and why we need to resist). *English Journal, 90*(1), 61–67.

Williamson, P., Carnahan, C., Birri, N., & Swoboda, C. (2015). Improving comprehension of narrative using character event maps for high school students with autism spectrum disorder. *Journal of Special Education, 49*(1), 28–38. https://journals.sagepub.com/doi/10.1177/0022466914521301

Wills, H., Wehby, J., Caldarella, P., Kamps, D., & Swinburne Romine, R. (2018). Classroom management that works: A replication trial of the CW-FIT program. *Exceptional Children, 84*(4), 437–56. https://doi.org/10.1177/0014402918771321

Wilson, B., & Moffat, N. (Eds.). (2014). *Clinical management of memory problems* (2nd ed.). Psychology Press. https://doi.org/10.4324/9781315774800

Wilson, M. G. (2008). *Math course taking and achievement among secondary students with disabilities: Exploring the gap in achievement between students with and without disabilities* [Unpublished doctoral dissertation]. University of Maryland, College Park.

Winn, R. (2021, April). *2021 Podcast stats and facts: New research from April 2021*. Podcast Insights. https://www.podcastinsights.com/podcast-statistics

Witzel, B., Mercer, C. D., & Miller, M. D. (2003). Teaching algebra to students with learning difficulties: An investigation of an explicit instruction model. *Learning Disabilities Research & Practice, 18*(2), 121–31.

Witzel, B., Riccomini, P., & Schneider, E. (2008). Implementing CRA with secondary students with learning disabilities in mathematics. *Intervention in School and Clinic, 43*(5), 270–76.

Witzel, B. S. (2020). Executive functioning disorder and mathematics: Three strategies to implement. *Children and Adults with Attention-Deficit/Hyperactivity Disorder* (CHADD). https://chadd.org/attention-article/executive-functioning-disorder-and-mathematics/

Witzel, B. S., & Little, M. E. (2016). *Teaching elementary mathematics to struggling learners*. Guilford.

Wixson, K. K. (2017). An interactive view of reading comprehension: Implications for assessment. *Language, Speech, and Hearing Services in Schools, 48*(2), 77–83.

Wolfe, K., Pyle, D., Charlton, C. T., Sabey, C. V., Lund, E. M., & Ross, S. W. (2016). A systematic review of the empirical support for check-in check-out. *Journal of Positive Behavior Interventions, 18*(2), 74–88. https://doi.org/10.1177/1098300715595957

Wolk, S. (2003). Teaching for critical literacy in social studies. *Social Studies, 94*(3), 101–6.

Wolter, D. R. (1975). *Effect of feedback on performance on a creative writing task* [Unpublished doctoral dissertation]. University of Michigan, Ann Arbor.

Yeo, S. (2010). Predicting performance on state achievement tests using curriculum-based measurement in reading: A multilevel meta-analysis. *Remedial and Special Education, 31*(6), 412–22.

Youth Radio Media. (2021, November 23). YR Media. https://yr.media

Zeidler, D. L., & Kahn, S. (2014). *It's debatable! Using socioscientific issues to develop scientific literacy, K–12*. NSTA Press.

Zeidler, D. L., & Newton, M. H. (2017). Using a socioscientific issues framework for climate change education: An ecojustice approach. In D. Shepardson & R. Roychoudhury (Eds.), *Teaching and learning about climate change* (pp. 56–65). Routledge.

Index

Note: Numbers in italics refer to information in figures, tables, and textboxes.

academic standards, 7–8, 13
acrostic letter strategies, 158–59, 161
ACT argumentative essay, 118–21
active engagement, 5, 67, 82, 147, 172, 178–79, *184*
Adams, Gary L., 224
affix learning, 17, 32–33, 35, *36*
Aleixandre, María Pilar, 151
algebra, 64, *234*; Algebra 2, 44, 46–47, 63; algebraic computation, 51, 63, 76, 77–78, 82; algebra of polynomials, 47, 48; arithmetic to algebra gap, 45, 50; CWPT and improvement in algebra performance, 81–82; Project AAIMS, monitoring student progress via, 82–83; structured worksheets and, 79. *See also* mathematics instruction
Algebra Assessment and Instruction: Meeting Standards (AAIMS), 82
Alter, Peter, 176
American College Testing (ACT) exam, 108
American Institutes for Research (AIR), 13, *223*
Anchor (app), 97, 103
Archer, Anita L., 17, *233*
area models, 58–59
argumentative writing: case study example using SRSD, 118–22; CCSS and increase in teaching of, 90, 91; genre-specific writing strategy for, 114; TREE strategy, use of, 115, 116, *117*
Aristotle, 169
at-risk students, 1, 24, 25, 27, 82, 109, 189
Attention-Deficit Hyperactivity Disorder (ADHD), 64
attention-seeking behavior, 198, 199, 202
Audacity (app), 103, 104
automaticity, 33, 115

Bandura, Albert, 170
Bazerman, Charles, 88
Beck, Isabel, 16
behavioral intervention: behavioral interventions, 199, 207, *236*; behavior contracting, 5, 180, 189, 199–200; daily behavior report cards, 200–202; explicit social skills instruction, 191–94; FBA-based intervention, 202–3; foundational learning theory for, 204–5; group contingencies, 197–98; High-P sequence, 195–96; intensive interventions, adding, 198–99; relevant educational policy, 203–4; self-monitoring intervention, 196–97
behavioral intervention plan (BIP), 202–3, 204
behavior contracting, 5, 180, 189, 199–200
behavior-specific praise (BSP), 179, 180, 181, 182, 183
Bell, Randy L., 131
Bellezza, Francis S., 158
benchmark assessments and benchmarking, 12–13, 27
Berry, Gwen, 219, 220
blending practice, 30
blocked practice, 55, 56
Bowman-Perrot, Lisa, 160, 199
box method, 58
Bulgren, Janis A., 156, 224
burnout, 5, 168

C3 Framework (C3 Inquiry Arc), 136–37, 138, 151–52, 154–55
calculus, 63
Canvas (learning management service), 97, 104
Cariveau, Tom, 182–83

Carnahan, Christina R., 159
CARS rubric (credibility, accuracy, reasonableness, support), 141
cause-and-effect routine, 155
CBM-Writing (CBM-W), 109, 111
Center on English Learning and Achievement (CELA), 93
Centers for Disease Control and Prevention (CDC), 138
Chard, David J., 75
check-in/check-out, 5, 195
Chow, Jason C., 198
CICO intervention (Behavior Education Program), 5, 195, 196, 197, 200
Ciullo, Stephen, 148–49, 160
classroom management, 168; appropriate behaviors, acknowledging, 179–81; classroom structure, maximizing, 173–75; evidence-based management, theoretical foundations of, 169–71; inappropriate behaviors, responding to, 181–83; observable ways to actively engage students, 178–79; professional standards of educational practice, 172, 206–7; relevant educational policy associated with, 171–72; rules and expectations, positively stating, 175–78; Tier 2 evidence-based interventions, 194–98; universal classroom management practices, 189–90
Classroom Management Skills (CMS), 168
classwide function-related intervention (CW-FIT), 180, 198
Classwide Peer Tutoring (CWPT), 81–82, 158, 160, 161
climate change, 34–35, 37, 131
"clues and undos" approach, 59
coefficients, 45, 47, 48, 67, 78–79
cognitive supports, 2–3, 57, 61, 148, 170
Collaboration for Effective Educator Development, Accountability, and Reform Center (CEEDAR), 148, 172, 203
college- and career-ready writing, 93
combinatorics, 46, 47
Common, Eric Alan, 179
Common Core State Standards (CCSS), 7–8, 23, 54, 67, 82, 90, 91, 108, 132, 152
comprehension-building practices, 26. 37
Concept Comparison Routine, 153
Concrete-Representation-Abstract Integration, 3, 82

Concrete to Representational to Abstract (CRA) instruction, 74, 76, 78
Conference on College Composition and Communication (CCCC), 93
confirmation inquiries, 131
connected text reading, 30, 32, 33
Connor, Carol M., 25
constructivism, 113, 133, 170, 171, 204–5
content acquisition interventions, 4, 149, 158–61
content-area knowledge, 35, 39, 218
Content-Enhancement Routines (CERs), 4, 152–53
context clues, 37
Cook, Bryan G., 148
cookbook labs, 131
correct minus incorrect word sequences (CIWS), 110
correct word sequences (CWS), 110
co-teaching, 10, 12, 222
Council for Exceptional Children (CEC), 148, 172, 195, 206, 207
Council of Chief State School Officers (CCSSO), 8
Council of Writing Program Administrators (CWPA), 93
COVID-19 pandemic, 94, 96
CRA-I strategy, 75–76
CRAMATH strategy, 76–77
criterion validity, 82, 111
cross-curricular argumentation, 157–58
crosscutting concepts, 132
Crujeiras, Beatriz, 151
cue cards, 71, 73–74, 77, 81
Cuenca, Alexander, 151
Curlee, Amber, 2, 3
curriculum-based assessments, 66, 67, 72, 81
curriculum-based measurement (CBM), 27–28, 82, 109–11

daily behavior report cards (DBRC), 5, 197, 200–201, 202
data-based instruction (DBI), 26–27, 28, 65, 233
Deci, Edward L., 174
decision-making, 28, 110, 131, 207; assessments for guidance in, 13, 26–27; Decision-Making Routine, 156–57; in MTSS framework, 13; in PBIS system, 206; in SSI framework, 133
decoding, 3, 30, 32, 37, 88; in Frayer model, 16, 17; IES Educator's Practice Guide,

skill-building via, 25–26; repetitive word reading practice for, 31; in SVR system, 8, 24
DeJager, Brittaleigh, 183
Deshler, Donald D., 219, 220, 221
Dewey, John, 133. 169
Dexter, Douglas D., 160
diagnostic assessment, 12, 13, *14*, 26, 27, 28–29, 30
differential reinforcement (DR), 181–82, 183
differentiated instruction (DI), 14–15, 18
direct behavior rating (DBR), 220
Direct Instruction (DI), 25, 174
DRA (reinforcement of alternative behavior), 181, 182, 183
DRO (reinforcement of other behaviors), 181, 182, 183
Durlak, Joseph A., 193

Education for All Handicapped Children Act, 203–4
Education Sciences Reform Act, 25
effective instruction, 52, 152; components and principles of, 1, 15; EI as an instructional practice, 66; strategies for math instruction, 74, 81
Elementary and Secondary Education Act of 1965, 171
emotional behavioral disorders (EBD), 159, 160, 274
English language arts (ELA), 6, 10, 11, 18, 87, 90; academic standards guiding, 7–8; high-quality ELA instruction, 15; reading assessment and instruction, 12–13; vocabulary instruction as a key component, 16
Every Student Succeeds Act (ESSA), 7, 8, 171, 204
evidence-based interventions, 2, 123, 194, 198–99, 207, *233–35*
evidence-based practices (EBP), 148–49, 151, 196, 203, 205, 206
expected rate of improvement method, 27
explicit instruction (EI), 2, 3, 5, 16, 77, 147, 152, 222; effectiveness of, 15, 66; explicit social skills instruction, 191–94; in IEP example scenario, 82; in Question Exploration Routine, 155; reading outcomes, positive effect on, 11; sample explicit instruction lesson, 67–72; in sentence construction, 123; in teaching good study strategies, 214, 216–18, 224
expository text, *12*, 17–18, 64, 90, 91, *117*, 159, 216

Fabiano, Gregory A., 201
factoring, 2, 45, 47, *49*, 58, 67, 72, 76
FBA/BIP intervention, 202–3
five-paragraph essay instruction, 87
flash cards, 30, 71, 81, 115, *119*, 159, 216, 224
fluency building activities, 11, *12*, 26, 32, 33, 34–35. 39
formative assessments, 12, 26, 60, 109–12, 140, 141–42, *143*, 207
fractions, 45, 52–53, 55, 75
Framework for Success in Postsecondary Writing (NCTE), 93
Frayer model, 16, *17*
free appropriate public education (FAPE), 7, 171, 204
Freeman, Jennifer, 172
functional behavioral assessment (FBA), 202–3, 204, 207

Gage, Nicholas A., 2, 176
GarageBand (app), 103, 104
garbage in, garbage out (GIGO) principle, 213
Gardasil vaccine, 138, 139, *140*, 143–44
Garwood, Justin D., 160–61
Geary, David C., 3
generic rubrics, 112
genre frameworks, 88, 90, 94
genre mastery, 3, 4, 94
genre theory, 88–89
Gersten, Russell, 75
Get the Gist Routine, 38
Gilmour, Allison F., 10, 198
Good Behavior Game (GBG), 180, 190
Google Classroom, 123
grade-level expectations, 7, 44
Graham, Steve, 90, 109
grapheme-phoneme correspondence (GPCs), 30–31
graphic organizers, 16, 18, 115, 141, 155, 158; ACT writing prompts and, *119*; as a cognitive strategy, 29, 148; as a content acquisition intervention, 4, 149, 161; in the ORDER Routine, 224; science-based graphic organizer

research, 160–61; student development of, 114, 144, 220
Greek and Latin root words, 37–38
guided instruction, 116, 131, 150
guided notes, 178, 179

hand-raising, 182
hands-on instruction, 54, 75, *140*, 141, 142, 145, 150
Haydon, Todd, 176, 179
Henry, O., 14–15, *17*
hero procedure, 197
Herrera, Sarah, 11
higher-order skills, 150, 151, 158, 161
Higher-Order Thinking and Reasoning (HOTR), 152–53, 154, 157
high-leverage practices (HLPs), 4, 147, 148, 149, 161, 172, 203
High Leverage Practices for Inclusive Classrooms (McLeskey et al), 214, 218
High-Probability (High-P) Sequence, 195–96
high school, 23, 24, 89, 123, 174, 182, 189; algebra taught in, 45, 51, 76, *234*; CCSS expectations upon graduation, 7, 91; college dorm life, preparation tips for high schoolers, *98–101*; reading assessment and instruction case example, 12–13; reading intervention case scenario, 26–27; students with disabilities in, 63, 118
HIT SONGS writing strategy, 114, *117*, 118, *120*, 122
holistic ratings system, 111
Hosp, Michelle K., 110
Hott, Brittany L., 195
Hudson, Melissa E., 160
Hughes, Charles A., 220
human papilloma virus (HPV), 138, *140*

Individualized Education Plans (IEPs), 7, 67, 82, 83, 149, 204
individual OTR, 178
Individuals with Disabilities Education Act (IDEA), 149, 171, 204
Individuals with Disabilities Education Improvement Act (IDEIA), 7, 8
Inquiry Arc, 136, 142–44, 150, 151, 152
inquiry-based instruction, 66, 130, 136, 145, 147, 150–51, 158
Inside-Out debates, 144
Institute of Education Sciences (IES), 10, 25, *233*, *234*

interleaving (cumulative reviews), 56
International Literacy Association (ILA), 87
interrater reliability, 197
Intervention Central, 57, 109, *236*
intra-individual rate of improvement method, 27
IRIS Center, 159, 214, 218, *233*
ISOLATE mnemonic, 78

Jameson, John Matthew, 160
Jang, Hyungshim, 174
Jimenez, Bree A., 160
job satisfaction, 5, 168

K-12 schools: K-2 and primary grades transition, 8; mathematics instruction in, 81, *234*; reading achievement of K-12 students, 10; science education in, 131, 132; social studies classes in, 127, 150; writing instruction in, 89, 90
Kahn, Sami, 4, 139
kinesthetic descriptions, 133, 141
King-Sears, Margaret E., 159
Kunsch, Catherine A., 81

Lane, Kathleen Lynne, 189
Laraux, Michelle, 224
learning disabilities (LD), 65, 66, 77, 118, 159, 160
Least Restrictive Environment (LRE), 7, 204, 206
lecture-read-write model of instruction, 137
Lee, Ahhyun, 176
Lenz, B. Keith Ben-Hanania, 5, 220, 224
letter-sound review, 30
LINCS Vocabulary Strategy, 222
Listening and Note-Taking Strategy (Berry et al), 219, 220
listening/note-taking system, 219–20
LISTS mnemonic device, 217, *221*, 226
Locke, John, 169
low-frequency content specific words, 16
low-intensity behavior management practices, 189
low-p (non-preferred) tasks, 195, 196

macrostructure of text, 14, 17–18
MacSuga-Gage, Ashley, 5, 178
Maggin, Daniel M., 180
Mastropieri, Margo A., 159, 160
mathematics difficulties (MD), 64, 77

mathematics instruction: assessment to drive differentiation, 60–61; fraction division, task analysis example, 52–53; instructional strategies, 57–60; issues in math learning, where they begin, 44–46; planned outcomes, 47–50; practice and homework, 55–57; practice standards, 53–55; progressions across grade and content, 50–52; setting goals in secondary mathematics, 46–47

mathematics interventions for students with disabilities, 3, 63, 80; classwide peer tutoring, 81–82; CRA strategy, 74–77; guided practice worksheet, 72–73; progress monitoring, 82–83; quadratic functions cue card, 73–74; sample lesson on solving quadratic equations, 67–72; strategy instruction, 77–79; taxonomy of intervention intensity, 65–66

mathematics learning disabilities (MLDs), 3, 64, 65, 66, 74, 79, 83

Mercer, Cecil D., 78

meta-analysis, 25, 160, 176, 201; of active supervision, 175; of behavior contracts, 180, 199; of mnemonics research, 159; of reading achievement, 10, 11

metacognitive strategies, 57, 113, 118

Me–We–Two–You release of information, 2, 52, 53

micro-credentialing, 5, 172

middle school, 23, 24, 123, 189; algebra taught in, 45, 51, *234*; co-teaching ELA classes, 10; SOLO taxonomy, applying, 48

Miller, M. David, 78

mind-mapping programs, 122–23

mnemonics, 148, 149, 213; content acquisition, as a strategy for, 4, 158–59, *161*; first-letter mnemonic technique, 221, 226, 229; ISOLATE mnemonic device, 78–79; as a retrieval strategy, 214, 217; in SRSD instruction, 115, *119*; strategy instruction, using for, 3, 77; as a support strategy, 148, 161

Moffat, Nick, 159

Moore Partin, Tara C., 196

multiple-choice exams, 135, 137

multisyllabic word reading fluency, 31, 39

Multi-Tiered Systems of Support (MTSS), 12, 13, 18, 195, 207

Myers, Jonté, 3

Nagel, Dana Robbins, 221–22
National Assessment of Educational Progress (NAEP), 6, 23, 44, 63, 89
National Association of Student Personnel Administrator (NASPA), *98–99*
National Center for Education Statistics (NCES), 89
National Center on Intensive Intervention (NCII), 12–13, 65, *233*, *236*
National Commission on Writing (NCW), 89
National Council for the Social Studies (NCSS), 139, 150
National Council of Teachers of English (NCTE), 87, 93, *234*
National Council of Teachers of Mathematics (NCTM), 53, 63, 66
National Education Association, 5, 172
National Governors Association Center for Best Practices (NGA CBP), 8
National Mathematics Advisory Panel (NMAP), 45, 46, 63
National Professional Development Center on Autism Spectrum Disorders, 232
National Reading Panel (NRP), 25
National Research Council (NRC), 150, 151
National Science Teaching Association (NSTA), 130, *234*
National Writing Project (NWP), 93
Neglected "R": The Need for a Writing Revolution (report), 89
Newton, Isaac, 123, 169
Next Generation Science Standards (NGSS), 131, 132, 134, 139, *140*, 150, 151, 152, 154
No Child Left Behind Act, 90–91
number lines, 45, 46, 51
number rays, 51

Odom, Samuel L., 148
Office of Special Educations Programs (OSEP), 172, *236*
off-task behavior, 174, 183, 191, 198
one-on-one teacher-student meetings, 182
on task behavior, 15, 174, 175, 178, 180, 183, *192*
open education resources (OERs), 225
open inquiry, 131
operant behavior, 205
oral reading fluency (ORF), 27, 33–34
ORDER Routine, 224
OTR (opportunities to respond) classroom management practice, 178–79, 182

out-of-seat behavior, reducing, 182
Overt Strategy, 17

Paired Associates Strategy, 222
Pavlov, Ivan, 170, 202
peel off reading, 32, 33
Peer-Assisted Learning Strategies (PALS), 160, 161
peer-mediated support strategies, 4, 160–61
peer tutoring, 81–82, 158, 160, 161
pegwords, 158, 159, 161, 222
Petscher, Erin S., 183
phonemic awareness, 30
phonics, *14*, 25, 29, 30, 31
Piaget, Jean, 170
planned ignoring, 181, 182
Plato, 169
podcasts, 3, 37, 93; CCSS standards, addressing in podcasting unit, *91–92*; college experience podcast assignment sheet, *97*; college experience podcast script, *98–100*; digital tools for podcasting, 103–4; extending the podcast, 104–5; finding focus for your podcast, 102–3; podcast scriptwriting template, *63*; sample podcast assessment rubric, *100–101*; teaching the podcast genre, 94–96
Podsafe music, 104
Pólya, George, 57
Positive Behavior Interventions and Supports (PBIS), 195, 198, 206, *235*
positive behavior supports, 171, 203
posttests (curriculum-based assessments), 72
Pouliot, Norman, 224
POW writing strategy, *113*, 114, 116
prerequisite skills instruction, 30, 39
pretests (curriculum-based assessments), 67, 81
Prior, Paul, 88
professional standards, 172, 206–7
progress monitoring, 13, 60, 66, 214, 221; CBW method, 82–83, 109–10, 111; in DBI process, 26, 27–28, 65; studying and, 226–29
project-based learning (PBL), 4, 133, 138, *140*, 143
prompt cards, 3, 64, 66, 79
prosocial behaviors, 169, 193–94
prosody, 33–34
Putnam, Adam L., 158

quadratic formula, 46, 49–50, 66, *67–69*, *71*, 72, 73
Question Exploration Routine, 4, 154, 155

Rademacher, Joyce A., 220
Ray, Amber B., 3–4, *117*
read-alouds, 16
reading instruction: comprehension instruction, 17–18; core reading instruction, 14–15; foundational theories, 8–10; guiding research, 10–11; pre-reading supports, 35; in secondary ELA classrooms, 6–7, 12–13; vocabulary instruction, 16–17
reading intervention, 39; evidence base on reading interventions, 25–26; foundational skills routine, 30–31; Get the Gist routine, 38; instructional decision-making guidance, 26–29; oral reading fluency routine, 33–35; peel off reading, 32–33; theories informing reading interventions, 24–25; topic introduction routine, 36–37
Reading Systems Framework (RSF), 9, 15
Reciprocal Peer Tutoring (RPT), 160, *161*
Reeve, Johnmarshall, 174
remembering systems, 212, 214, 217–18, *221*, 222–23
respondent behavior, 205
Responsive Classroom, 171, 184
reteaching, 33, 111, 176, 178, 182
retrieval strategies, 214, 218
Riccomini, Paul J., 76
Roberts, Brian, 131
Rohrer, Doug, 56
Romig, John, 3, 4
Royer, David J., 180
Ruhl, Kathy L., 220
rules-and-routines matrix, 176, *177*

scaffolded instruction, 55, 113, 136, 154, 161; explicit instruction, as part of, 15, 152, 193; gradual release of information, 2, 52; in inquiry-based science, 130–31, 145, 151; in secondary mathematics, 45, 46, 50, 51
Scammacca, Nancy K., 25
Scanlon, David, 220
Schneider, Elke, 76
school suspensions, 171, 176, 204
schoolwide positive behavior interventions and supports (SWPBIS), 176

Schumaker, Jean B., 219, 220, 221
Science, Technology, Engineering, and Mathematics (STEM), 4–5, 141, 161, *234*
science instruction, 131, 217, *234*; best practices in science case study, 138–44; content acquisition for science classes, 149, 158–61; EBP and HLP in science studies, 148–49; general literacy interventions for science studies, 149, 150–58; Greek and Latin Roots in science texts, 37–38; key instructional methods in science education, 133–34; quality assessment in science education, 132–33; science, describing and defining, 129–30; social studies, linking science with, 4, 127–29, 145, 147
screeners, 13, *14*
scriptwriting, 94–95, *96*, 102–4
Scruggs, Thomas E., 150, 159
secondary writing instruction. *See* writing instruction
self-monitoring, 29, 78, *113*, 115, 118, 148, 195, 196–97
self-regulated strategy development (SRSD): ACT exam-writing case study, 118–22; SRSD instructional model, 113–18; writing skills, improving through, 4, 112, 124, 213
self-reinforcement, *113*, 115, 118
self-testing, 214, 220, 221, 223–24, 225, 226, 229
sentence construction, 123
short-answer responses, 108
Sierens, Eline, 174
signal words, 18
Simonson, Brandi, 178
Simple View of Reading (SVR), 8–9, 24
Singer Early, Jessica, 3
single-case research designs, 148
skillstreaming, 193–94
Skinner, B. F., 170, 202, 205
small group instruction, 14, 15, 38, 173, 174, 176, 197, *226*
SMART Boards, 179
SMARTER planning, 149
Smith, Stephanie, 264
social studies instruction, *235*; best practices case study, 138–44; C3 framework for social studies state standards, 136–37; content acquisition for social studies, 149, 158–61; EBP and HLP in social studies, 148–49; general literacy for, 149, 150–58; Greek and Latin root words in social studies texts, 37–38; key instructional strategies, 137–38; nature of social studies, 134–35; science and social studies, teaching together, 127–29, 144–45; social studies inquiry, 4, 135, 147, 150–51, 151–52
socioscientific issues (SSI), 133–34, *140, 143*
specially designed instruction (SDI), 7, 10, 149
Speedy Read instructional practice, 33
S-R-S (three-term contingency), 205
STAR reading assessment, 12–13, 14
STAR strategy (search, translate, answer, review), 77, 78
stepwise approach, 3, *57, 75*
Stichter, J. P., 175
Stockard, Jean, 25
storage strategies, 214, 218, 219
story grammar, 9, *12*, 17–18
story maps, 17
Strategic Instruction Model (SIM), 152, 213
strategy instruction (SI), 3, 77, 78, 112, 213, 214, 215
Strickland, Tricia K., 3, 77
structured inquiry, 131, 150
structured outcomes of learning objectives (SOLO), 46, 47, 48, 61
students with disabilities (SWDs), 6, 7, 8, 10, 11, 13, 168
student-to-student OTR, 178
study skills, 45, 212; good study strategies, 215–16, 216–18, 229; listening and note-taking, 219–20; overall study plan, 225–26; poor study strategies, teaching students with, 213–15; progress monitoring and studying, 226–29; structuring good study practices, 220–25
summative assessments, 13, 93–94, 109, *140, 143*, 207
Swanson, Elizabeth, 11
systematic instruction, 2, 25, 52–53, 54, 55, 60, 61

target behaviors, 190, 191, *192*, 197, 198, 199, 200
taxonomy of intervention intensity, 3, 65–66, 83
Taylor, Jonte' C., 160
Taylor, Mary Jo, 4
Teachers Pay Teachers resource, 232

test-taking, 214
think-alouds, 66, 114, 116
Thorndike, Edward, 170
TIDE writing strategy, *113*, 114, *117*
Tier 1 instruction, 4, 13, 198; "The Gift of the Magi" example, 14–15; Tier 1 words, 16; universal screenings, 194, 195, 207
Tier 2 instruction, 13, 14, 198; Tier 2 interventions, 195; Tier 2 supports, 194, 207; Tier 2 words, 12, 16
Tier 3 special education services, 13, 16, 198, 207
time out situations, 181, 182, 183
"T" method for organizing, 219
Topic Introduction Routine, 36–37
topographical target behaviors, 182, 191
Torgesen, Joseph K., 10
Toste, Jessica R., 2, *233*
TREE writing strategy, *113*, 114, 115, 116, *117*
triadic reciprocity learning framework, 170
tutoring, 3, 81–82, 160, 161, 218

unison OTR, 178
universal classroom management, 2, 171, 184–85, 189–90
Universal Design for Learning (UDL), 4, 14, 15, 18, 140–41, 142, 149
US Department of Education (DOE), 1, 7, 25, 168, 171, 201, *236*

Vannest, Kimberly J., 201
Venn diagram, 18, 153, 161
Vernon, Sue, 225
virtual-representational-abstract (VRA) framework, 77
Vision I and Vision II of scientific literacy, 131
visuospatial deficits, 3, 64
Vocabulary LINCING Routine, 222
vocabulary routine, 35–36
Vygotsky, Lev S., 170–71, 205

Watson, John B., 205
Wexler, Jade, 10

What Works Clearinghouse (WWC), 109, 201, 202, *236*
whole-class engagement, 14, 116, 144, 152, 176, 180
whole number computation, 45, 48, 50, 58
Williamson, Pamela, 2, 159
Wilson, Barbara, 159
Witzel, Bradley S., 2, 3, 76, 78
word-building activity, 32–33
Word Mapping Strategy, 17
word problems, 3, 45, 47, 64, 77–78
word-recognition, 8, 9–10, 24, 31
words spelled correctly (WSC), 110
words written (WW), 110
worksheets, 71, 81, 108, 175, *223*; completion of, students avoiding, 182, *192*; guided practice worksheet, *69–70*, *72–73*; structured worksheets, 3, 66, 79
writing instruction, 108, 122; assignment examples, 96–101; celebrating writing and making it public, 104–5; digital tools as aids, 103–4; formative/summative assessment methods, 93–94; foundational learning theory, 88–89; guiding research and policy, 89–90; mentor texts, 101–2; podcast genre, teaching, 94–96; standards, connection to, 90–92; writing strategies for the writing process, 112–18. *See also* argumentative writing
writing intervention: curriculum-based measurement, 109–11; error analysis, 29, 111; exit slips, 60, 111; genre-specific elements, 112; self-regulation strategies, 113, 118; six stages of instruction, 114–16; SRSD intervention for ACT essay case study, 118–22; technology tools, 108, 122–23; writing strategies, 116–17

Yes/No T-Charts, 141
YouTube tutorials, 104

Zeidler, Dana L., 139

About the Contributors

Julie Atwood is a special educator and board certified behavior analyst (BCBA) who has worked in education for over fourteen years. She currently serves as a behavior specialist for a school district, supporting teachers and staff in the implementation of behavior interventions in the classroom. Julie has a master's degree in special education with an emphasis in applied behavior analysis, and is a doctoral student at the University of Oklahoma.

Dr. Brittany Batton earned her PhD in special education with a concentration in early childhood studies at the University of Florida. She has taught in public elementary, middle, and high schools as a special education and general education teacher. She is a board certified behavior analyst (BCBA) working with individuals age 2–19 with autism and emotional and behavior disorders both in home and in schools. She provides parent and teacher training in classroom management, positive behavior supports, and principles of applied behavior analysis.

Dr. Glenna M. Billingsley is an associate professor at Texas State University in San Marcos, Texas. She taught students with emotional and behavioral disabilities in a variety of educational settings for twenty-six years prior to her move to higher education. Dr. Billingsley's research primarily focuses on schoolwide and individual application of positive behavior interventions and supports as well as academic and behavioral interventions for students with emotional, mental, and behavioral health needs.

Brennan Chandler is a doctoral student in the Department of Special Education, the University of Texas at Austin, and a scholar with the National Center for Leadership in Intensive Intervention (NCLII). Before pursuing his doctoral studies, he was a special and general education teacher in public and private settings. His research interests include theory-aligned reading and writing interventions for students with dyslexia and other learning disabilities.

Amber Curlee is a doctoral student in the English education program at Arizona State University, and codirector of the Central Arizona Writing Project Summer Institute. She began her career teaching English at the high school and community college levels.

Erica Fry is a doctoral student in the Department of Special Education at the University of Texas at Austin and where she works on Project EXPERT in the Meadows

Center for Preventing Educational Risk. She worked previously as a special education teacher at the elementary and middle school levels and as a high school special education administrator. Her research interests focus on the pre-service and in-service professional development of special educators.

Dr. David Furjanic is the coordinator for Project EXPERT at the Meadows Center for Preventing Educational Risk at the University of Texas at Austin. He graduated from the University of Oregon with a PhD in school psychology and an MS in special education in 2021 and from Millersville University of Pennsylvania with an MS in psychology in 2017. His research interests focus on data-based decision-making, coaching, and capacity building.

Dr. Nicholas A. Gage is Senior Researcher in Special Education at WestEd focused on advancing rigorous research and evaluation in learner variability and special education. Gage's research interests are centered on the identification of policies and practices at the national, state, local, and classroom levels to support the academic, social, and behavioral needs of students with disabilities. This work is grounded in a multi-tiered systems of support (MTSS) framework, with a particular emphasis on positive behavior interventions and supports (PBIS).

Angela Green has been a classroom teacher, instructional coach, and special education administrator for twenty-nine years in Texas and Oklahoma public schools. She also trains principals, teachers, and paraprofessionals on implementation of IEPs and specially designed instruction. Currently, Ms. Green is a doctoral student in special education at the University of Oklahoma.

Dr. Brittany L. Hott is associate director of the Institute for Community and Society Transformation (ICAST) and associate professor of special education at the University of Oklahoma. She is a licensed behavior analyst and special education teacher with interests in rural school-based interventions and the effective translation of special education research to rural practice. Her publication record includes over sixty peer-reviewed articles and program evaluations and over 100 national presentations. Her work is predominantly with rural deep east Texas and south east Oklahoma schools. Dr. Hott is a member of the executive board of the American Council on Rural Special Education and past president of the International Council for Learning Disabilities.

Jasmine Justus is a licensed behavior analyst (LBA), board-certified behavior analyst (BCBA), and a special educator. For the past five years, she has taught in an elementary setting as a general and special education teacher. Currently, she is pursuing a doctoral degree in special education at the University of Oklahoma, where she focuses her research on rural classroom management and IEP implementation.

Dr. Sami Kahn, Executive Director of the Council on Science and Technology (CST) at Princeton University, works to promote scientific literacy for all through quality interdisciplinary course development, robust STEM education research, and creative programming. An award-winning STEM educator, teacher educator, and author, she uses her background in science education and law to inform her research and scholarship on inclusive science practices, socioscientific issues (SSI), argumentation, and social justice.

Dr. Ben-Hanania Lenz is an associate professor and coordinator of special education programs in the Department of Elementary, Literacy, and Special Education at the University of Central Arkansas. Dr. Lenz has over thirty years of experience in conceptualizing and connecting innovative research, developing interventions, and conducting professional development to improve instruction and outcomes for adolescents and adults with disabilities. His scholarship includes numerous publications and he has been a major contributor to and author in the development and validation of the Strategic Instruction Model (SIM), and SIM Learning Strategies Curriculum and Content Enhancement Routines.

Dr. Timothy Lintner is Carolina Trustee Professor of Education at the University of South Carolina Aiken. His research interests explore the intersections between social studies, special education, and literacy.

Dr. Ashley MacSuga-Gage is a clinical associate professor of special education at the University of Florida's College of Education in the Department of Special Education, School Psychology, and Early Childhood Studies (SESPECS). Her work centers on positive behavior support (PBS) applications to school settings and to providing professional development to in-service and pre-service teachers focusing on effective classroom management strategies. Dr. MacSuga-Gage has worked as a special education self-contained and resource teacher across NYC and Connecticut serving students with emotional behavioral disorders (EBD) as well as other disabilities.

Dr. Darren Minarik is an associate professor in teacher preparation and serves as codirector for the Virginia Inclusive Practices Center at Radford University. His areas of teaching and research include civic education and self-determination for youth with disabilities, instructional strategies, postsecondary transition, collaboration, inclusive practices, and the perceptual and pedagogical intersections between social studies, disability studies, and special education.

Dr. Jonté A. Myers is an assistant professor of special education at Georgia State University. He studies special education, mathematics instruction for students with learning disabilities, and teacher quality and effectiveness in mathematics. He has also conducted research on special education policy as it relates to teacher certification and preparation.

Jacquelyn Purser is a special education teacher. She currently serves as a special education teacher for a school district, serving students with extensive support needs. Jacquelyn has a master's degree in special education with an emphasis in challenging behaviors, and is a doctoral student at the University of Oklahoma.

Dr. Kathleen (Kathy) M. Randolph is an assistant professor at the University of Colorado Colorado Springs and board certified behavior analyst with doctoral distinction (BCBA-D). Her research focuses on using iCoaching to support teacher implementation of evidence-based classroom management practices in their classrooms.

Dr. Amber B. Ray is an assistant professor in the Department of Special Education at the University of Illinois at Urbana-Champaign whose research interests include writing and reading interventions and instruction to help students with disabilities and diverse learning needs succeed. Her research focuses on strategy and self-regulation approaches to instruction and methods of professional development for teachers and school leaders on effective writing and reading instruction. Dr. Ray works on developing evidence-based instruction to cultivate the learning of all students, including those with disabilities, and has conducted research with elementary through high school students and adults.

Dr. John Elwood Romig is an assistant professor at the University of Texas at Arlington. His research interests include literacy instruction and assessment. Specifically, he examines effective writing instruction, vocabulary instruction, reading instruction, and progress monitoring assessments to help students with high incidence disabilities. His teaching and research experiences focus on secondary grades.

Dr. Jessica Singer Early is a professor of English education at Arizona State University and the director the Central Arizona Writing Project. She began her career as a high school English teacher and is now a writing researcher and teacher educator.

Dr. Tricia K. Strickland is a professor of education at Hood College in Frederick, Maryland. Her area of research focuses on mathematics instructional interventions that assist elementary and secondary students with high incidence disabilities access the general education curriculum. Previously, Dr. Strickland spent twelve years teaching mathematics to middle and high school students with diverse learning needs.

Dr. Jonte' C. Taylor (JT) is an associate professor of special education at Pennsylvania State University (Penn State). His research includes examining effective strategies for inclusive STEAM education for students with disabilities and improving school/classroom climates for students, families, and teachers. His STEAM scholarship focuses on supporting inquiry-based STEAM instruction and using research-based interventions and practices.

Dr. Jessica R. Toste is an associate professor in the Department of Special Education at the University of Texas at Austin. She holds research affiliations with the Meadows Center for Preventing Educational Risk and the Texas Center for Equity Promotion. Her research is focused on methods for intensifying intervention for students with persistent reading challenges and reading disabilities. She is principal investigator on multiple research grants from the U.S. Department of Education, Institute of Education Sciences, and her research has resulted in more than 70 peer-reviewed publications.

Dr. Kelly J. Williams is an assistant professor of special education and the Dyslexia Graduate Certificate Program Coordinator in the Department of Curriculum and Instruction at Indiana University. Her research focuses on improving academic and postsecondary outcomes for students at risk for and identified with mild/moderate disabilities. Her main areas of expertise are reading instruction and intervention, dyslexia, and dropout prevention.

Dr. Pamela Williamson is department head and professor at the University of North Florida. Her research focuses on autism, reading instruction and intervention, and the preparation of special education leaders.

Dr. Bradley S. Witzel is an award-winning teacher and researcher who serves as the Adelaide Worth Daniels Distinguished Professor of Education at Western Carolina University. Dr. Witzel has authored ten books and over sixty other professional publications, developed over twenty multimedia resources, and delivered over 600 presentations and workshops.

www.ingramcontent.com/pod-product-compliance
Lightning Source LLC
Chambersburg PA
CBHW060337010526
44117CB00017B/2860